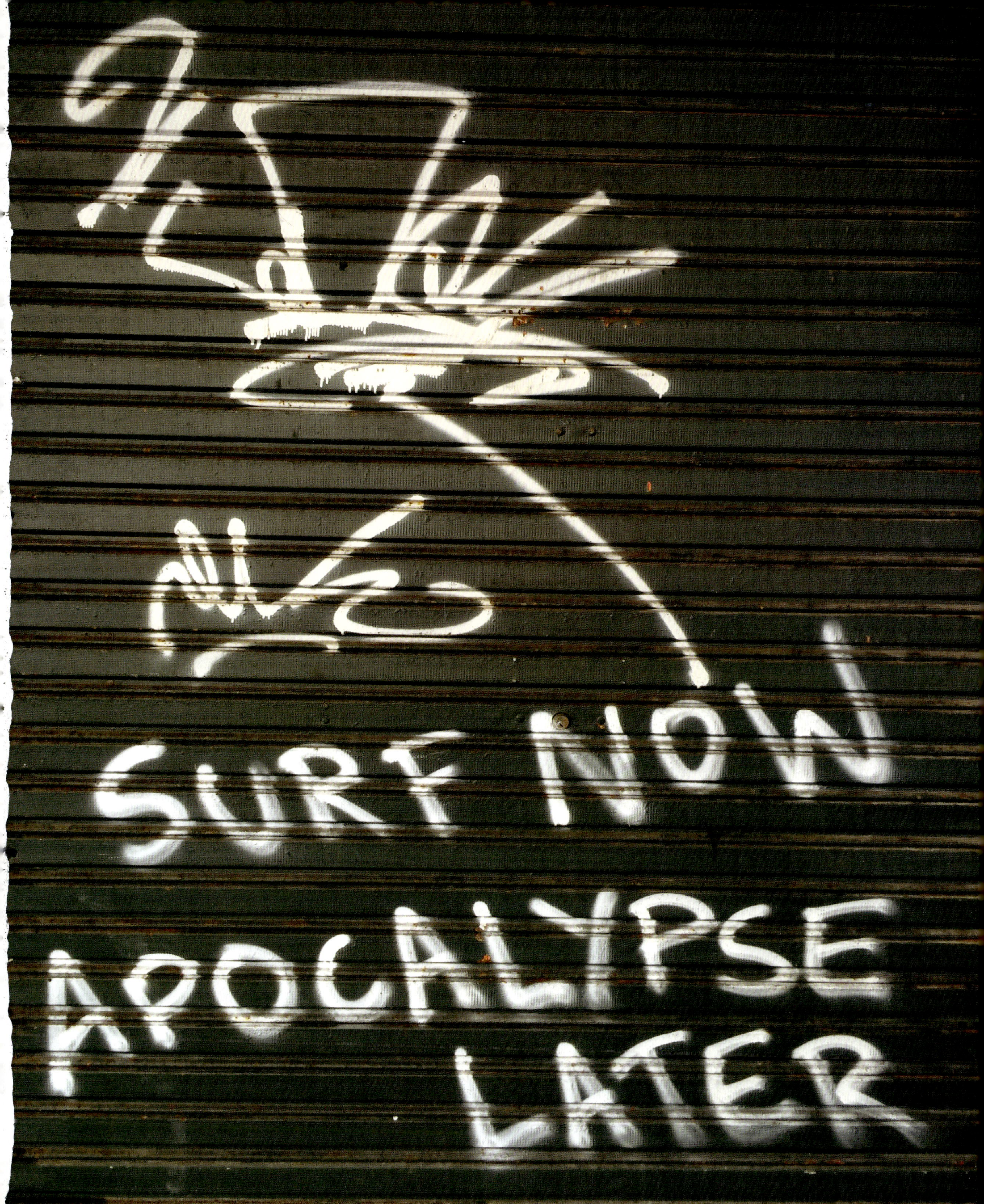

SURF NOW
APOCALYPSE LATER

SURF/SKATE

Art and Board Life

Steve Miller

Foreword by Michael Tolkin

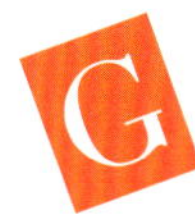

In a rare moment, a bright light can enter your life.
Mine is Jeanine Pepler. This book is dedicated to her.

First published in 2019 by

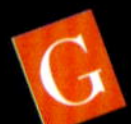

Glitterati Editions
311 West 43 Street
12th Floor
New York, NY 10036

www.glitteratieditions.com
media@glitteratieditions.com

First edition, 2019

Library of Congress Cataloging-in-Publication data
is available from the publisher.

Hardcover edition
ISBN: 978-1-943876-60-0

Printed and bound in China

10 9 8 7 6 5 4 3 2 1

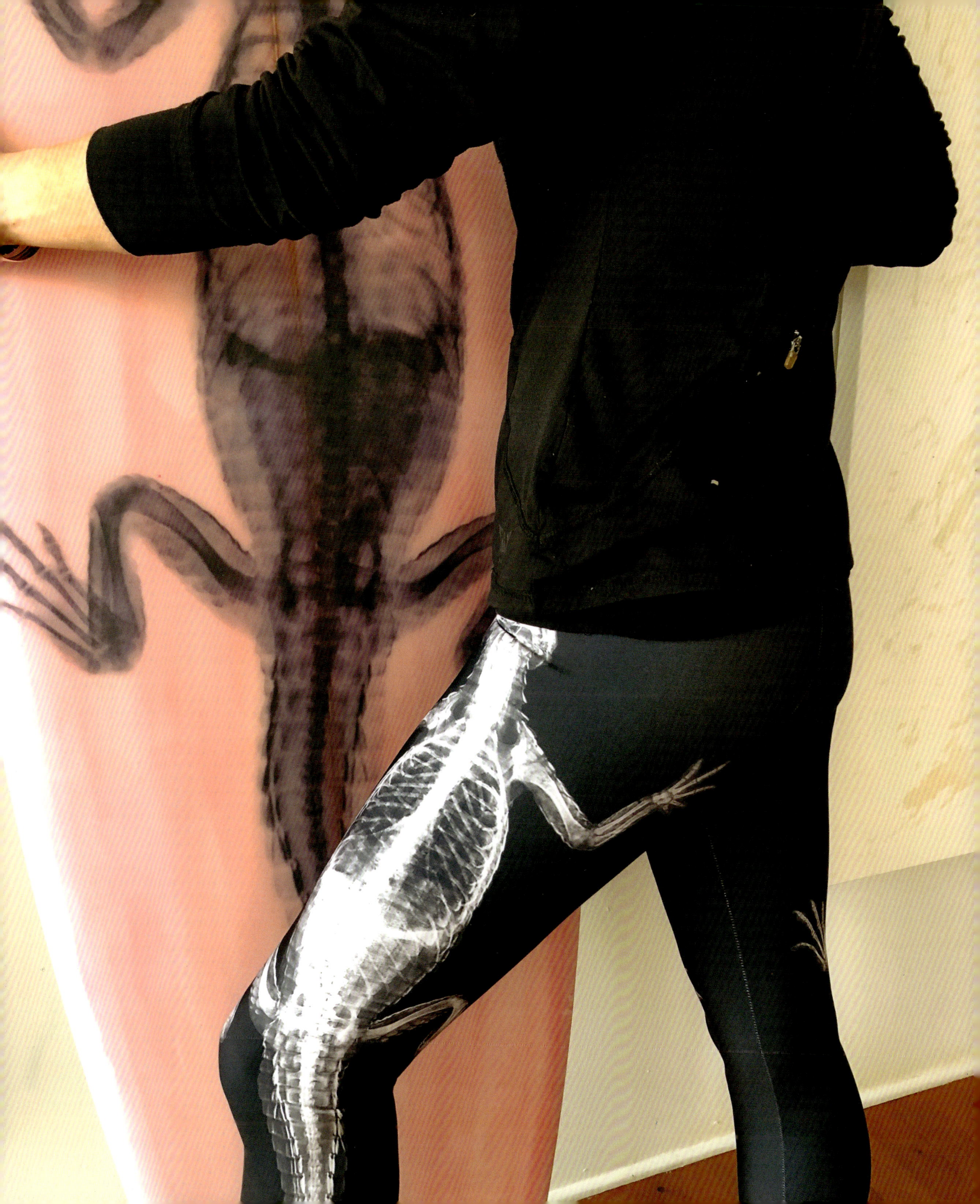

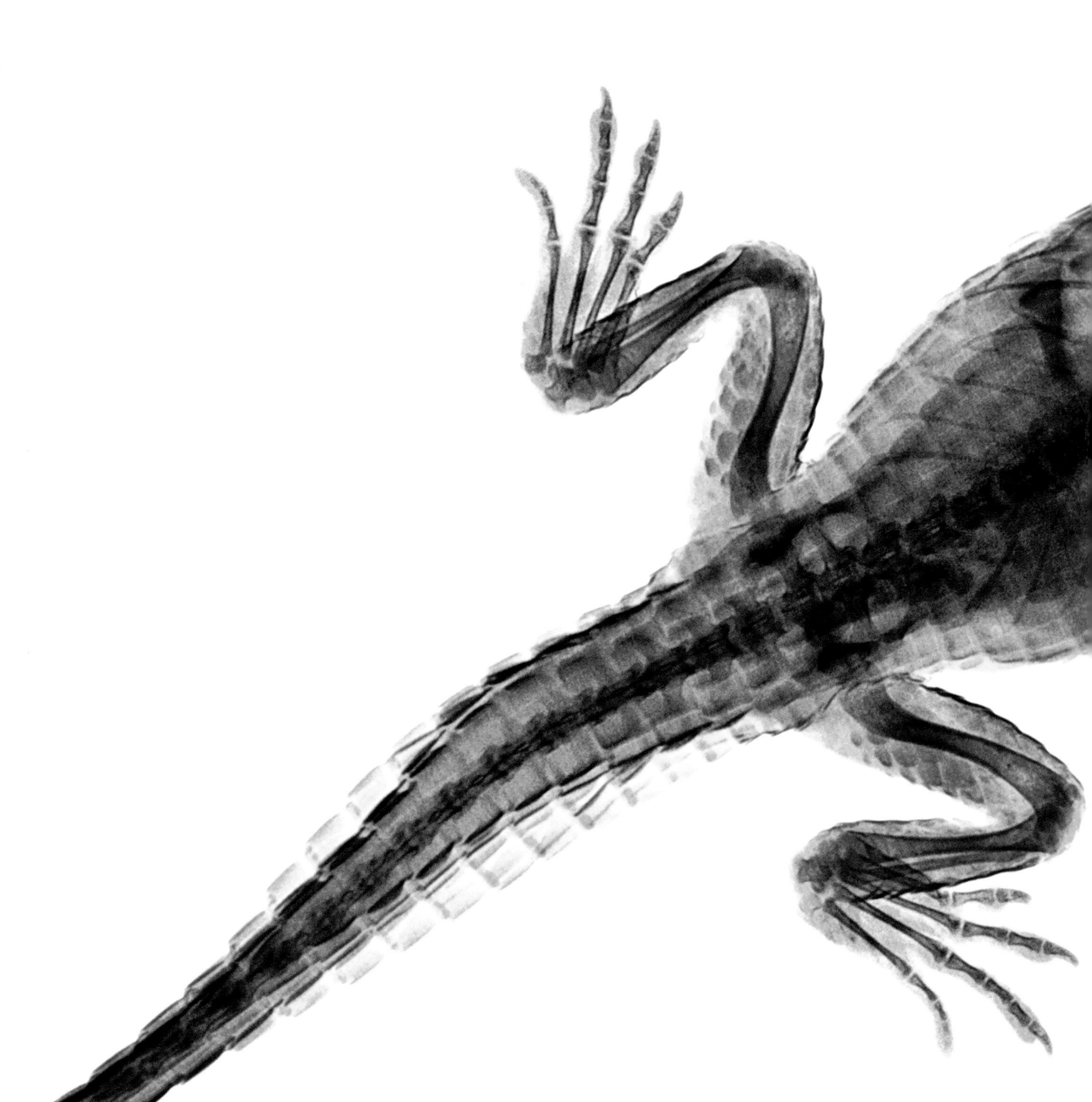

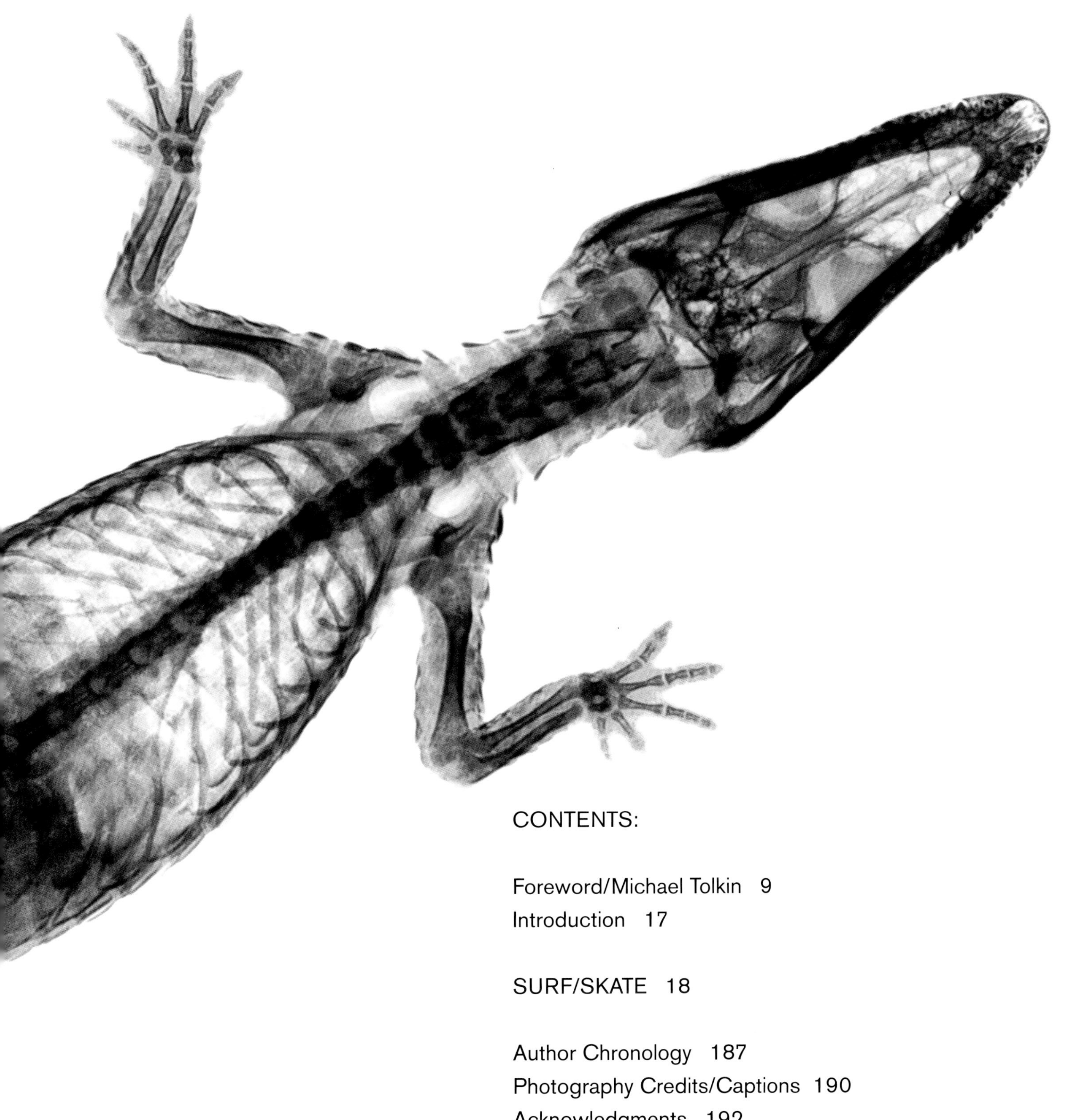

CONTENTS:

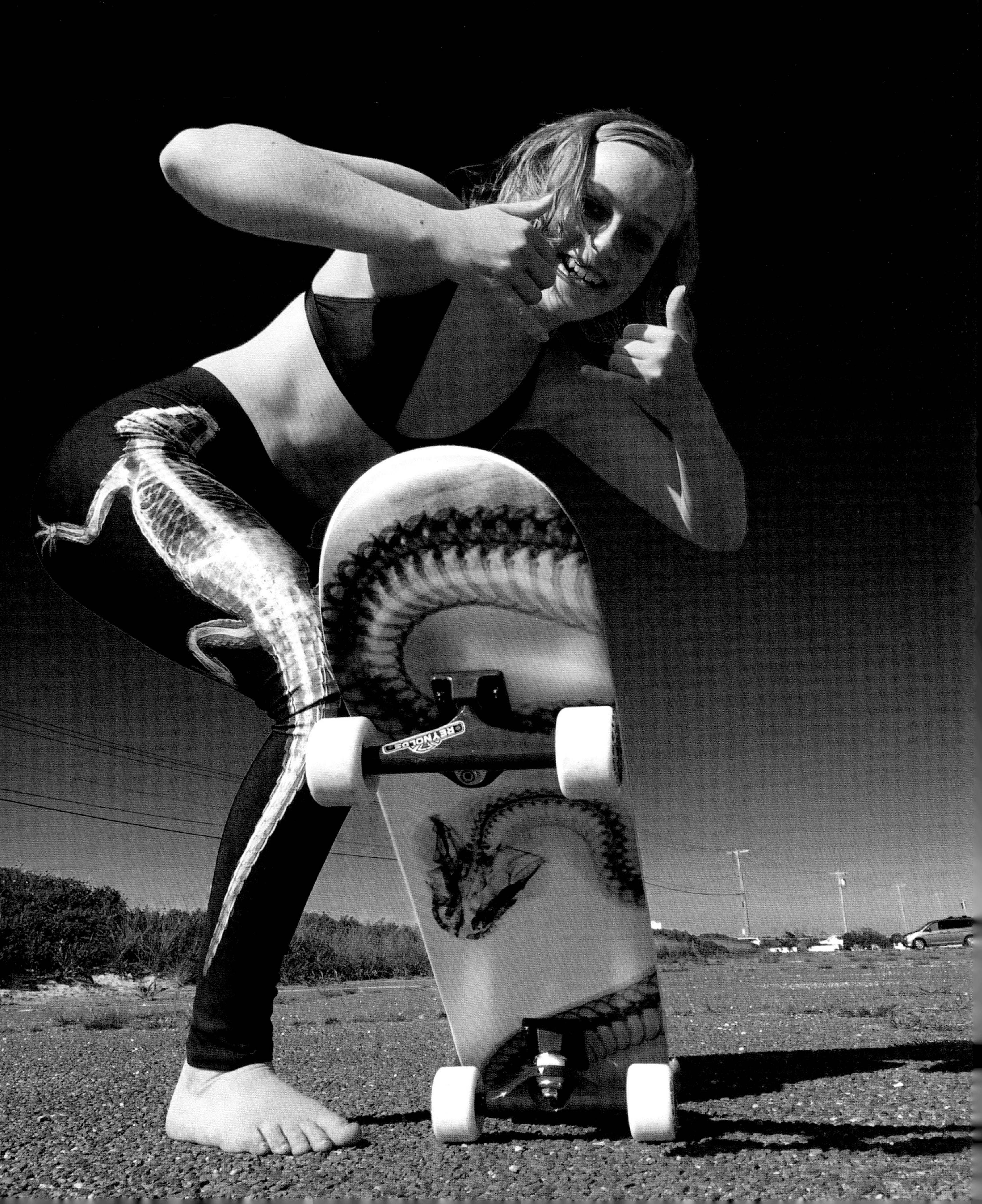

Inspiration.

It was the seventh grade.

1962.

I don't know who made my first skateboard or how much I paid for it. I bought it from someone at school. It was made of a solid piece of something like maple, stained in light and dark stripes, to look like four pieces of wood. The wheels came from roller skates, two steel plates, toe and heel screwed into the wood. It was noisy. It vibrated. It was unforgiving. I wasn't very good at it, but it made my dog happy. He pulled me around the block like an Evinrude speed boat, and I waterskied behind him.

I don't know when I threw it out. The wheels might have come off. There were no skateboard shops then. It was an artisanal project.

I didn't think much about skateboards until one day in the mid 1980s, when I saw a kid on a skateboard coming down the street carving a few wide S turns, like a surfer. He passed me, and the sound of his wheels was deeper than the metallic screech of the past.

Not long after, I read an article in the *LA Times* about the Vietnamese children who had arrived in the States as refugees at the end of the war and were now teenagers, rebelling in their way—the boys wearing leather motorcycle jackets, the girls in poodle skirts. I wanted to write a film about that world and spent a few days in Orange County, driving around the Vietnamese neighborhoods. The idea that began to form was to make an Orange County Vietnamese *Rebel Without a Cause* about the pressures driving families apart, with a sensitive Vietnamese war orphan bounced around the community as a foster child and getting into trouble because he was a bad model to the kids he grew up with.

I didn't know enough about the world of the boat people and didn't have the patience to learn it, and at the same time, I started to form a story about the change in tone from my old skate wheels to the sound of the modern board.

I ditched the Vietnamese family and made the rebel an orphan adopted by a white American family with a three-year-old. The orphan becomes their golden child, and the first born becomes the rebel, a bitter disappointment to his parents, a fuck up in every way. The story accelerates when the Vietnamese brother is murdered in a way that looks like suicide. The American brother skates around Orange County following clues, and in the end, brings down the villains. That part came together quickly, and to write it, I told myself that I needed to buy a skateboard and learn how to use it.

I went to a skate shop in Santa Monica, a fetish store for teenagers who knew what they wanted and needed no help in asking for it. I needed

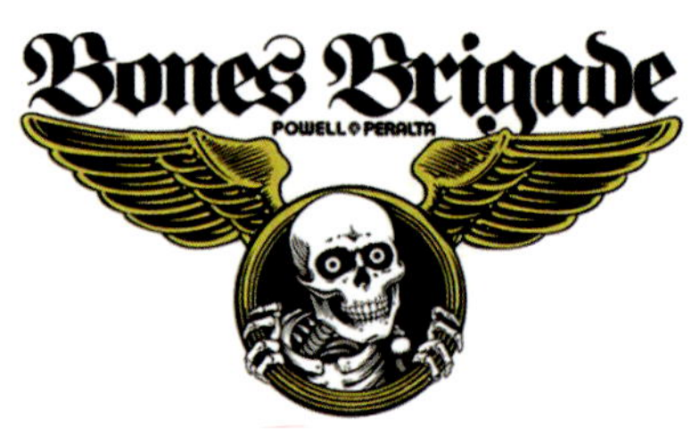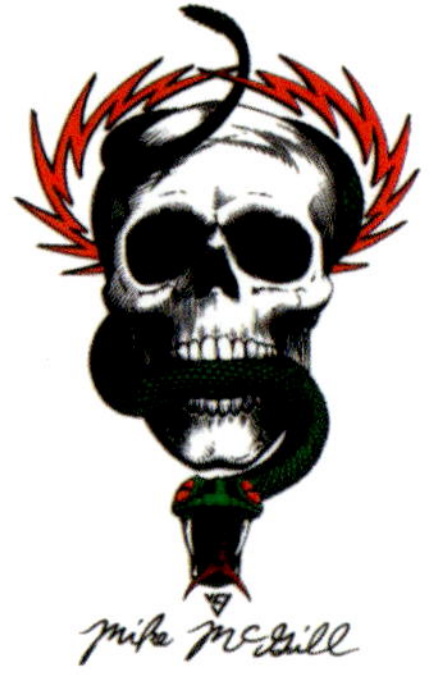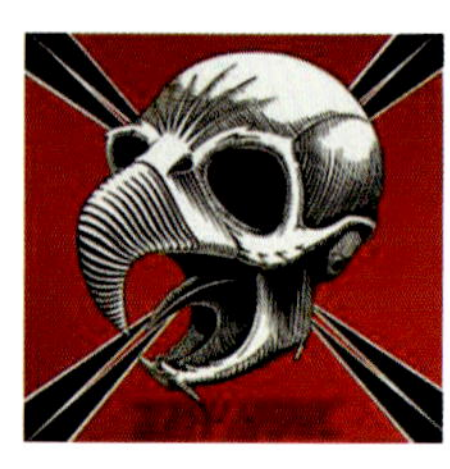

nothing but help. I had three choices to make: deck, the part you stand on; trucks, made of the base plate; the pivot and axle; and then the polyurethane wheels. I was told I would be safest on something wide and stiff. The selection of equivalent boards was set in front of me, and I was stuck with a dilemma that was aesthetic rather than practical. Any of ten boards would work equally well, and I was too much of a beginner to feel the subtle differences. There was no one board that was clearly the only choice for me, so I bought logo stickers from my dozen or so contenders and took them home.

It came down to two boards, the Tony Hawk and the Mike McGill. They were both skating with the Bones Brigade, the team sponsored by Powell Peralta Skateboards, and at the time Hawk was not yet the dominant skater of his generation. McGill had perfected the McTwist, which was an impossible skate ramp trick, the skater version of the four minute mile, a front flip, and a 540-degree rotation.

The basic Bones Brigade logo was a grinning skull clawing his way into a halo between two yellow wings. It combined the left facing skull and wings of the Hells Angels symbol and the Grateful Dead's top view of a skull with hair of roses framed as though inside a porthole.

Hawk's symbol was a hawk skull set on an Iron Cross. The bird skull was friendly, the beak dominant like a parrot's, like Disney's José Carioca. McGill's symbol took the Bones Brigade skull and a Grateful Dead lightning bolt and removed the frame. The skull was large and serious, fully human, no hint of glee. A thick green rattlesnake, tail above the skull, wraps around the back of the skull beneath a halo of lightning. The snake has wedged itself between the skull's teeth and then reached forward, fangs ready to sink into the viewer's face. Below the snake's head is McGill's signature.

The snake ennobles the skull by making it a home, as though the skull logo was finished before the snake crawled into the frame. Where did that snake come from? Who knows? I just know that one day it wrapped itself around Steve Miller's skateboard (snakeboard!) and stopped to have the artist take a picture of its bones.

Michael Tolkin

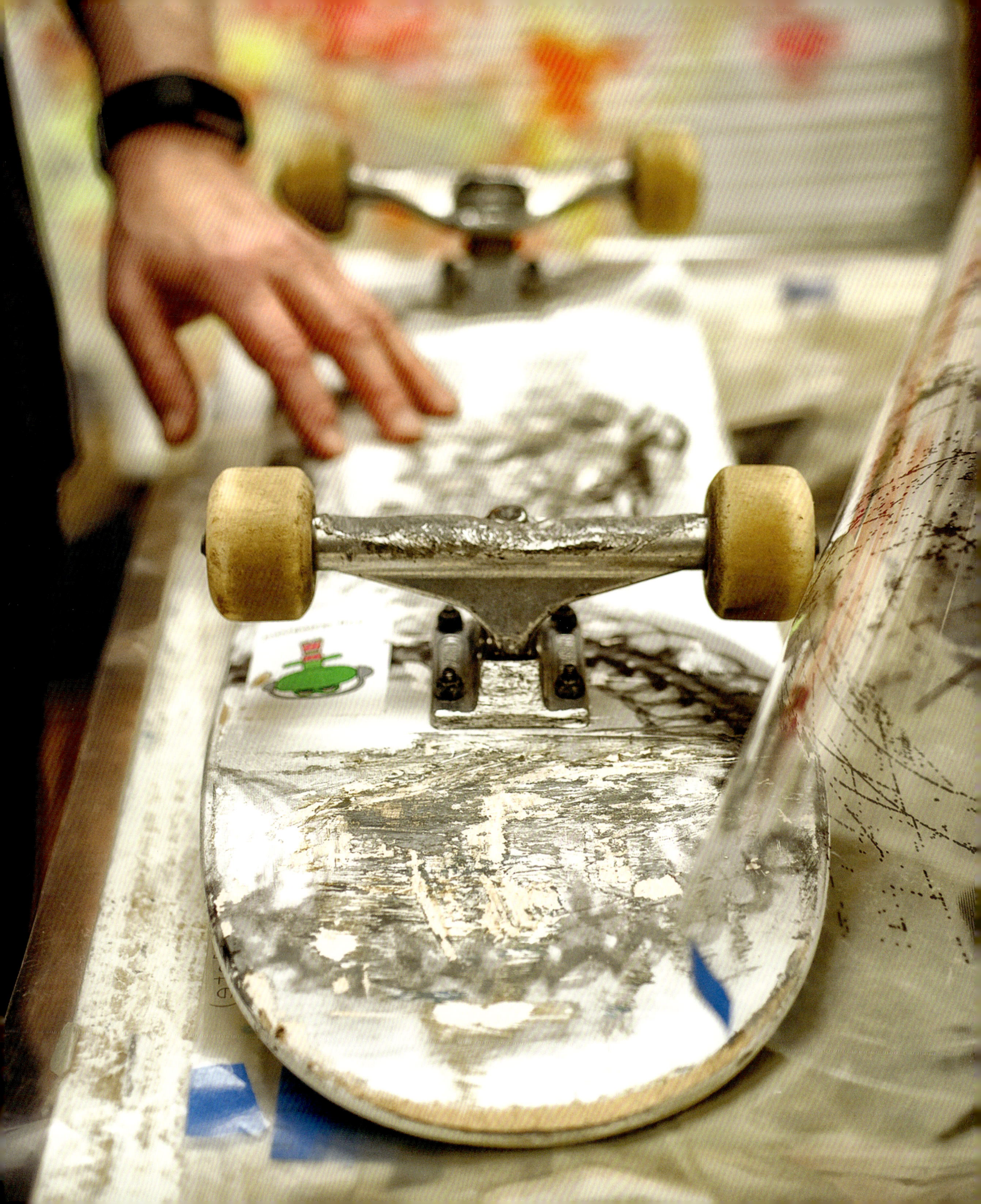

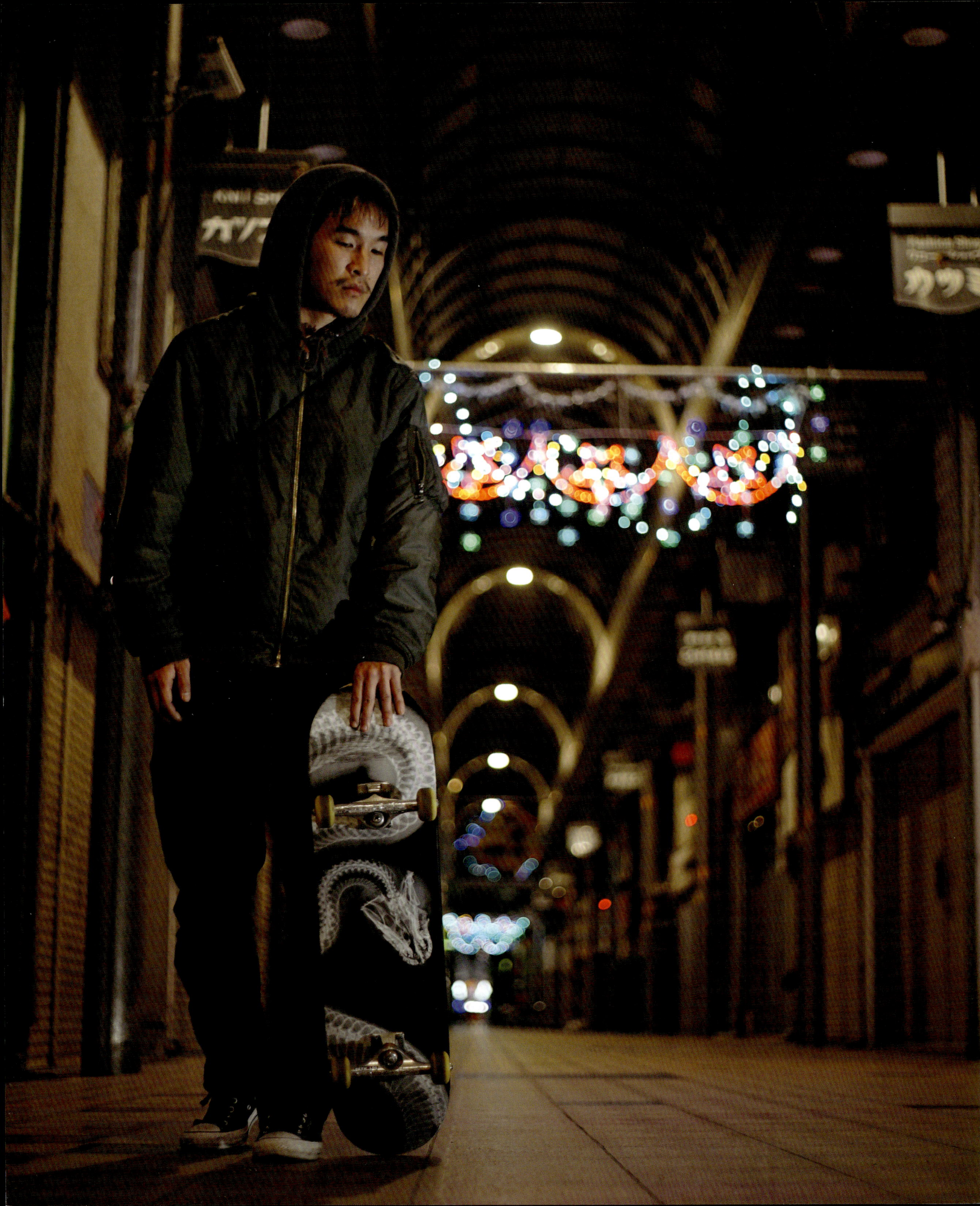

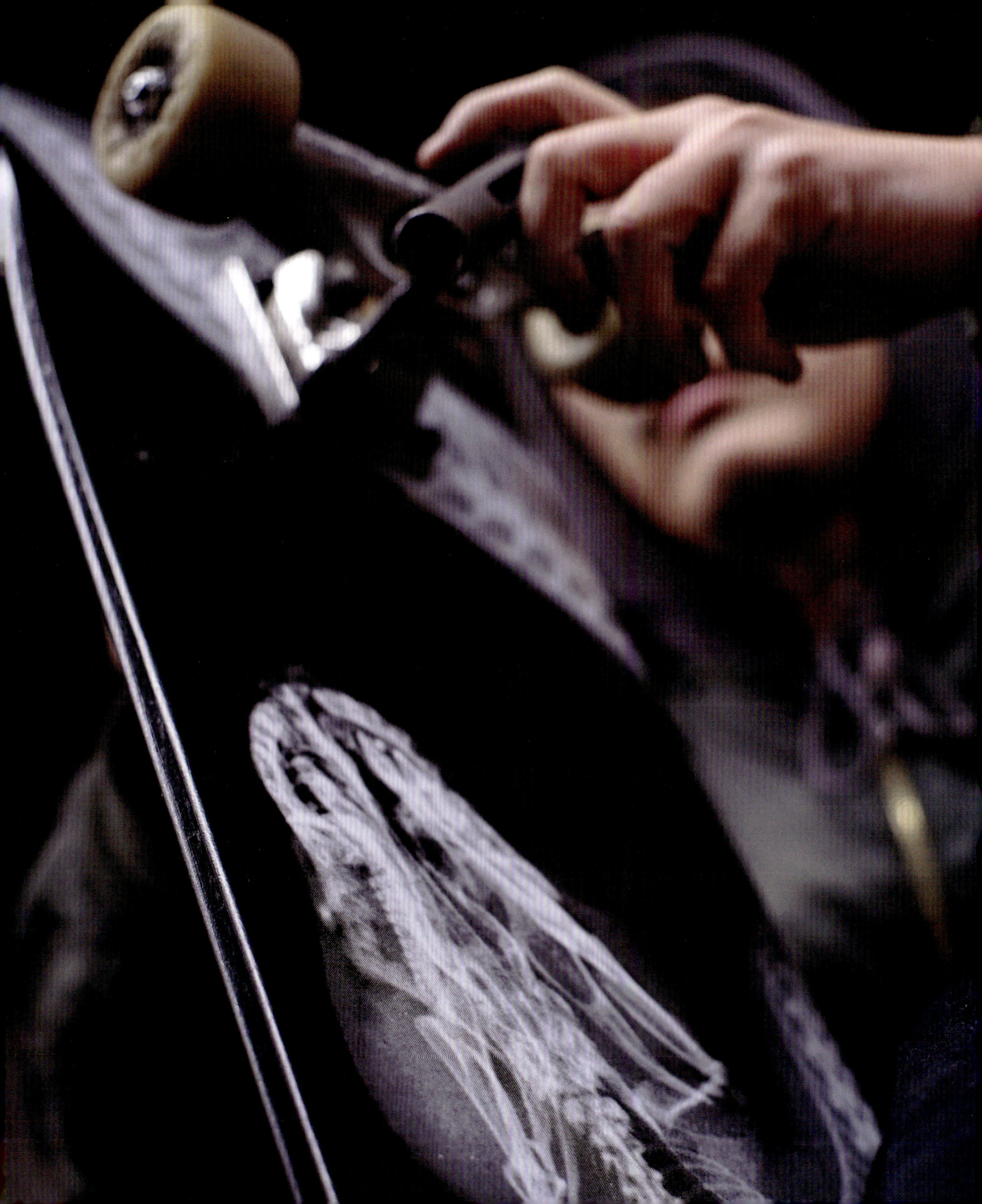

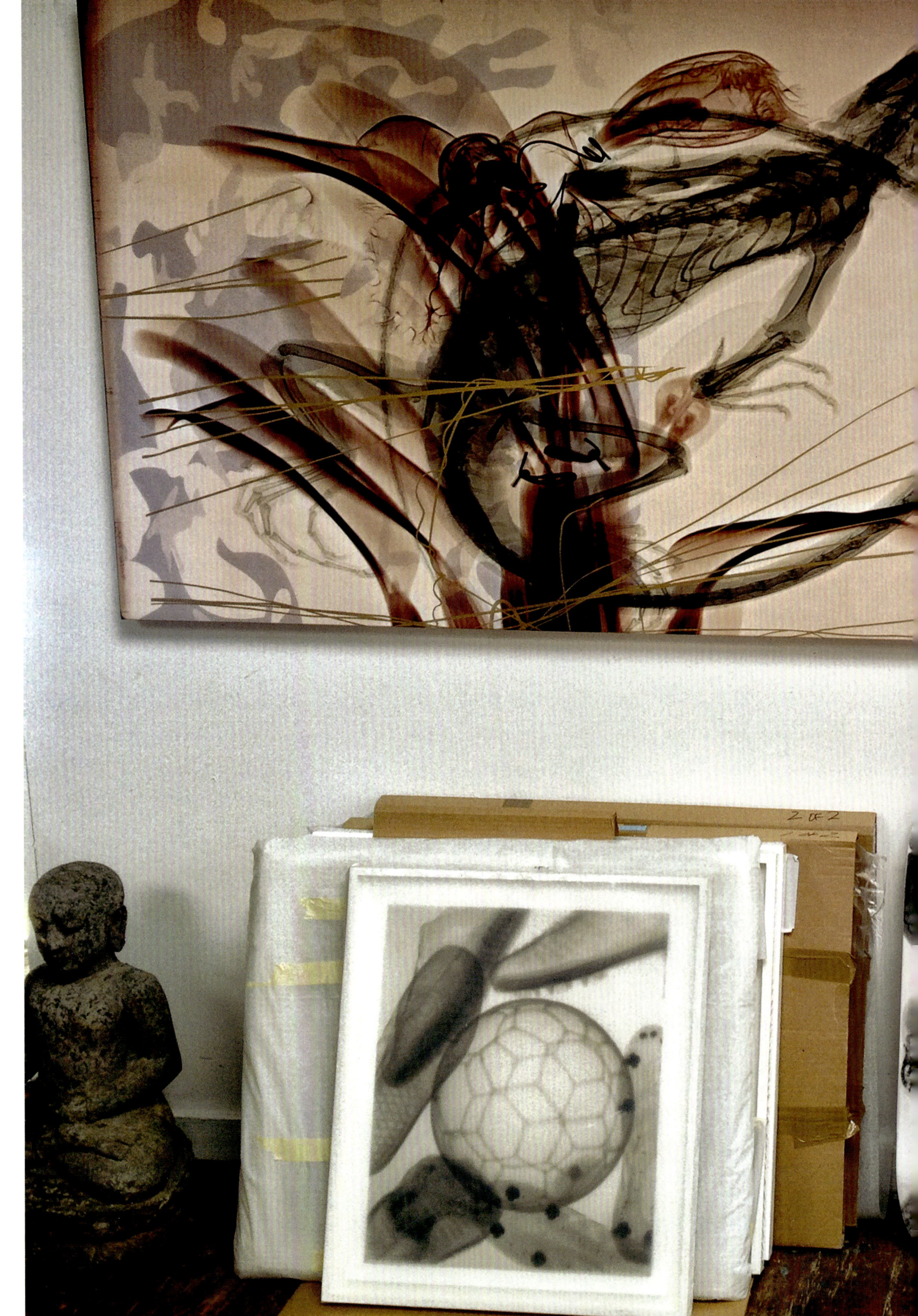

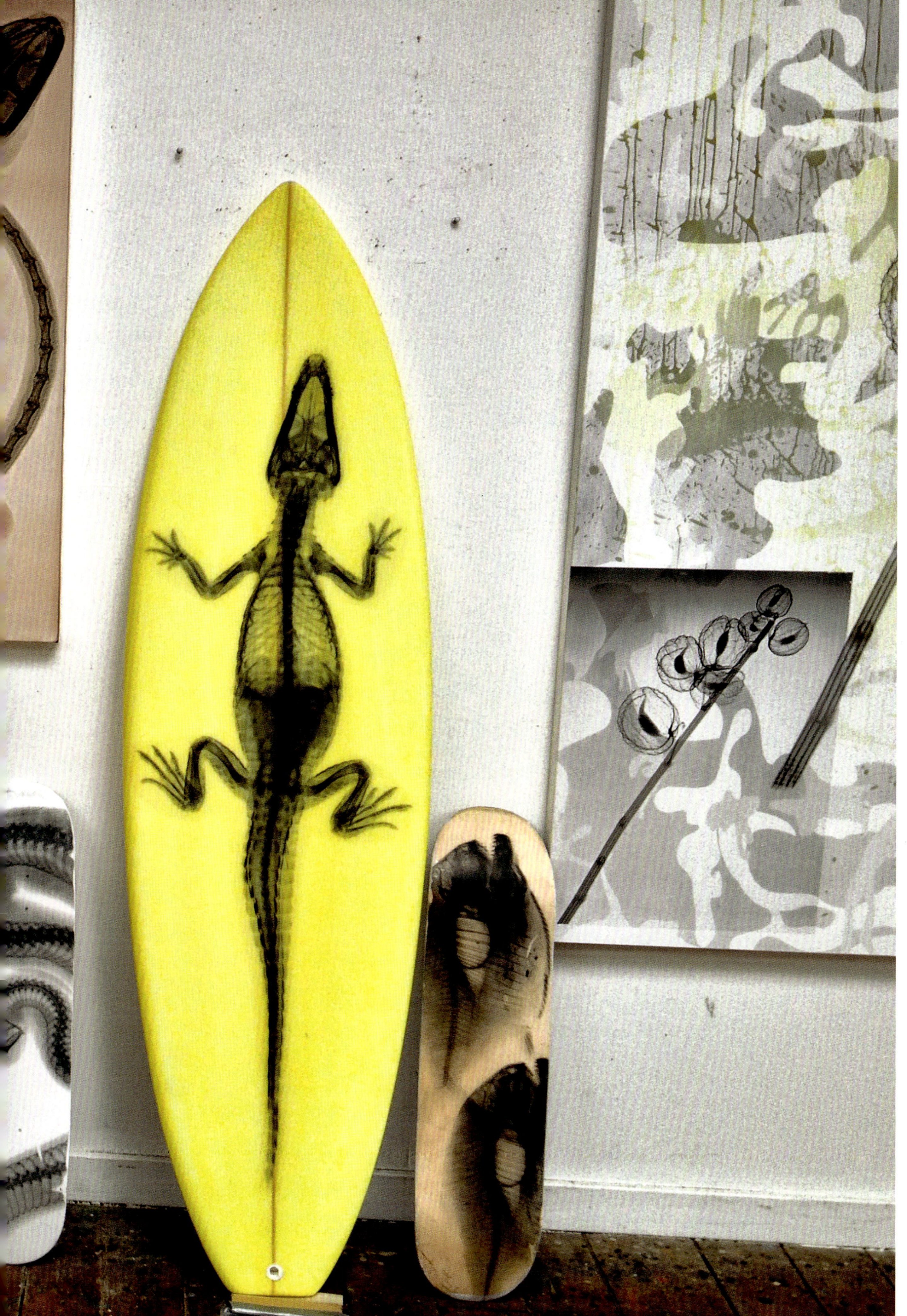

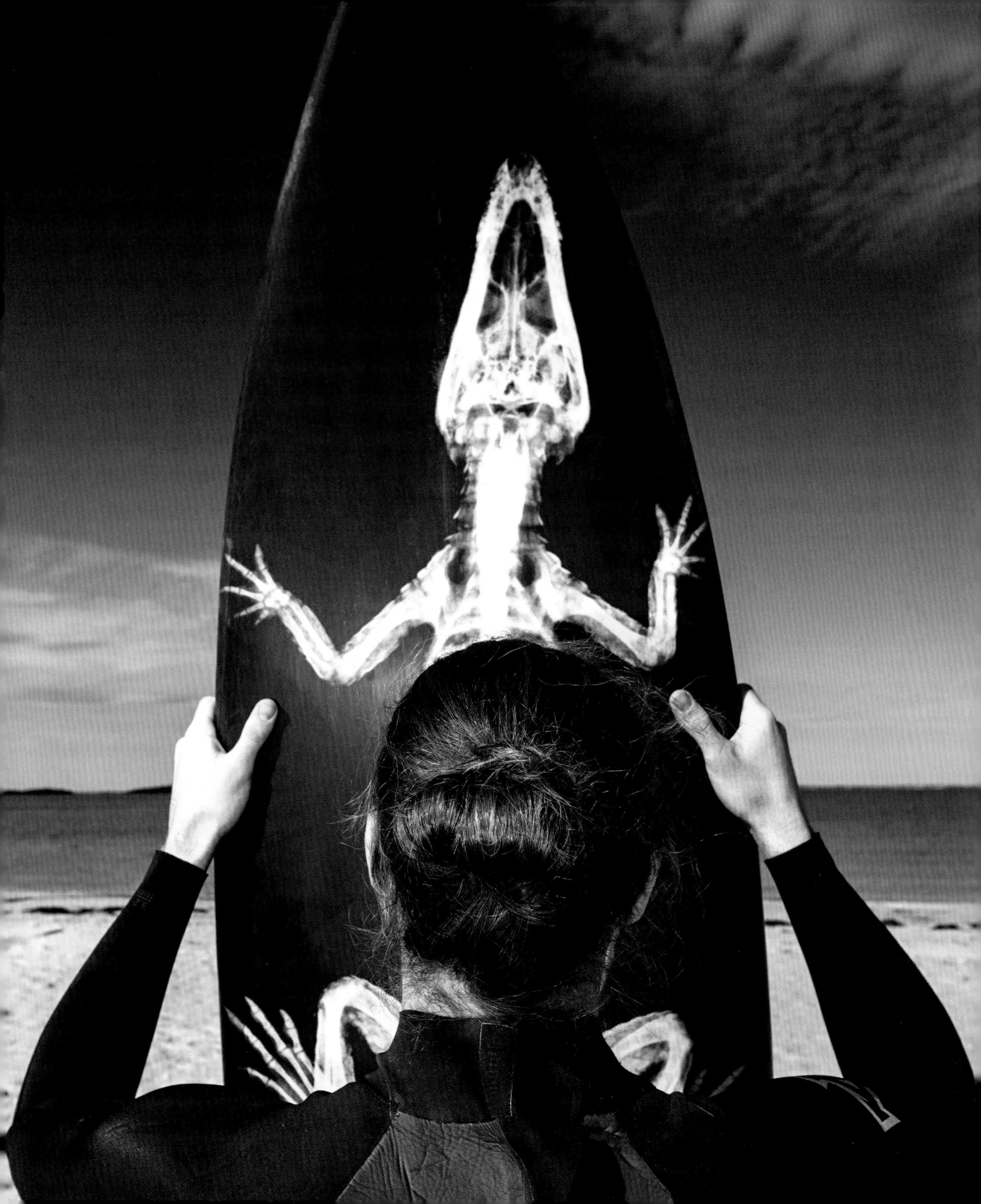

INTRODUCTION

It started out in 1995: while rushing to make an exhibition catalog entry deadline for a show in Paris about the shoe designer Roger Vivier, I decided to x-ray a pair of Vivier stilettos as my submission. I had one day to find the shoes in New York, make an x-ray, photograph the x-ray of the shoes on a light box to make a print (in the pre-digital era), develop the print, and send it off to Paris that evening. Through Dr. William Frosch, who chaired the Psychiatry Department at Cornell University Medical School, I reached Rick Perez, the head of radiology at New York Hospital. Rick provided the shoe x-rays I needed in short order, which started a friendship that reflects our mutual excitement of looking inside the world that fuels this book.

Thus began a study of objects, plants, and animals observed through the lens of technology.

Radiographic, the companion book to *Surf/Skate*, reviews a 20-year artistic journey that ends in Brazil in the body of work entitled, *Health of the Planet*. I'd like to thank the animals that gave me the opportunity to hang out with them—namely, the sloths, anteaters, alligators, turtles, and birds.

Surf/Skate is both an extension of the *Health of the Planet* project and a record of the energy that went into making the artwork itself. The x-ray alligator on a surfboard became the eco-trophy that stands as one of the icons of this project. At this point, multiple surfaces have become vehicles for *Health of the Planet*: surfboards, skate decks, clothing, coffee mugs, and cashmere. Letting the images infiltrate the world in different ways allows for an endless motion into life, as the body uses this art in different ways on different waves.

Steve Miller

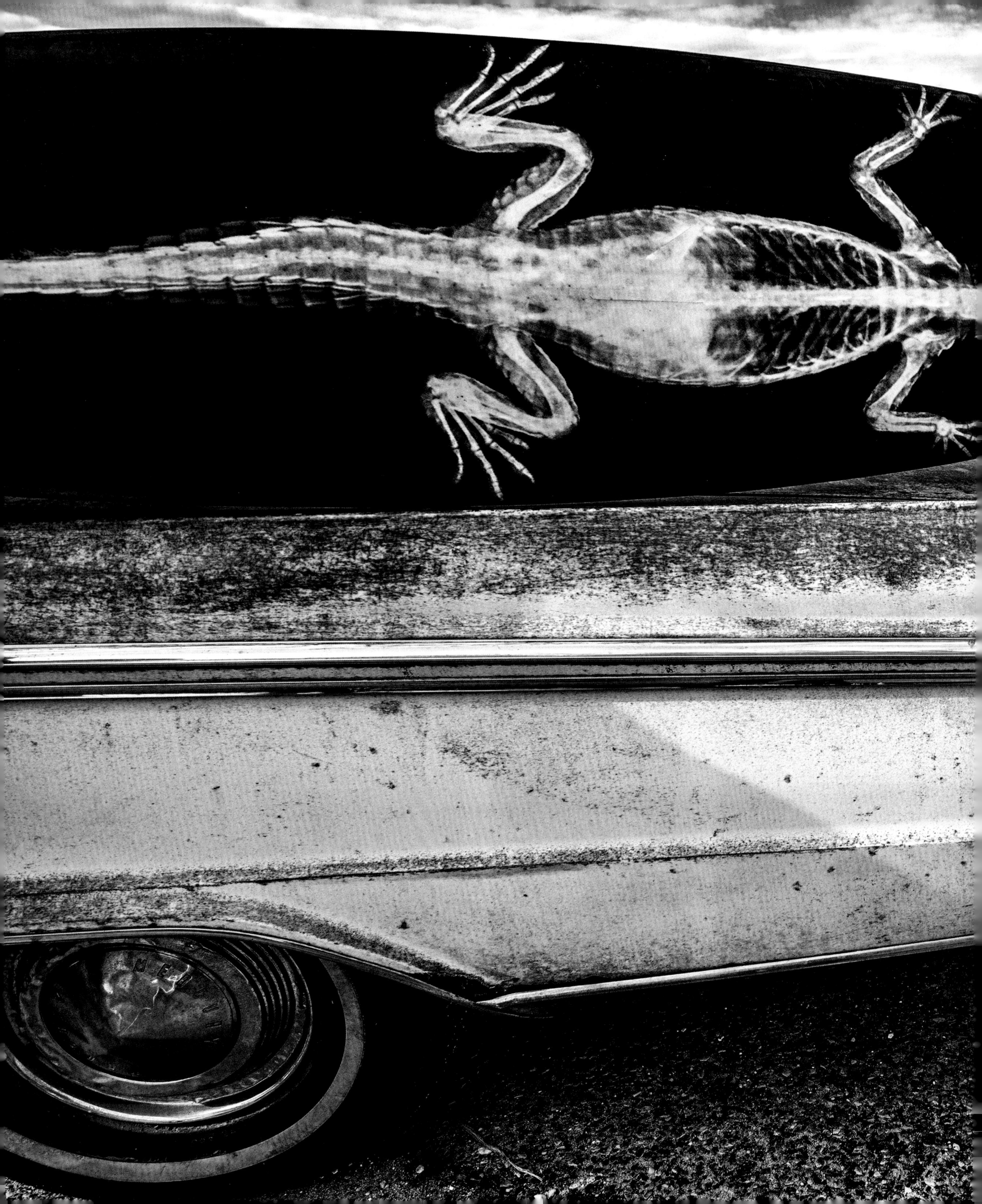

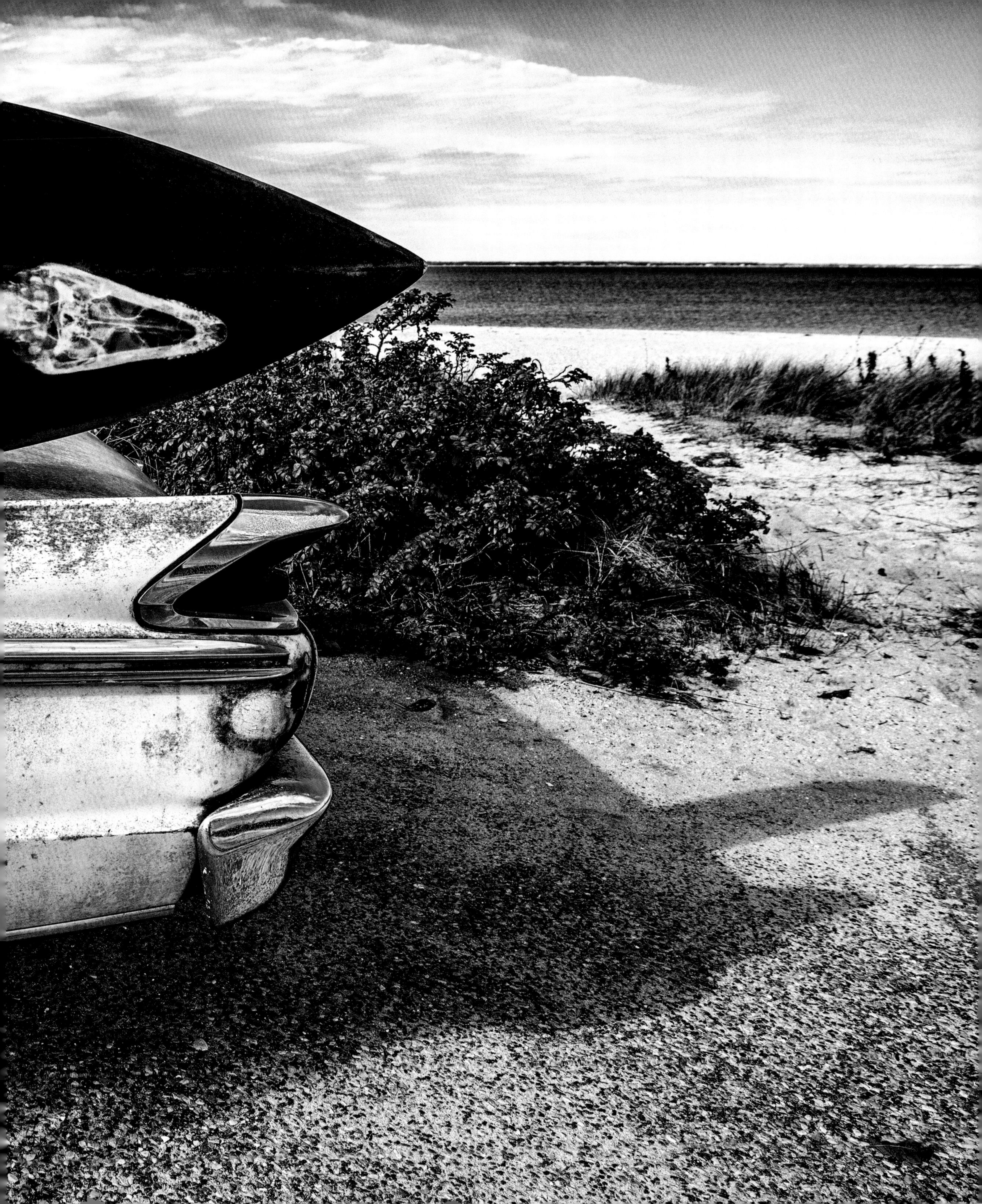

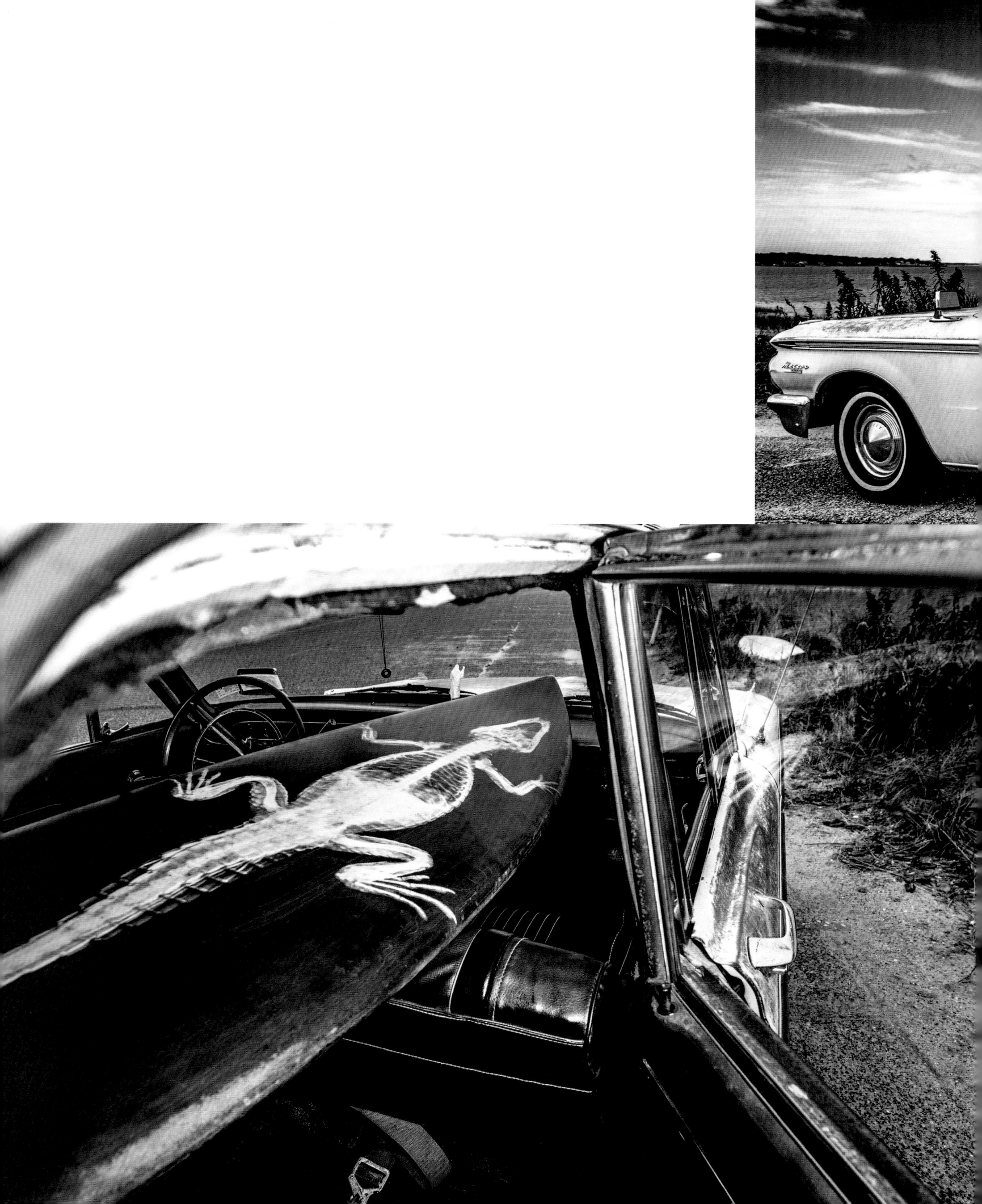

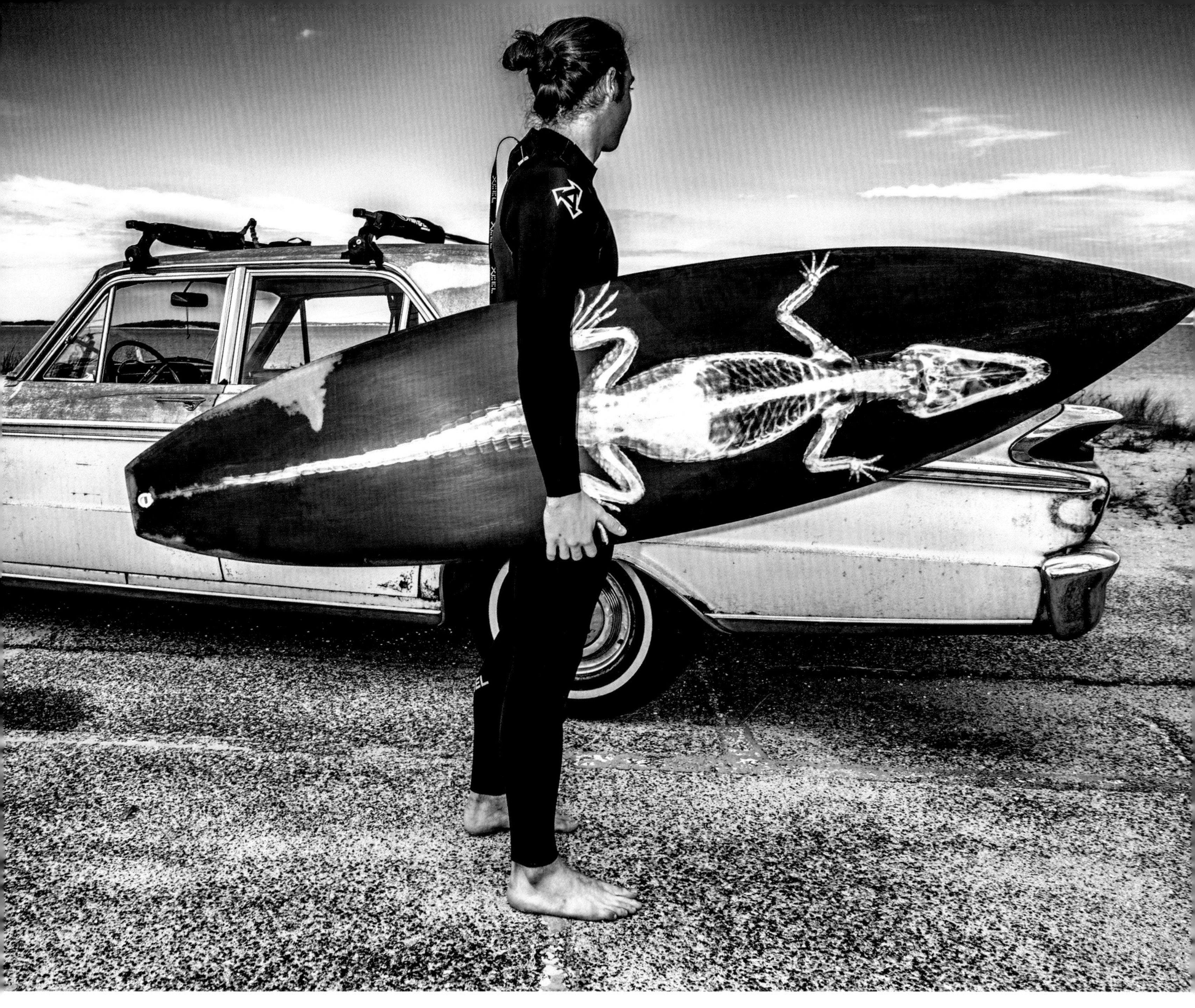

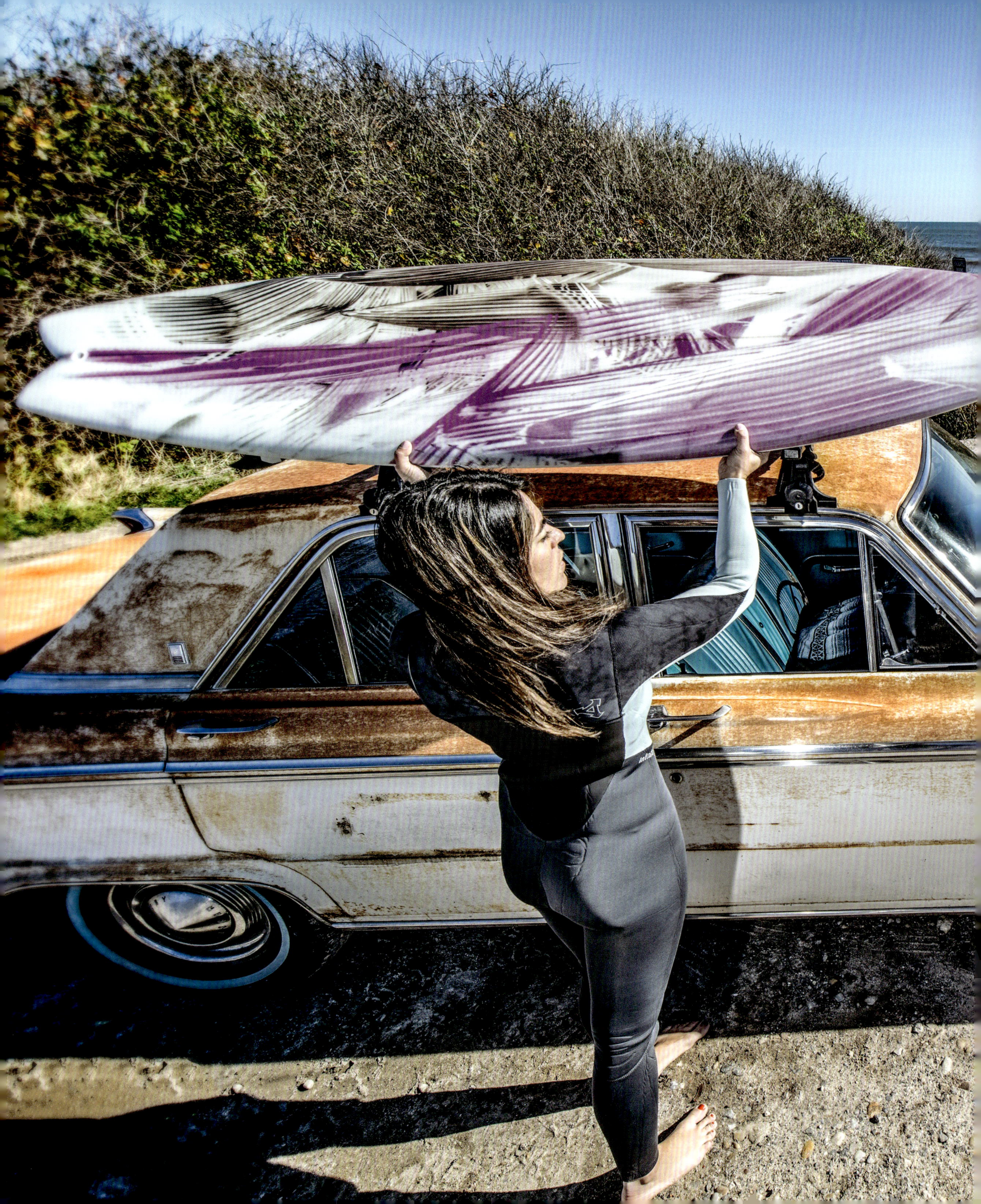

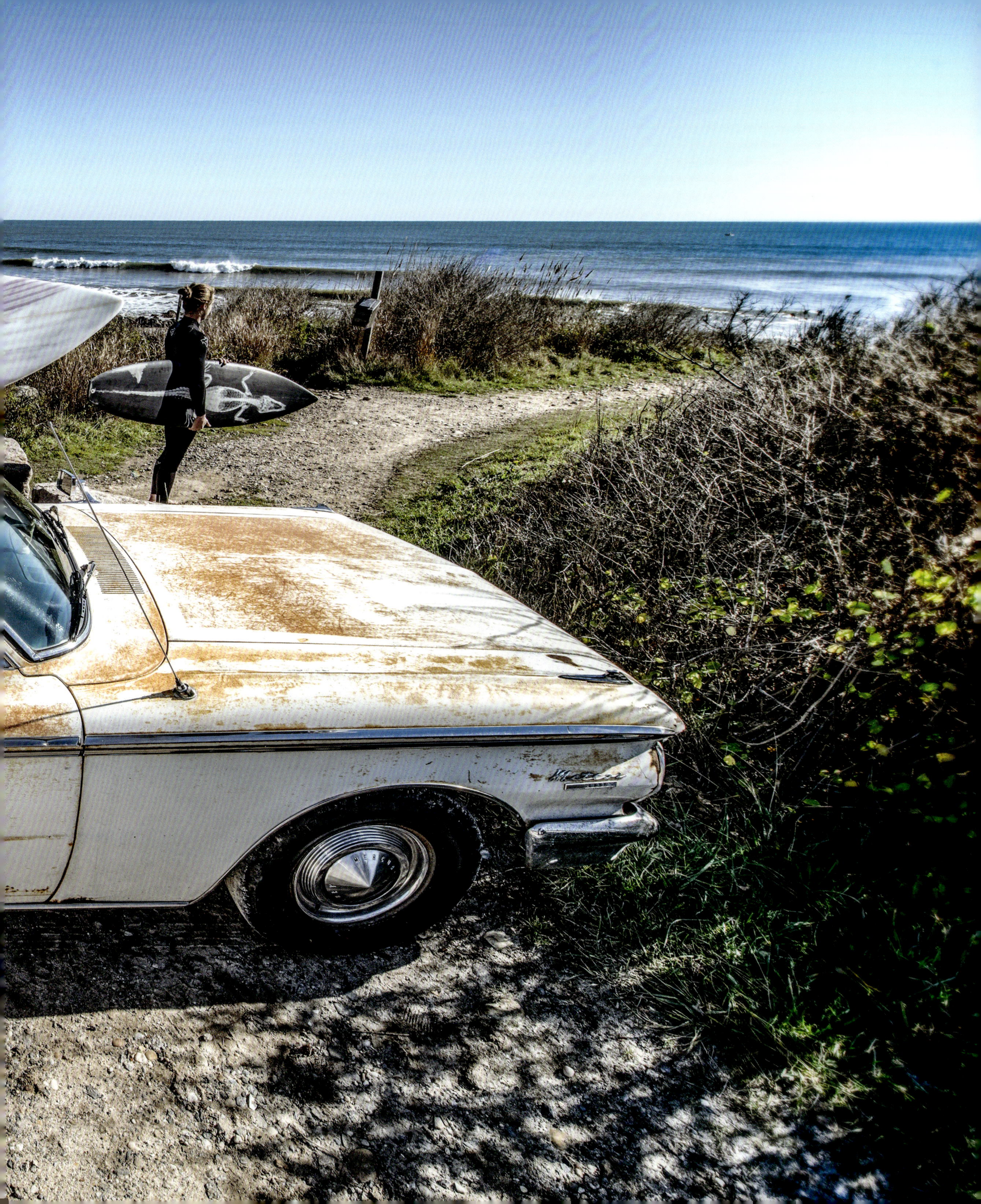

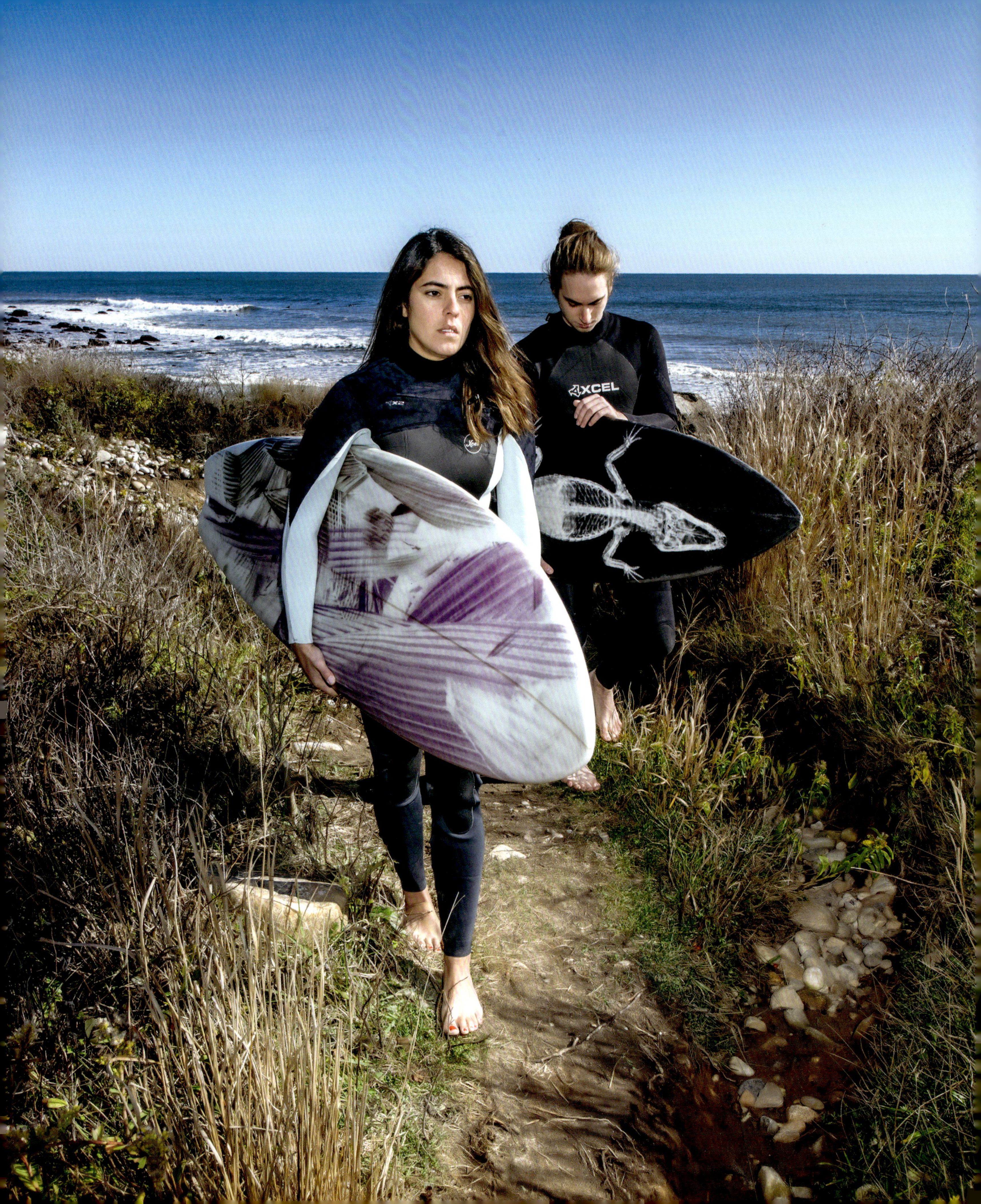

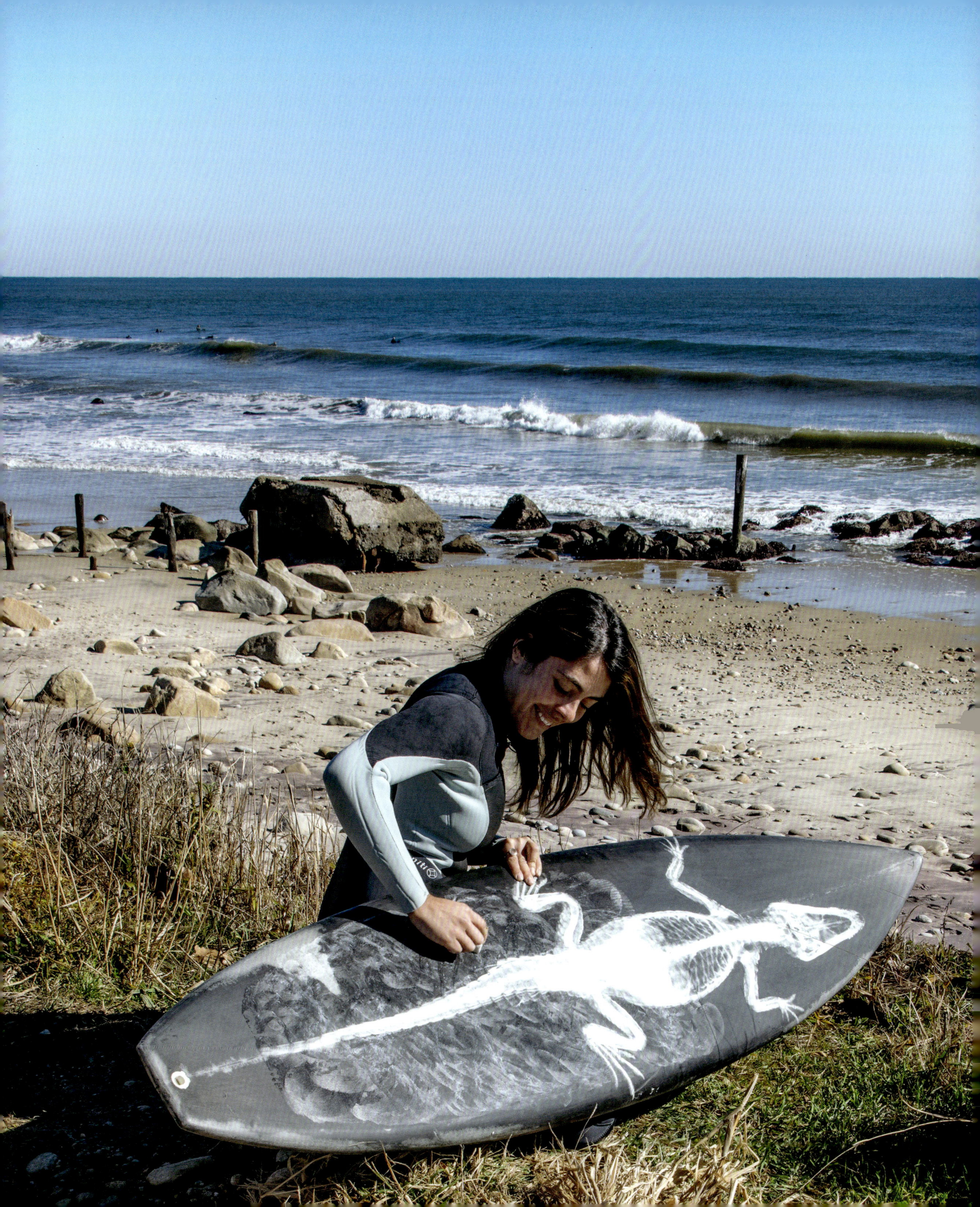

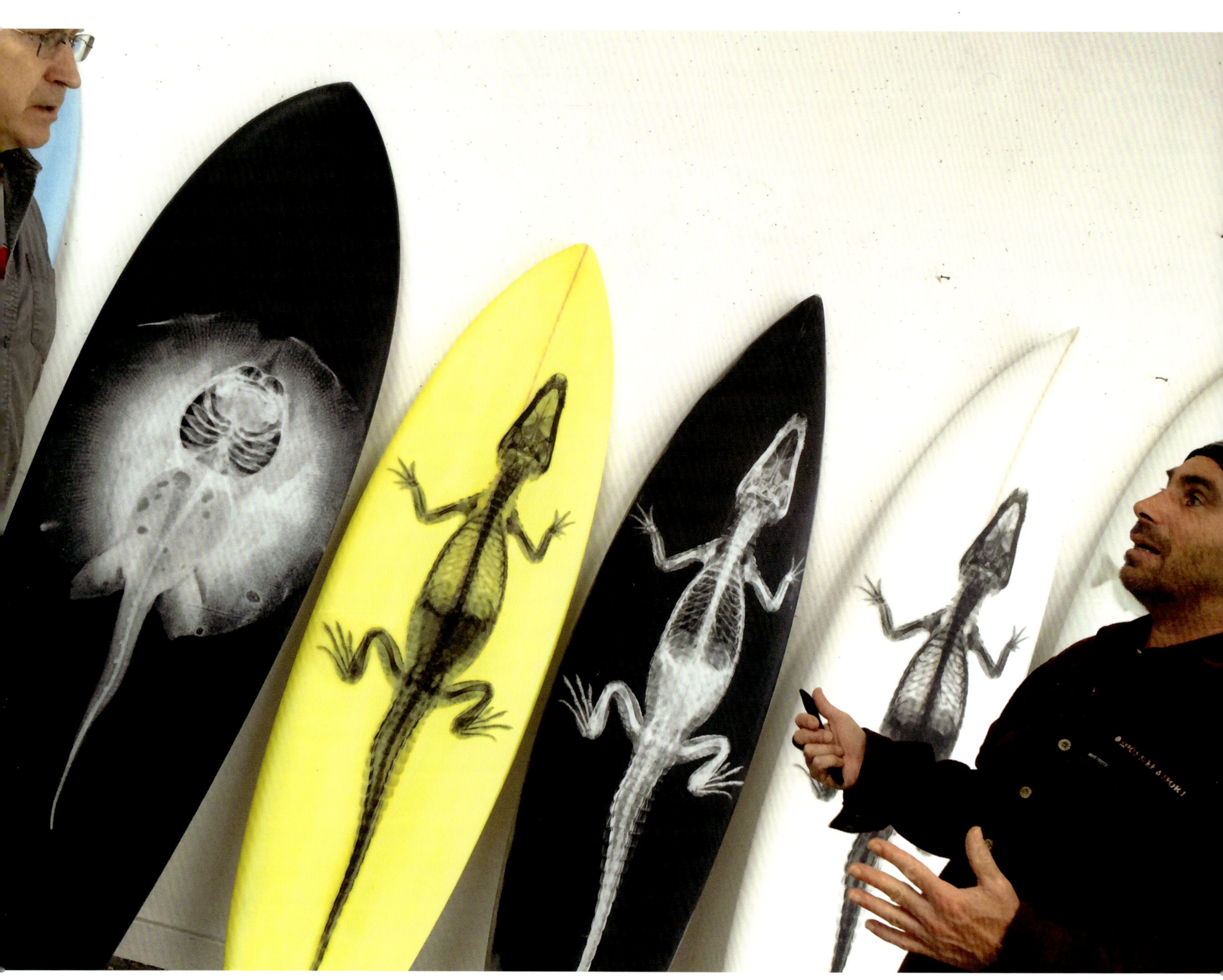

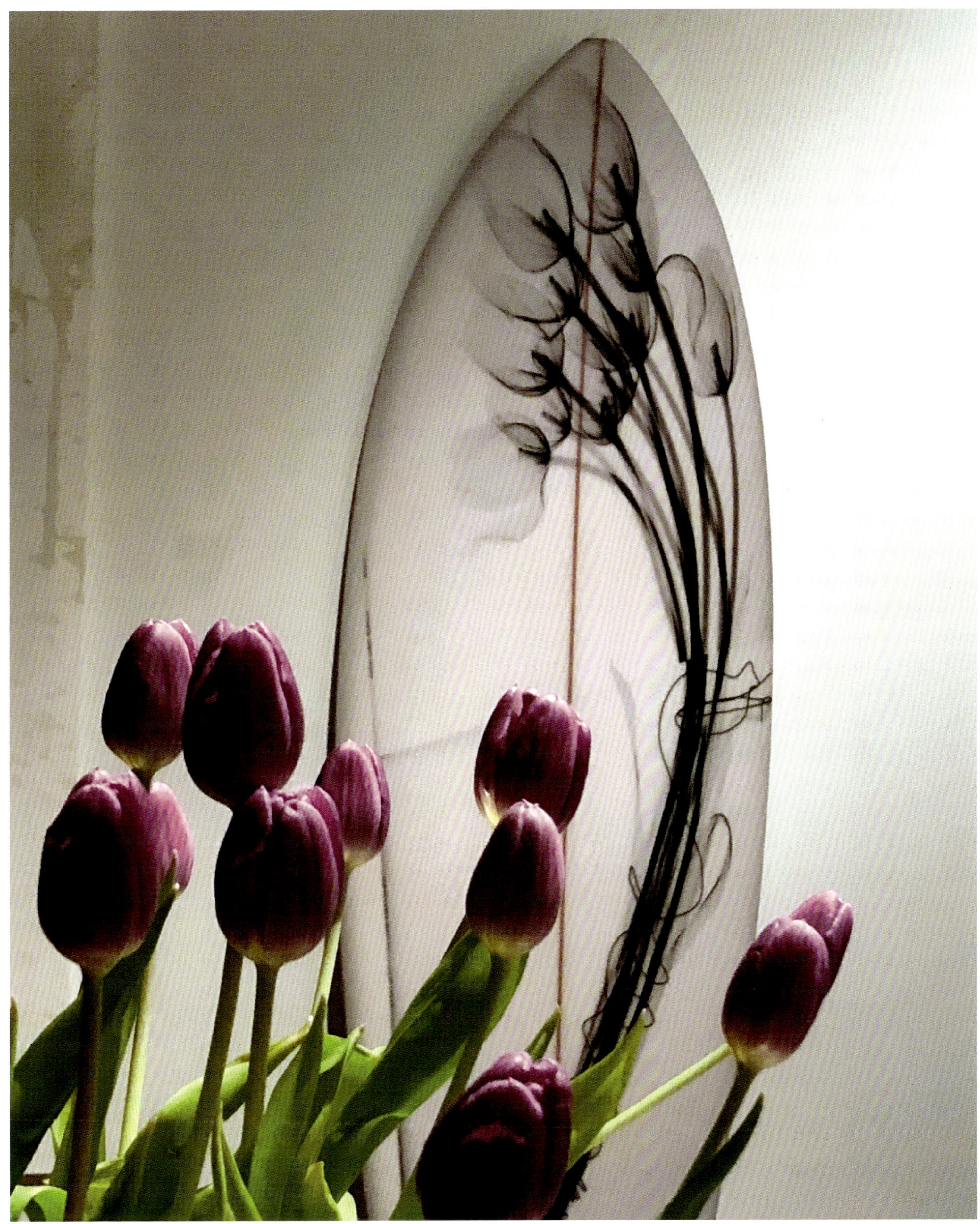

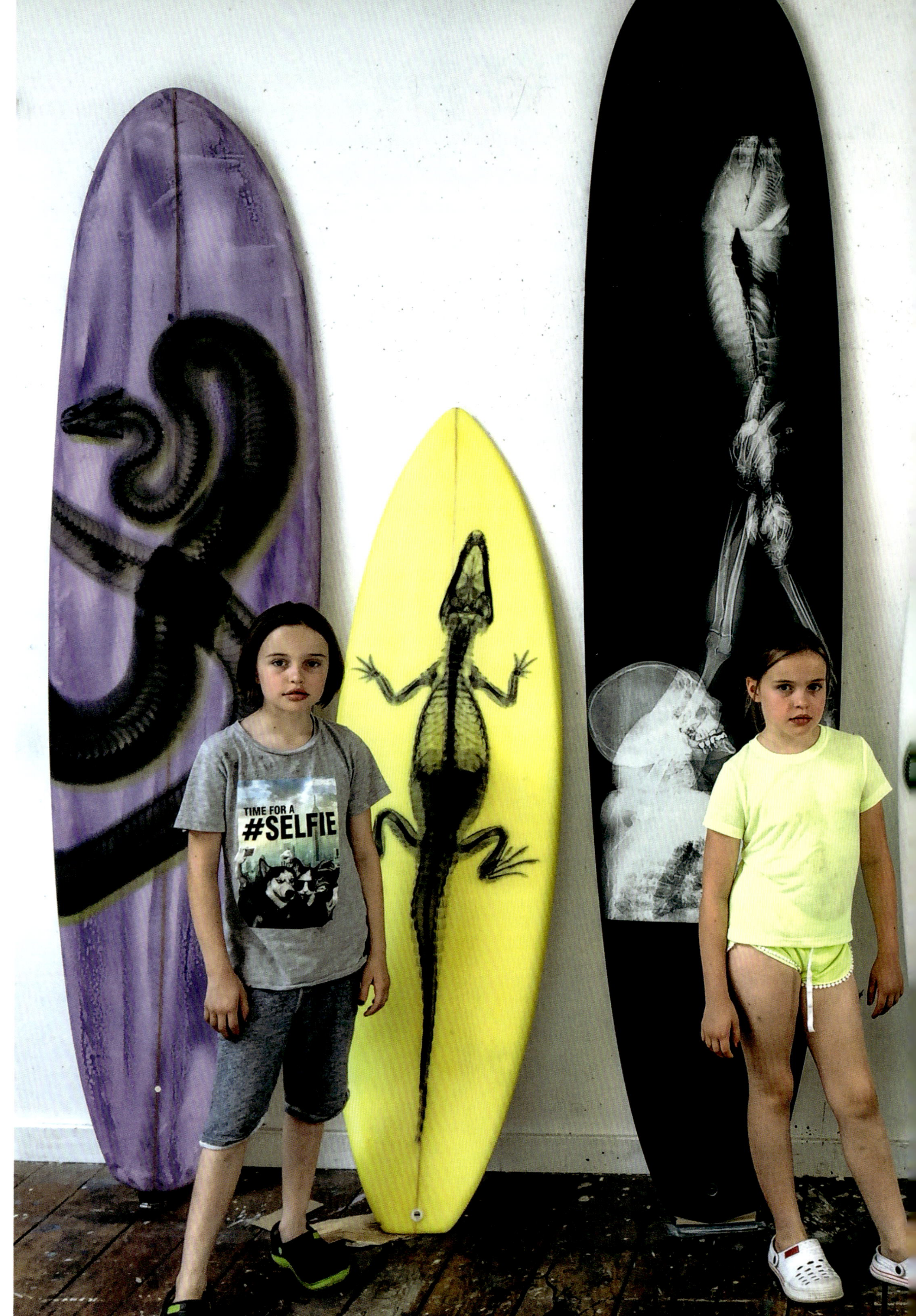

TIME FOR A
#SELFIE

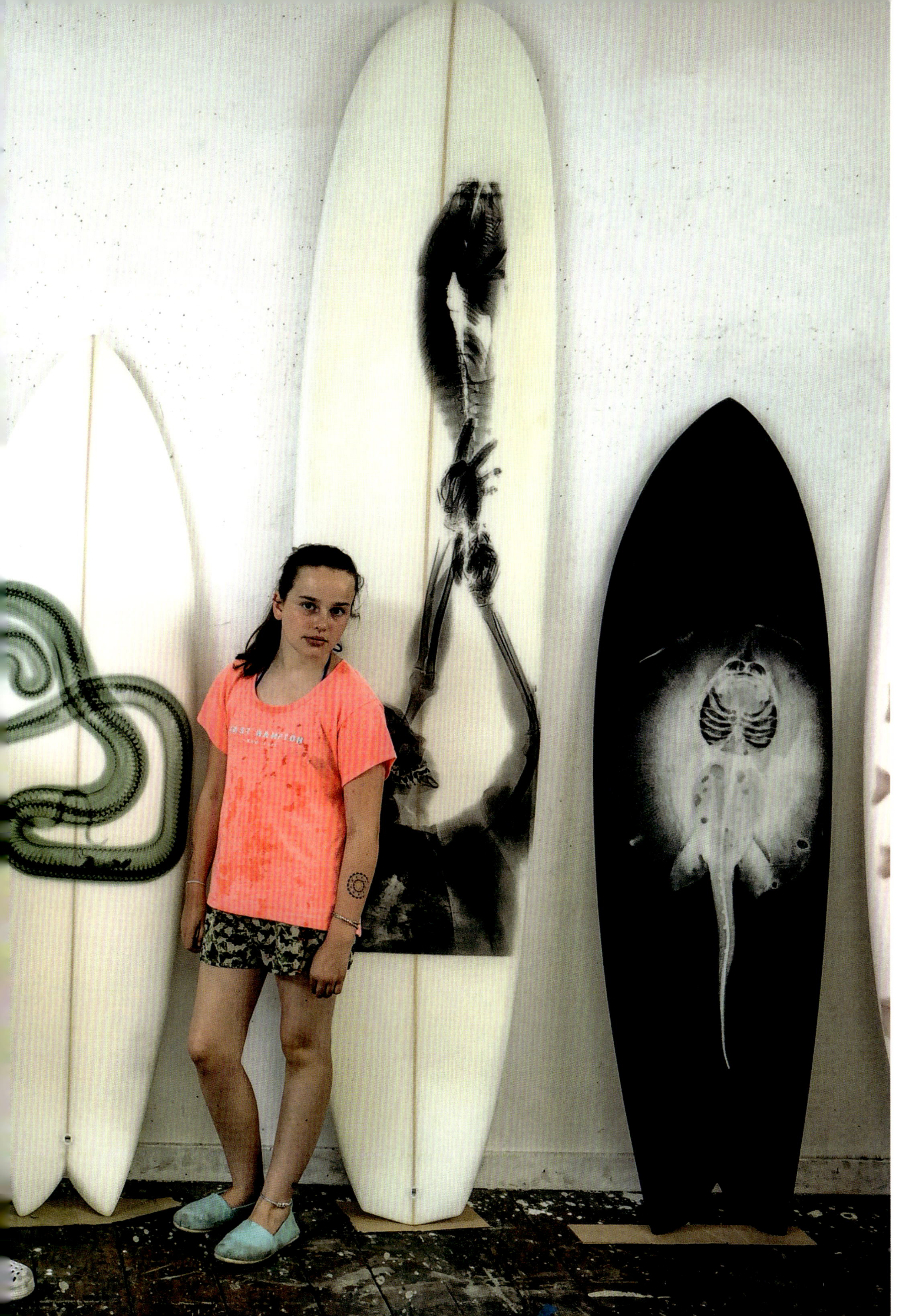

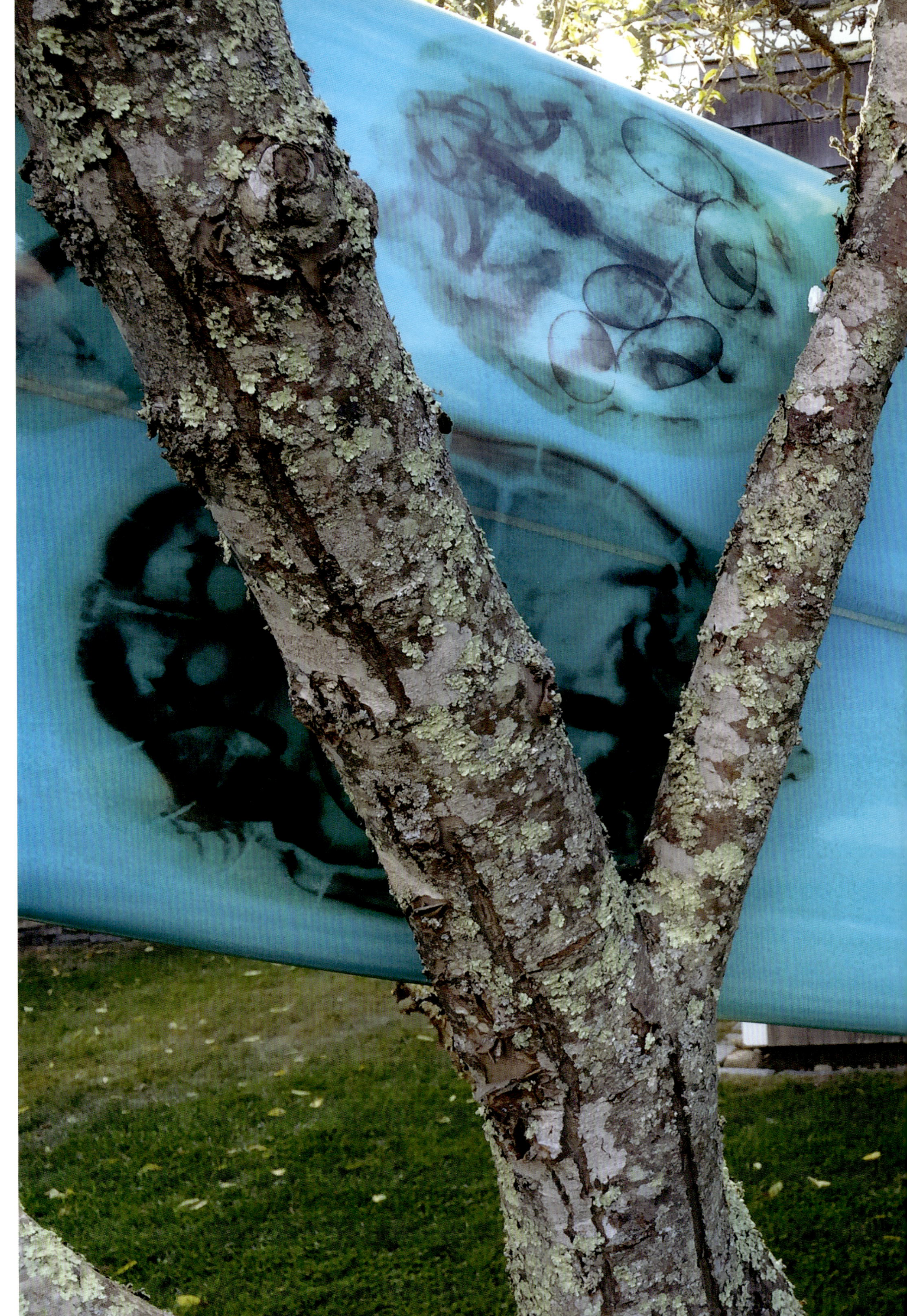

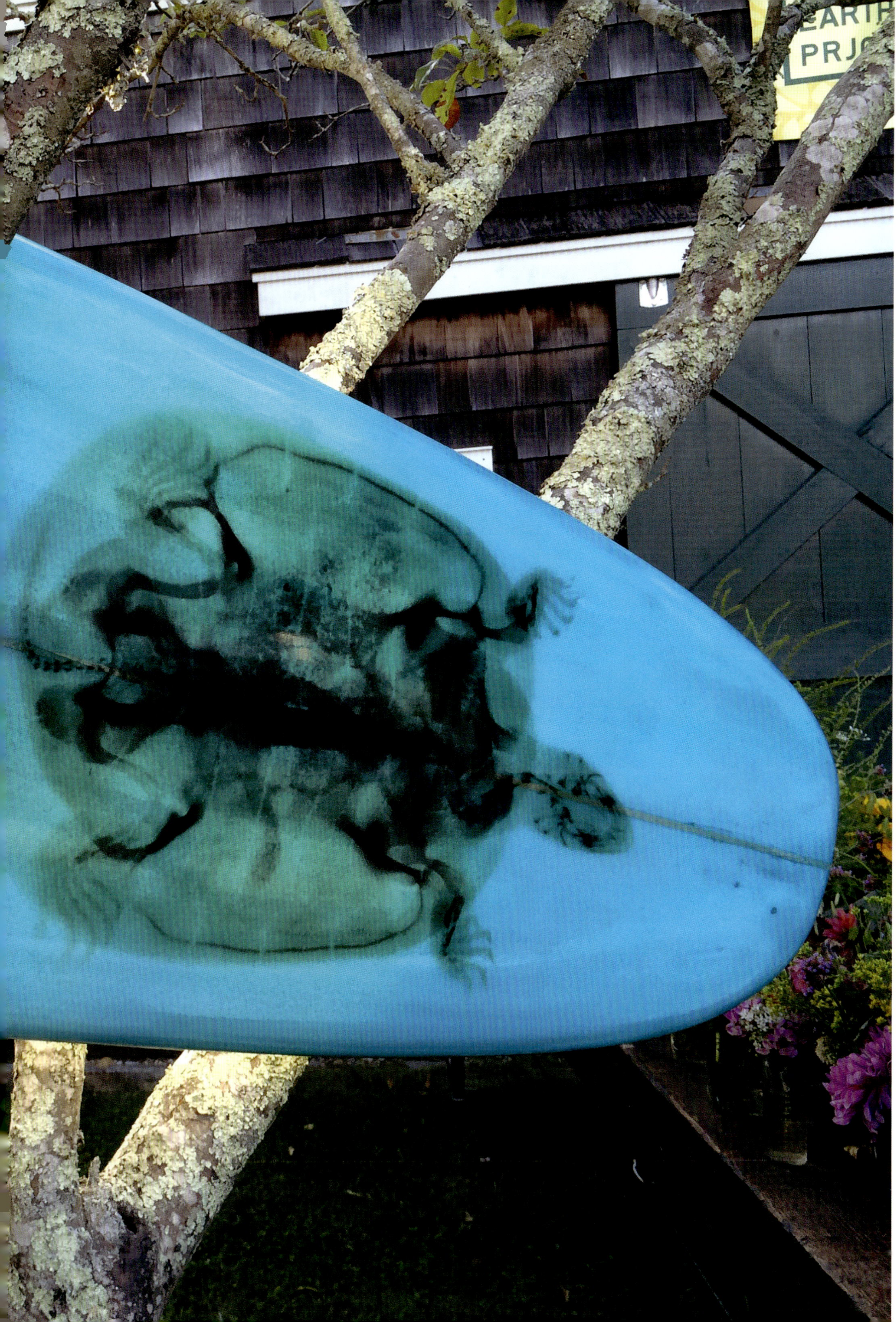

EARTH
PRJ

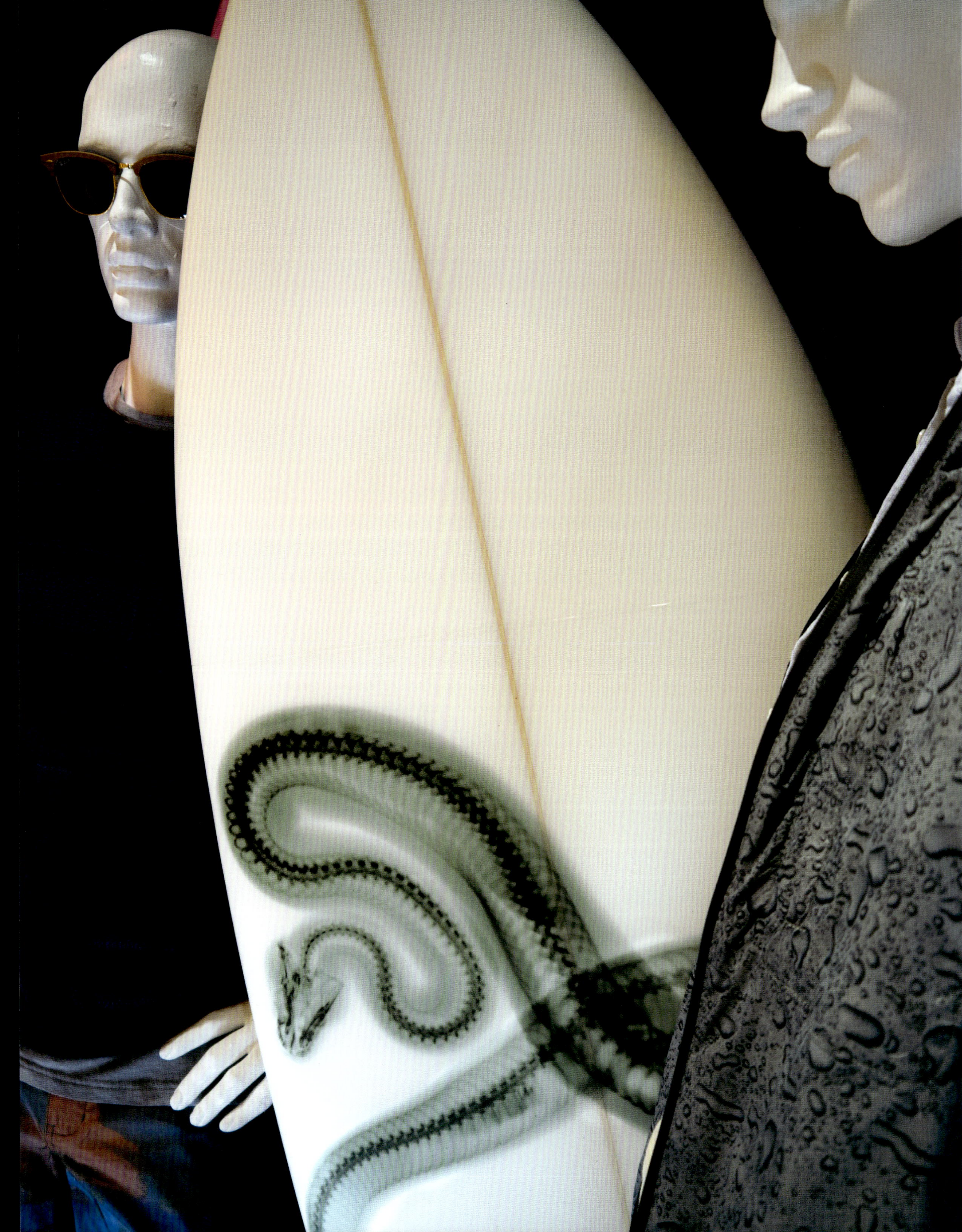

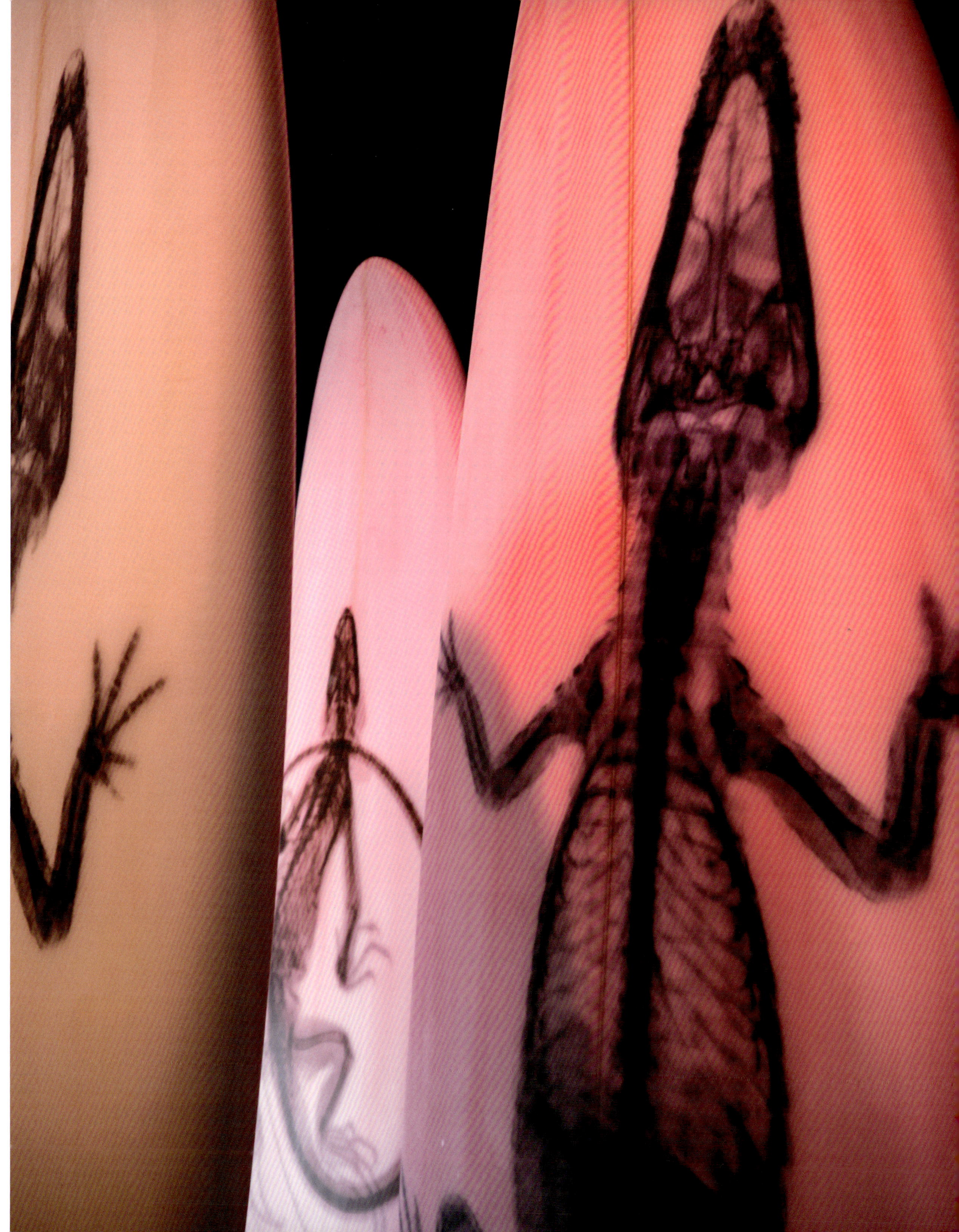

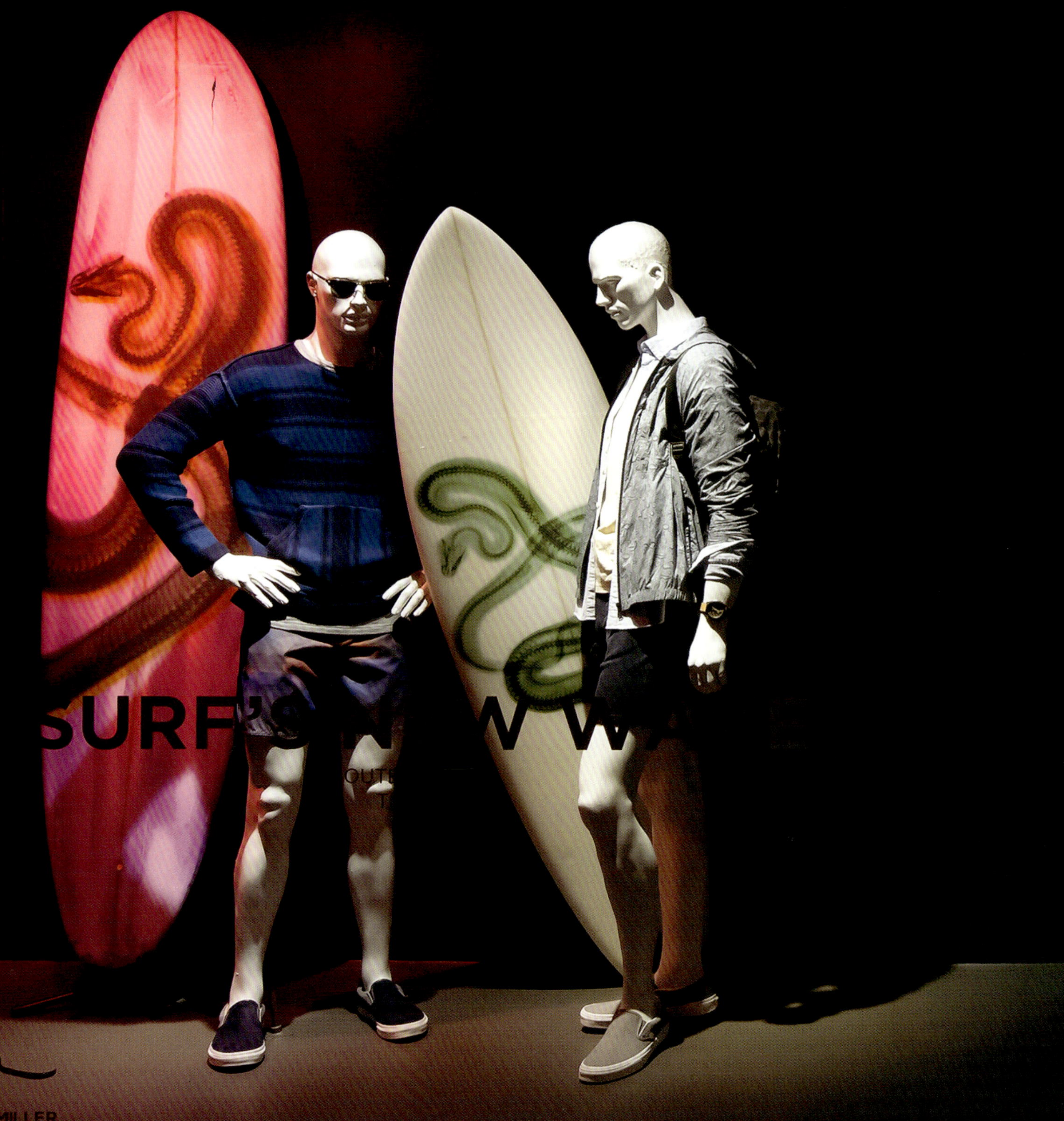

SURF'S NEW W
PLANET
esy of STEVE MILLER

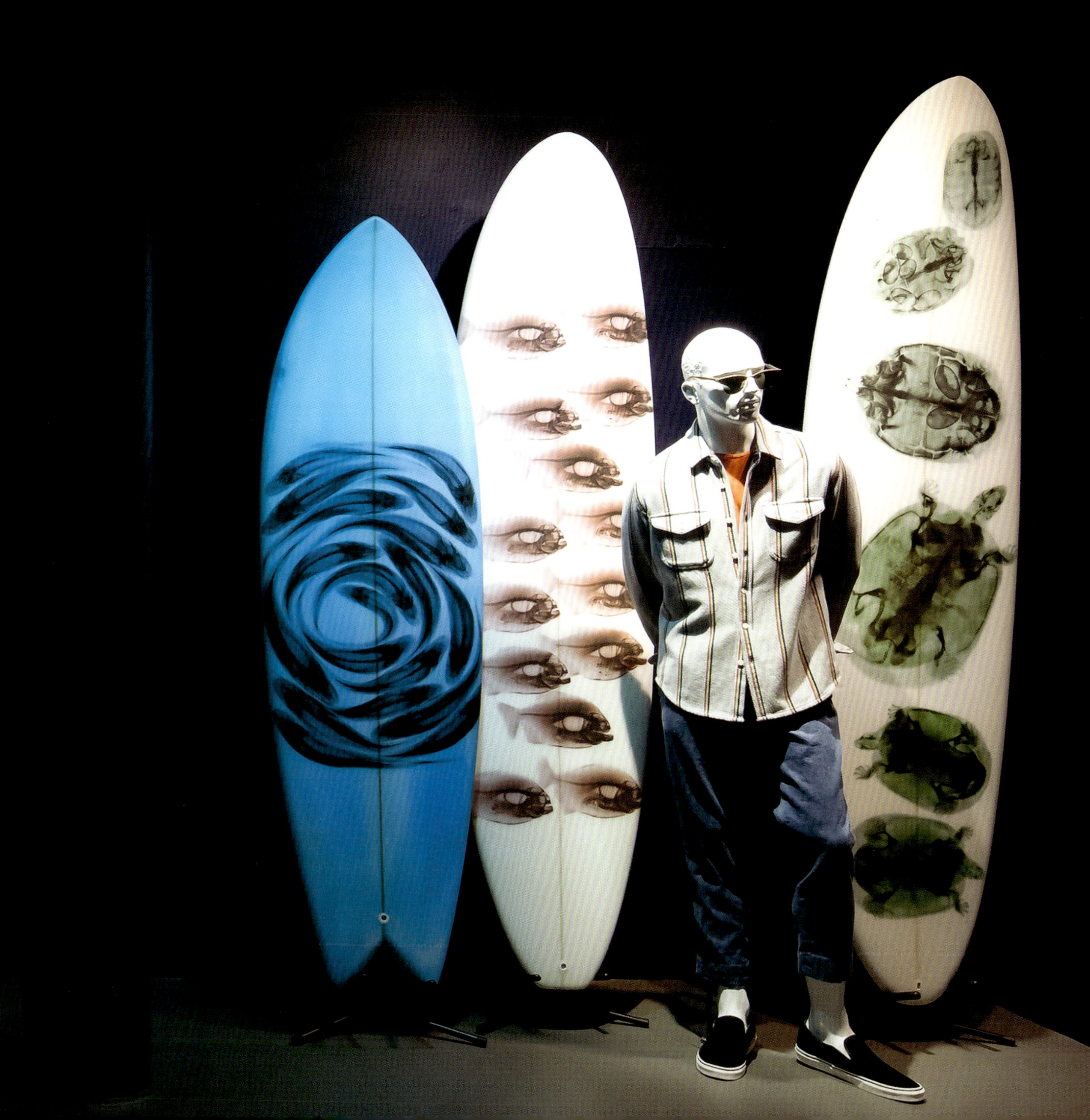

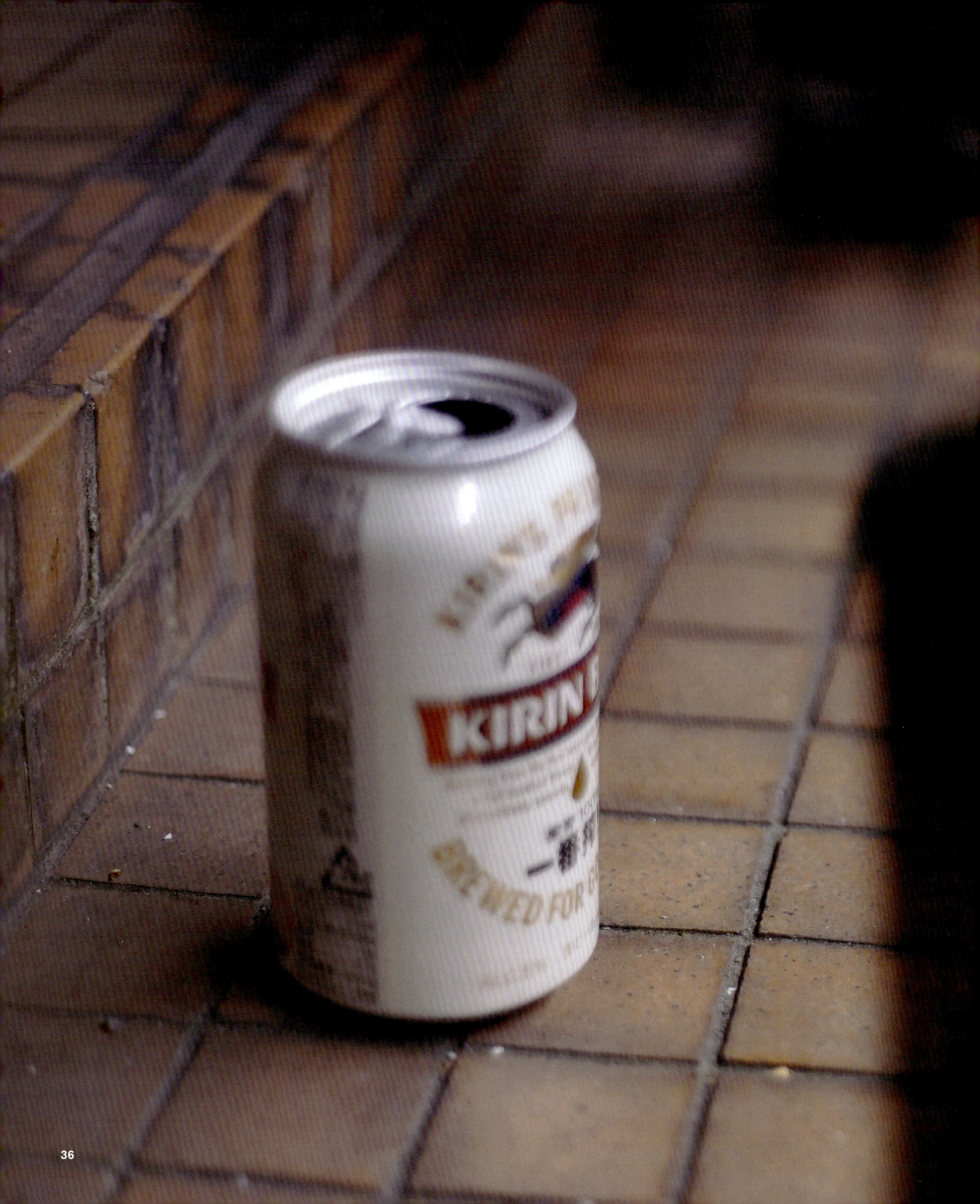

KIRIN
一番搾
BREWED FOR

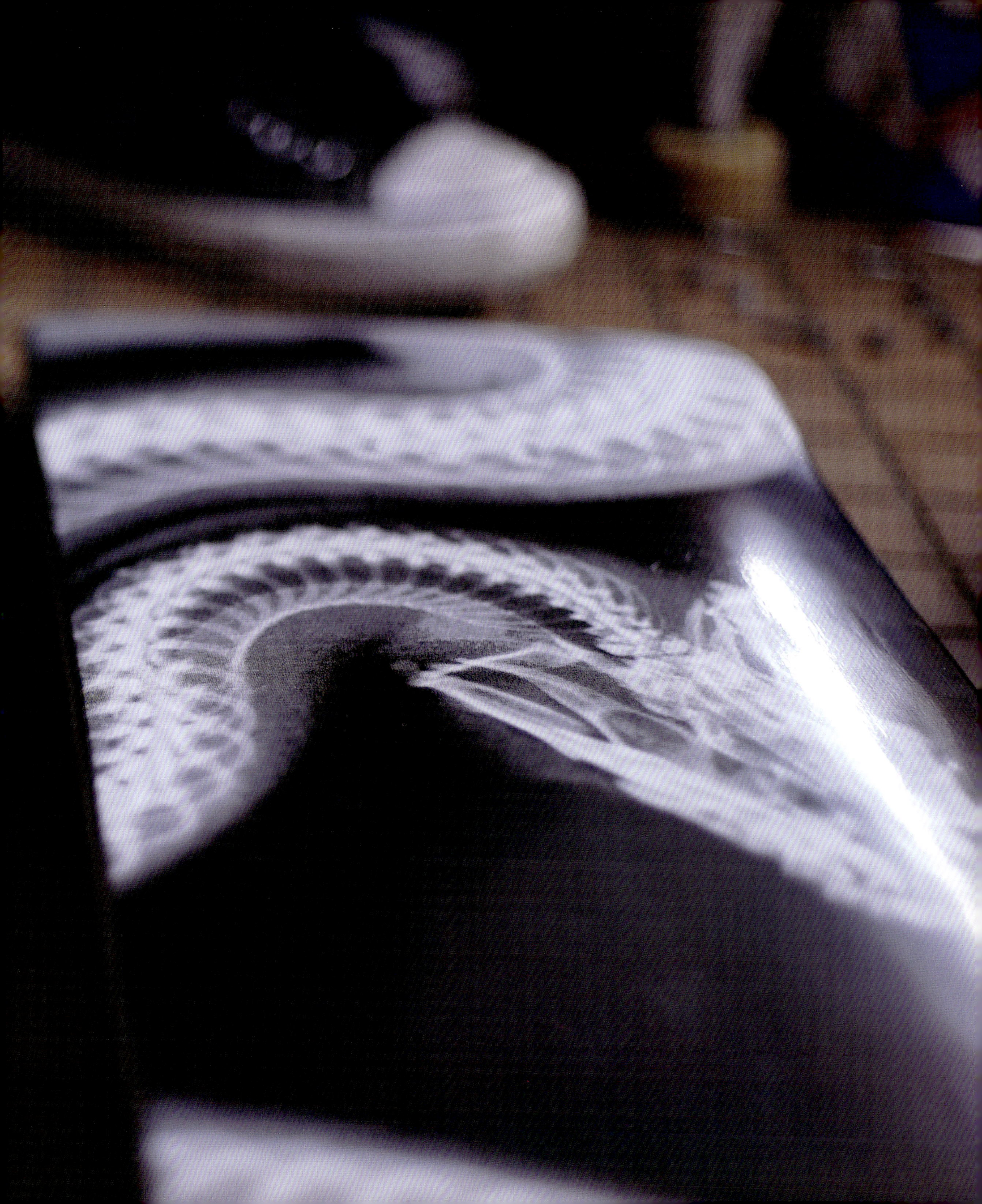

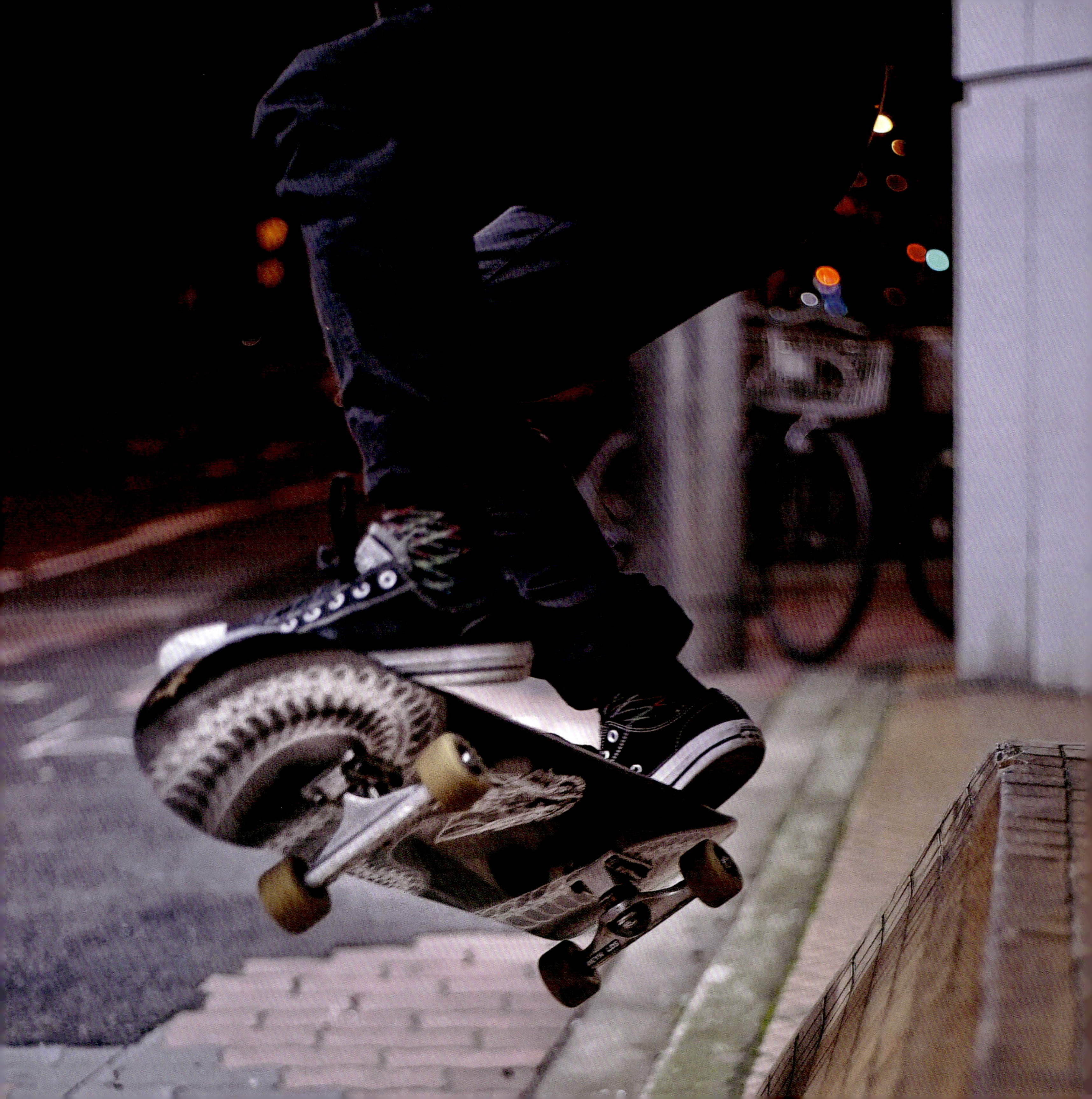

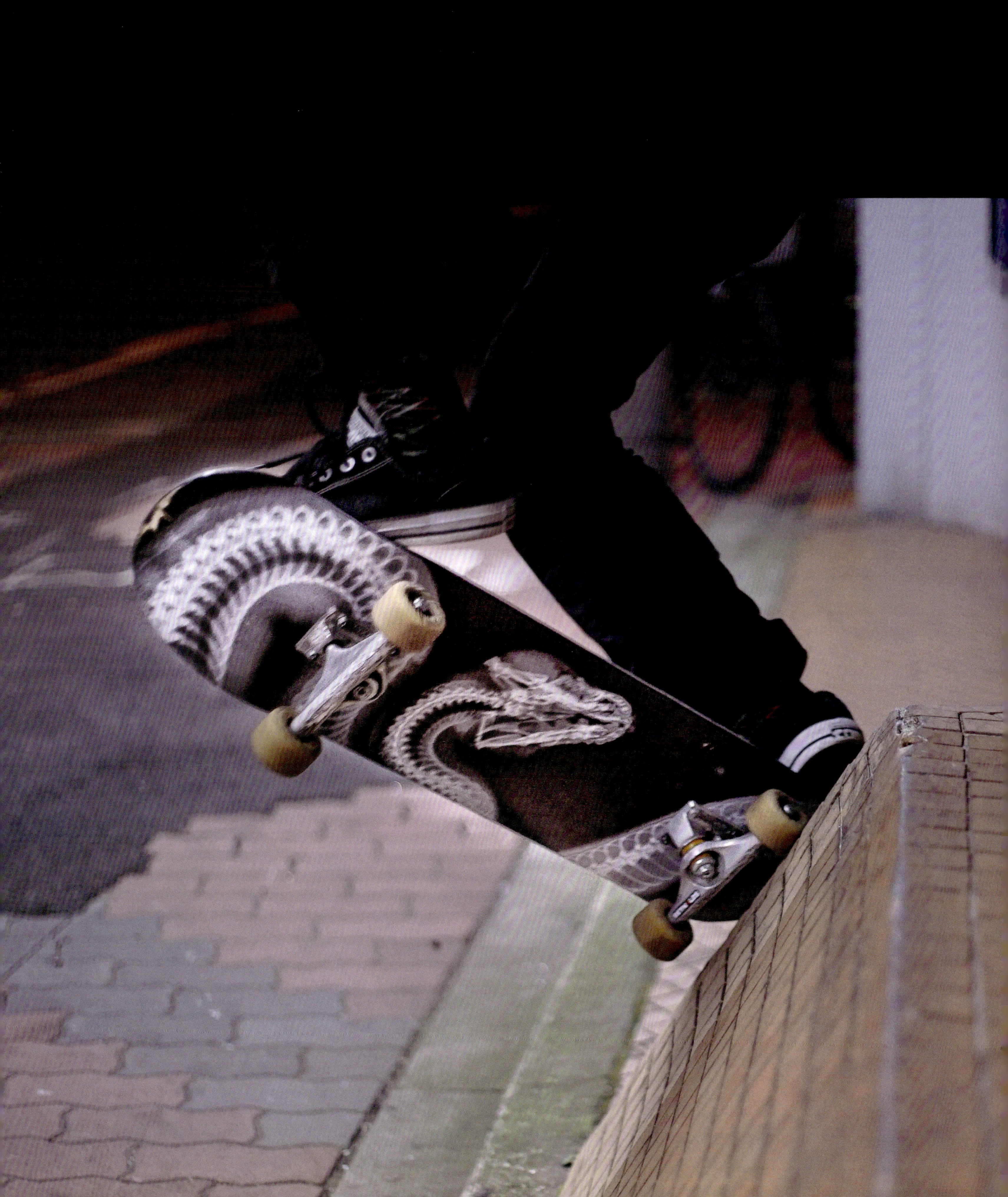

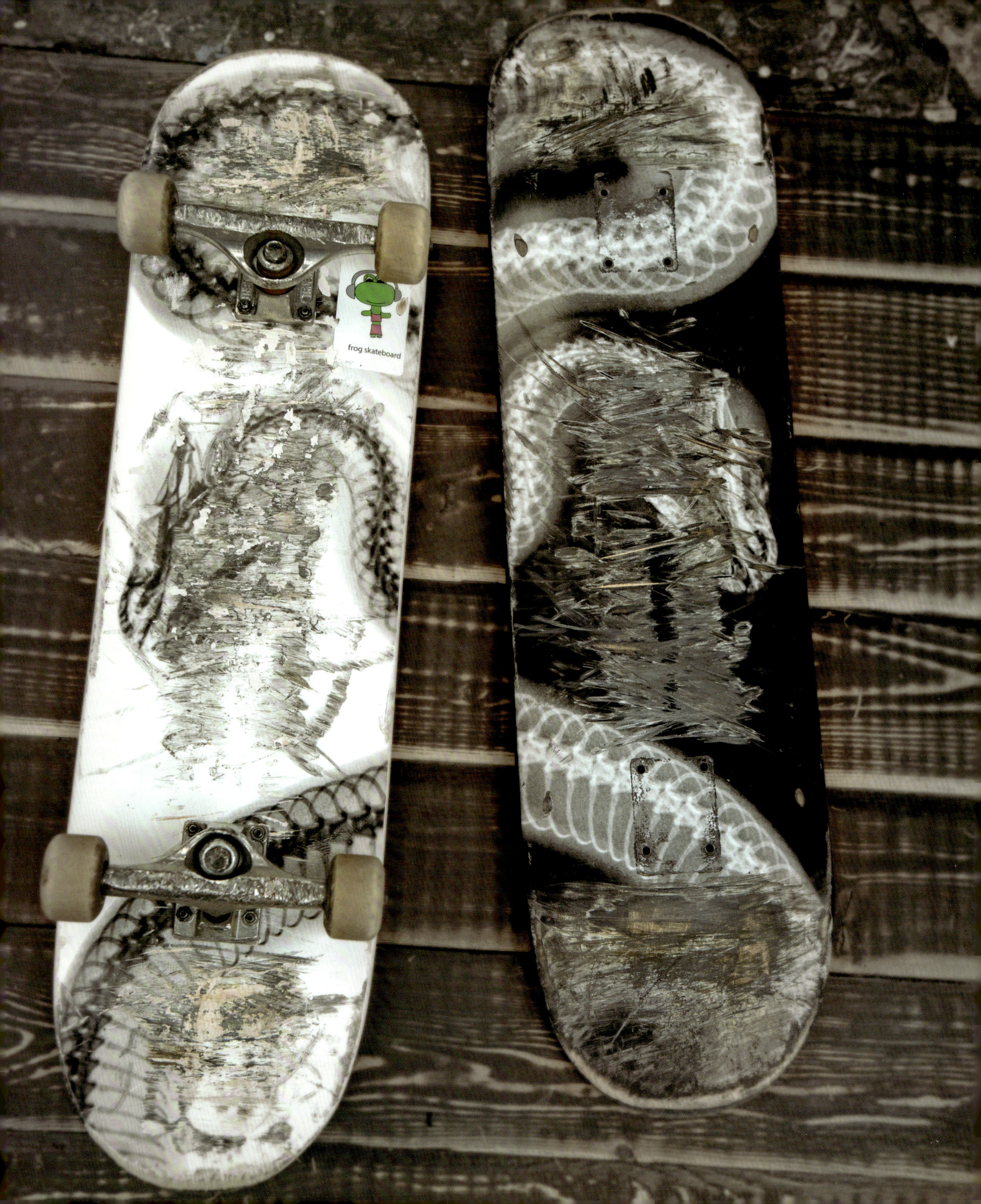

frog skateboard

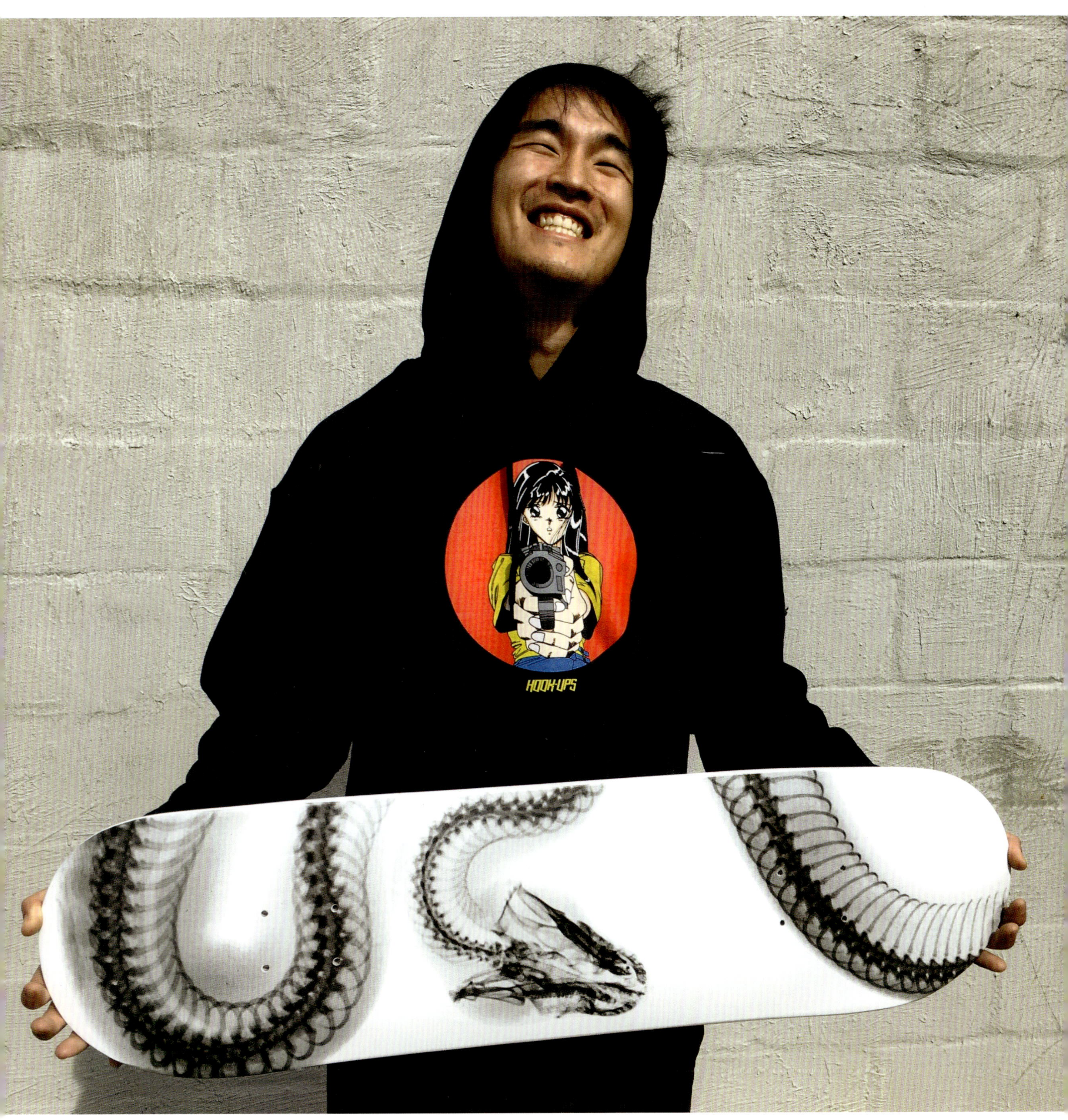
HOOK-UPS

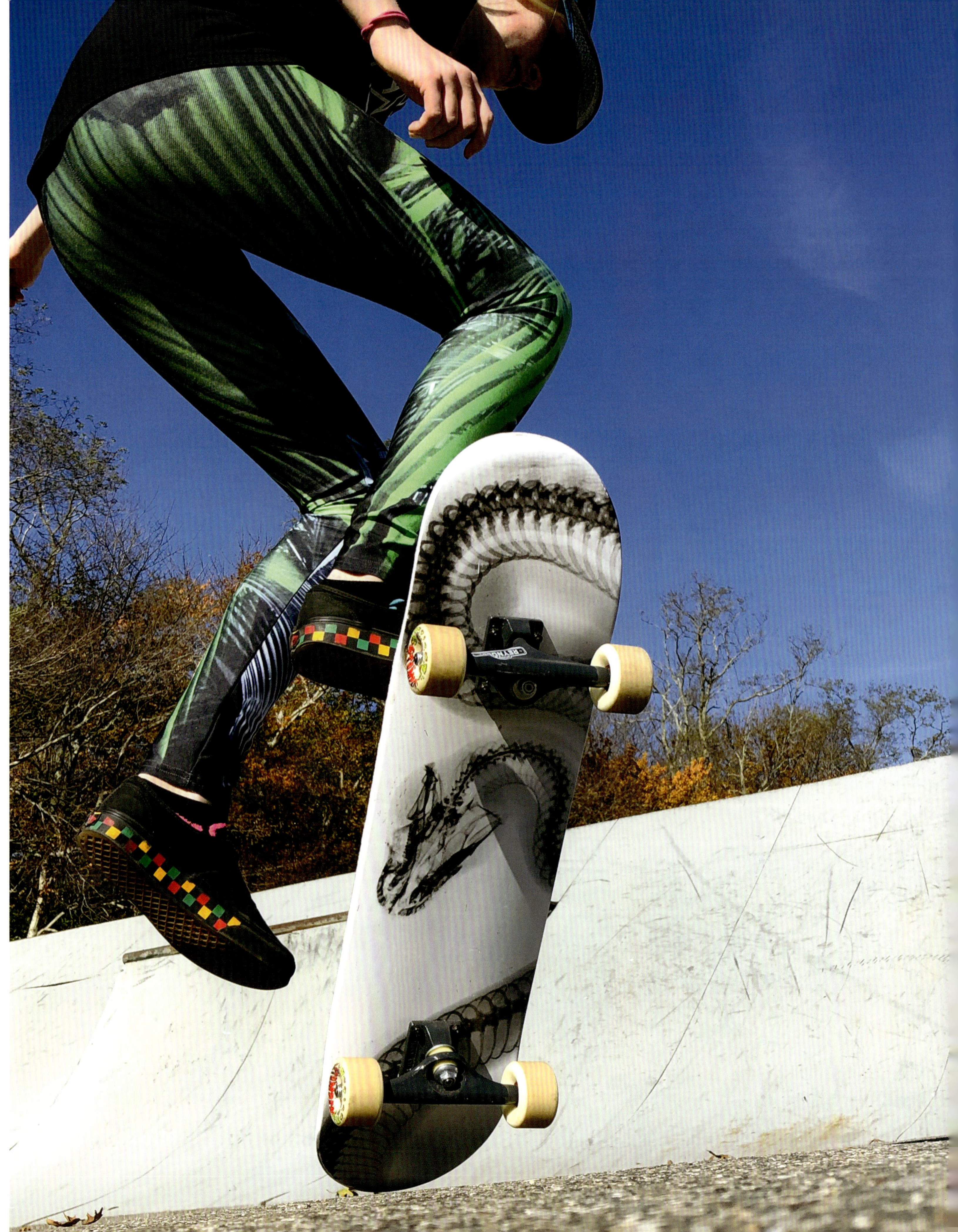

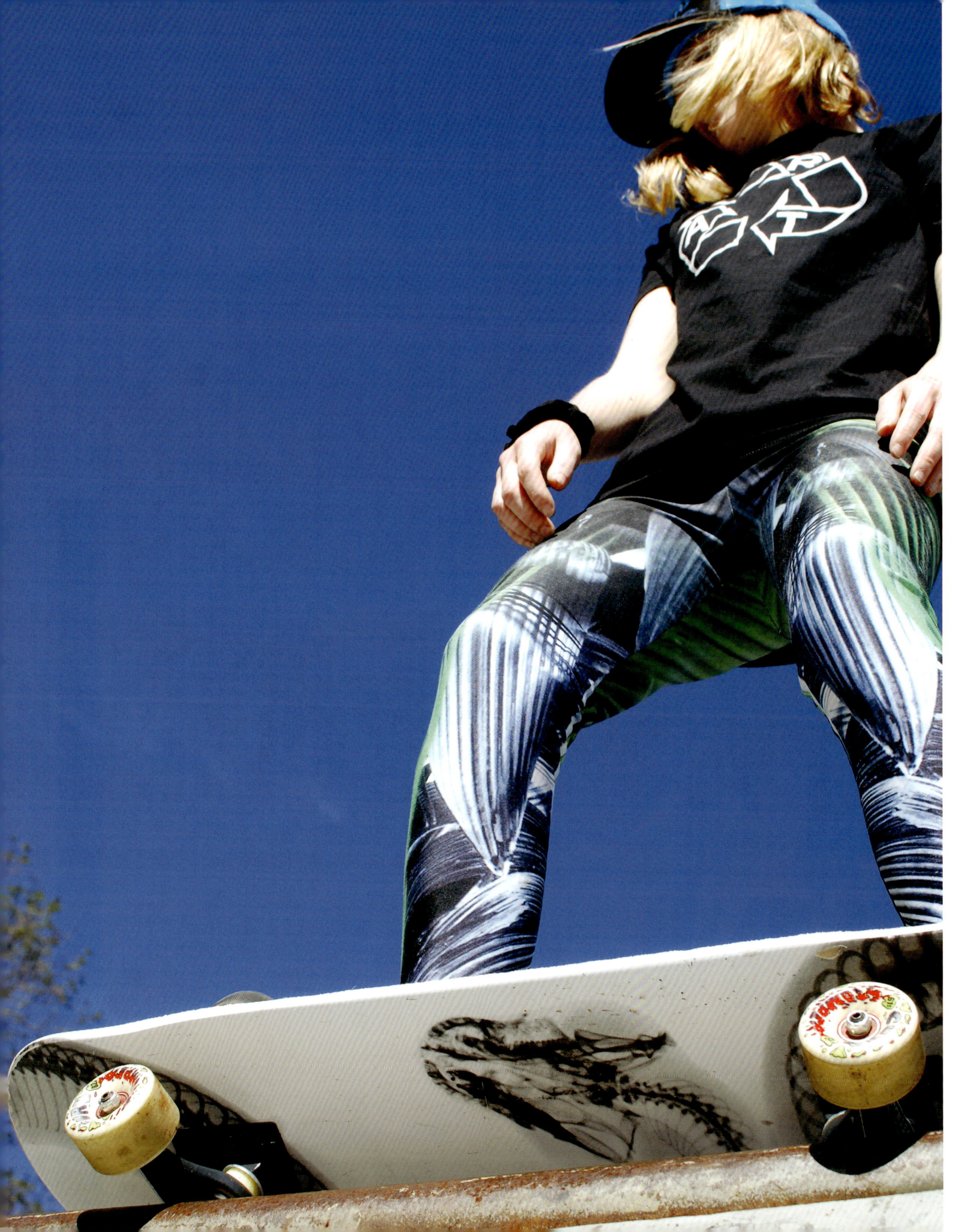

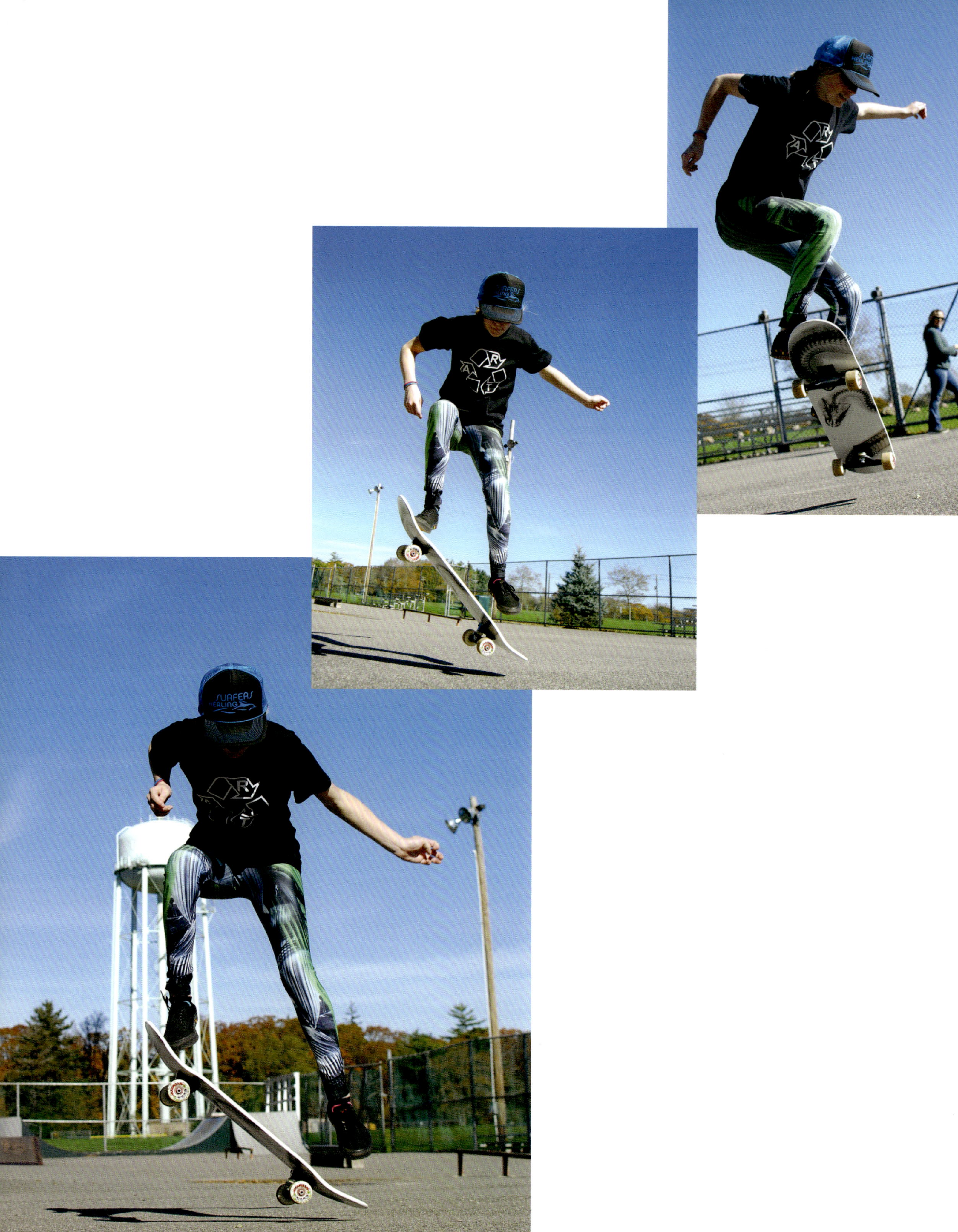

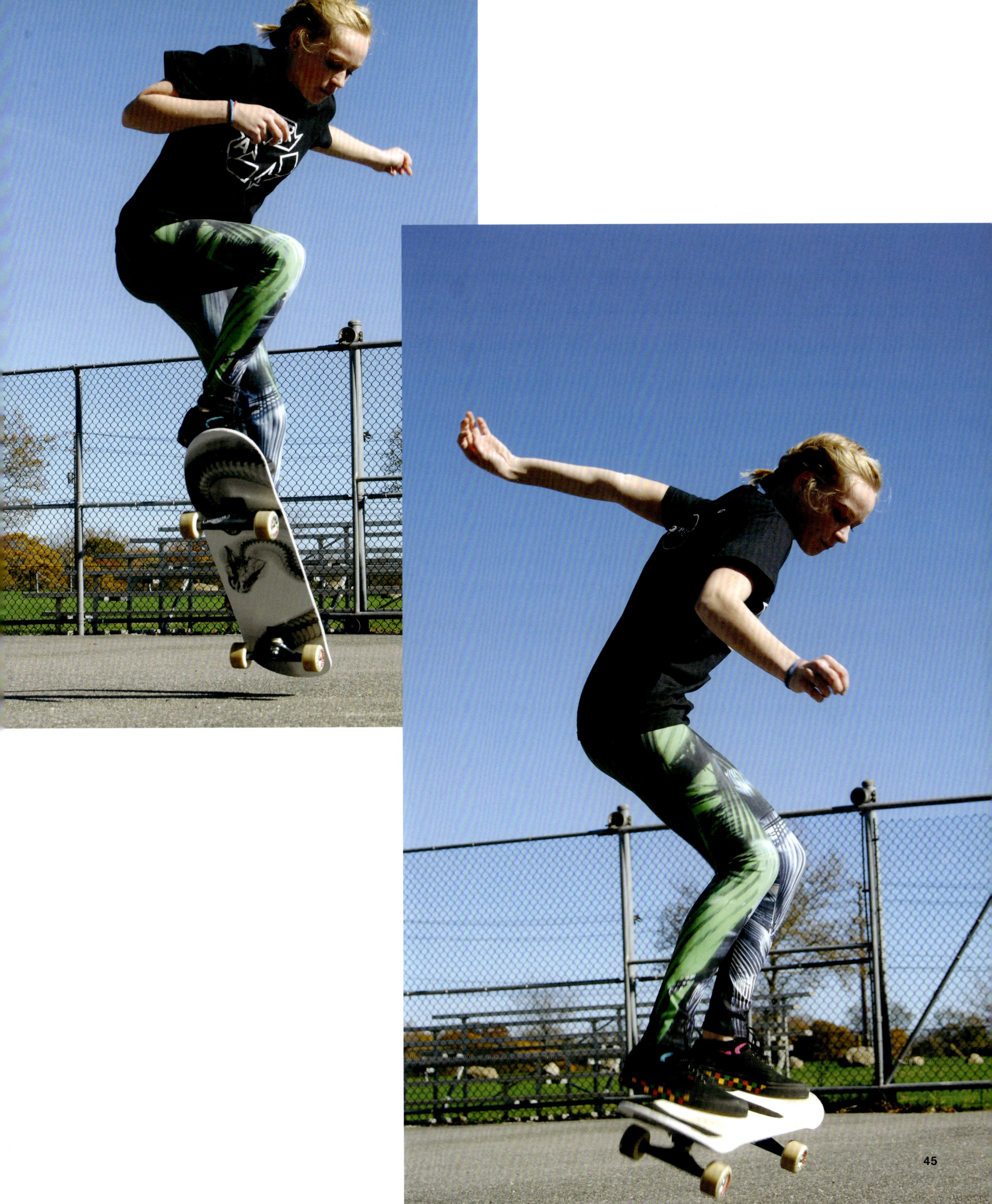

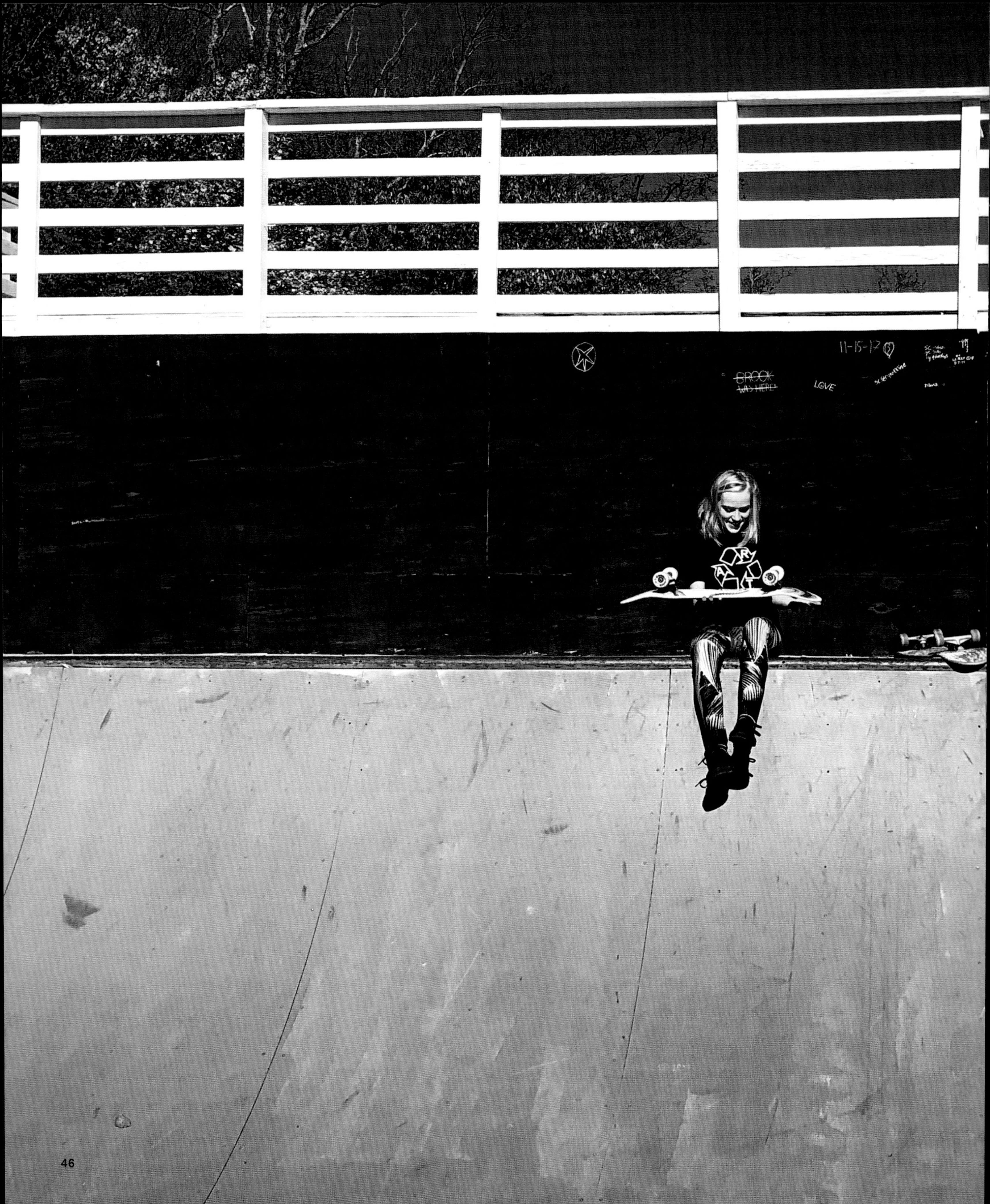
BROOK
WAS HERE
LOVE
11-15-17

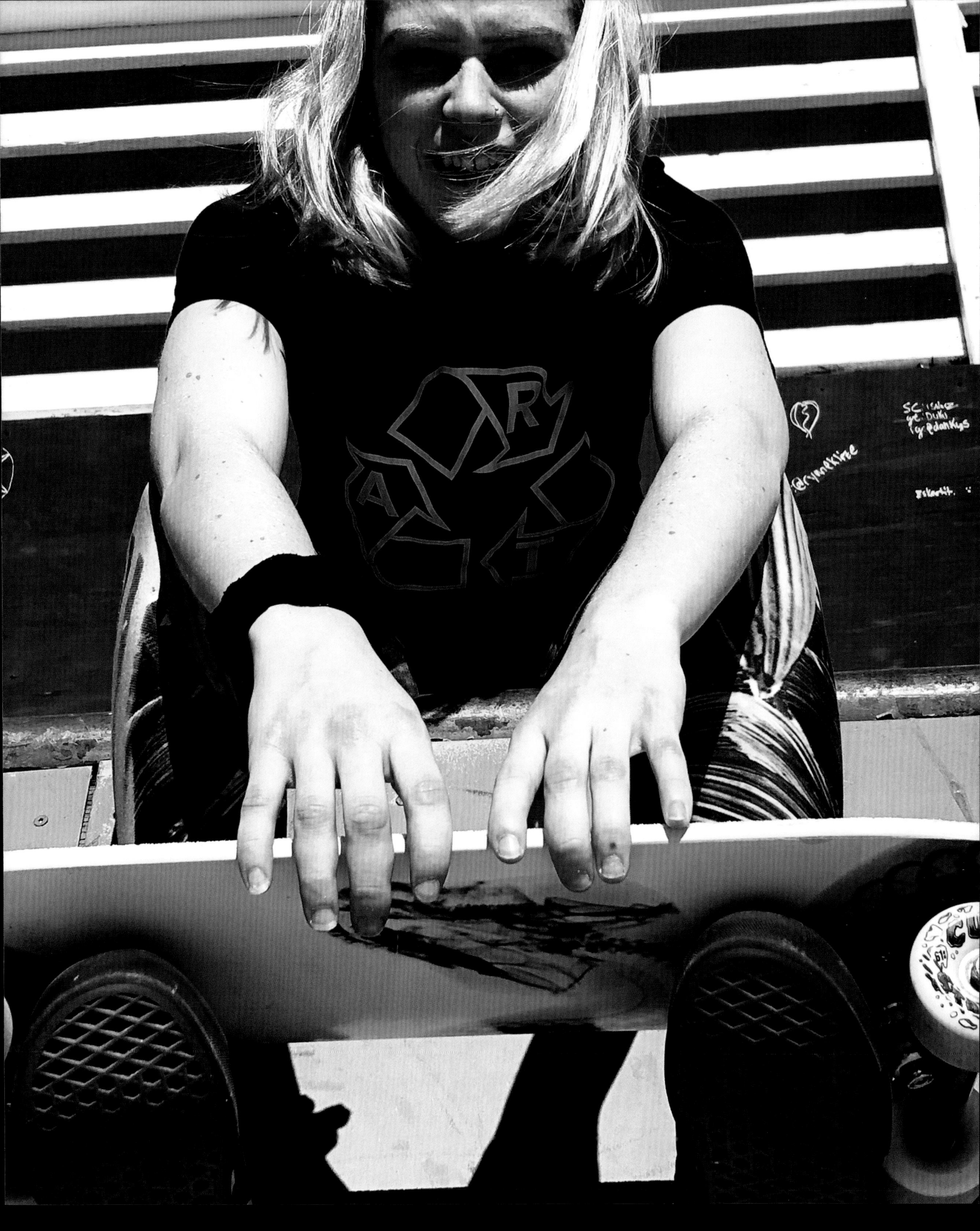

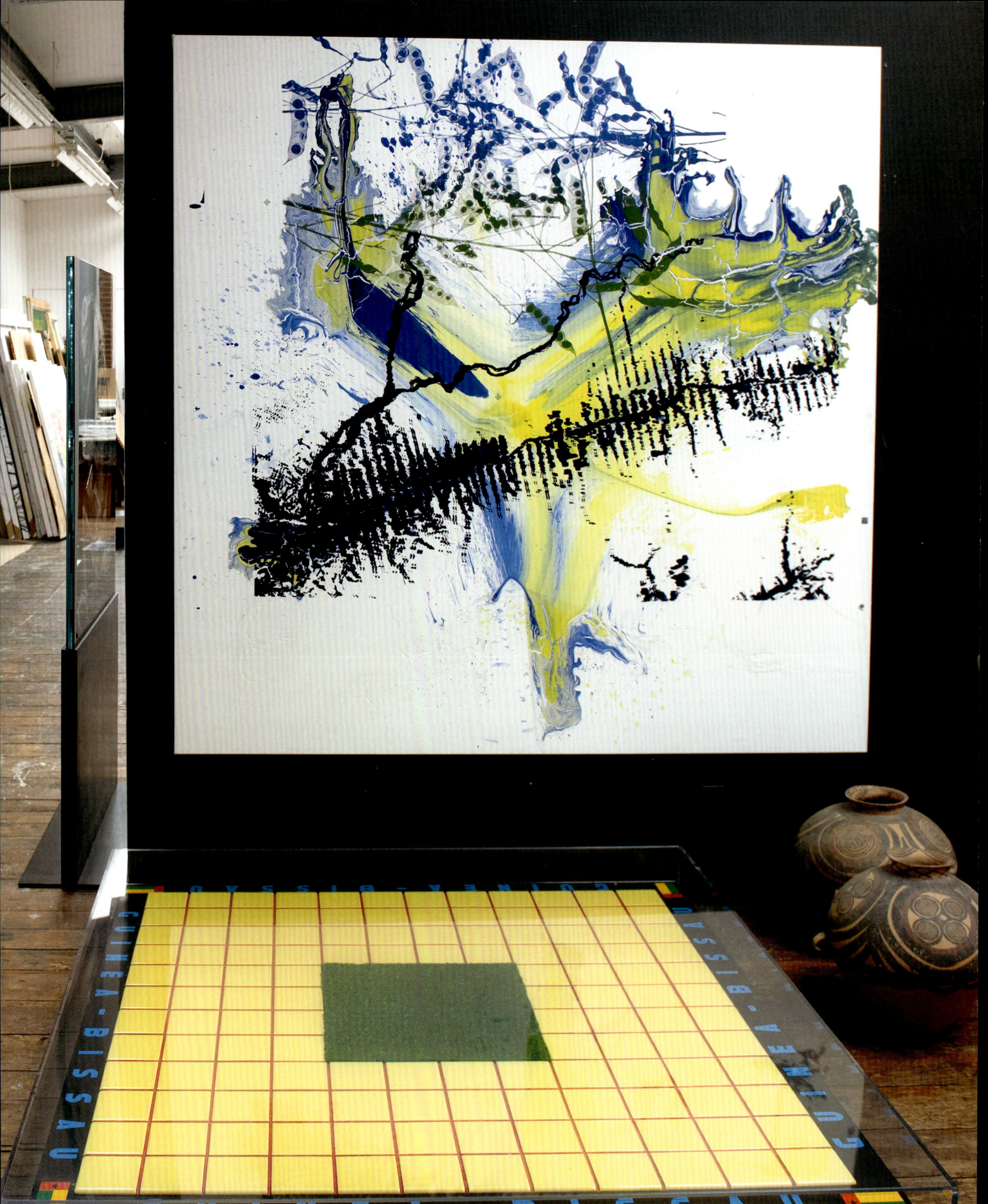
GUINEA-BISSAU
GUINEA-BISSAU
GUINEA-BISSAU

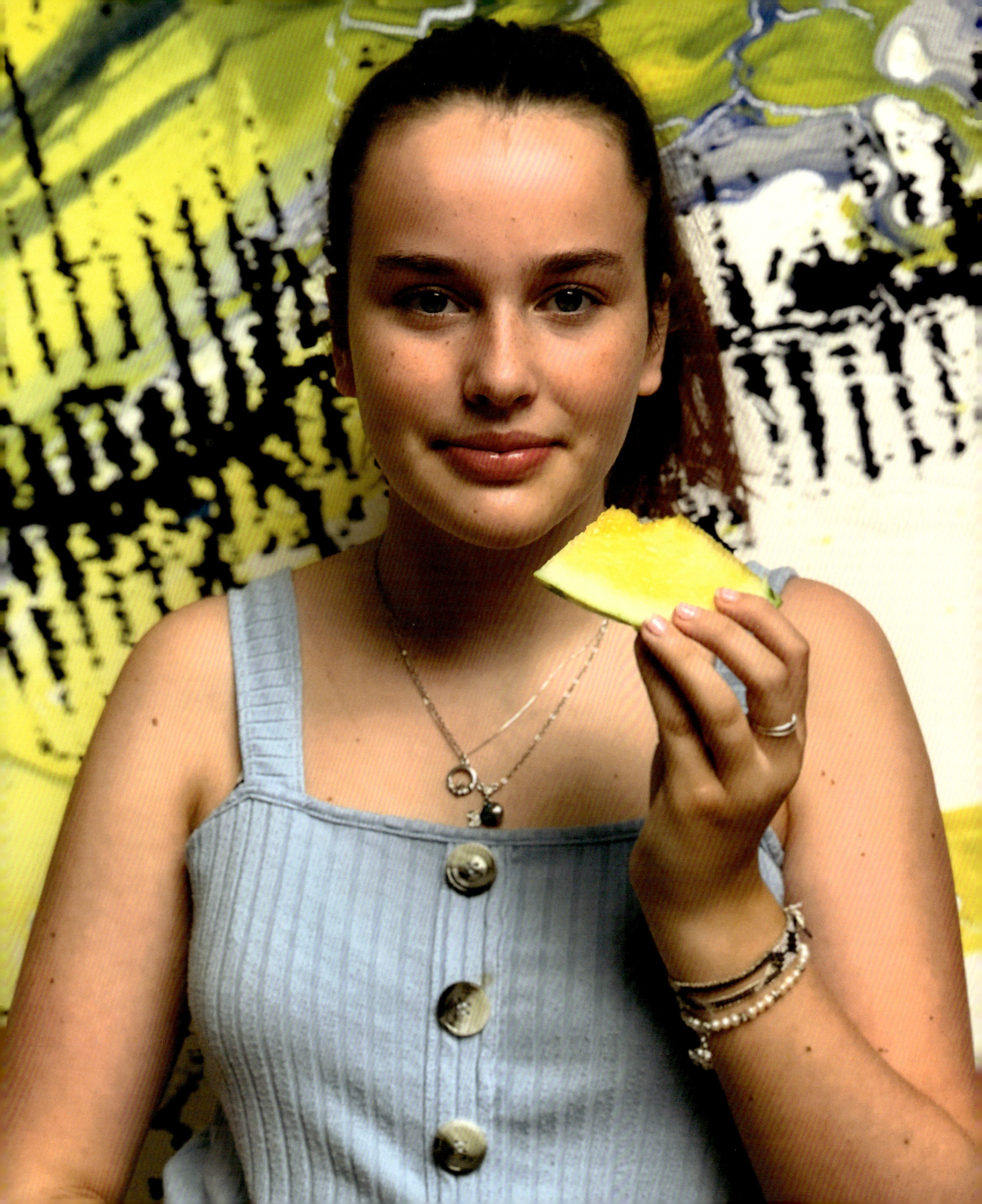

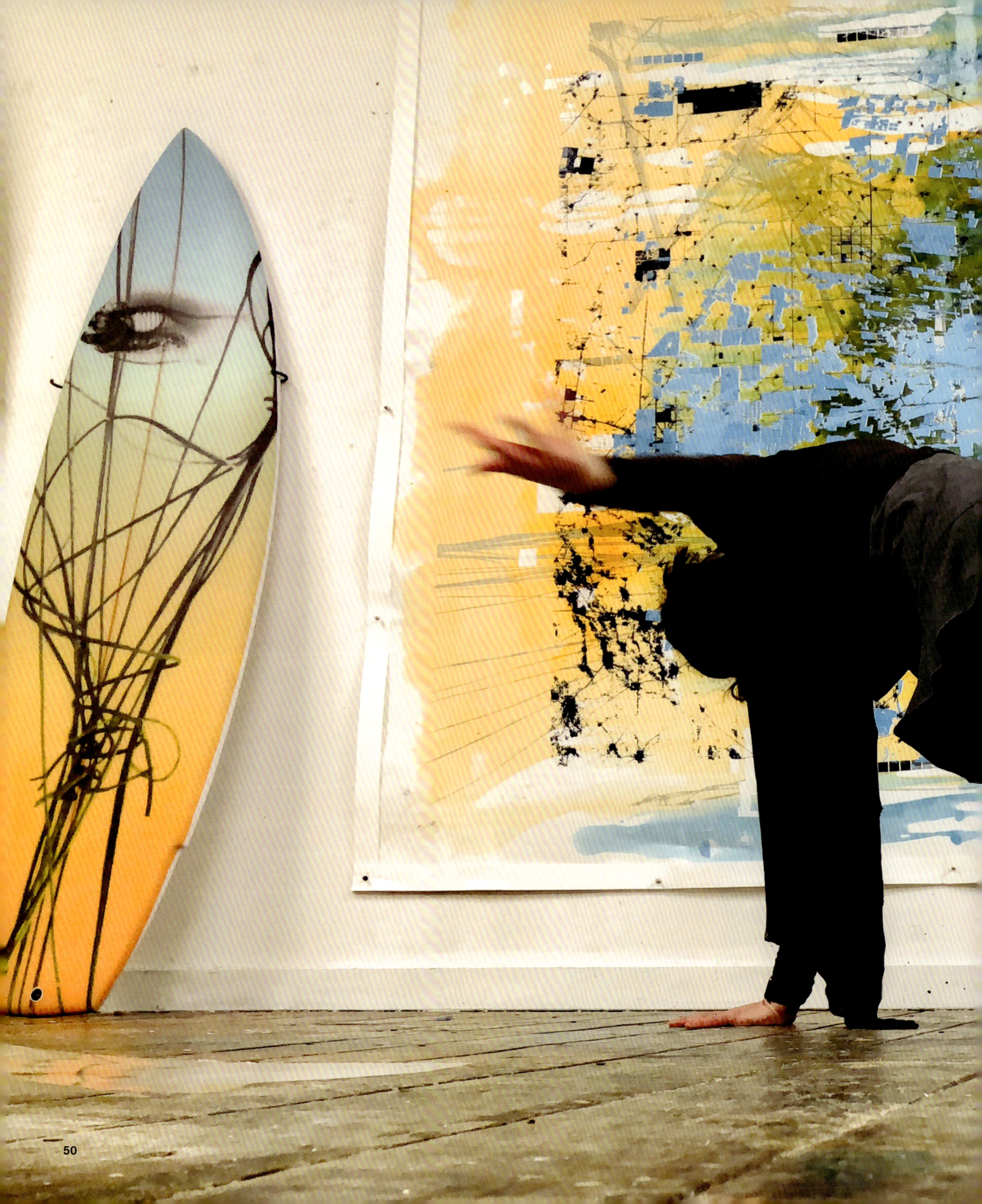

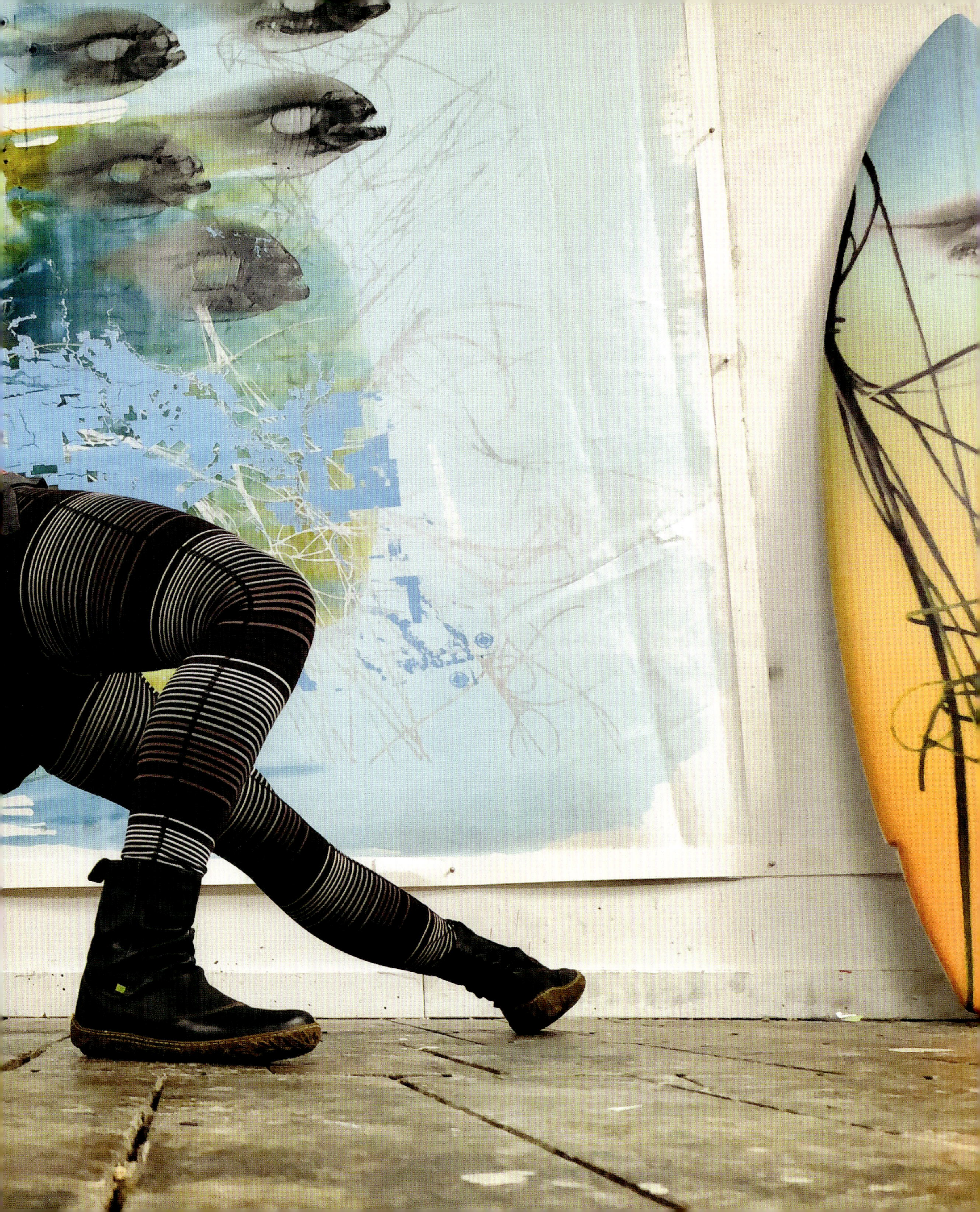

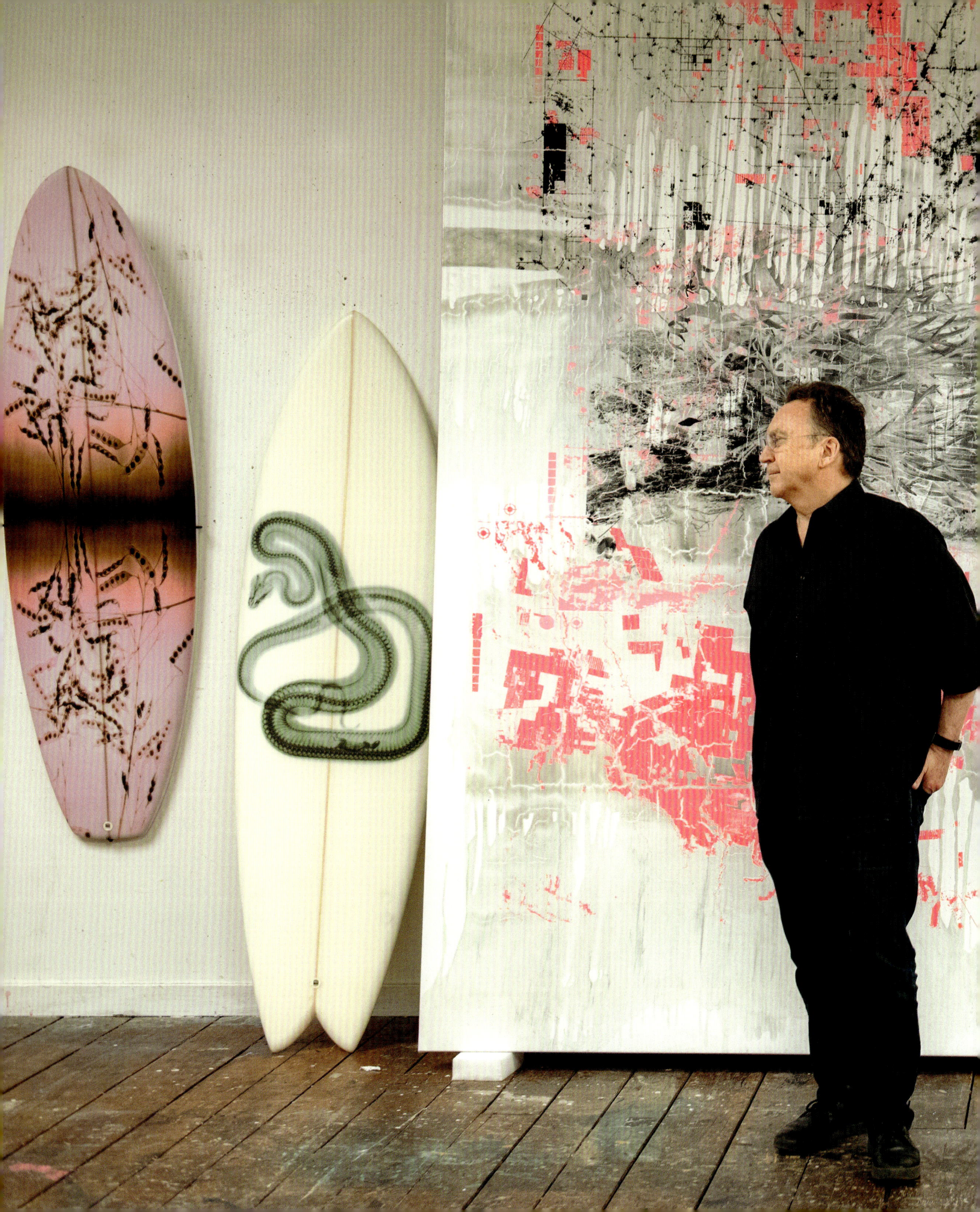

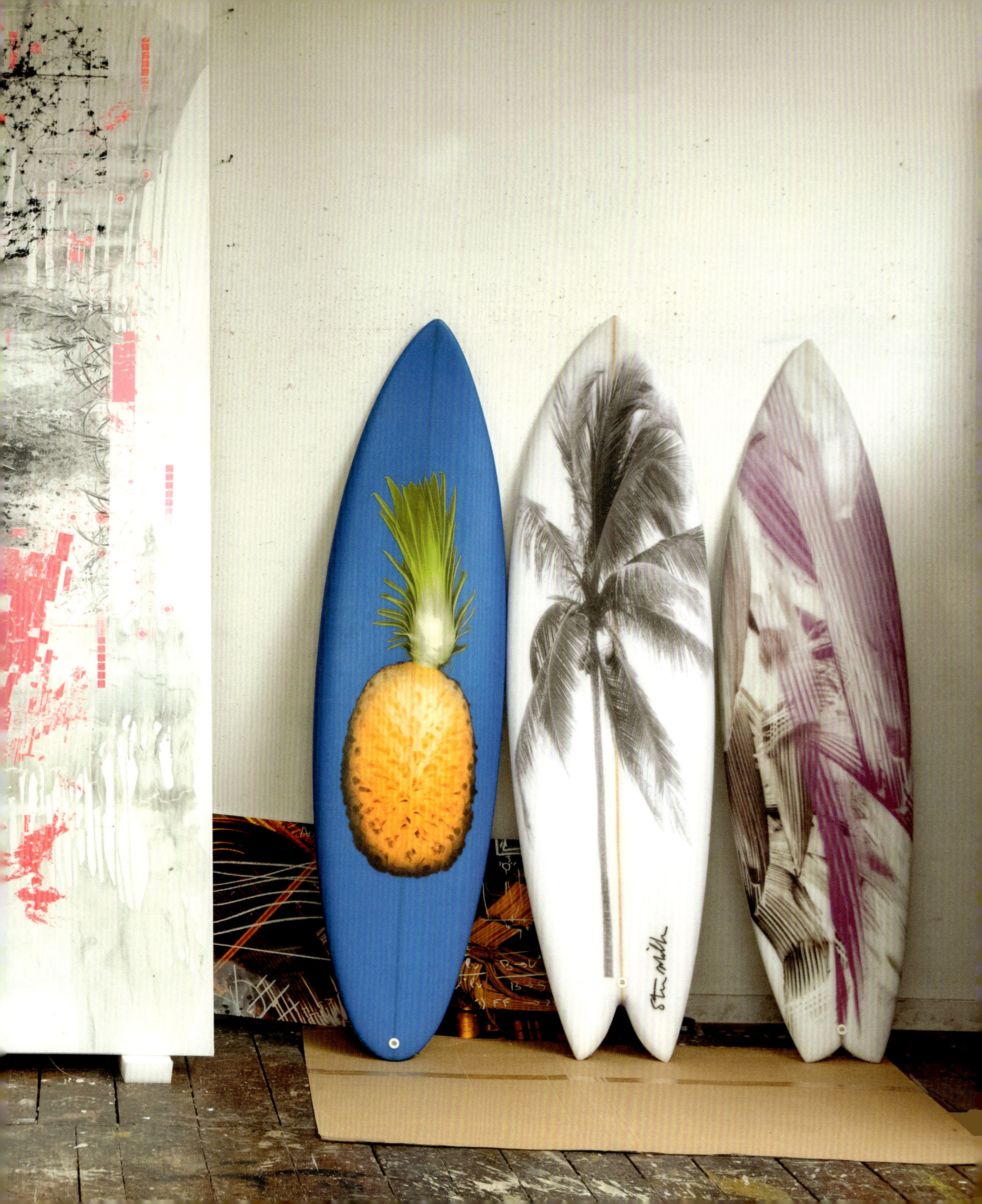

Stu.mill

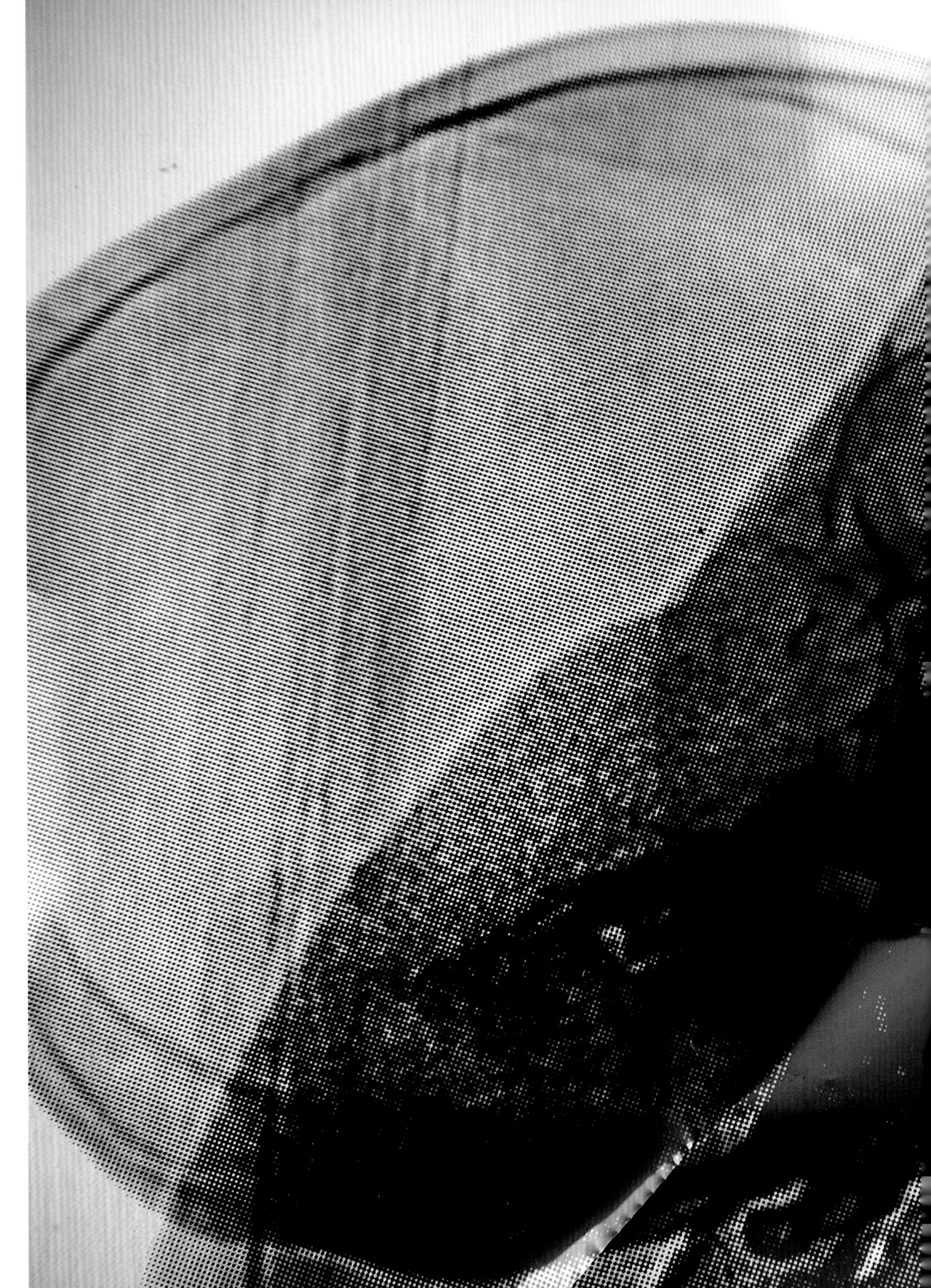

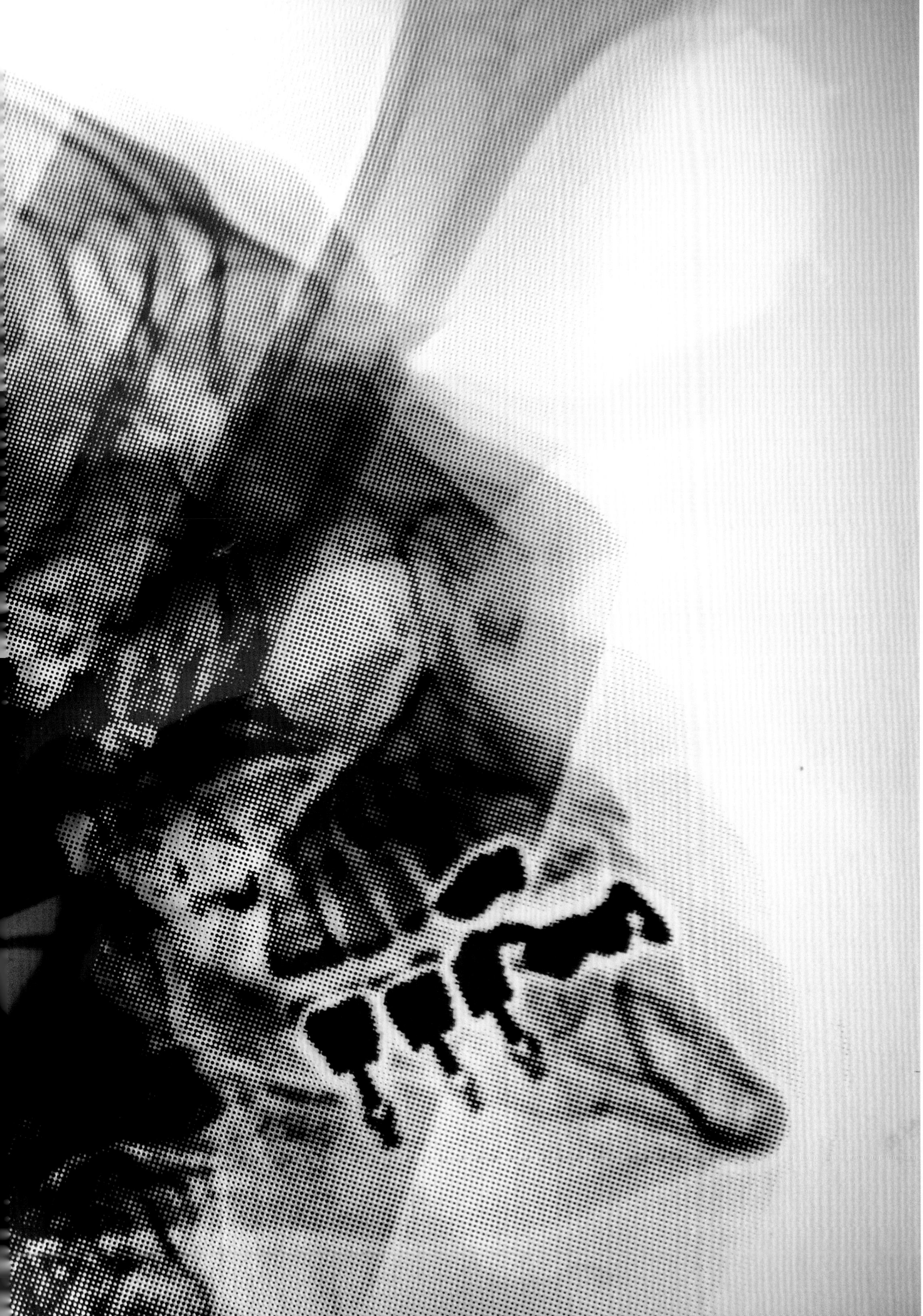

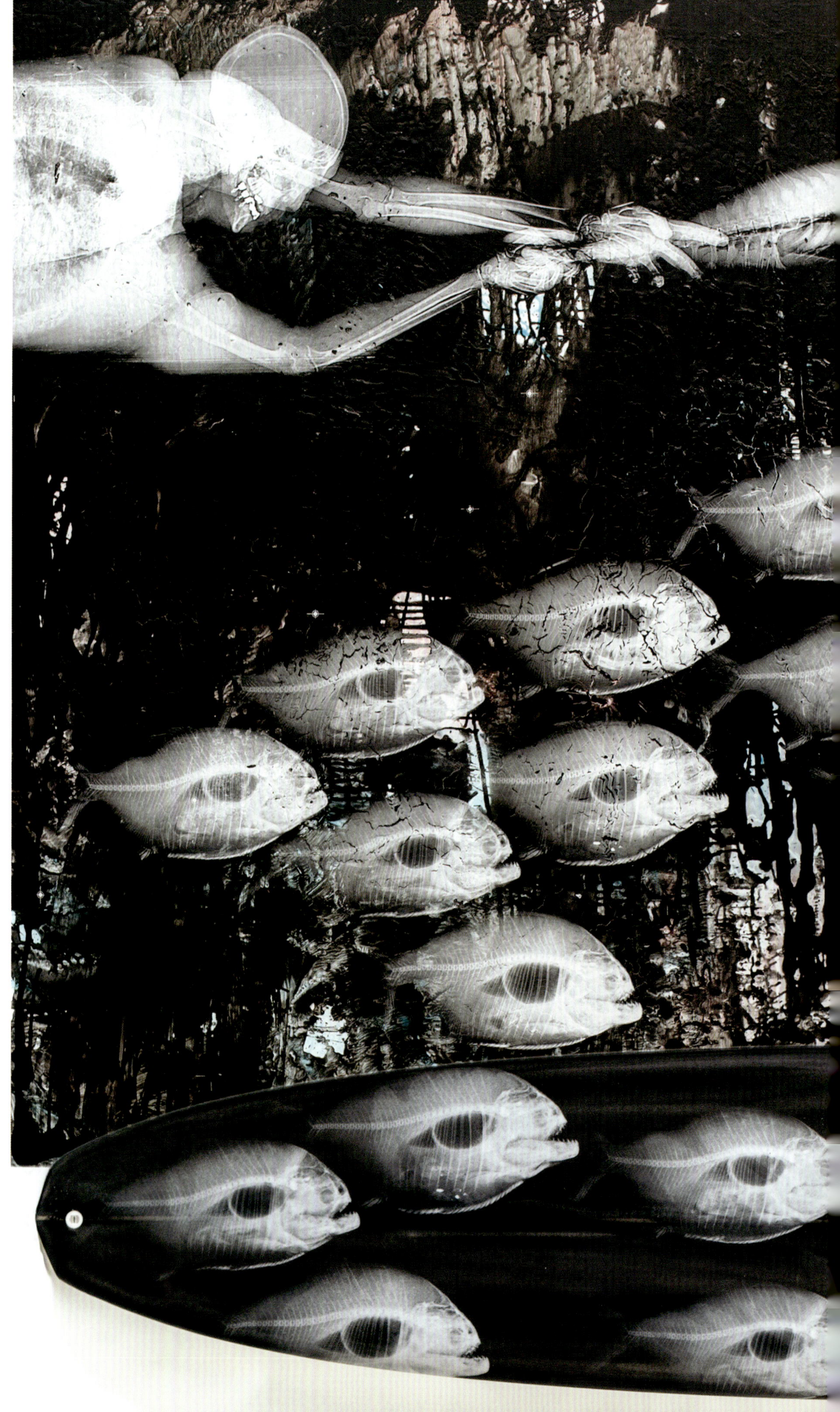

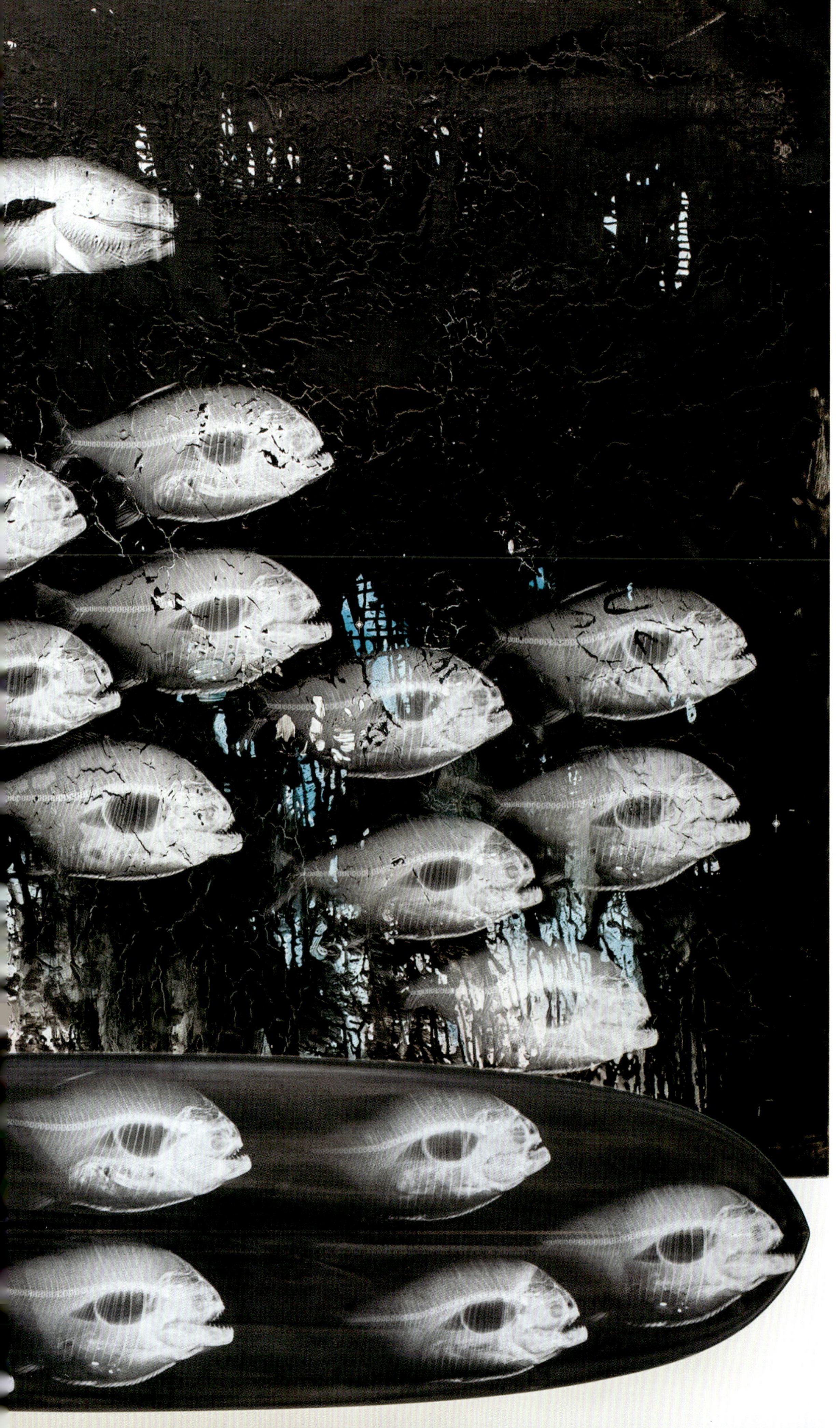

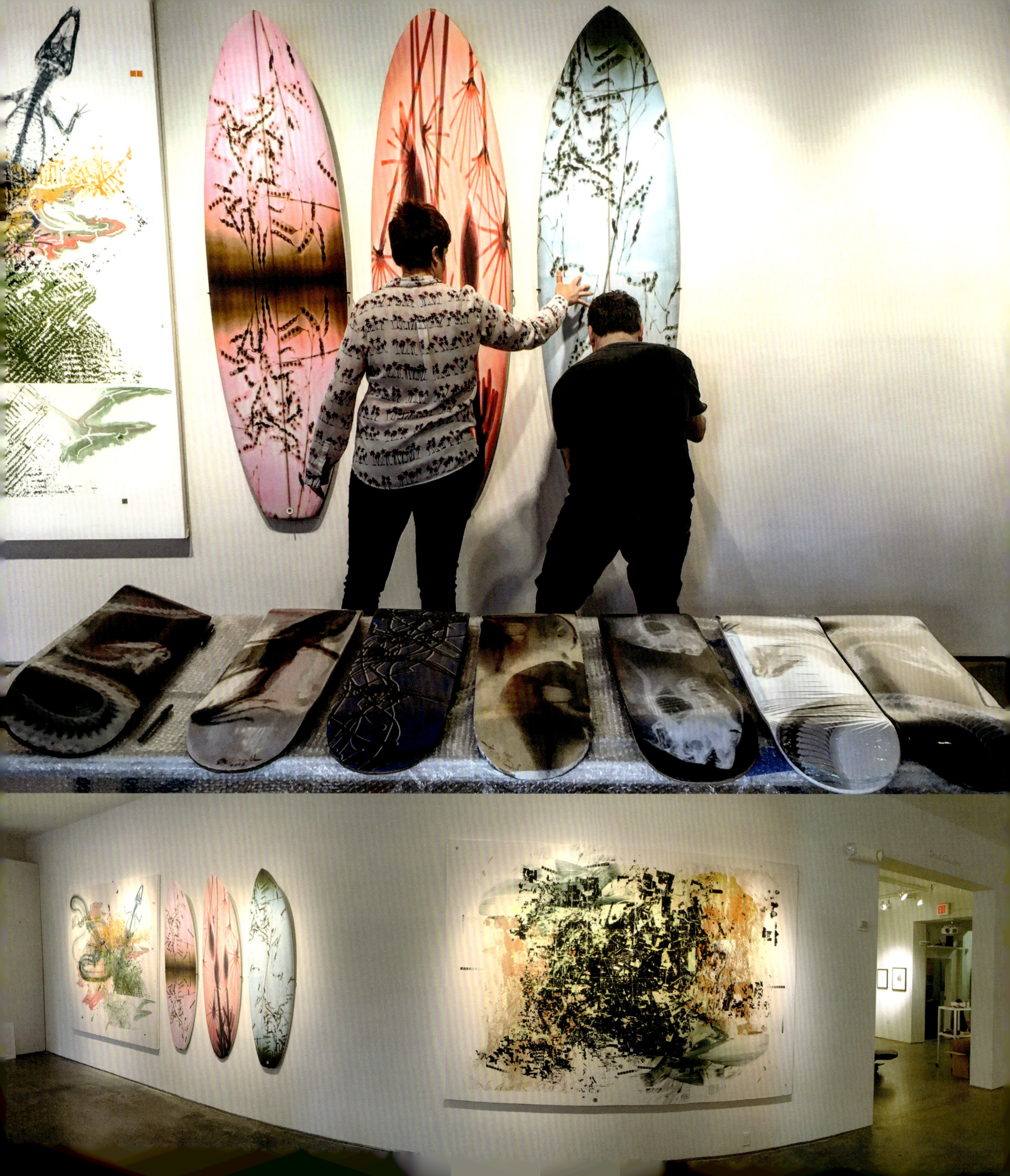

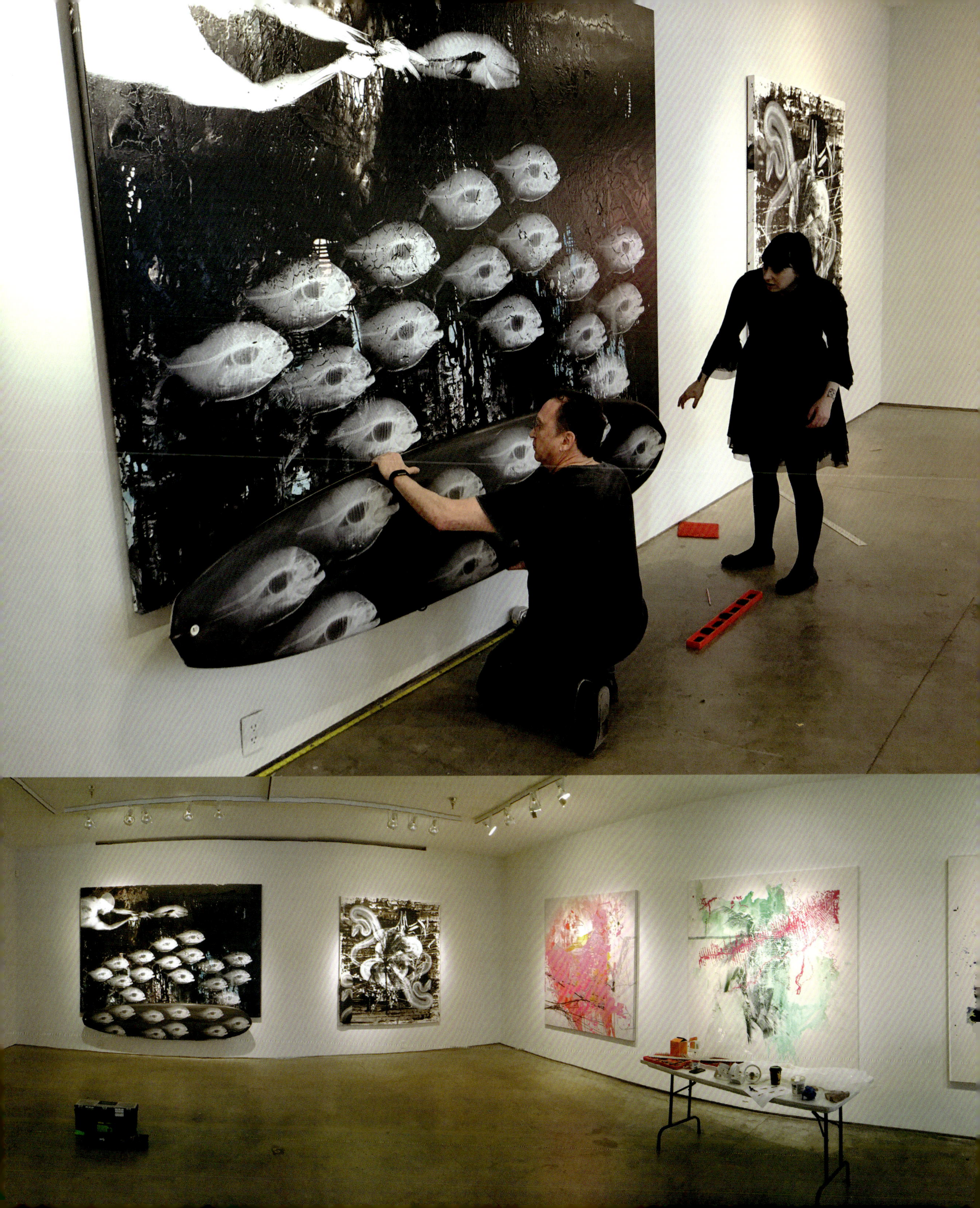

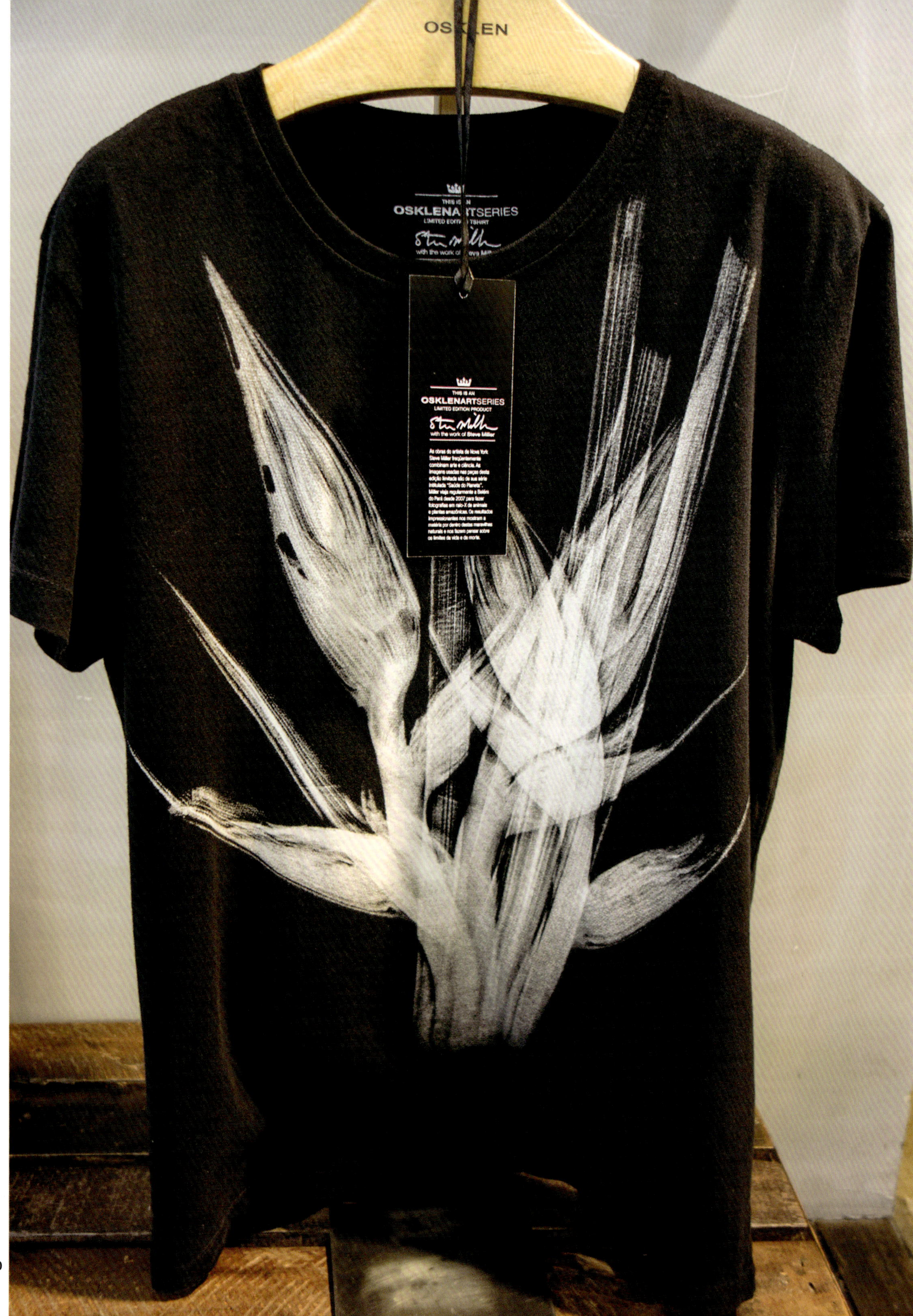
OSKLEN

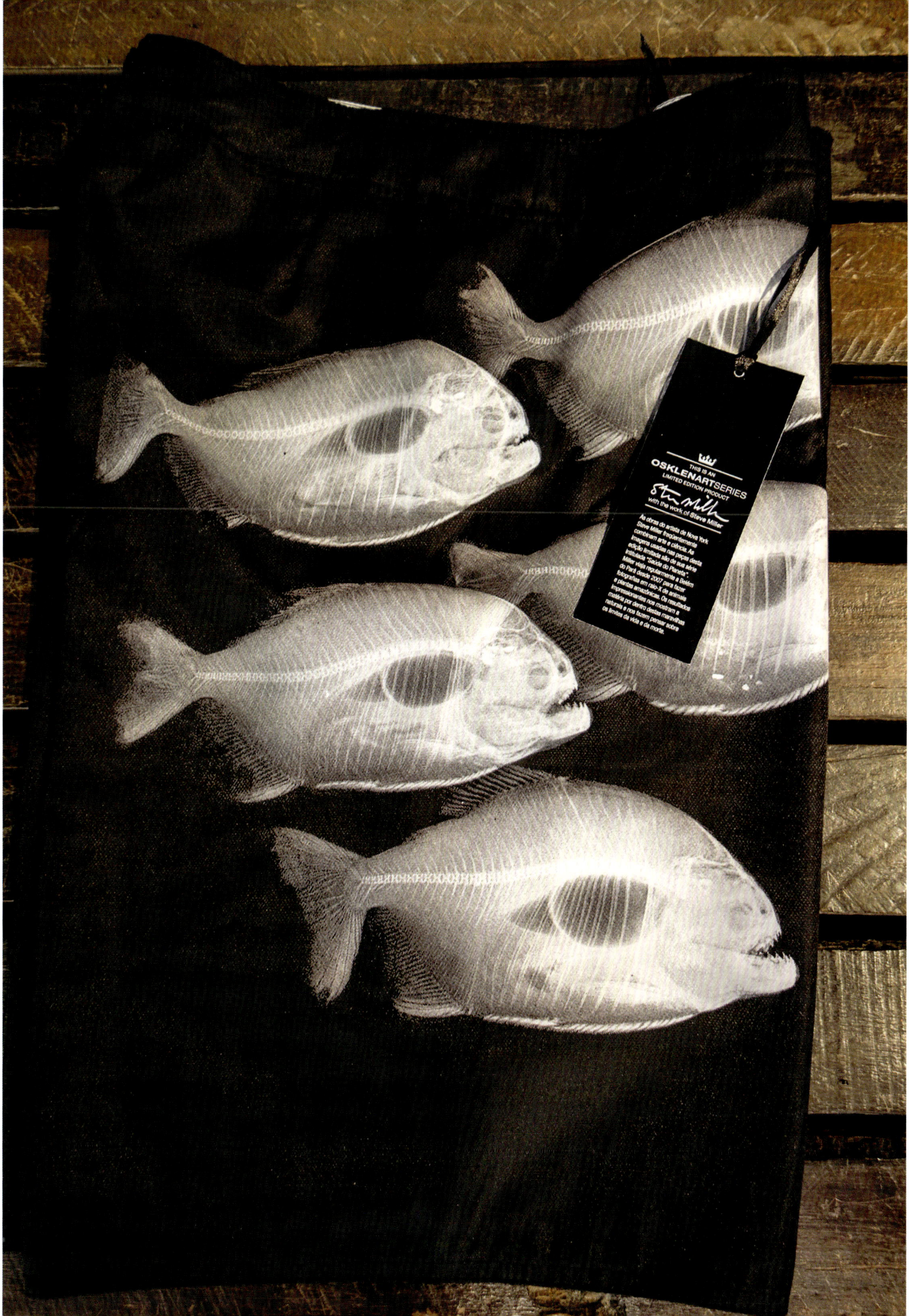

THIS IS AN
OSKLENARTSERIES
LIMITED EDITION PRODUCT
with the work of Steve Miller

As obras do artista de Nova York
Steve Miller freqüentemente
combinam arte e ciência. As
imagens usadas nas peças desta
edição limitada são de sua série
intitulada "Saúde do Planeta".
Miller viaja regularmente à Belém
do Pará desde 2007 para fazer
fotografias em raio-X de animais
e plantas amazônicas. Os resultados
impressionantes nos mostram a
matéria por dentro destas maravilhas
naturais e nos fazem pensar sobre
os limites da vida e da morte.

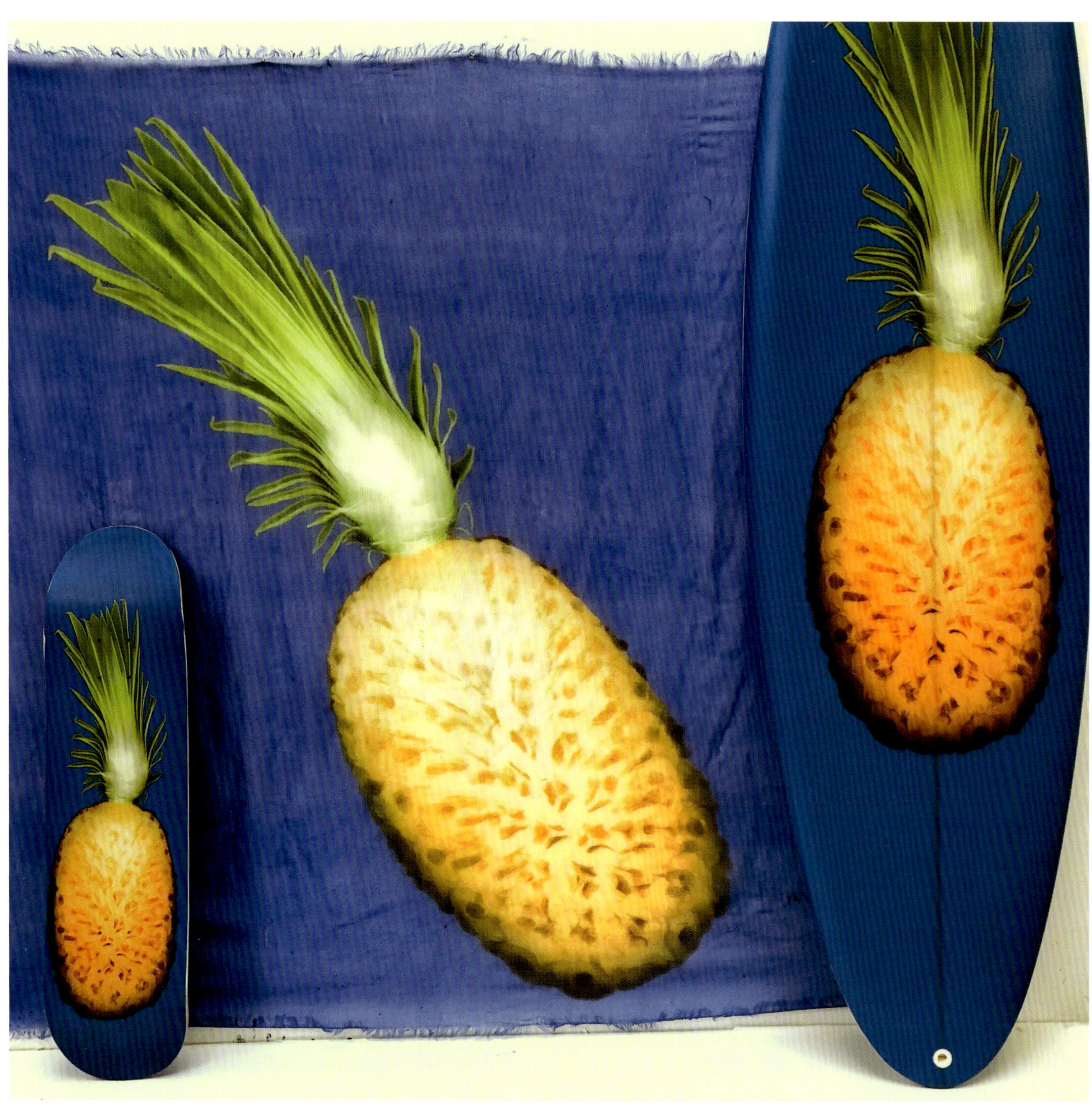

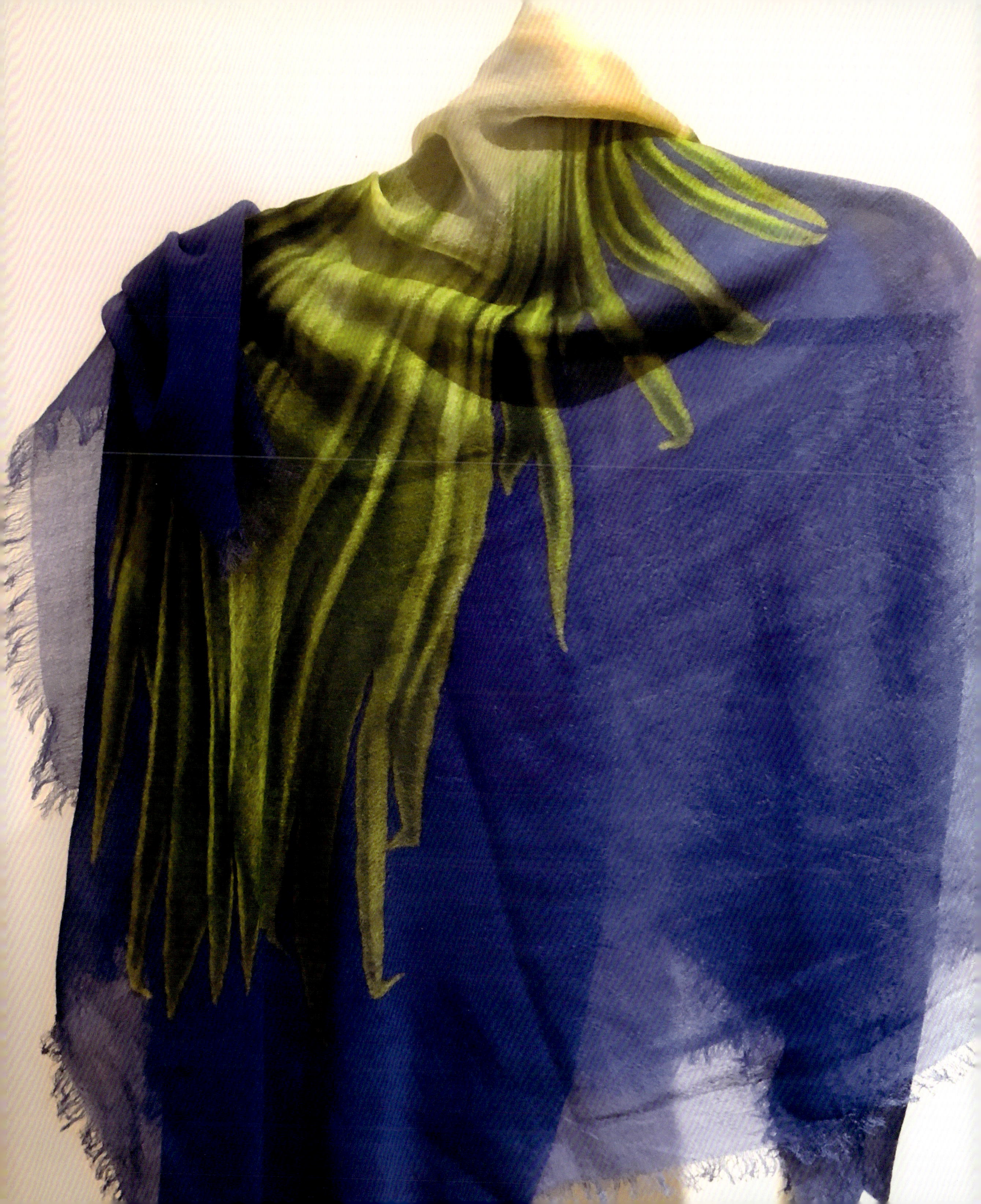

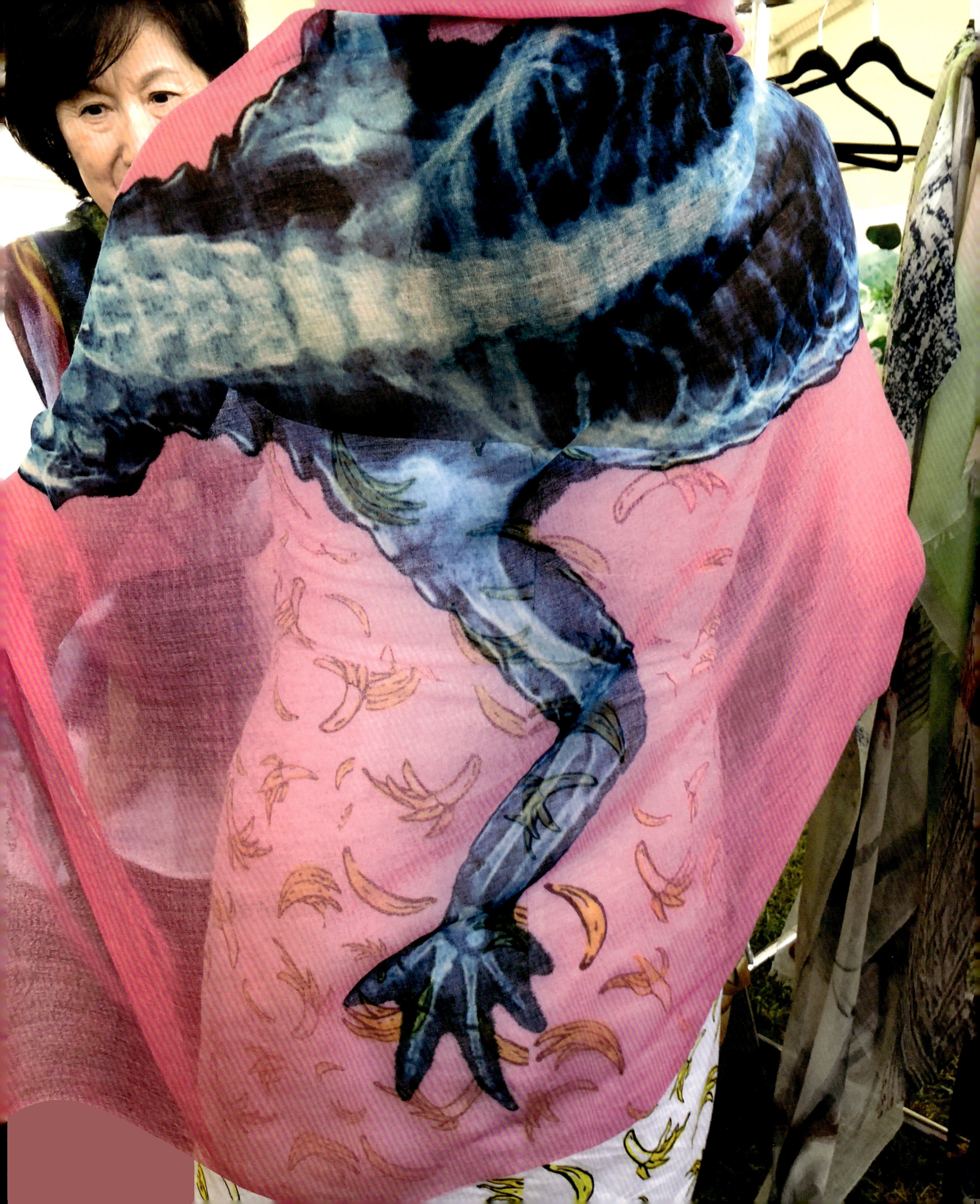

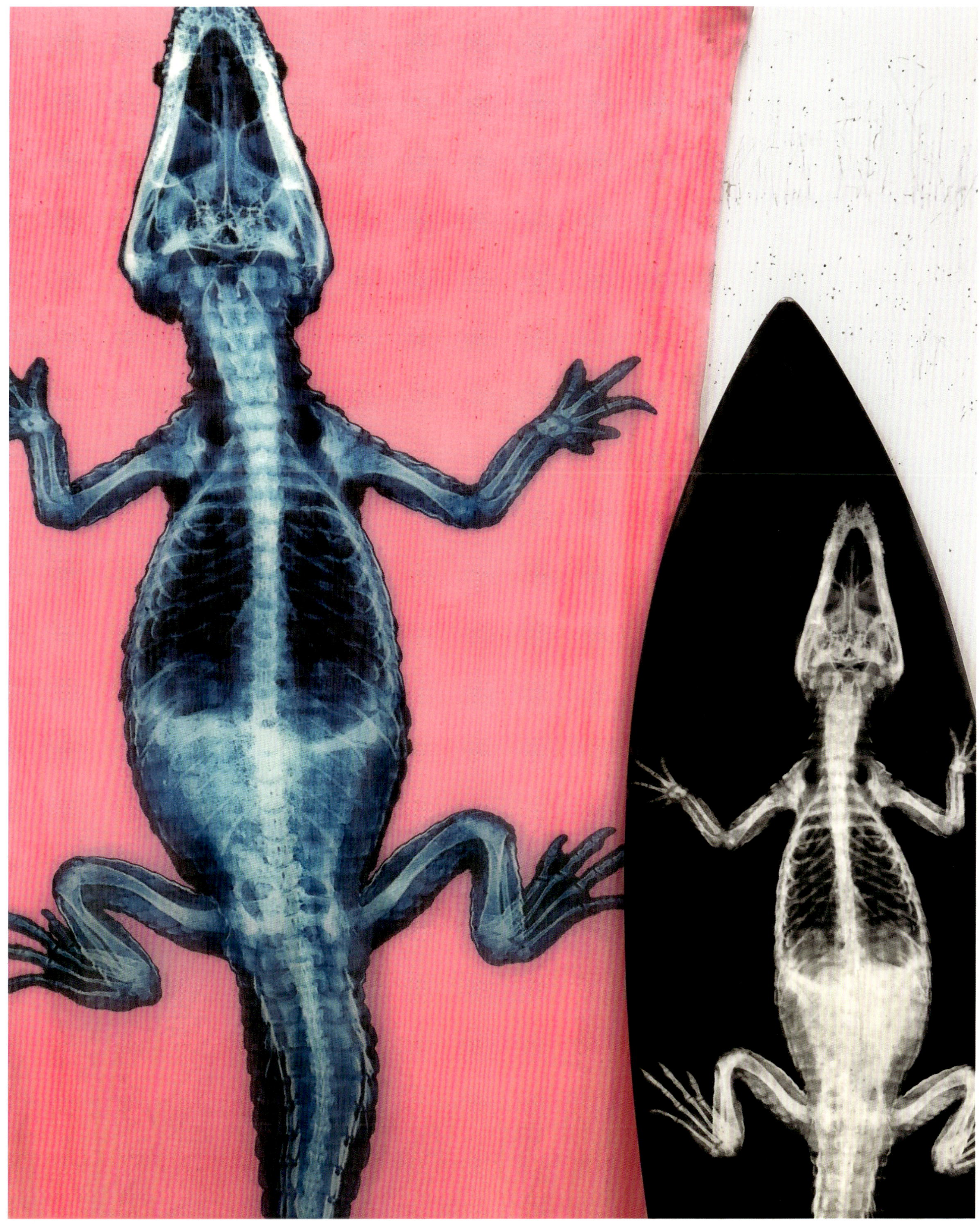

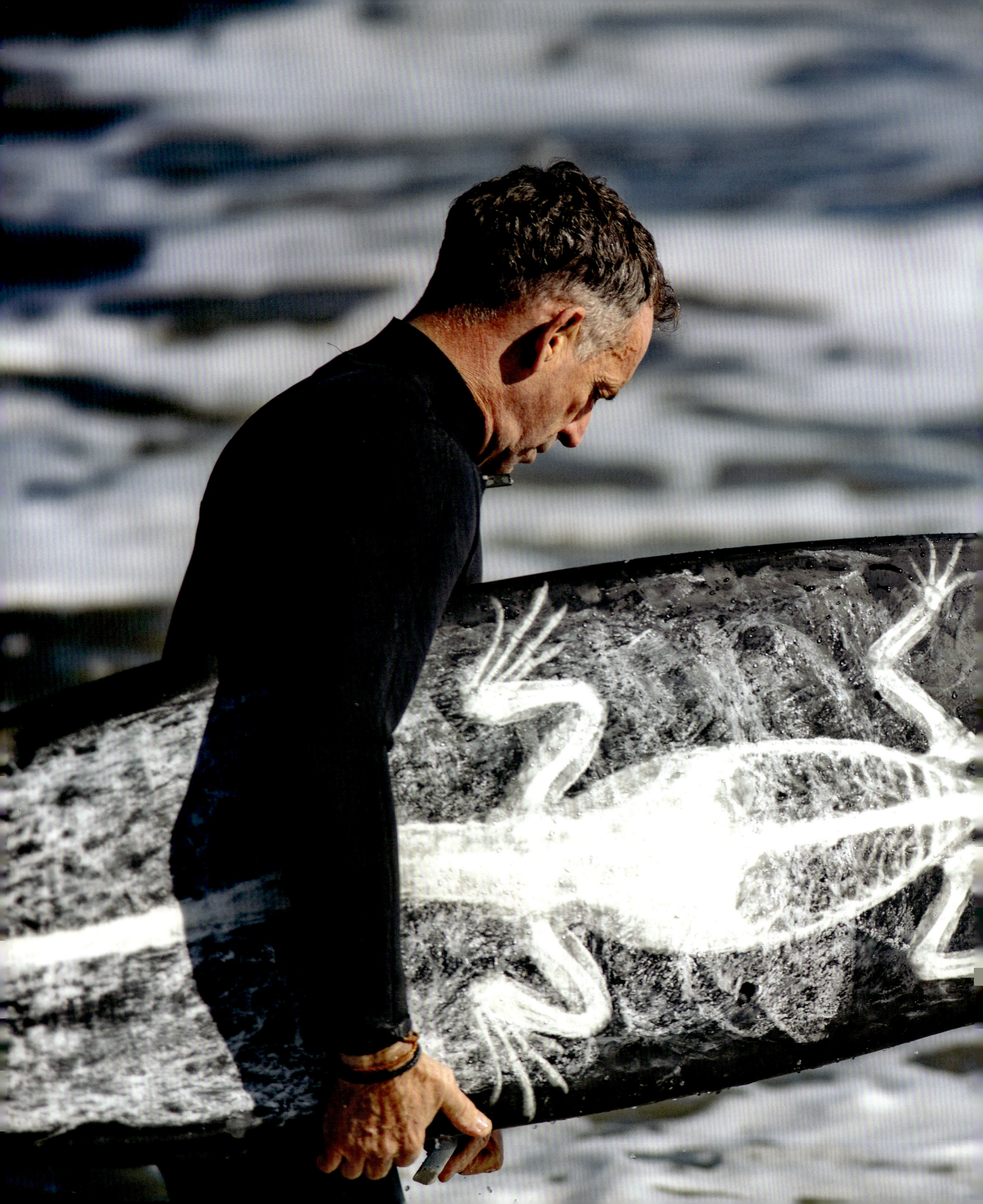

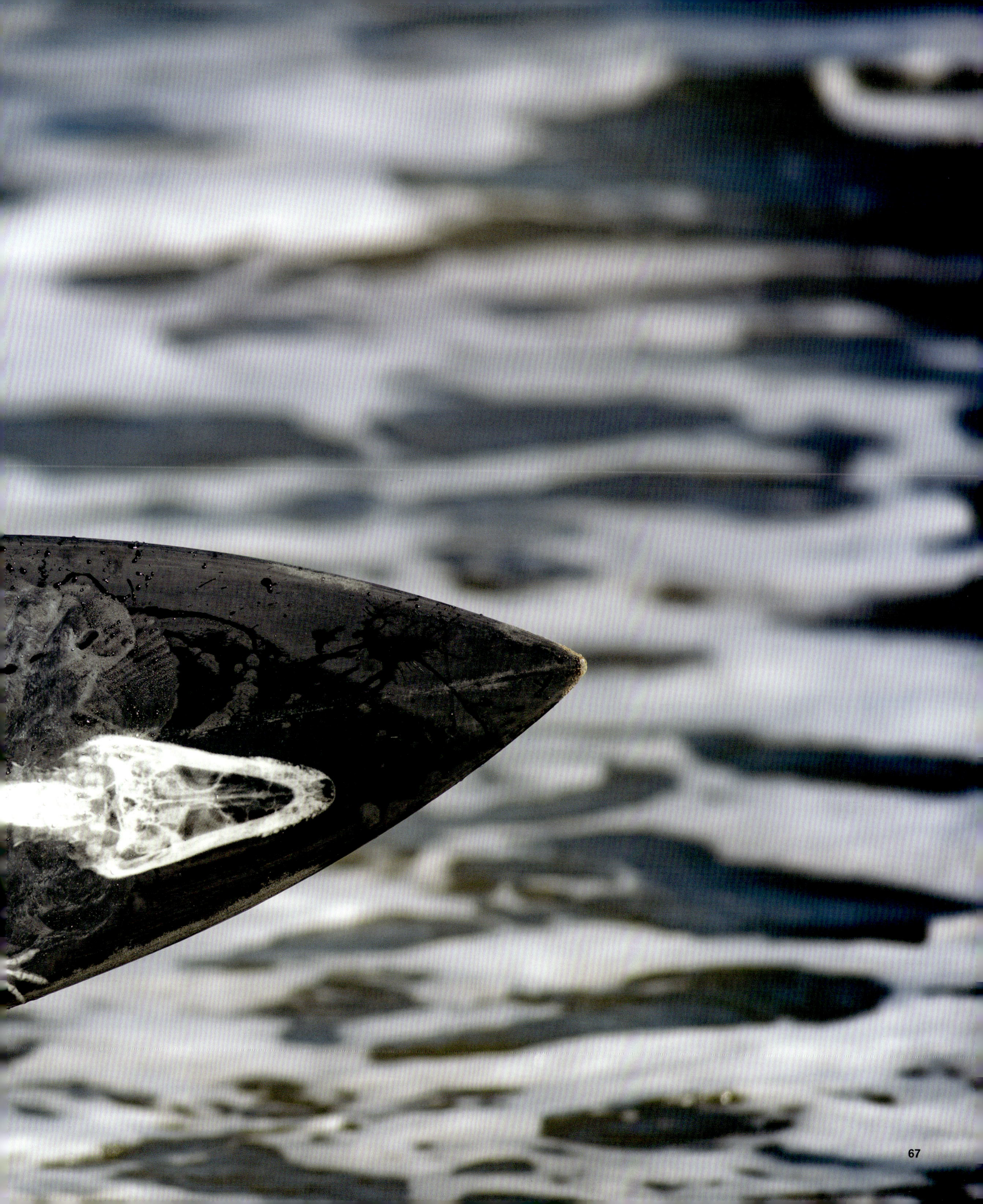

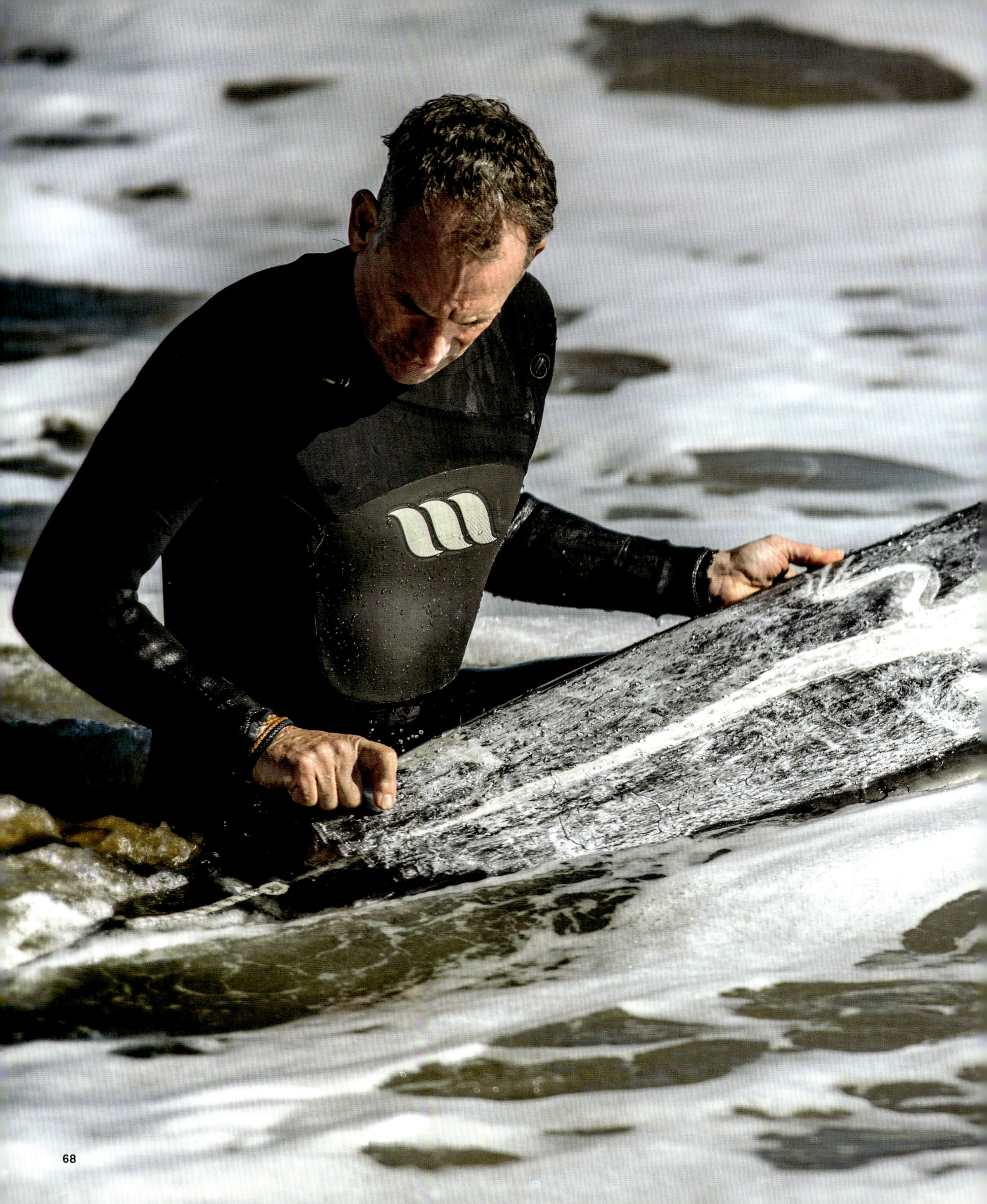

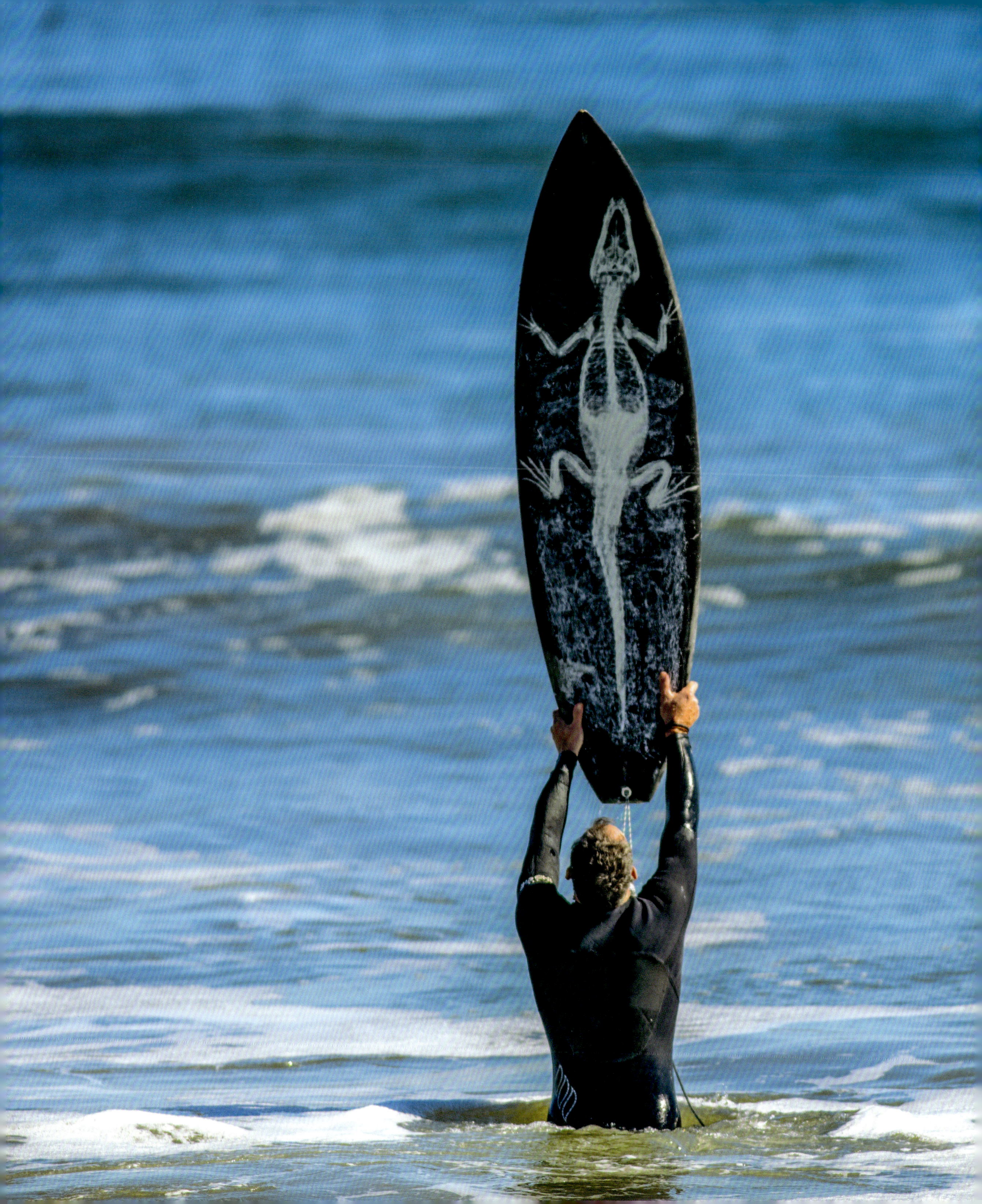

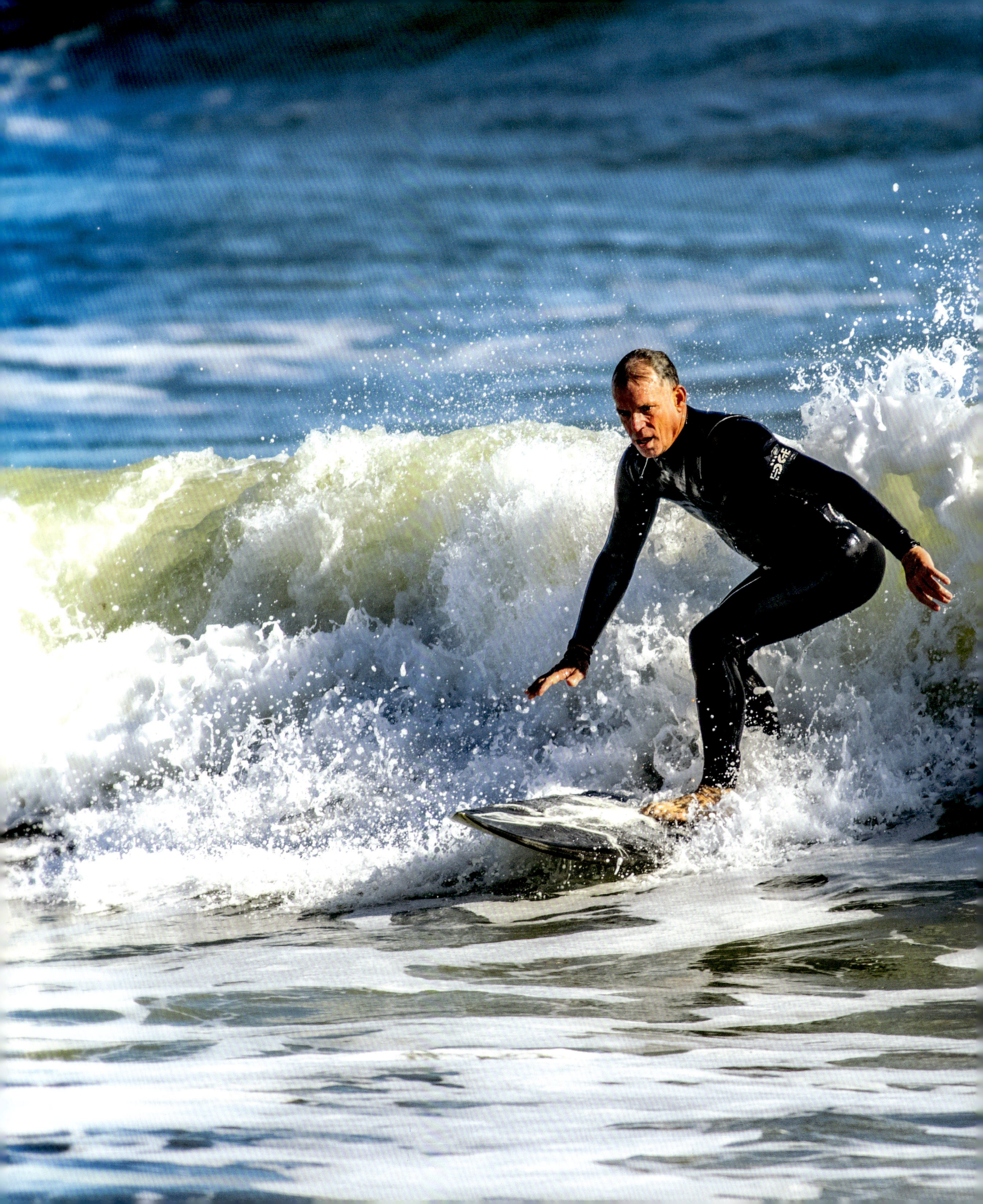

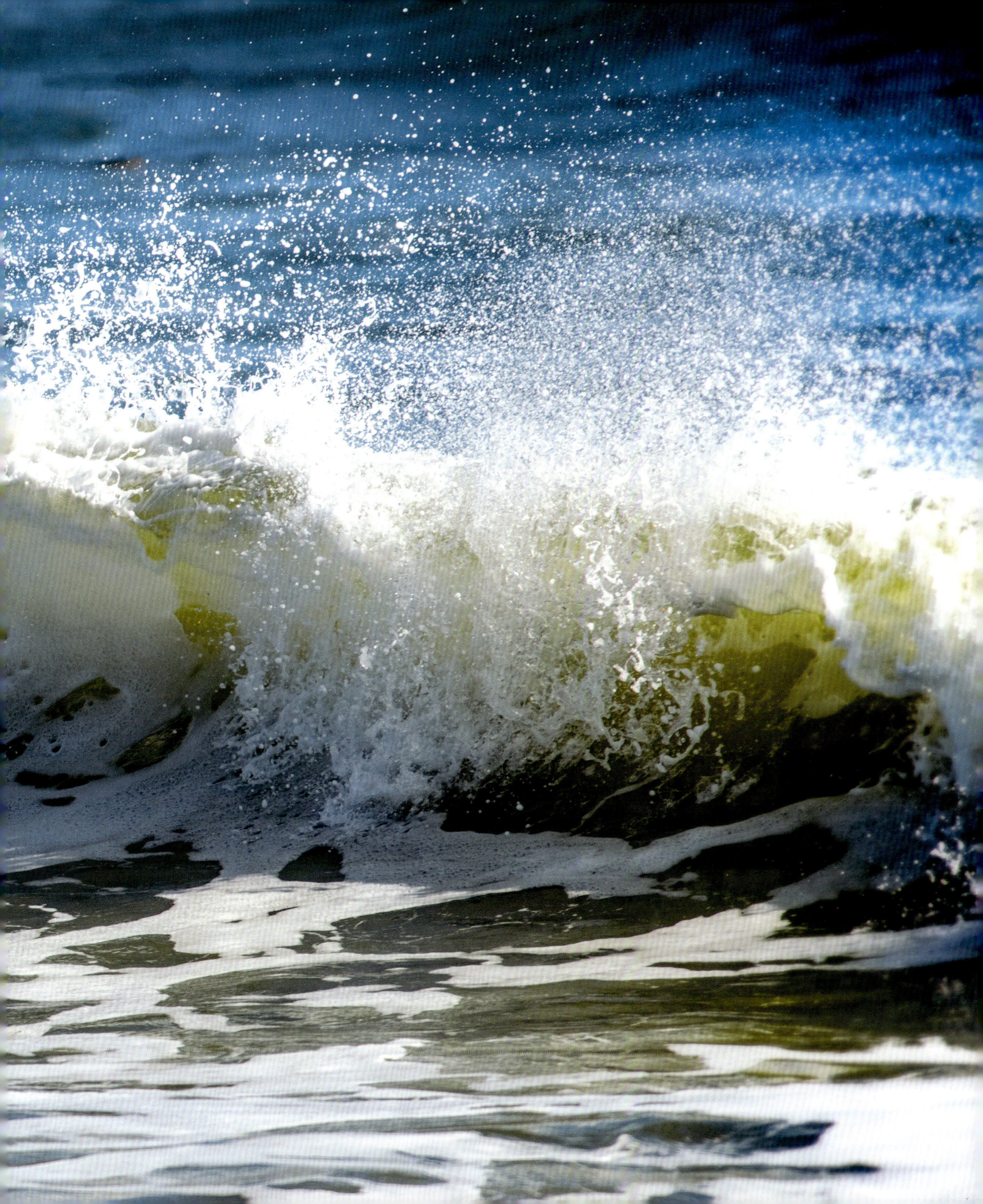

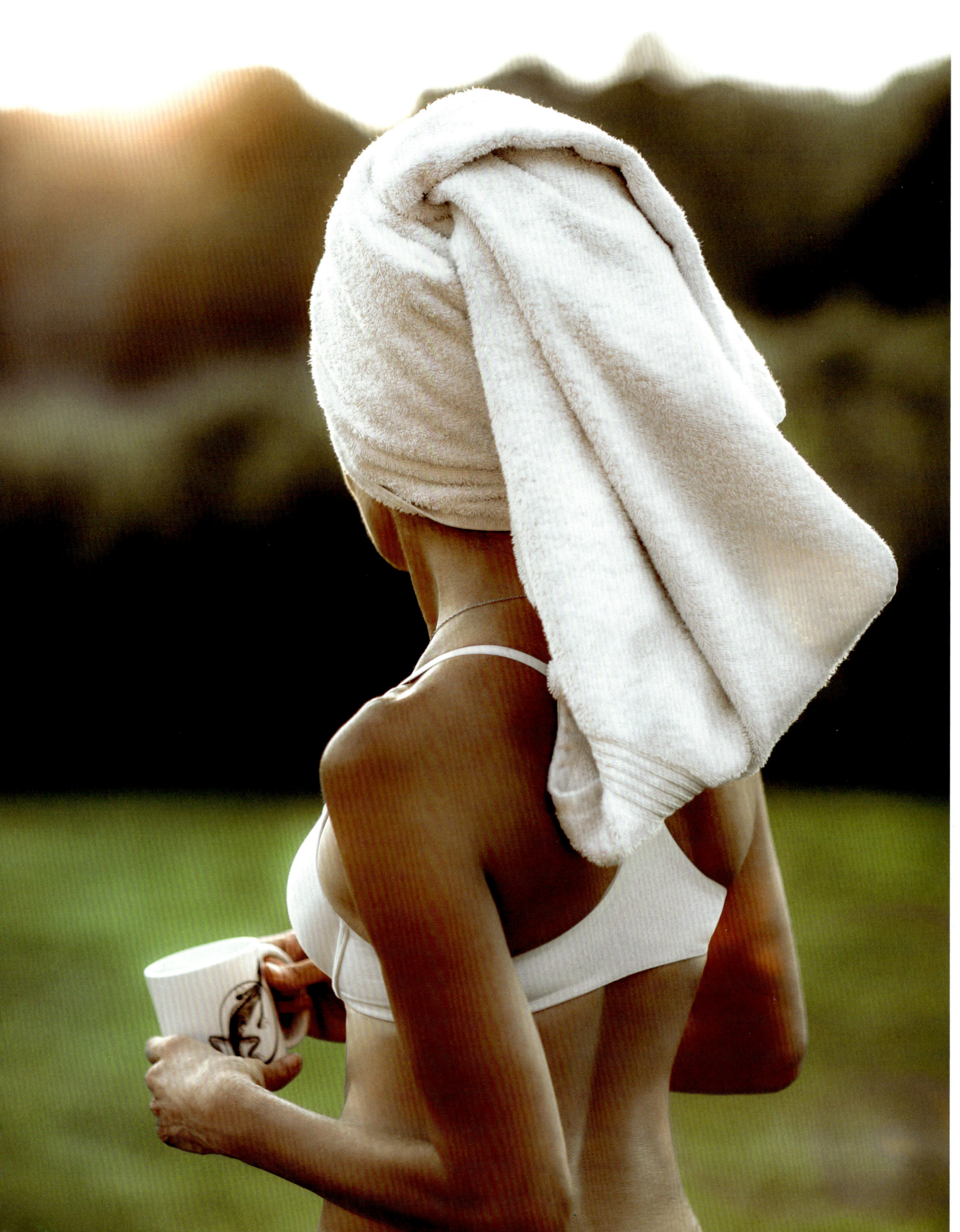

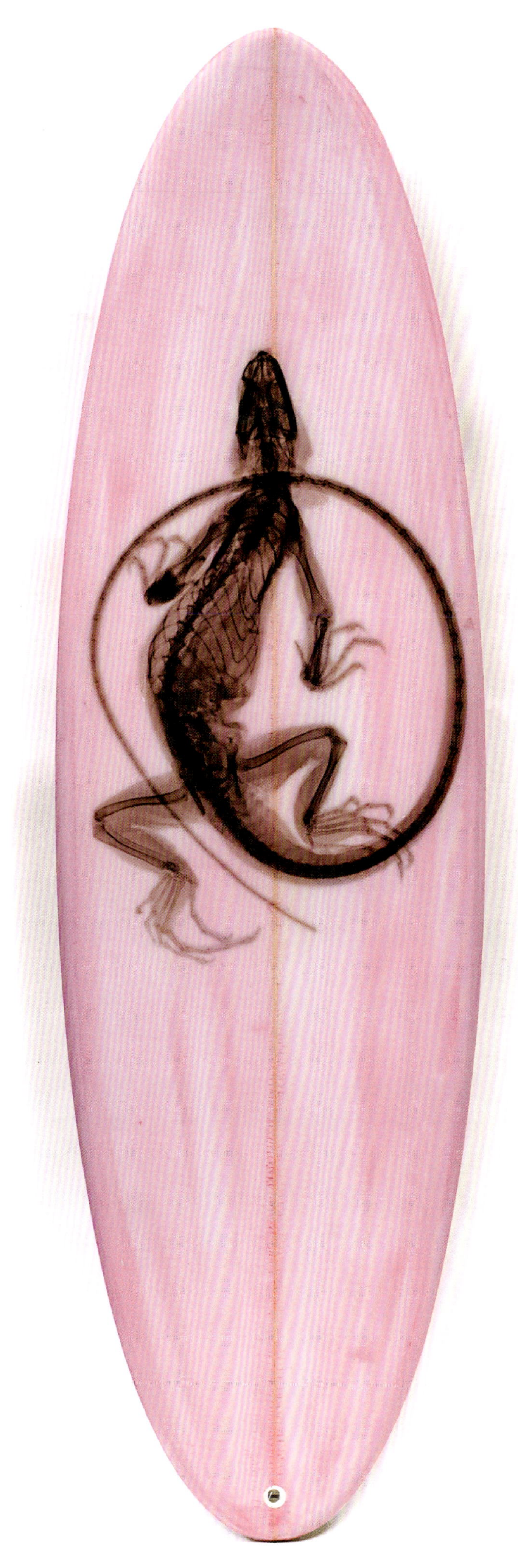

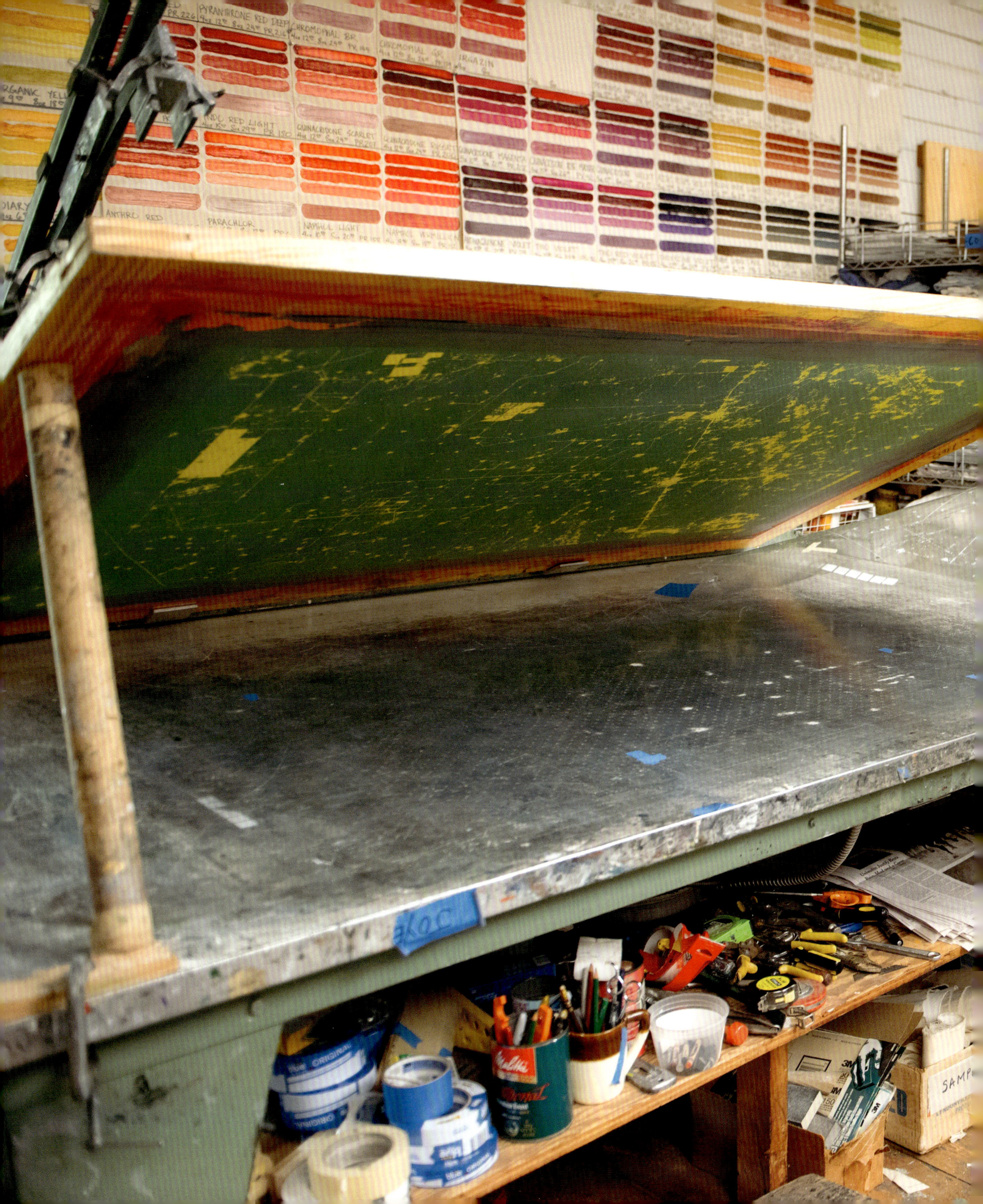

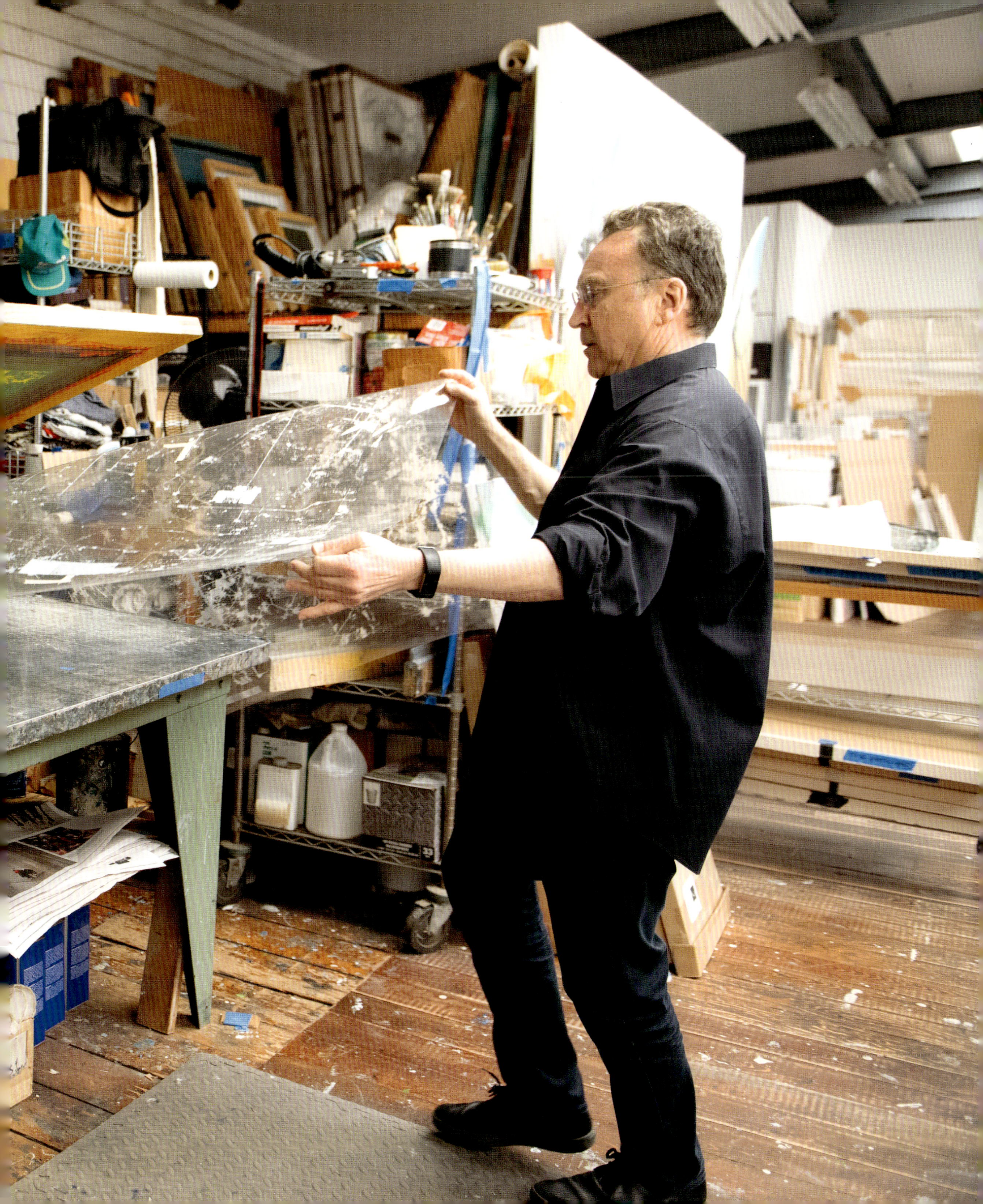

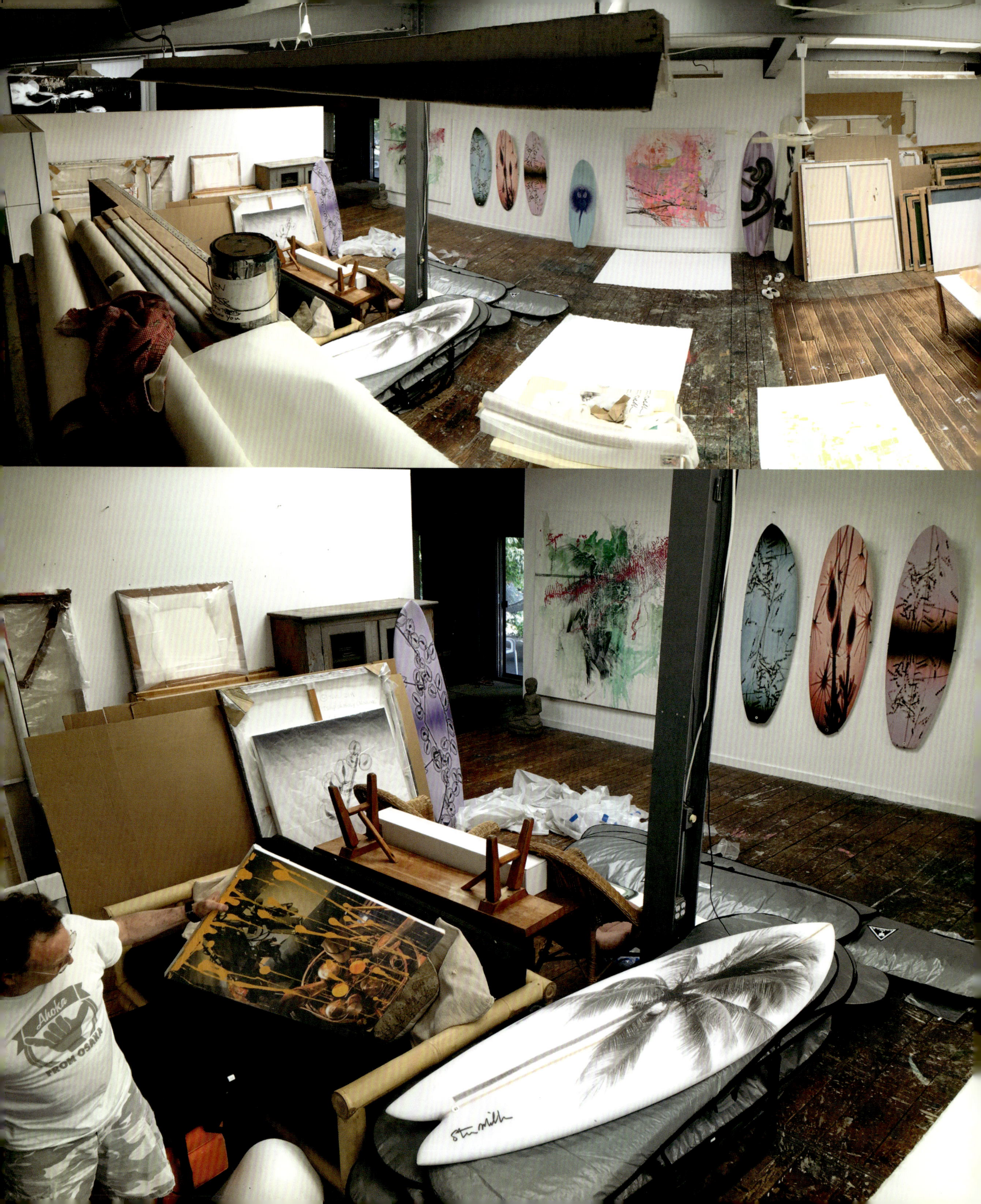

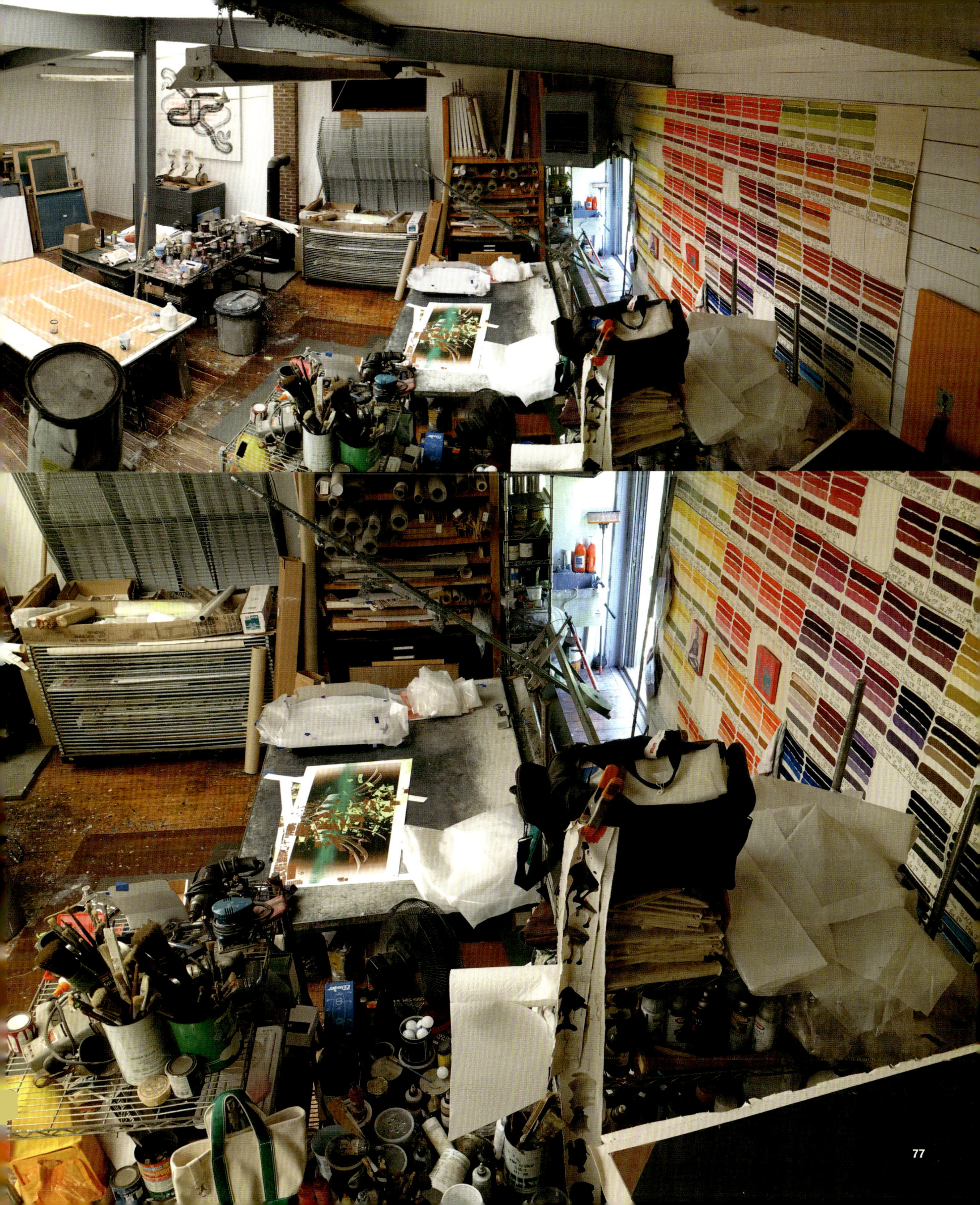

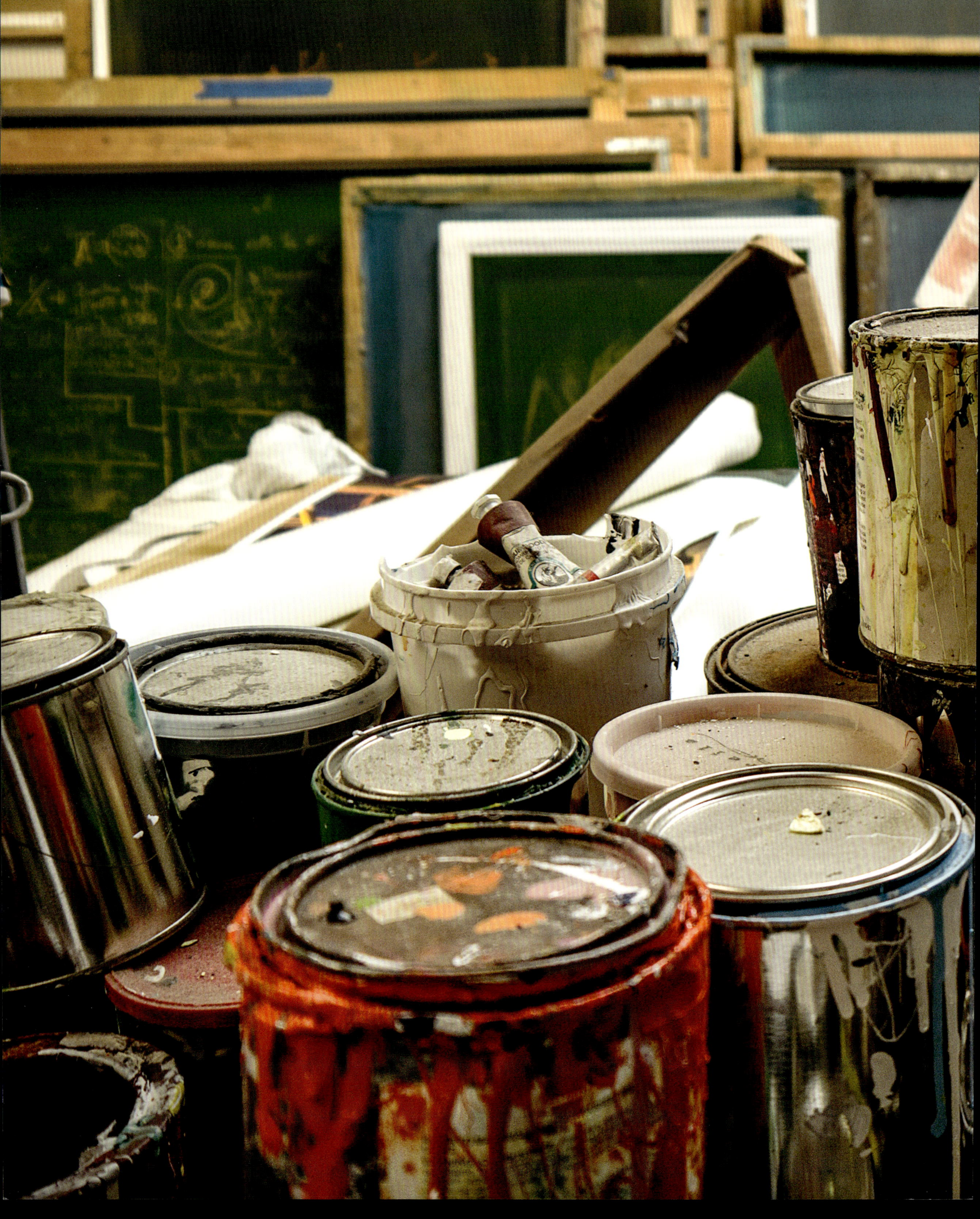

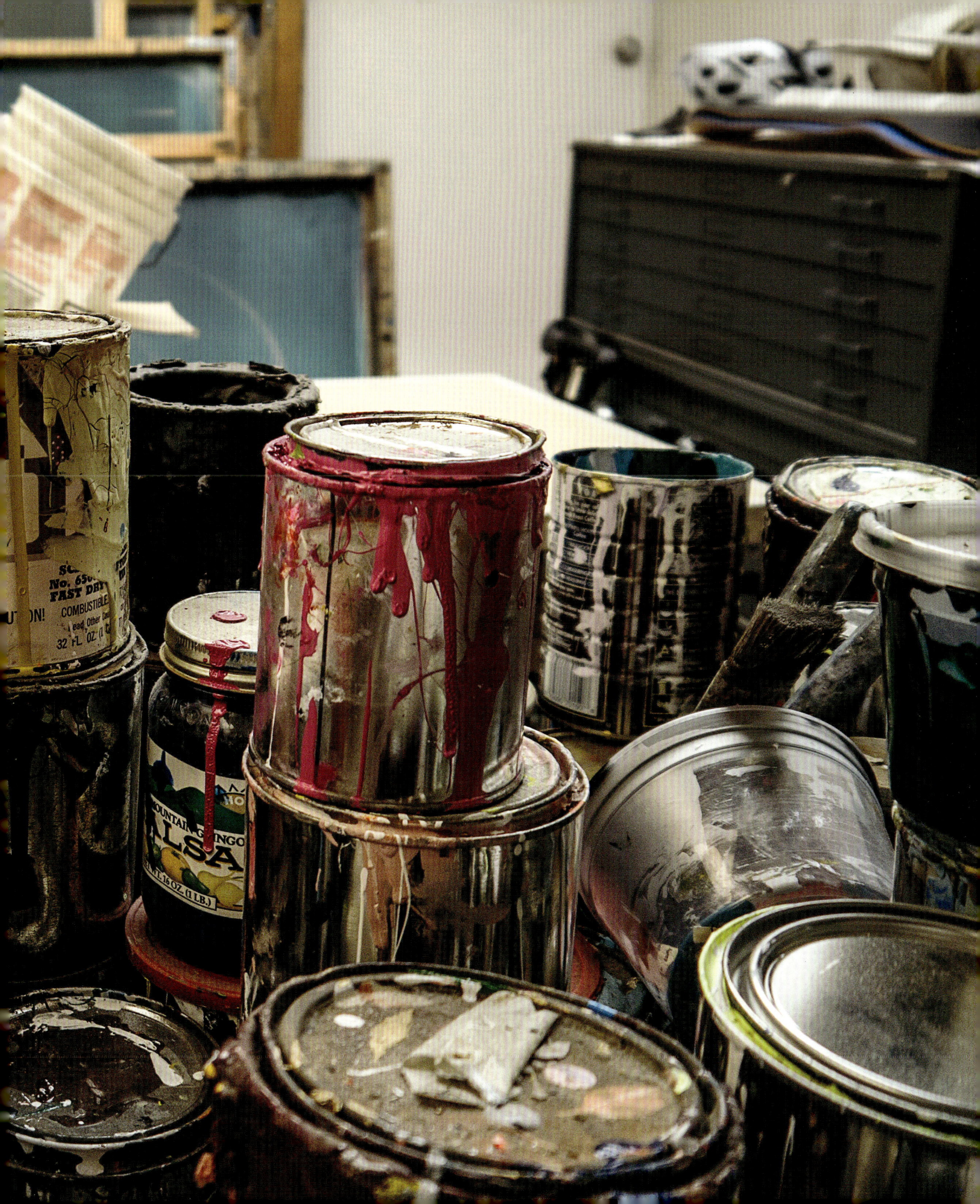

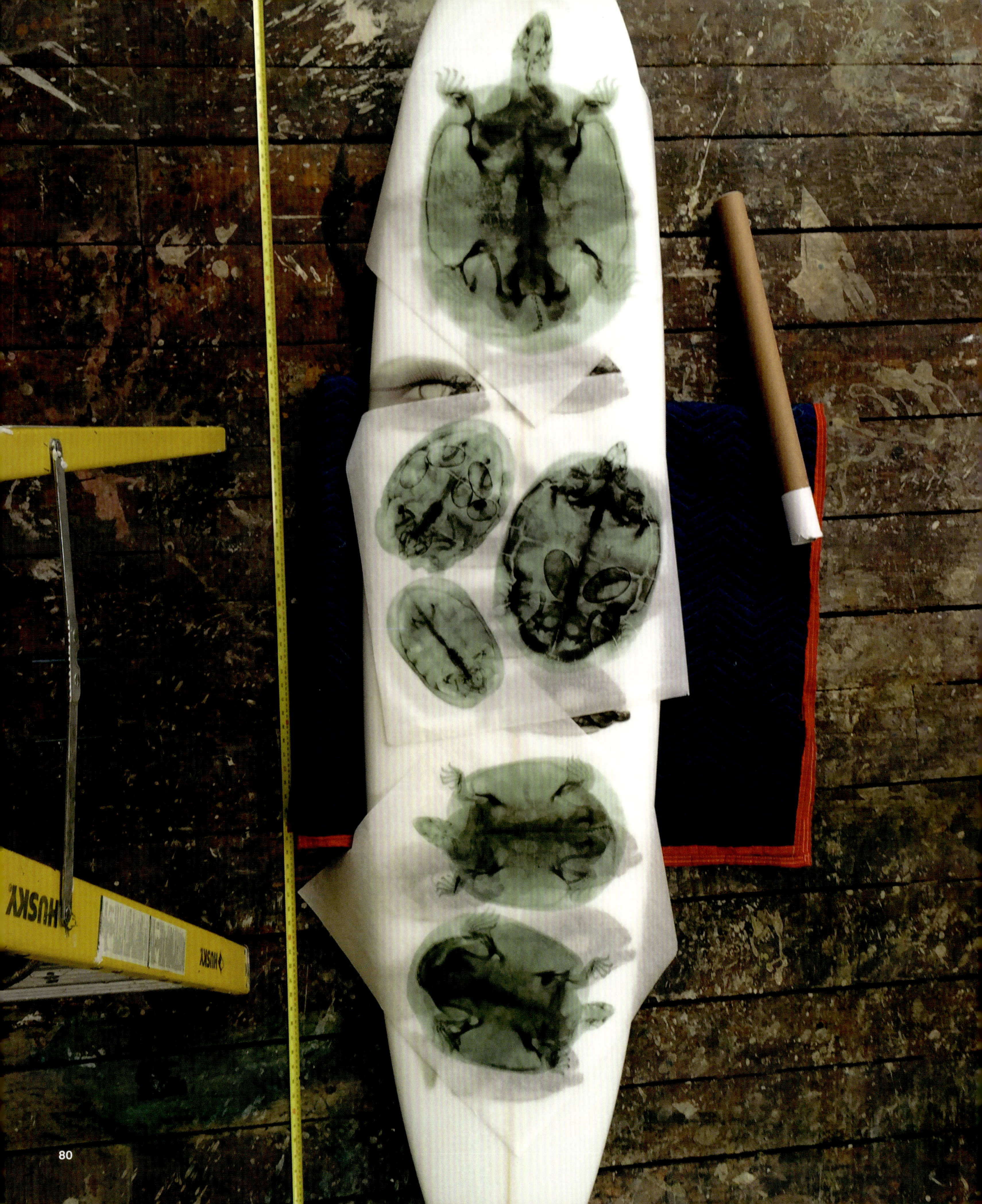

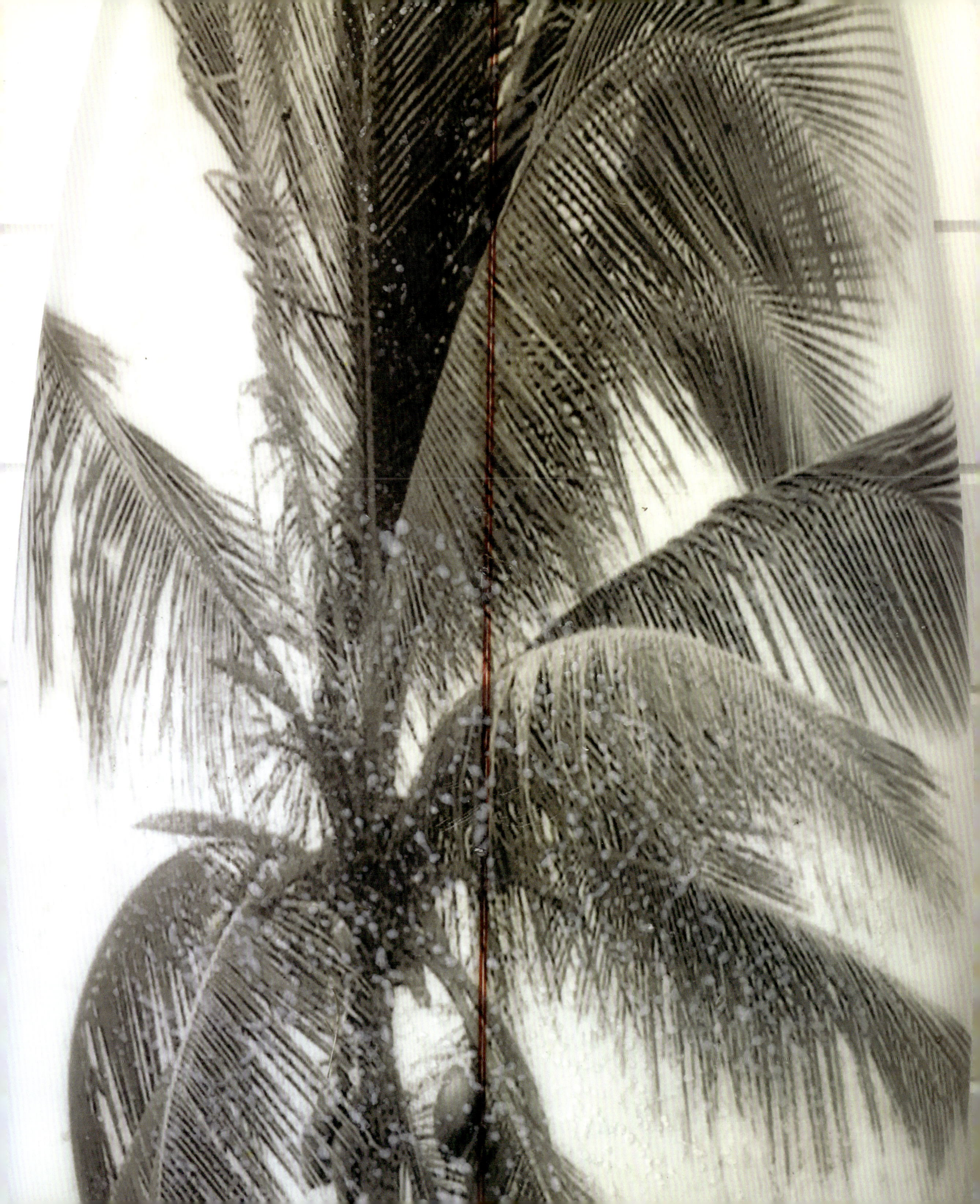

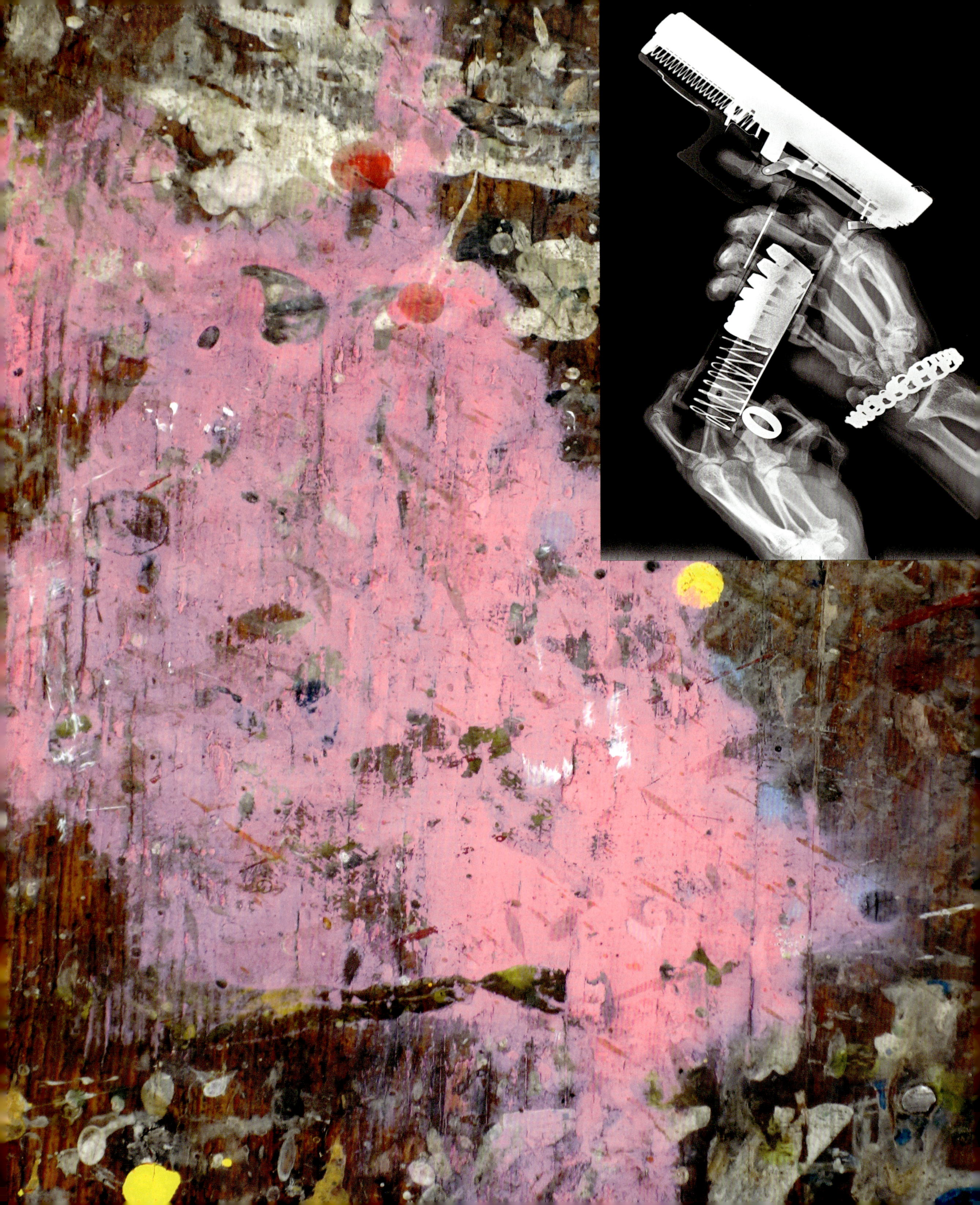

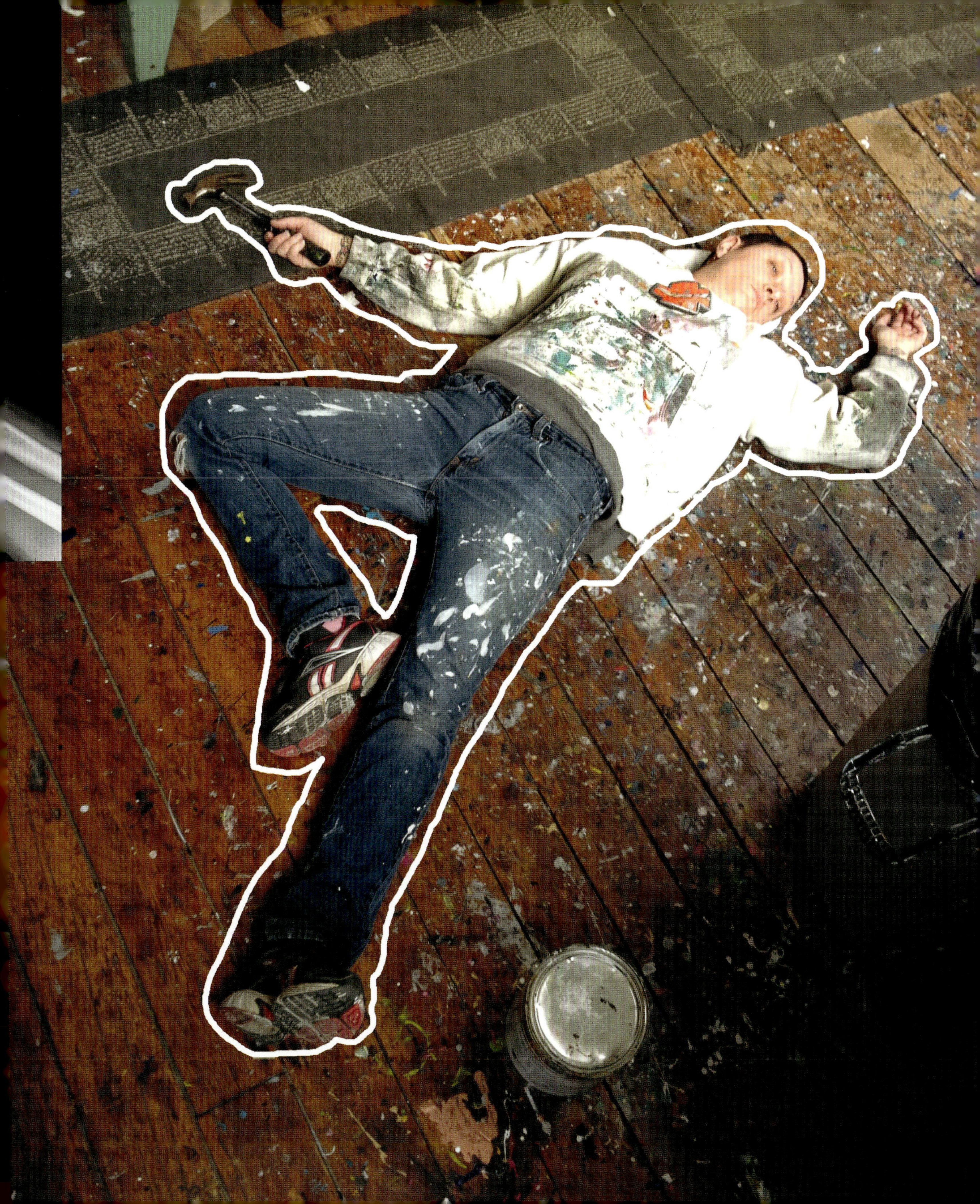

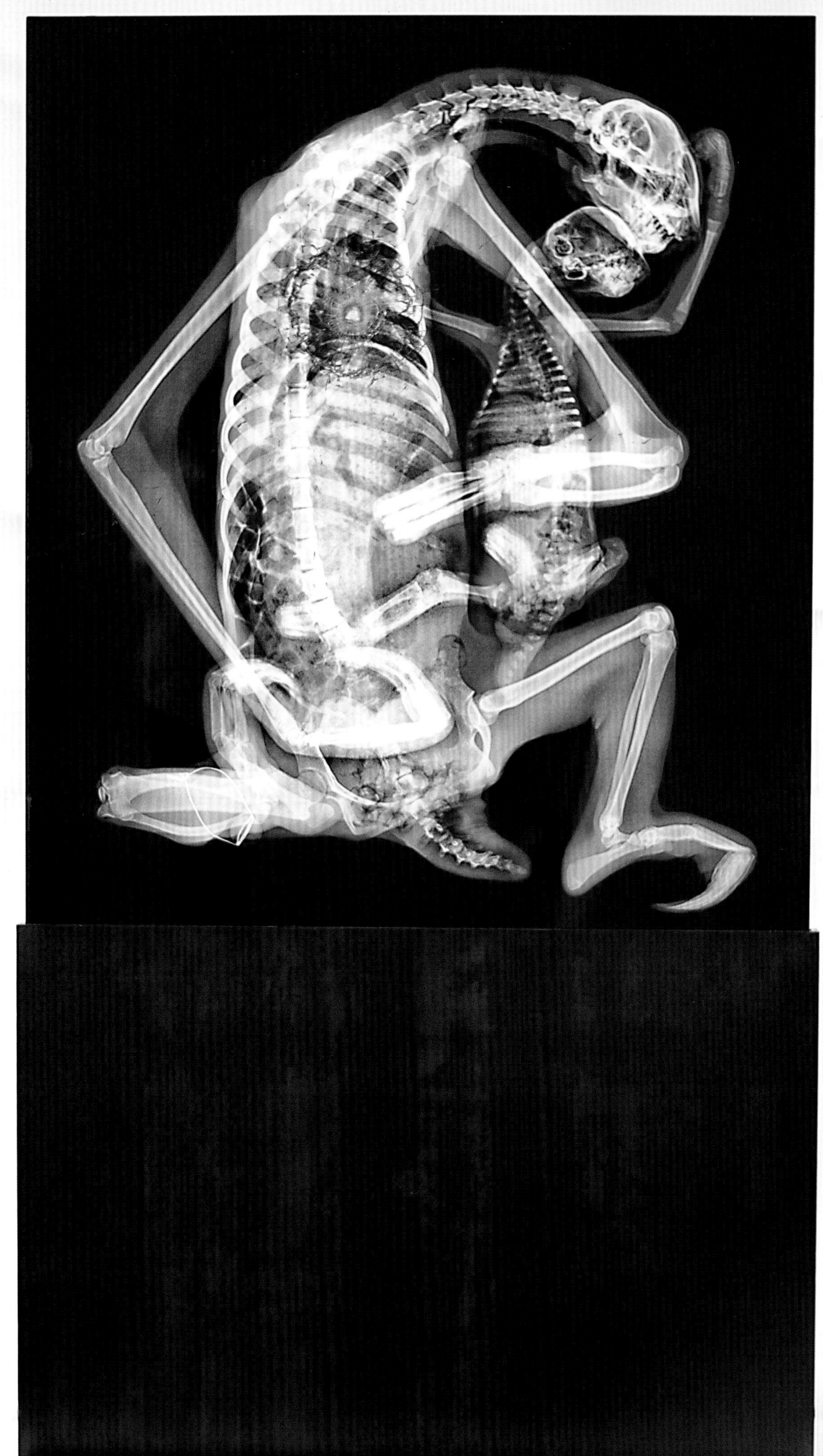

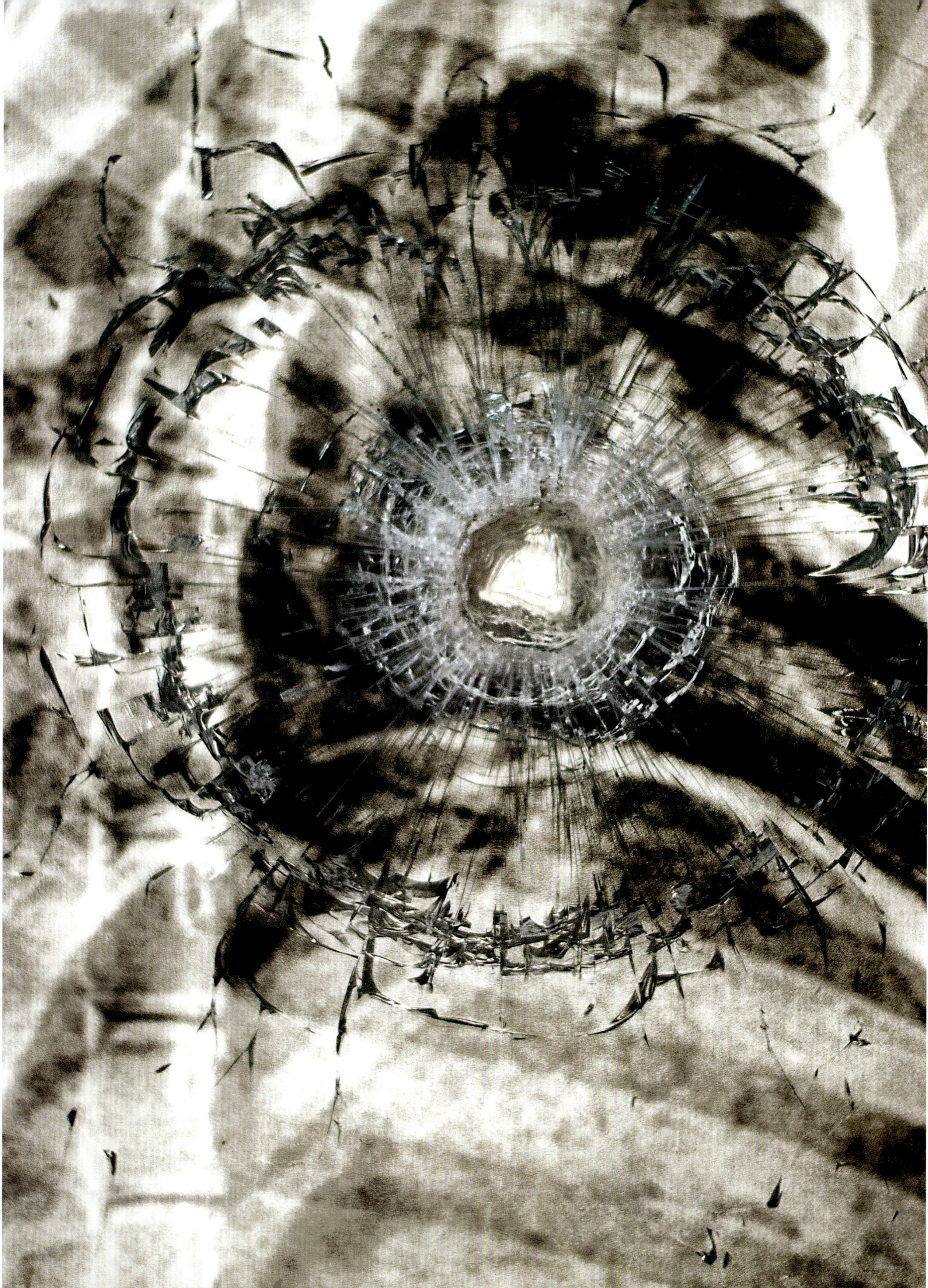

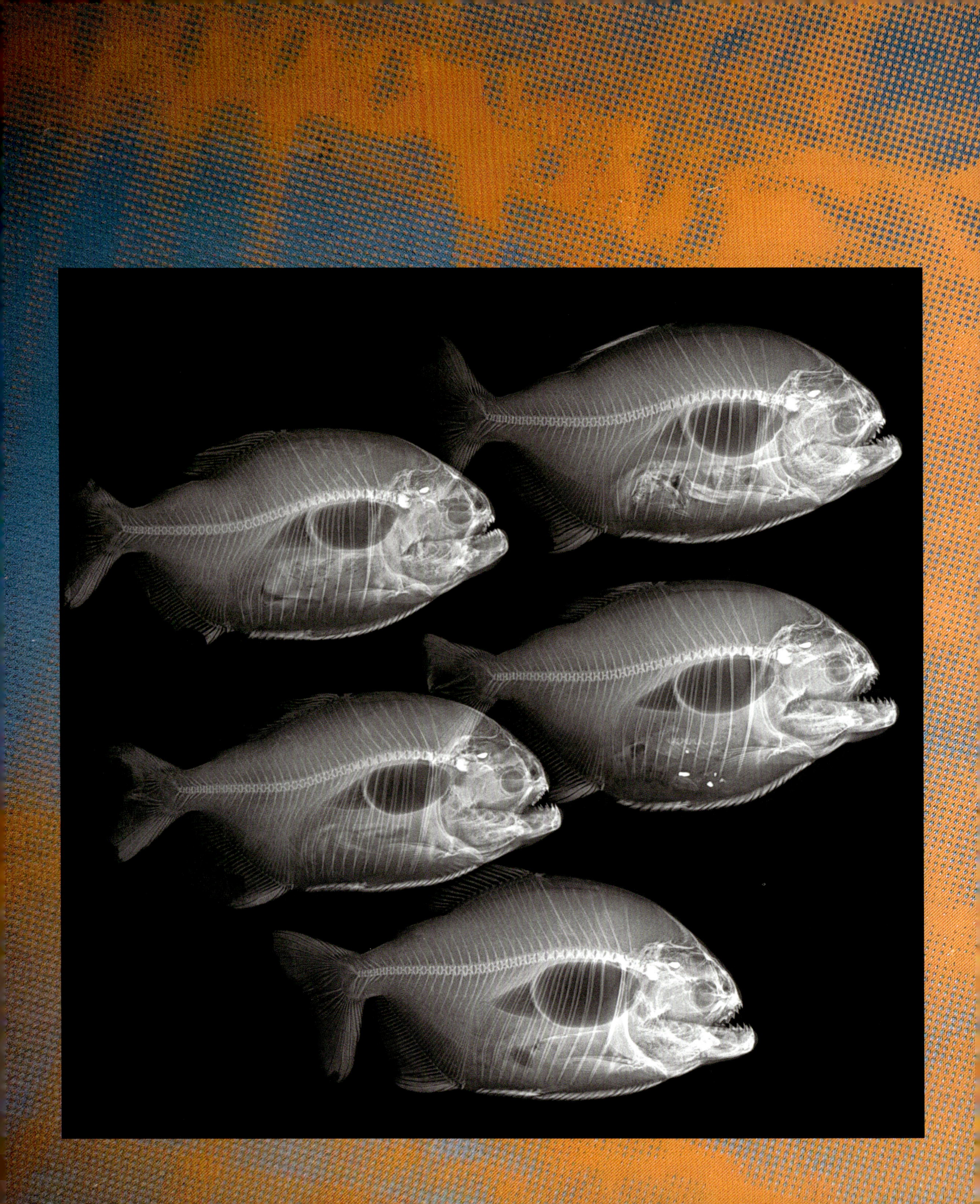

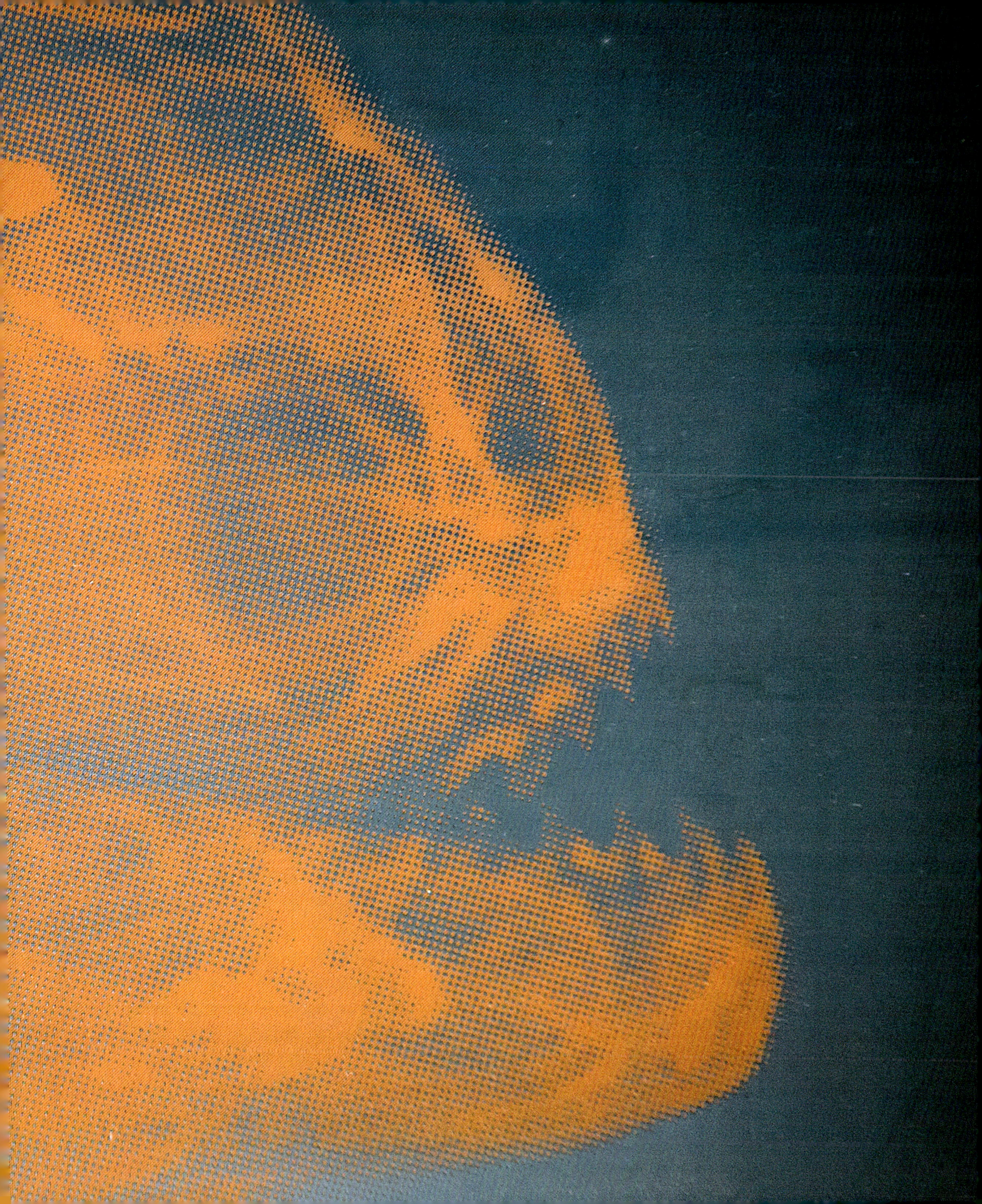

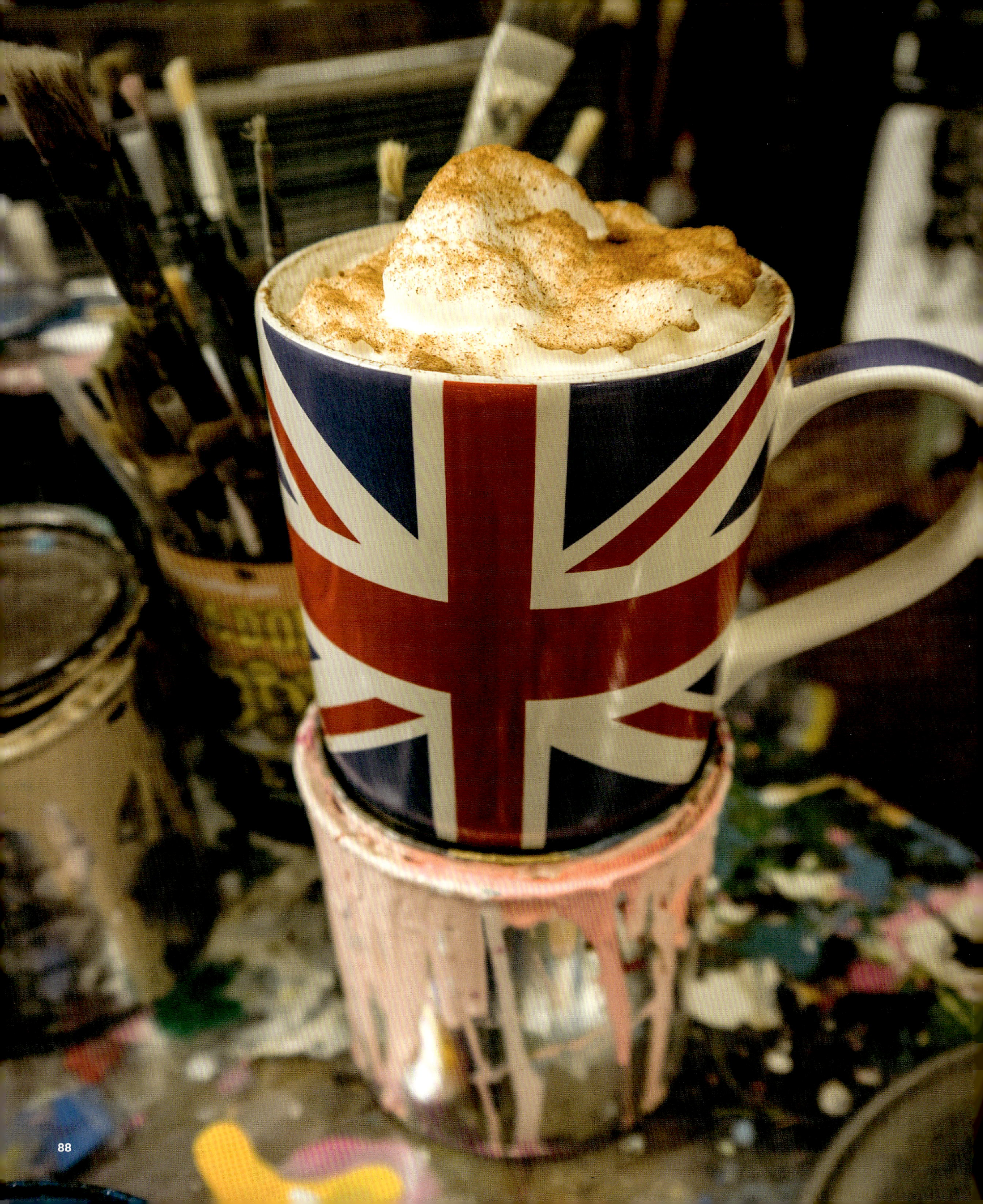

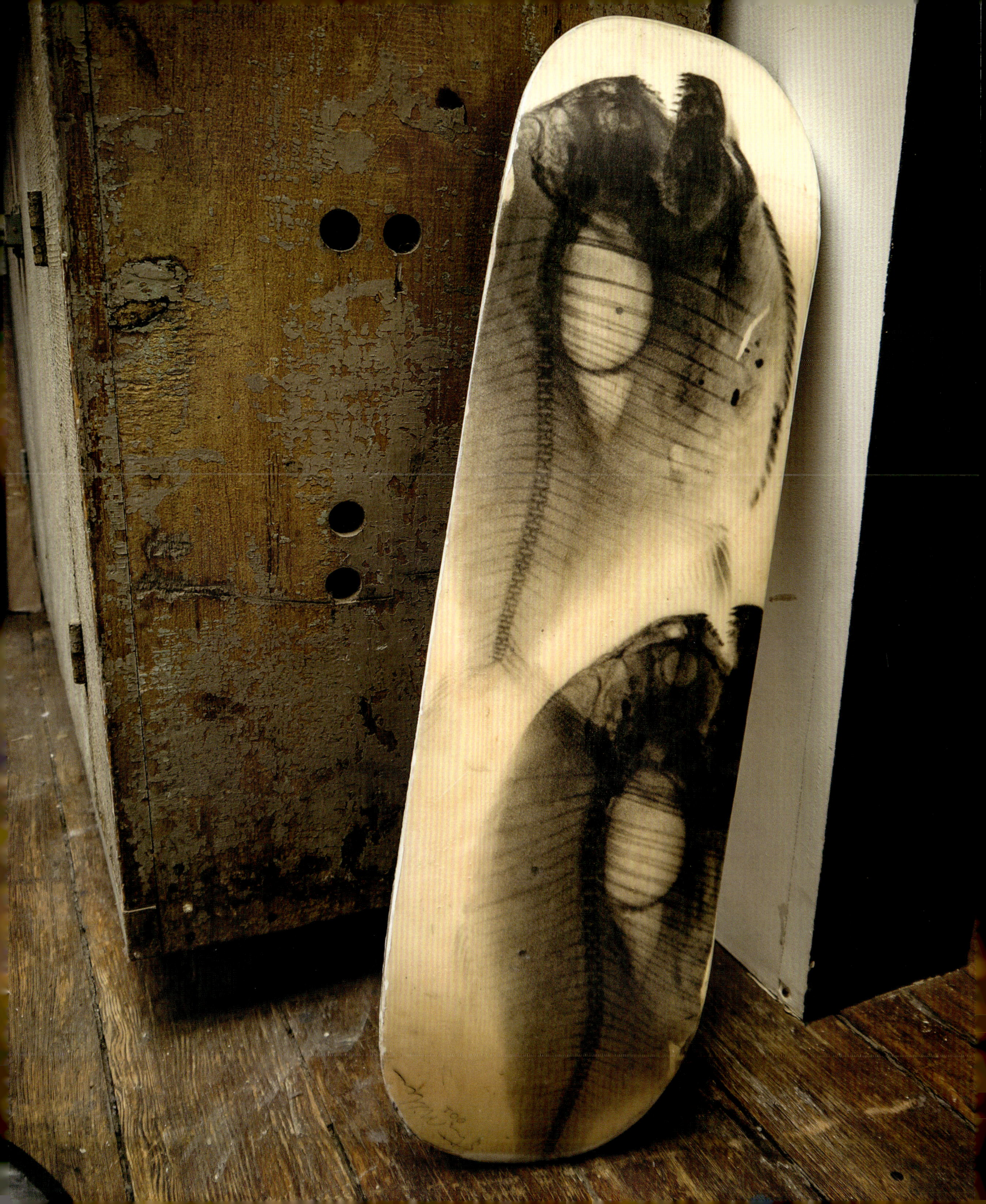

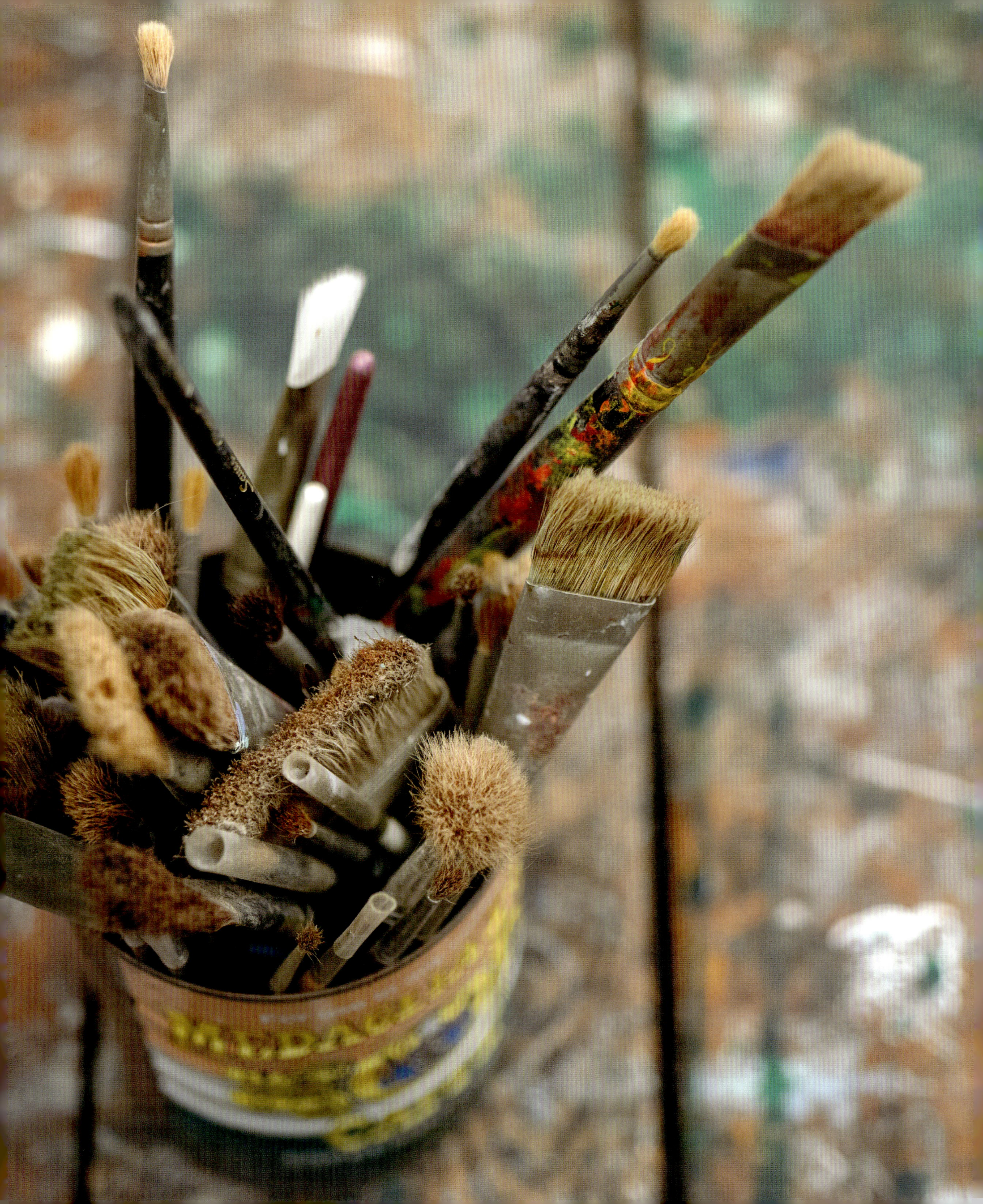

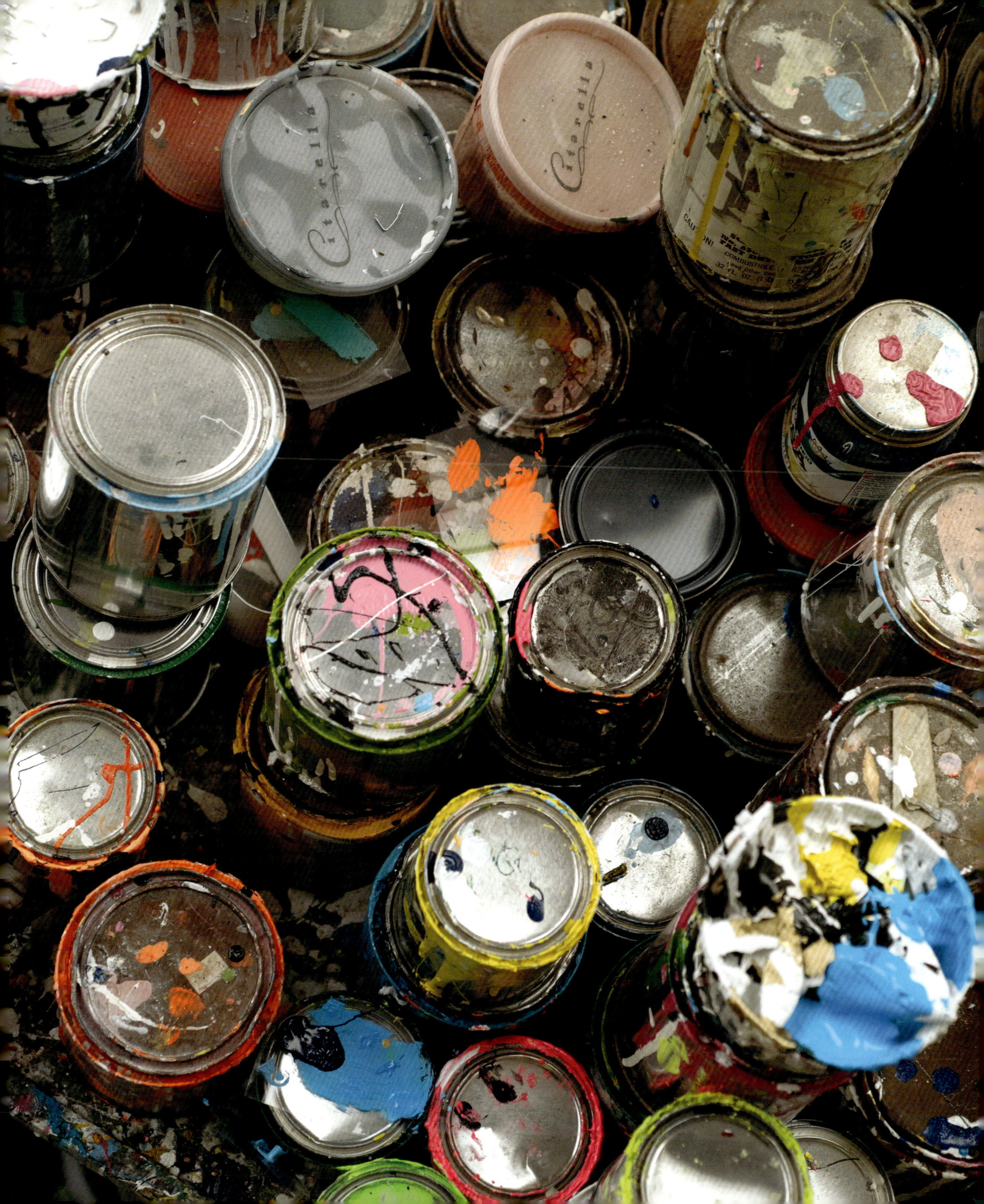
Citarella
Citarella

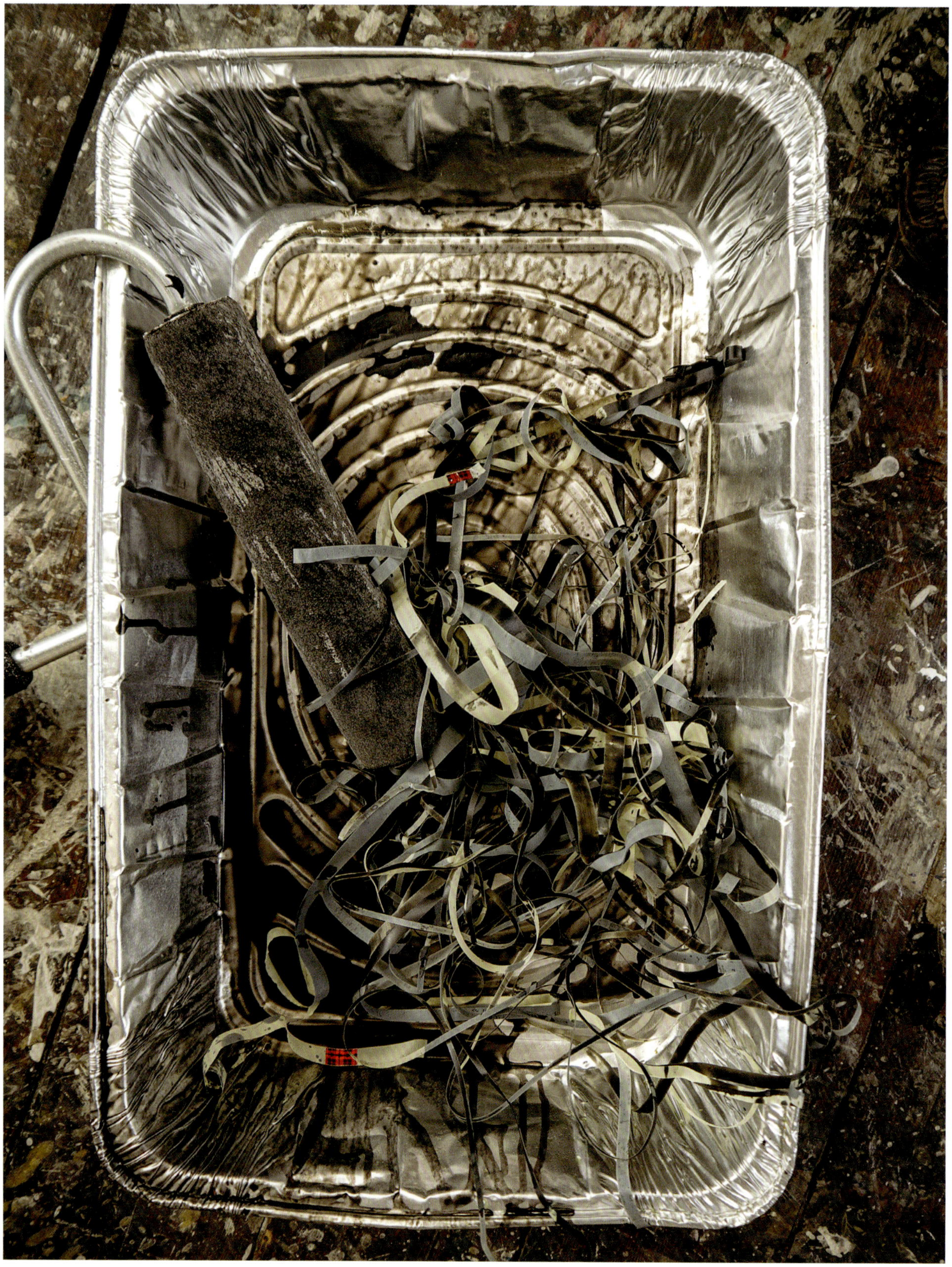

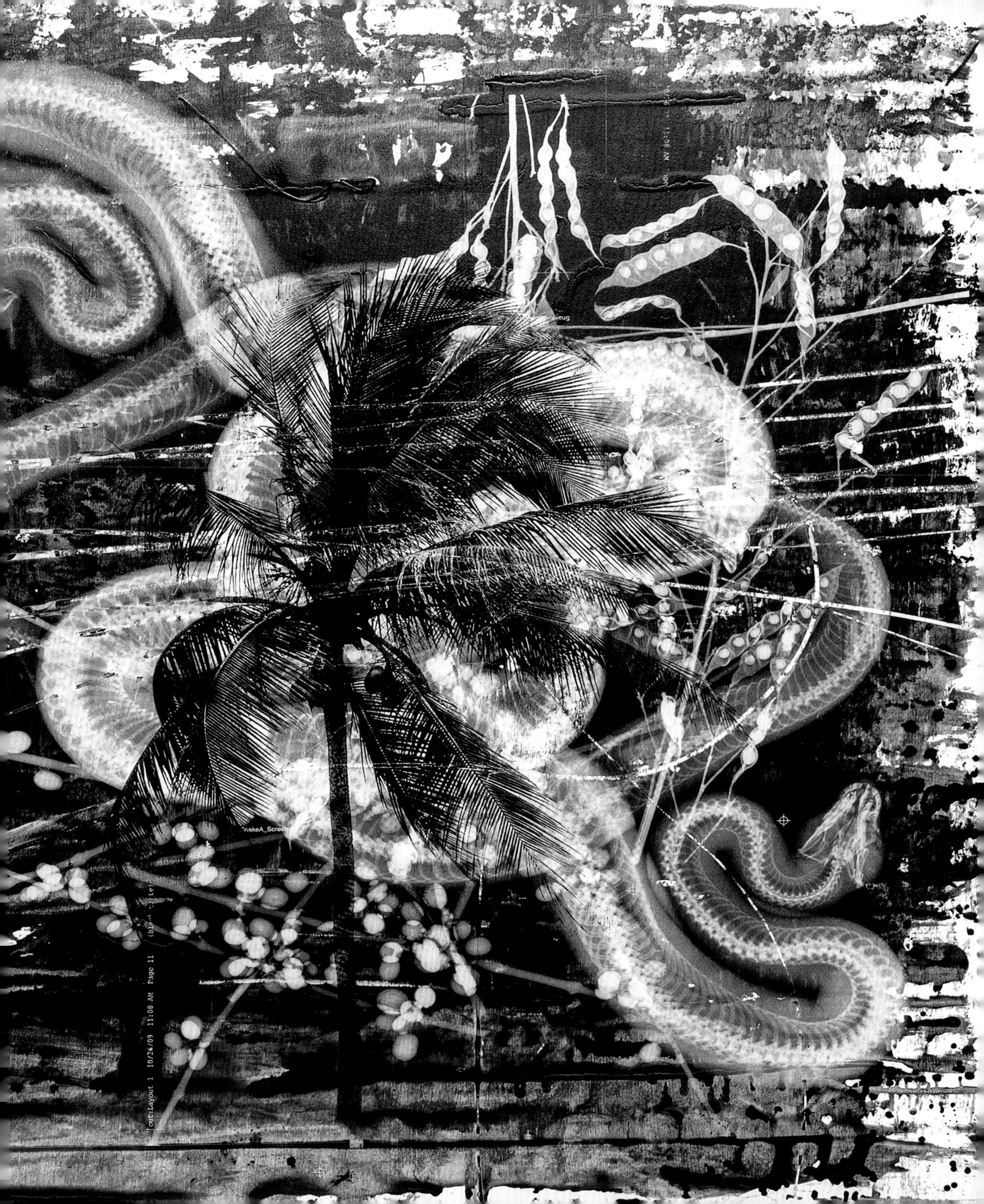

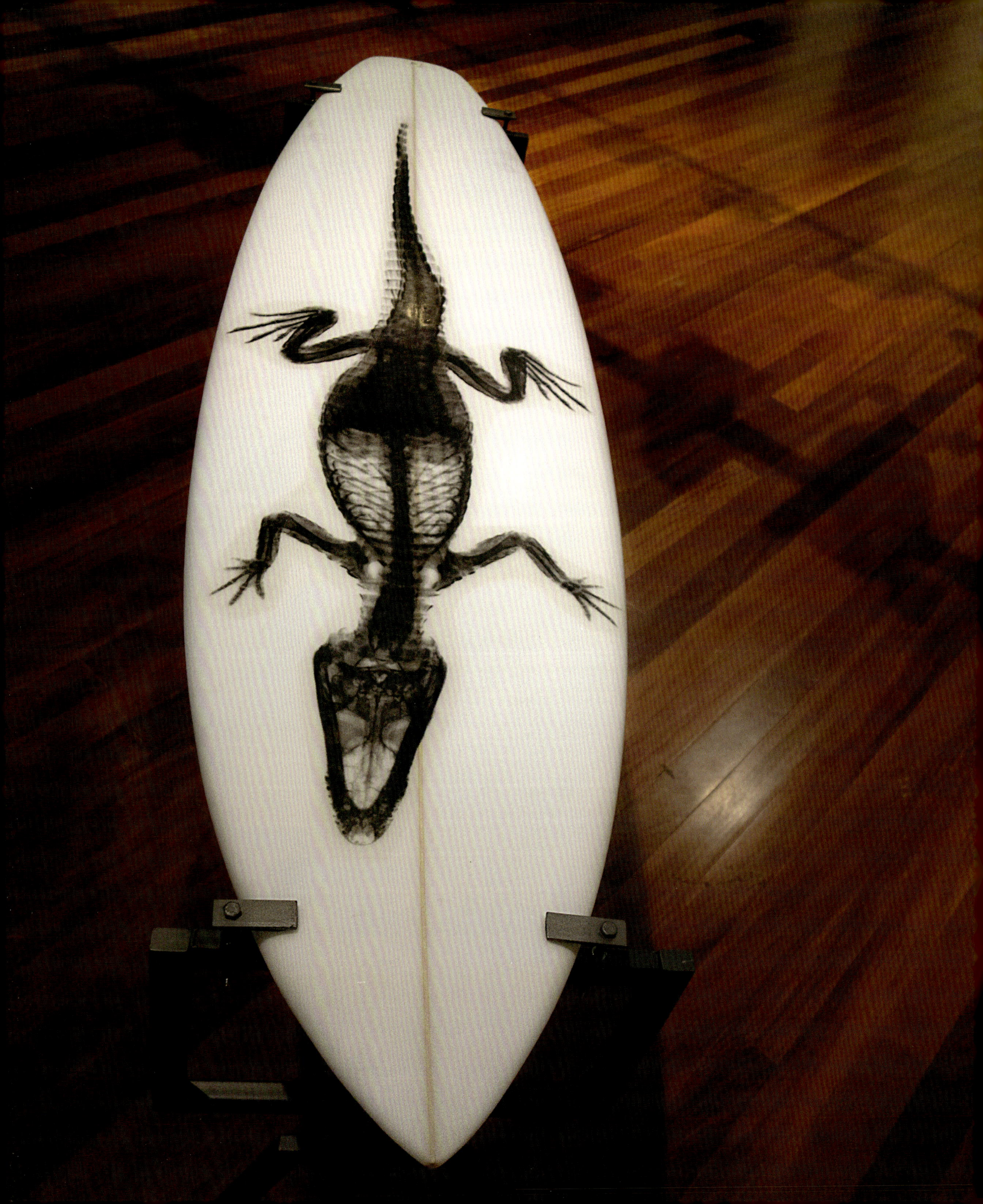

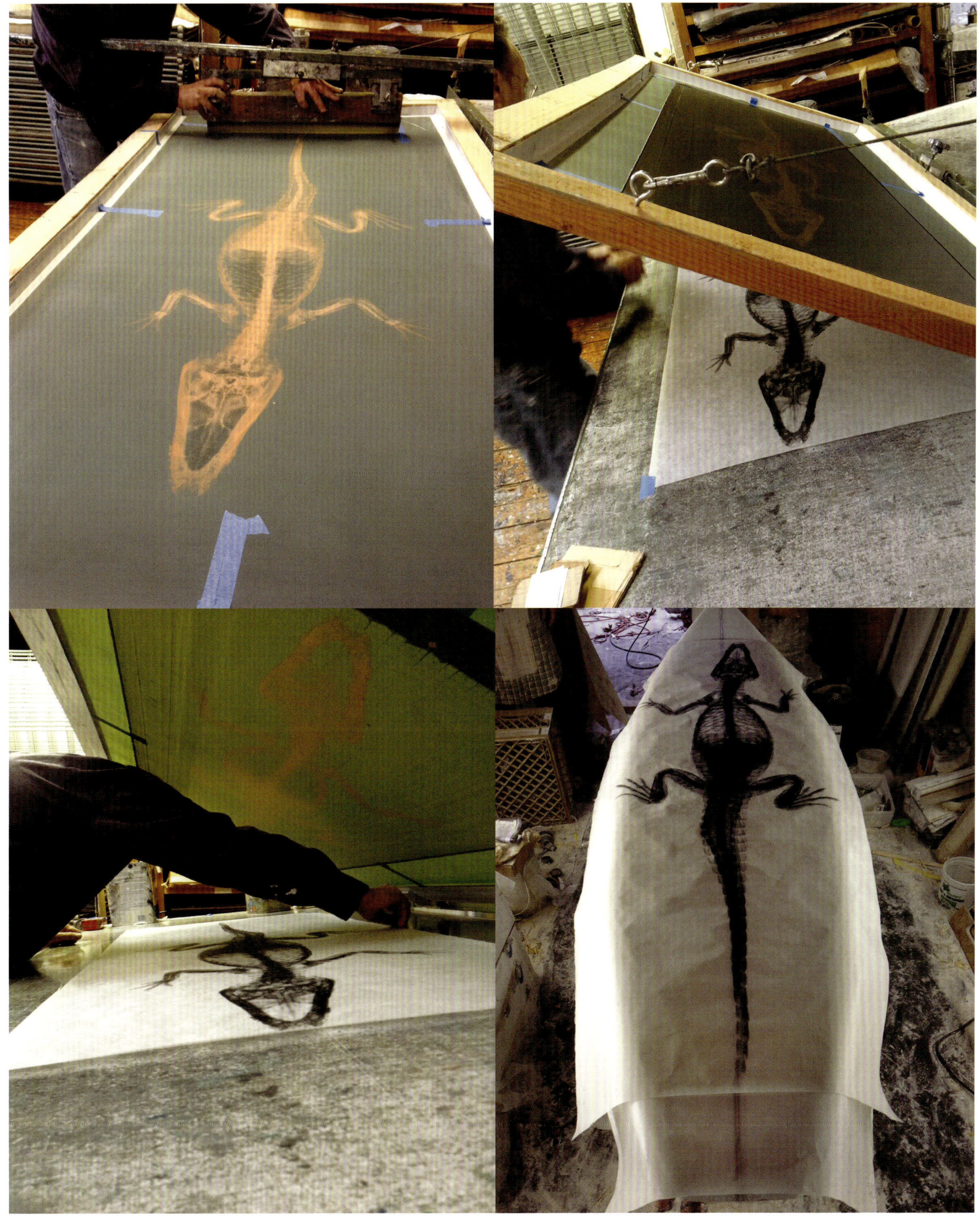

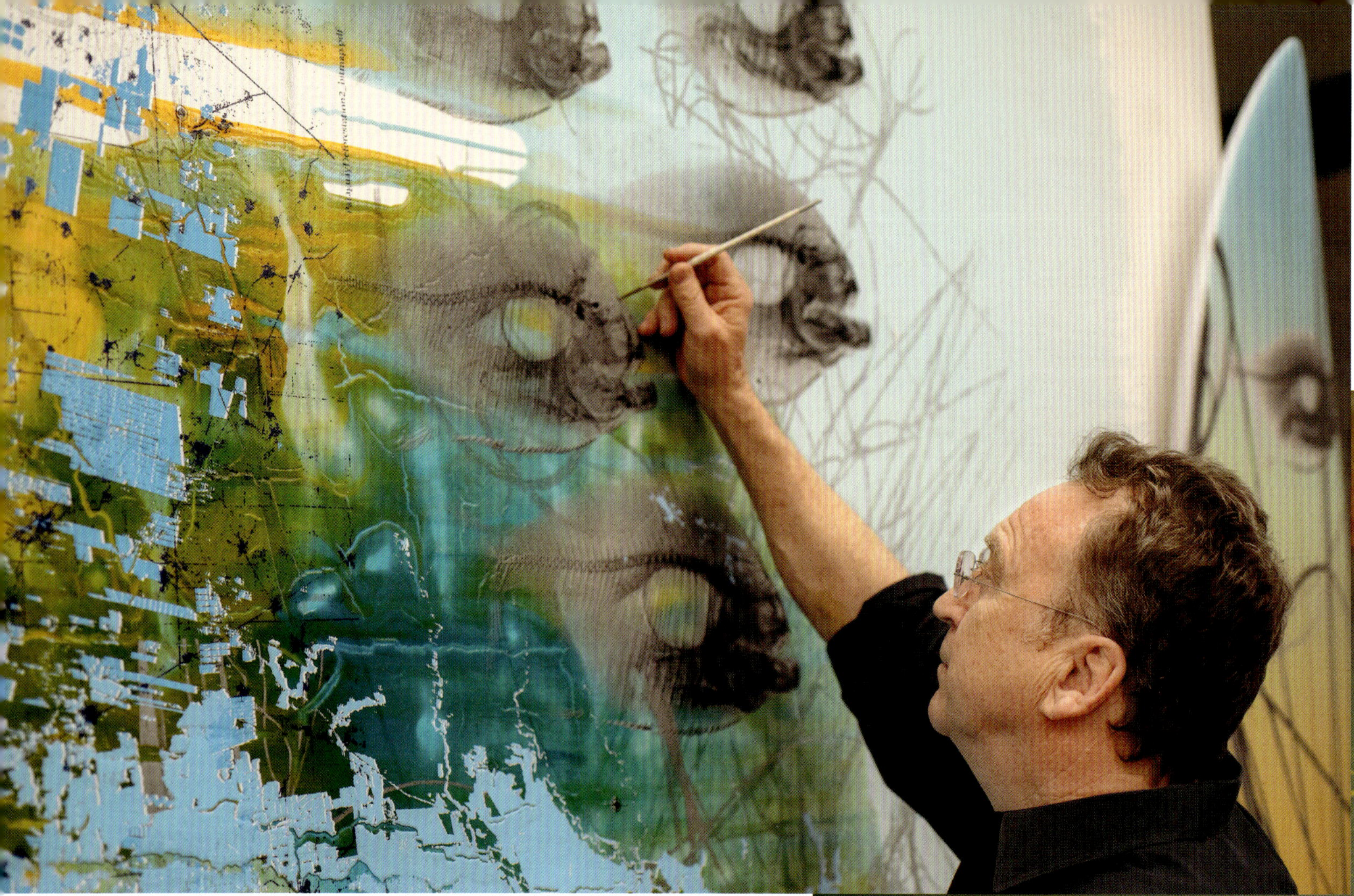

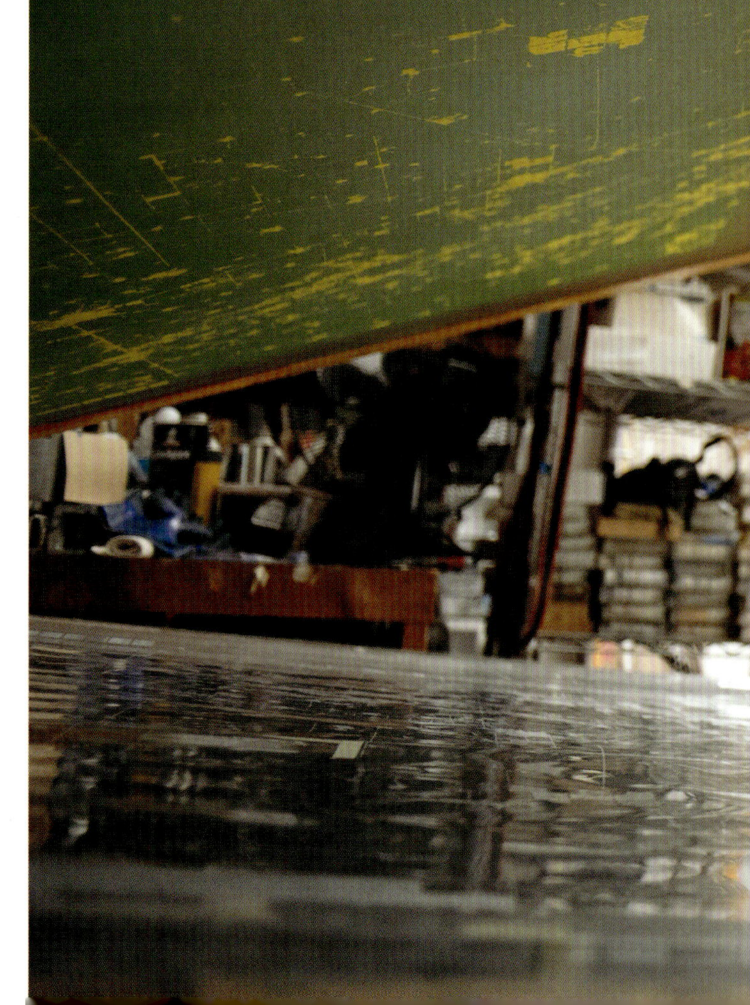

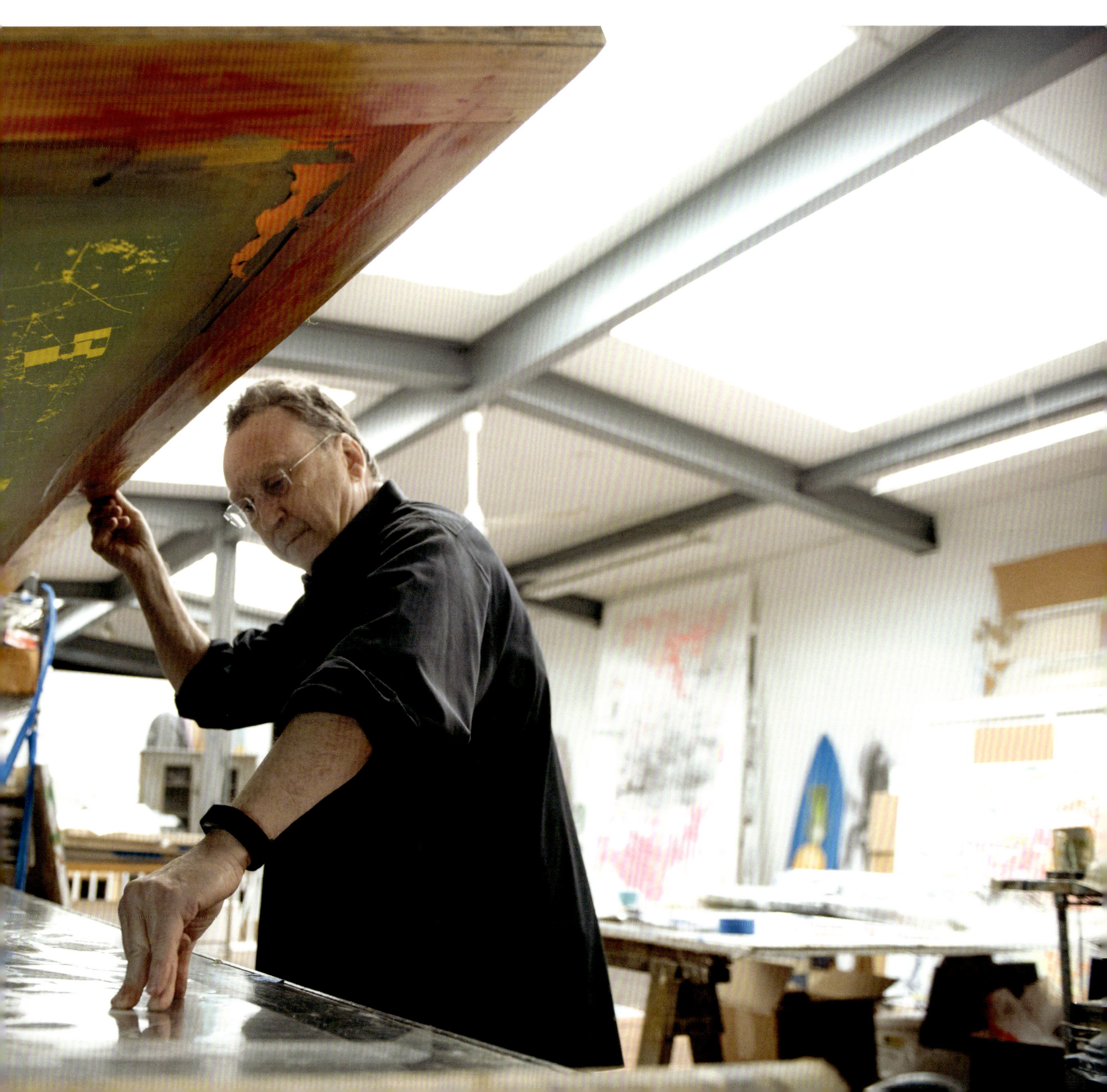

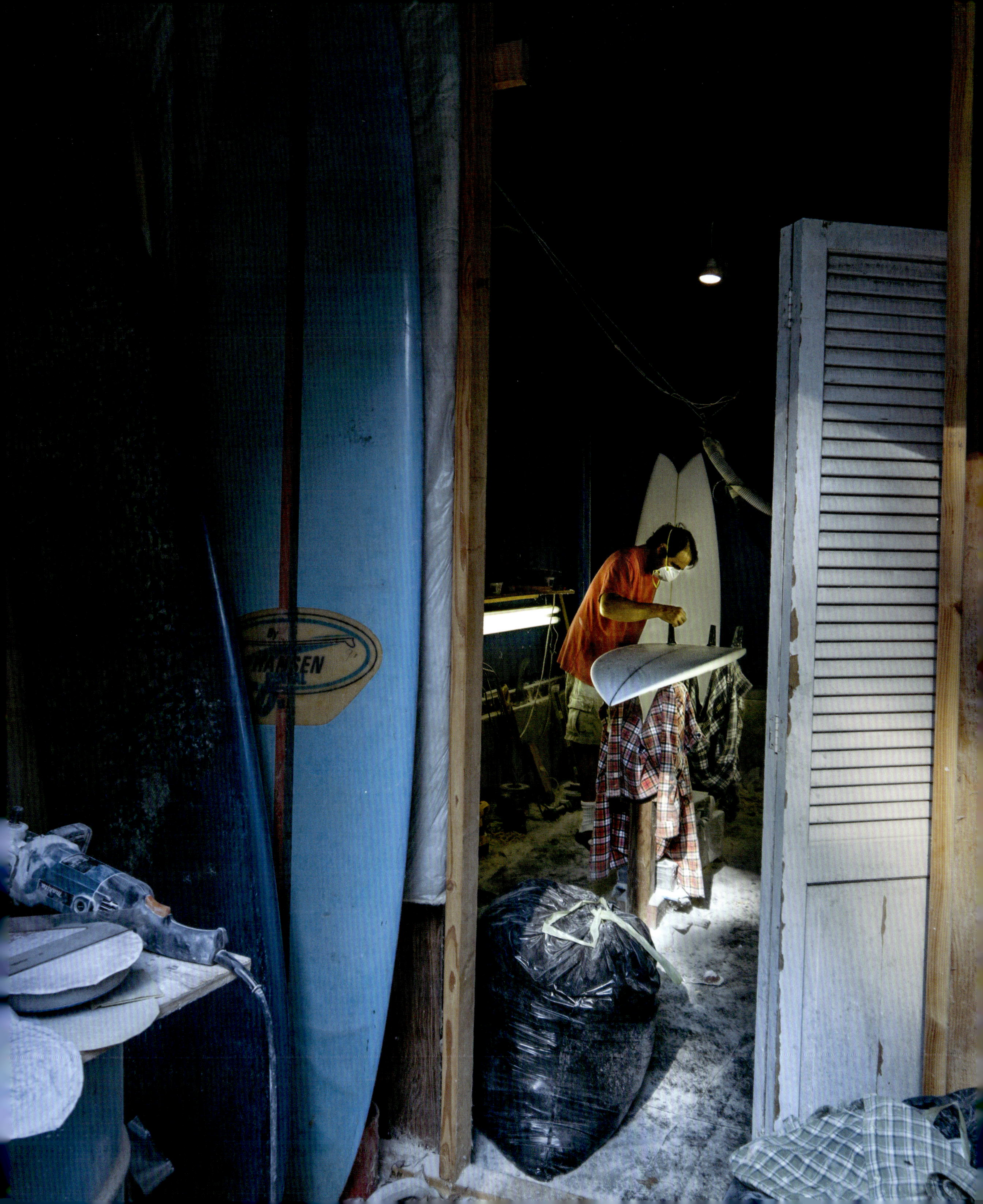

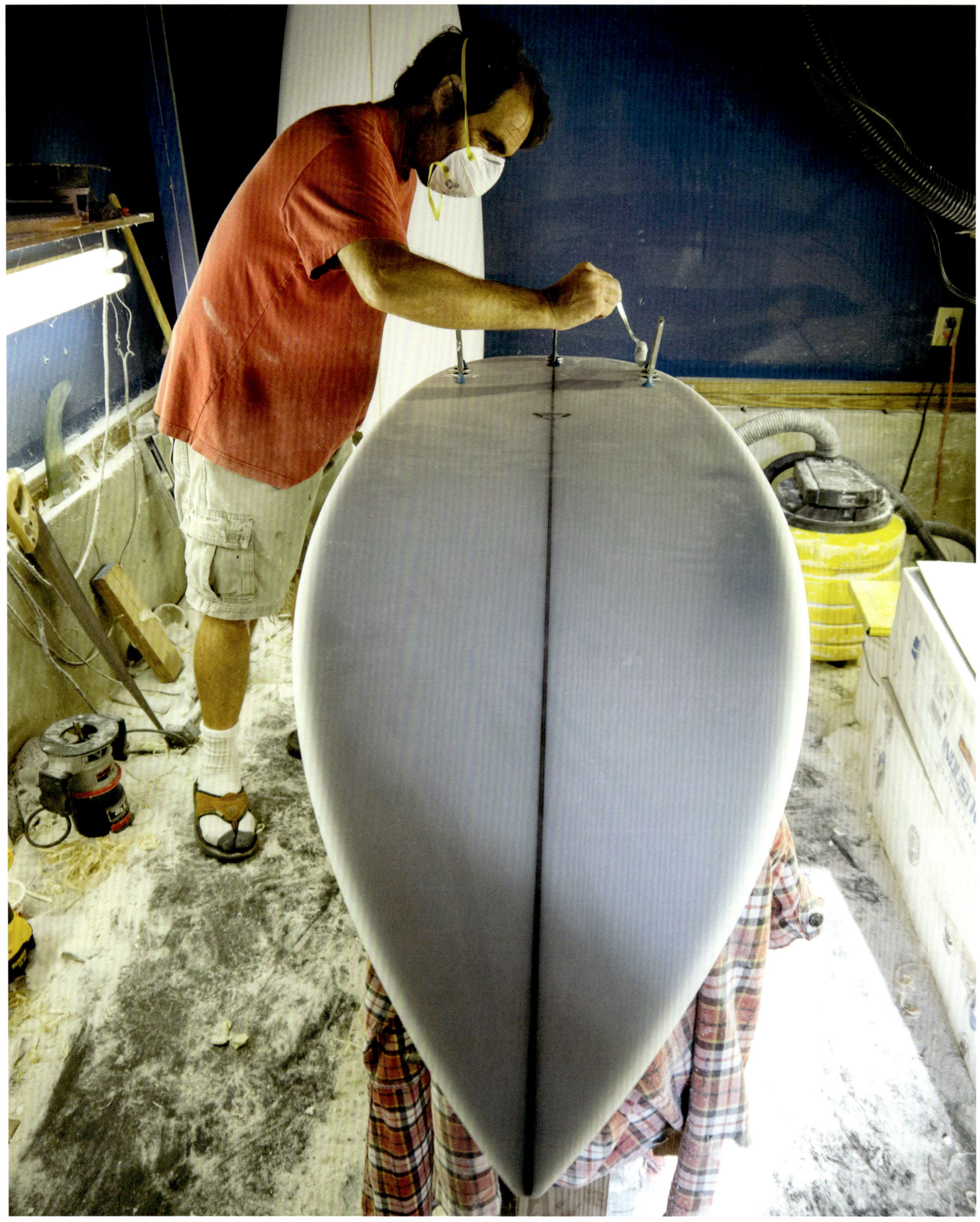

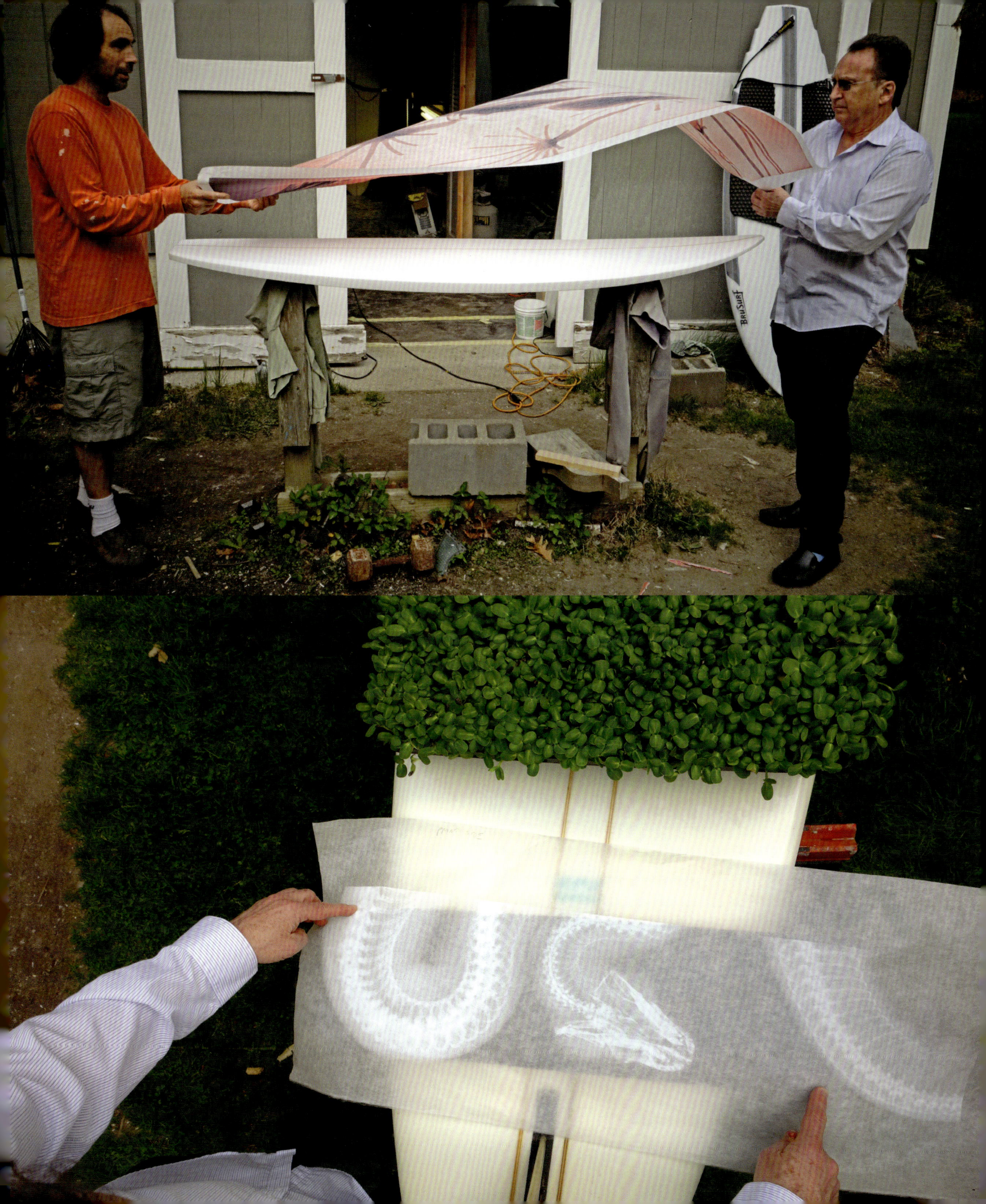

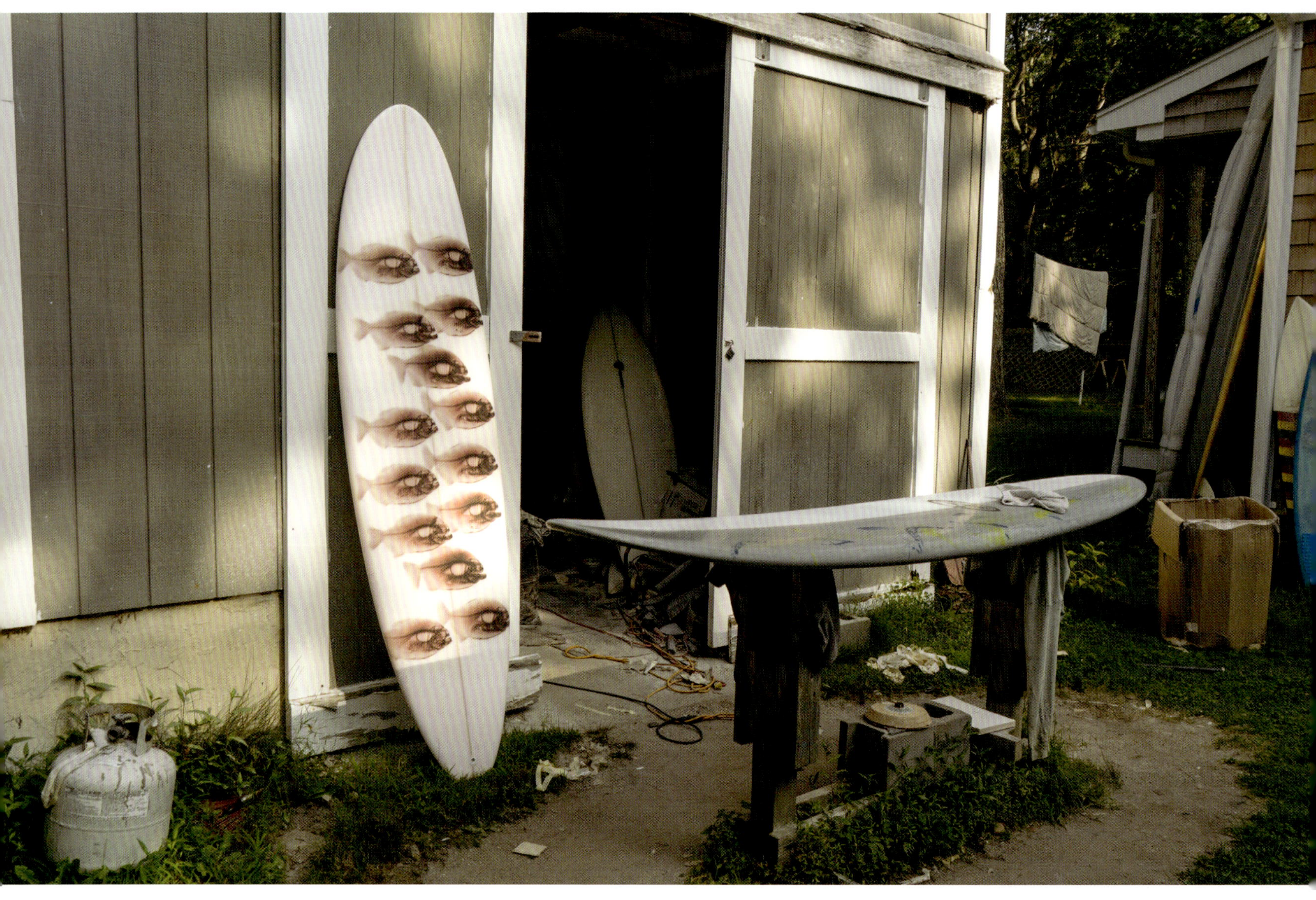

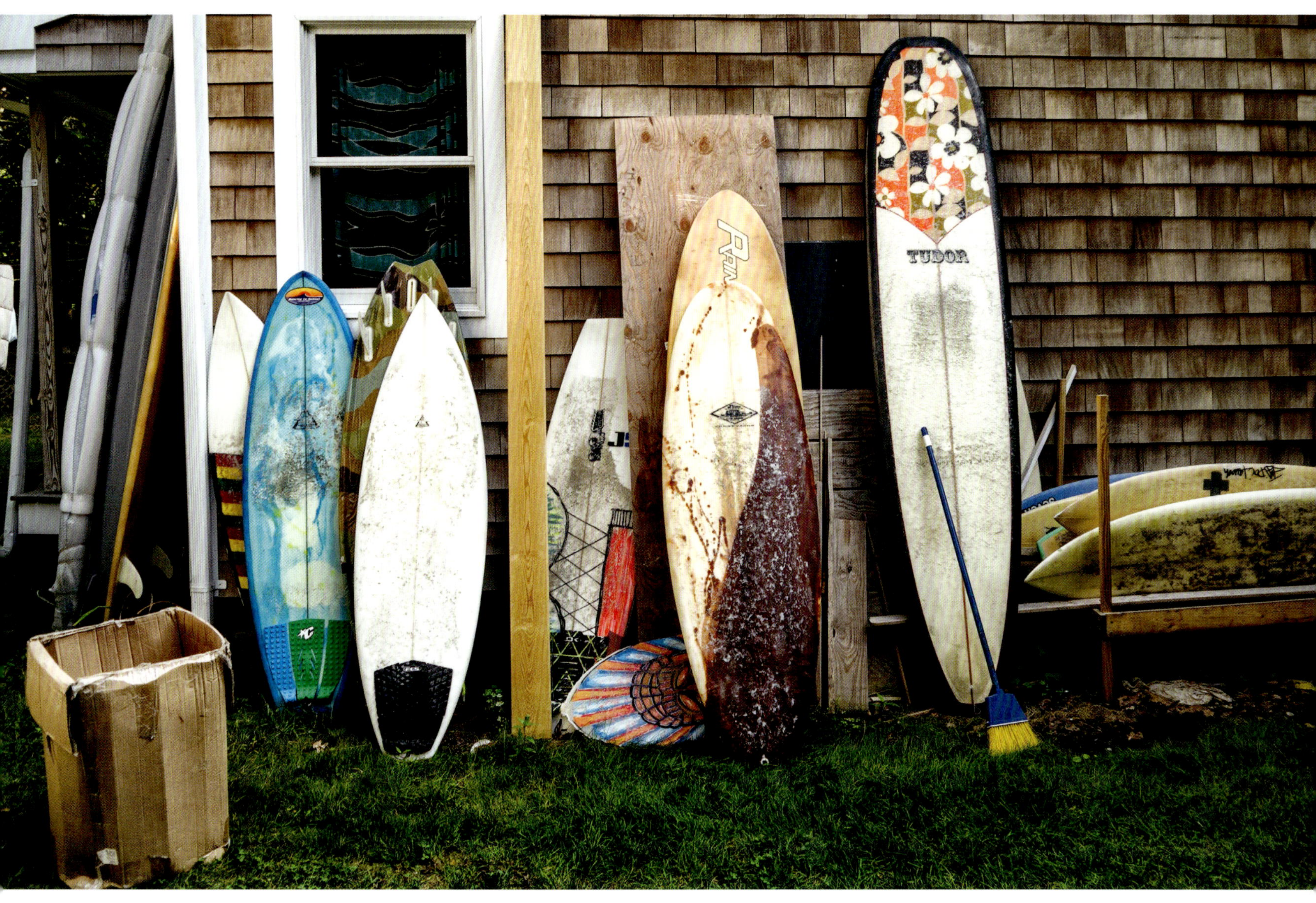

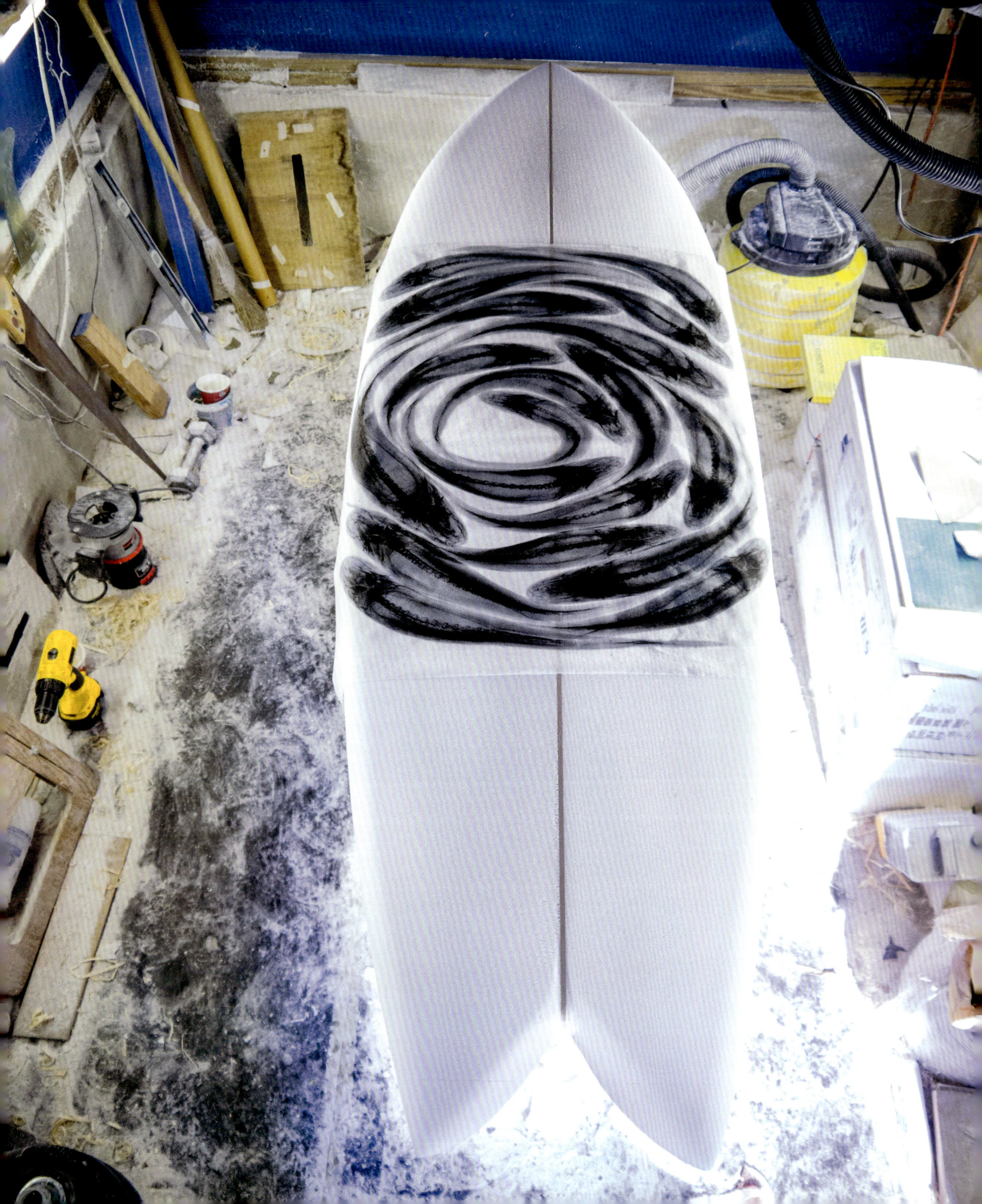

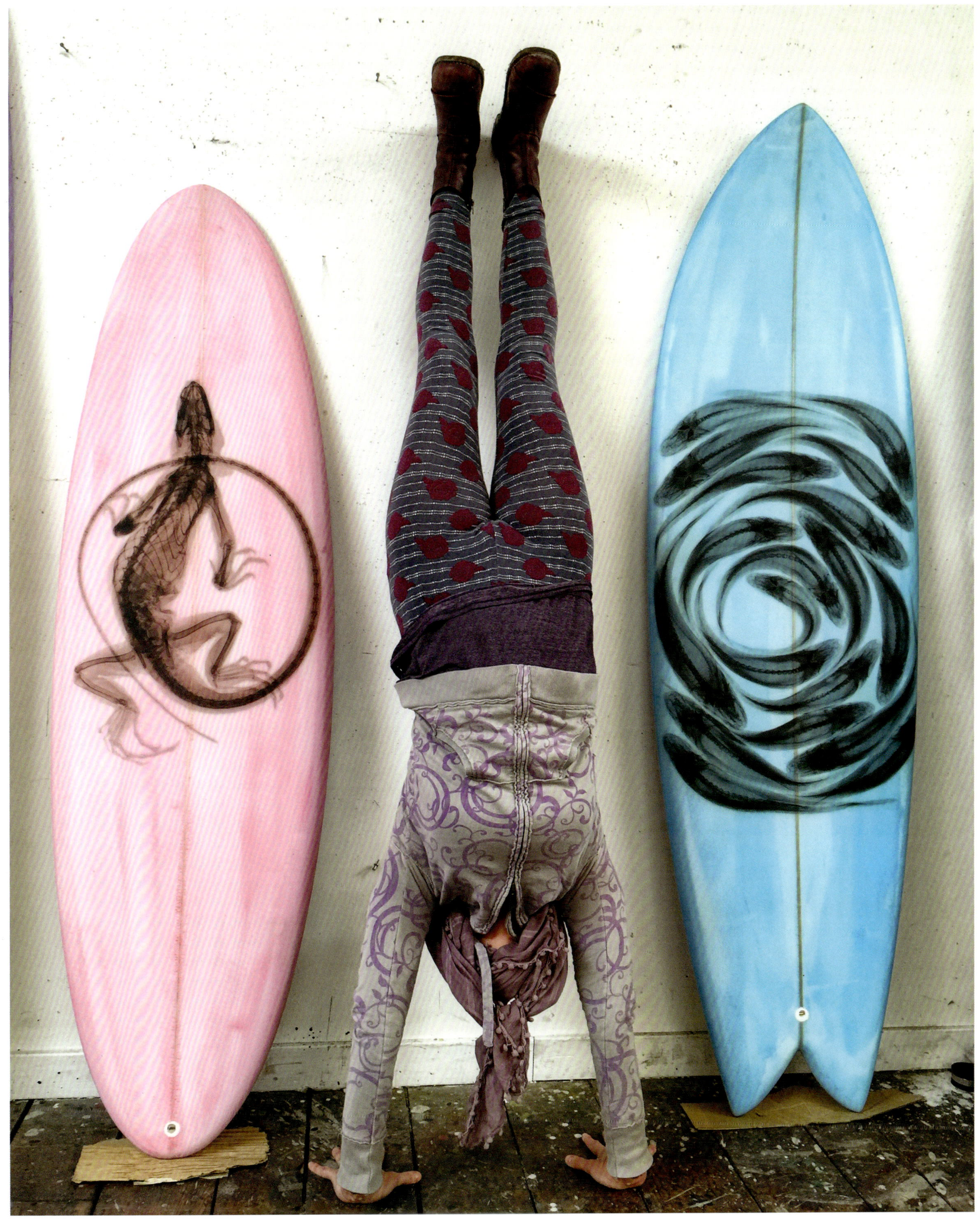

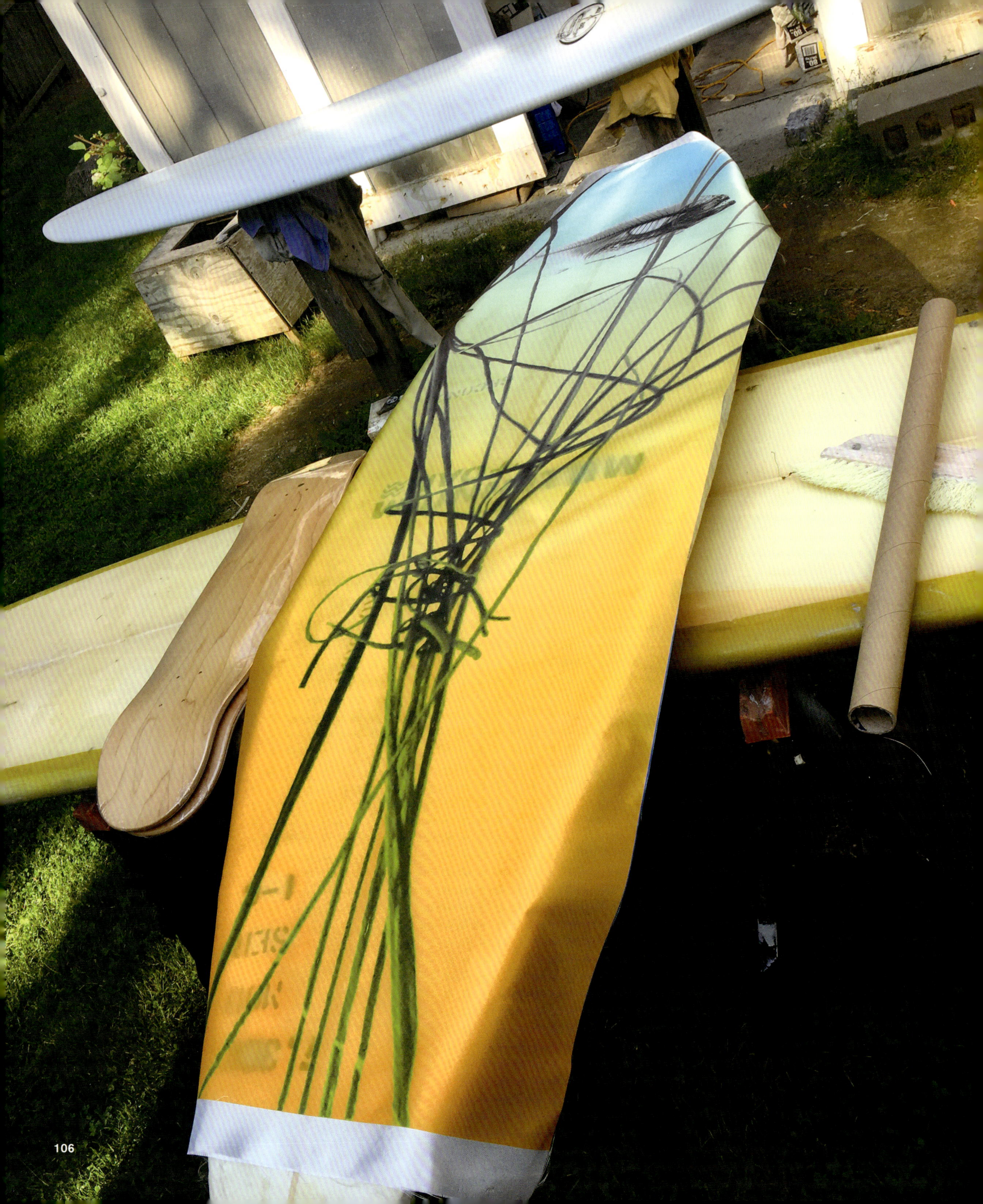

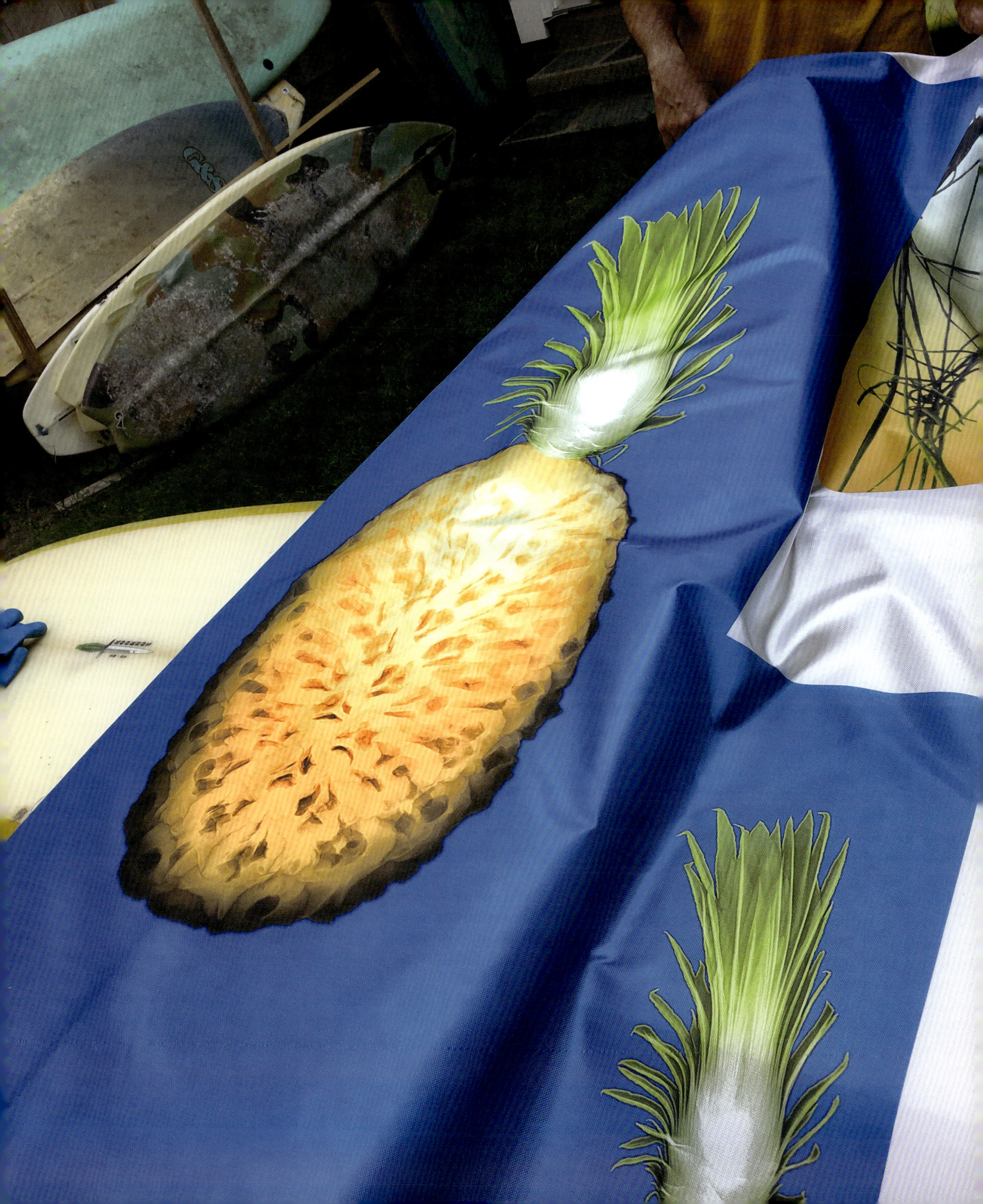

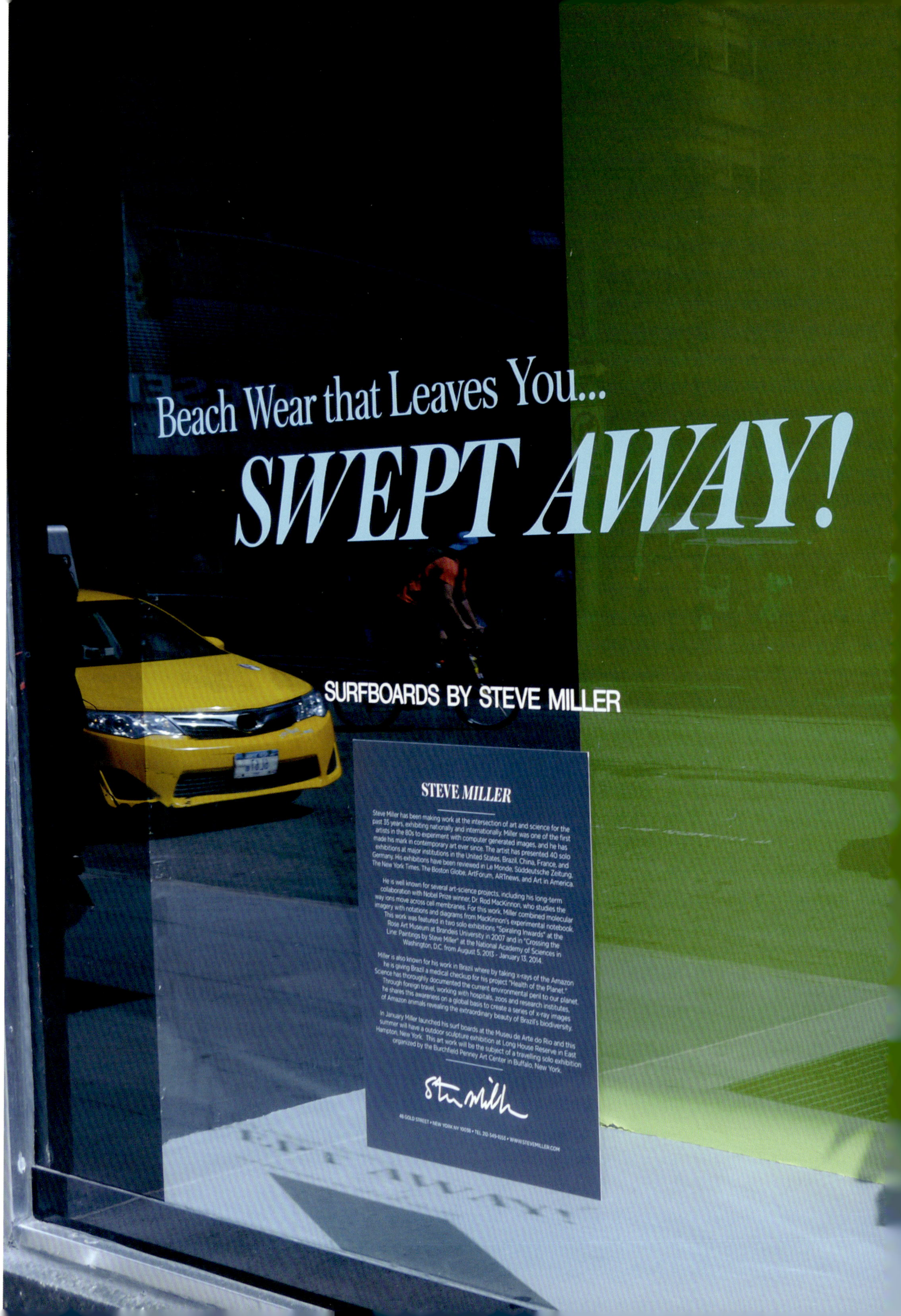

Beach Wear that Leaves You...
SWEPT AWAY!

SURFBOARDS BY STEVE MILLER

STEVE MILLER

Steve Miller has been making work at the intersection of art and science for the past 35 years, exhibiting nationally and internationally. Miller was one of the first artists in the 80s to experiment with computer generated images, and he has made his mark in contemporary art ever since. The artist has presented 40 solo exhibitions at major institutions in the United States, Brazil, China, France, and Germany. His exhibitions have been reviewed in Le Monde, Süddeutsche Zeitung, The New York Times, The Boston Globe, ArtForum, ARTnews, and Art in America.

He is well known for several art-science projects, including his long-term collaboration with Nobel Prize winner, Dr. Rod MacKinnon, who studies the way ions move across cell membranes. For this work, Miller combined molecular imagery with notations and diagrams from MacKinnon's experimental notebook. This work was featured in two solo exhibitions "Spiraling Inwards" at the Rose Art Museum at Brandeis University in 2007 and in "Crossing the Line: Paintings by Steve Miller" at the National Academy of Sciences in Washington, D.C. from August 5, 2013 - January 13, 2014.

Miller is also known for his work in Brazil where by taking x-rays of the Amazon he is giving Brazil a medical checkup for his project "Health of the Planet." Science has thoroughly documented the current environmental peril to our planet. Through foreign travel, working with hospitals, zoos and research institutes, he shares this awareness on a global basis to create a series of x-ray images of Amazon animals revealing the extraordinary beauty of Brazil's biodiversity.

In January Miller launched his surf boards at the Museu de Arte do Rio and this summer will have a outdoor sculpture exhibition at Long House Reserve in East Hampton, New York. This art work will be the subject of a travelling solo exhibition organized by the Burchfield Penney Art Center in Buffalo, New York.

46 GOLD STREET • NEW YORK NY 10038 • TEL 212-349-6155 • WWW.STEVEMILLER.COM

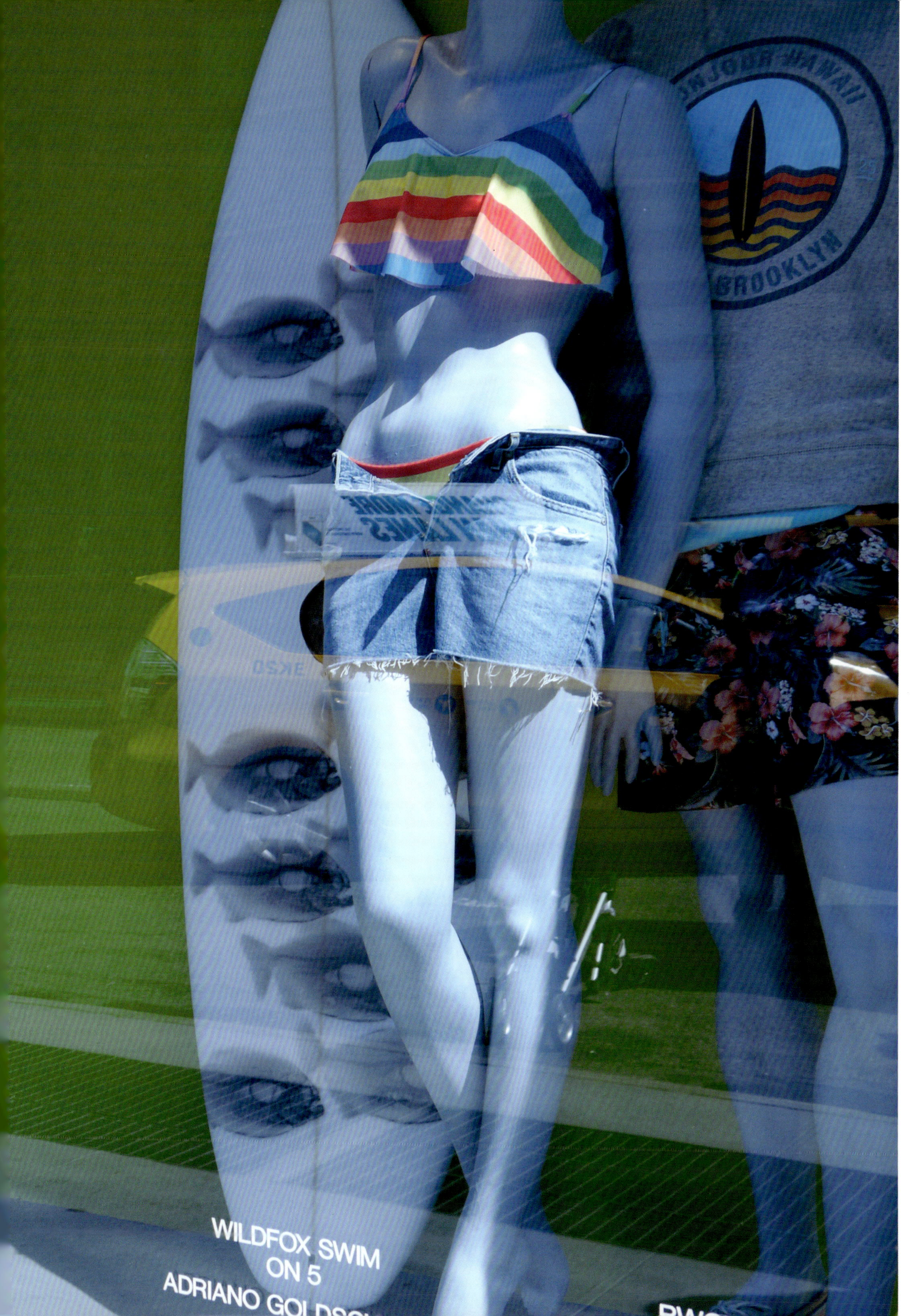
BROOKLYN
WILDFOX SWIM
ON 5
ADRIANO GOLDSC

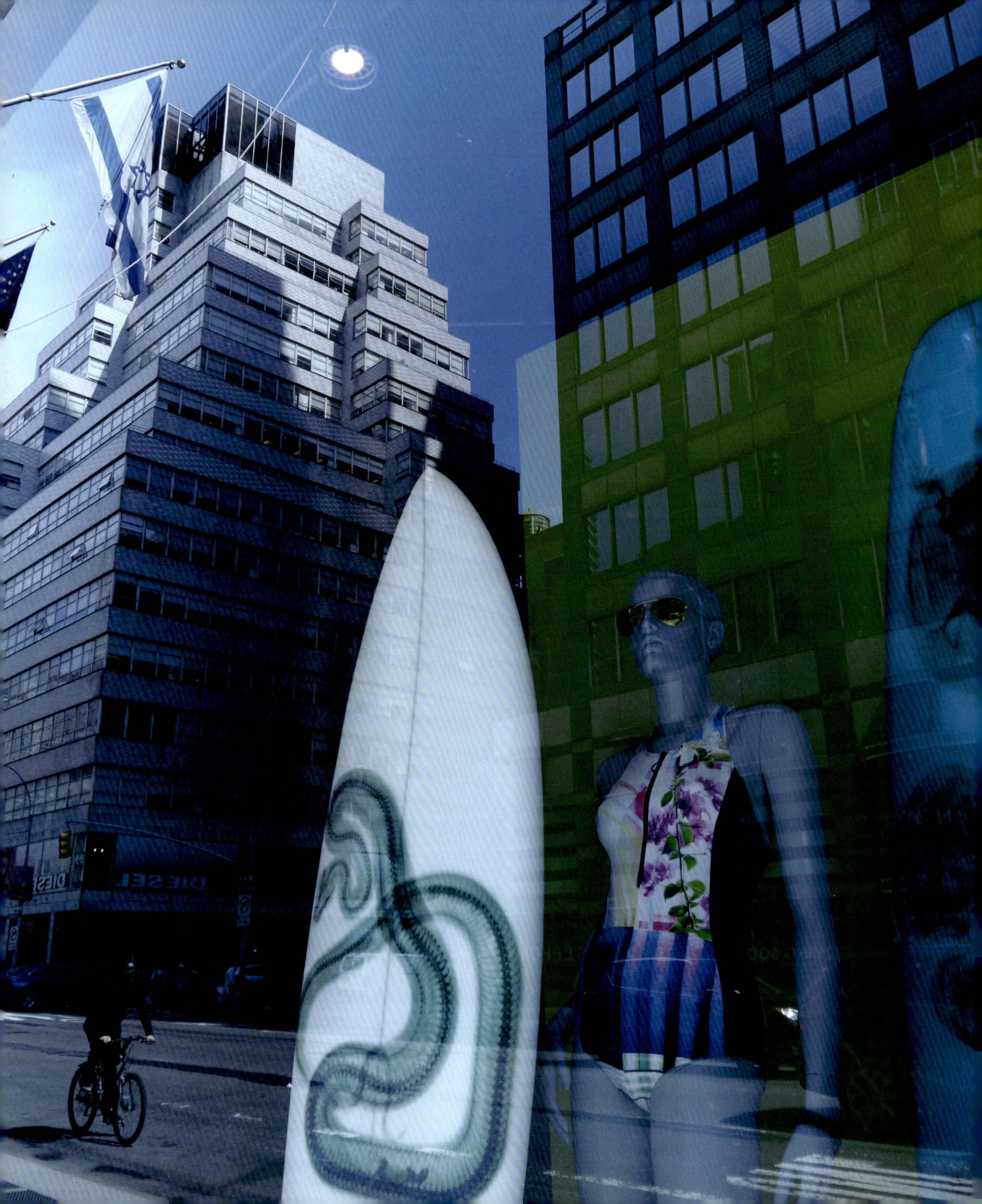

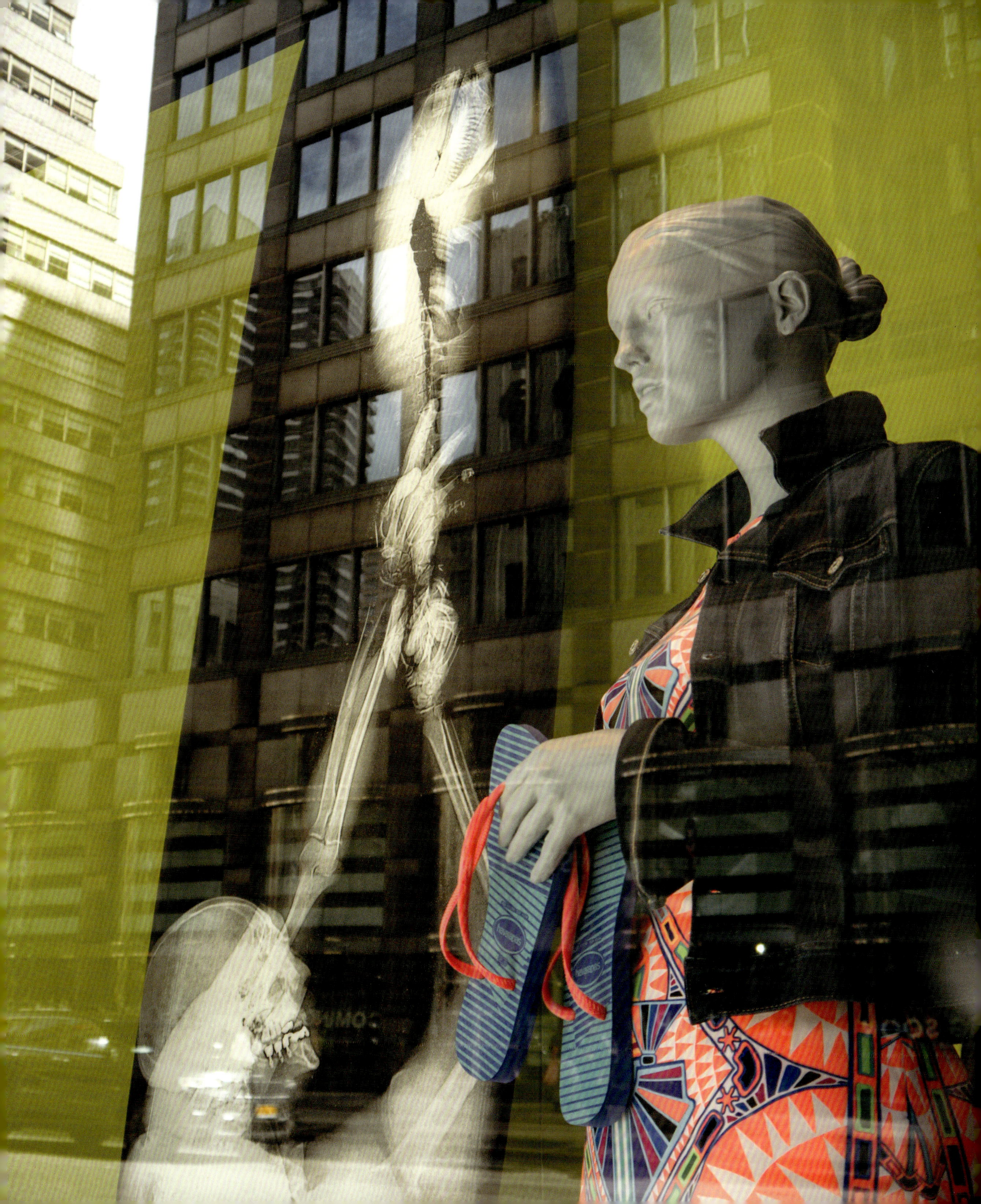

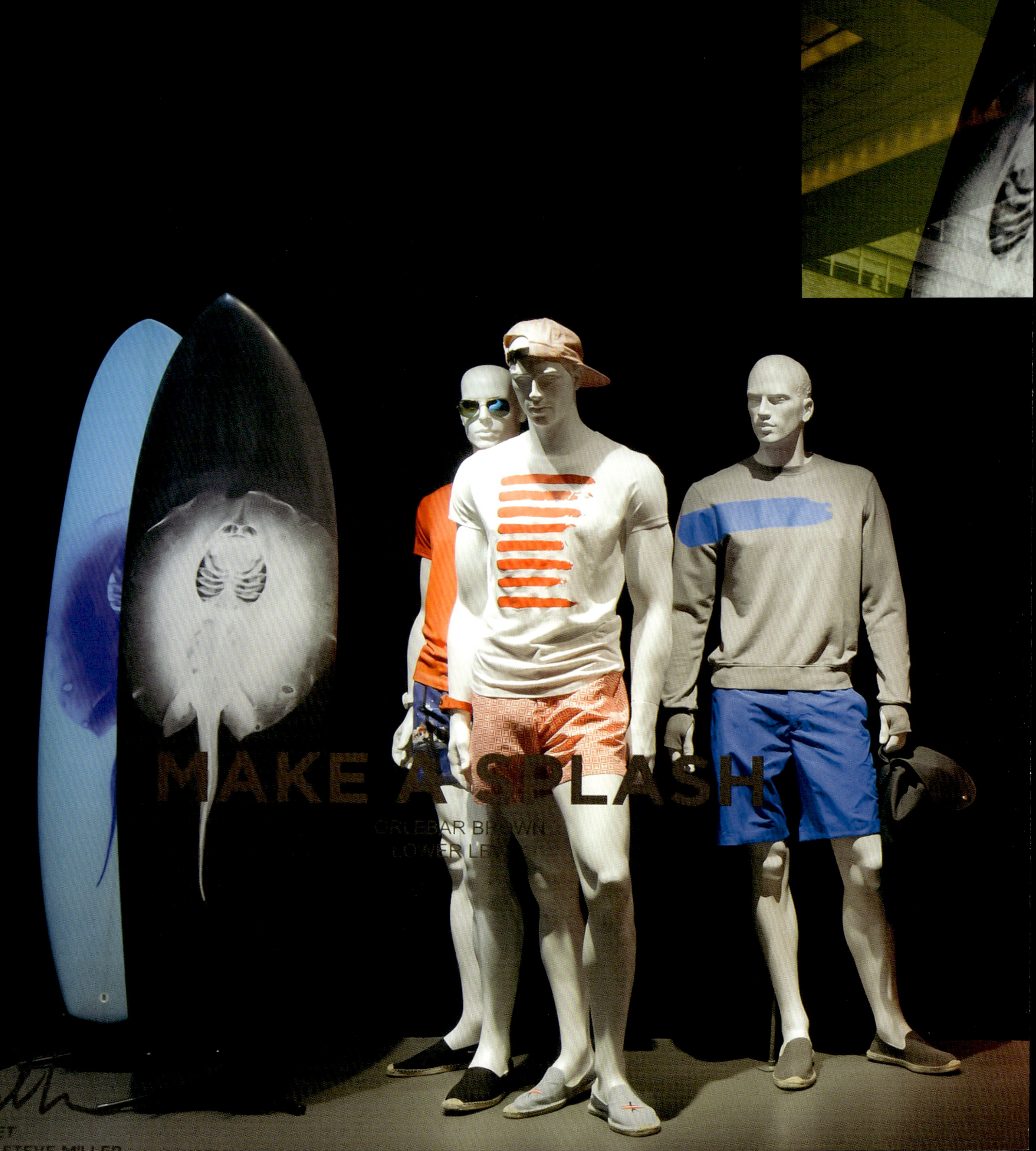

MAKE A SPLASH
ORLEBAR BROWN
LOWER LEVEL

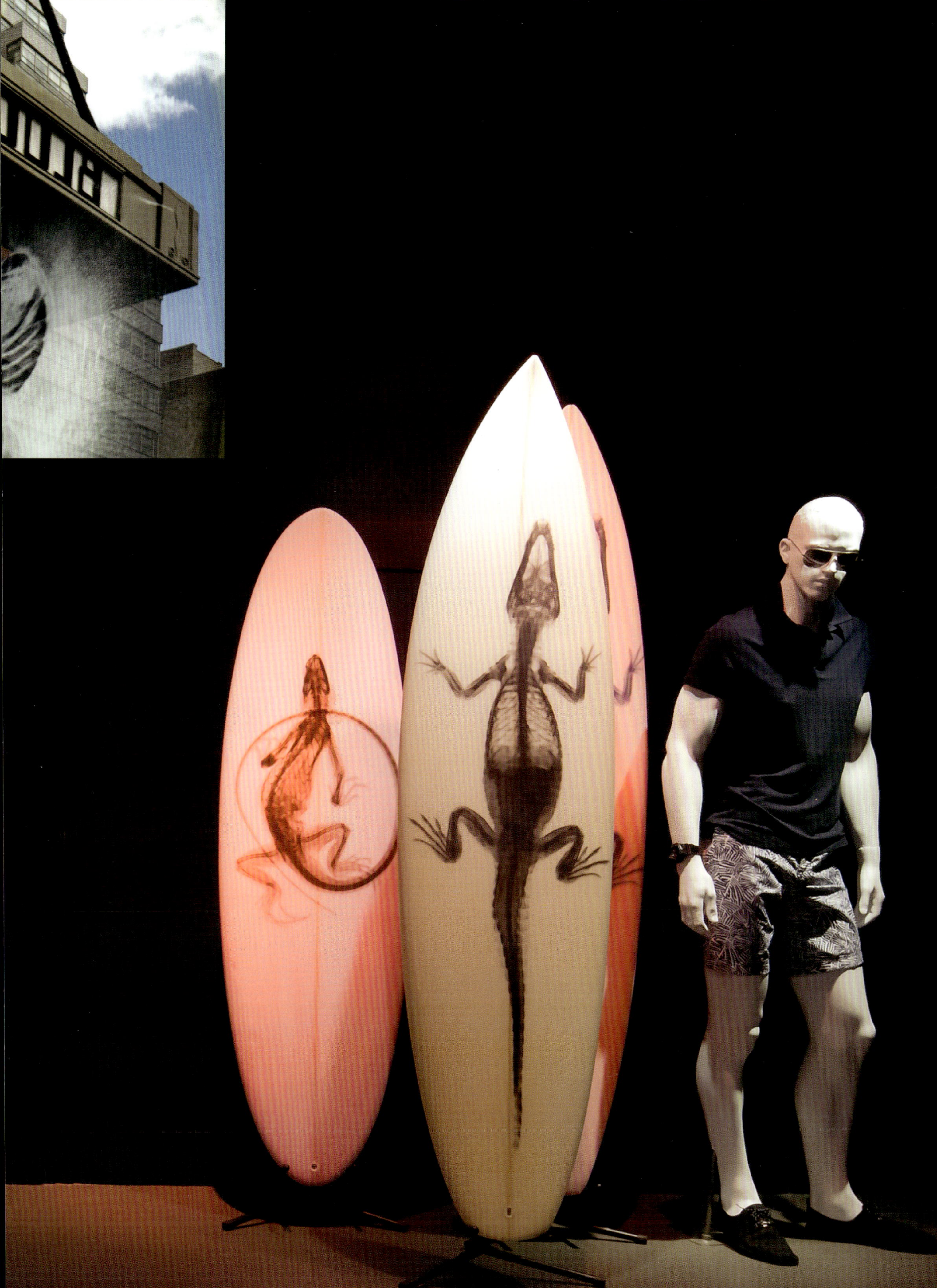

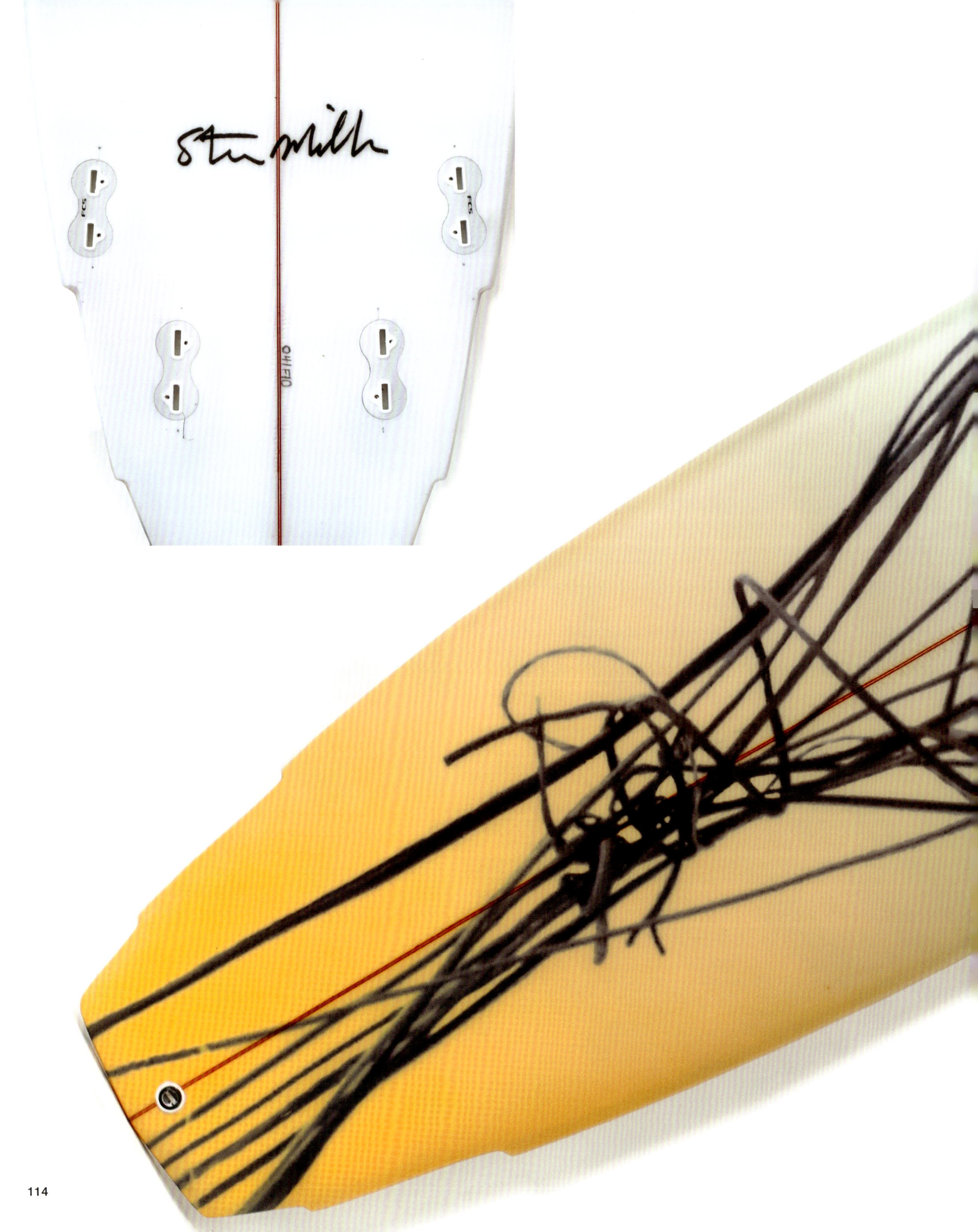

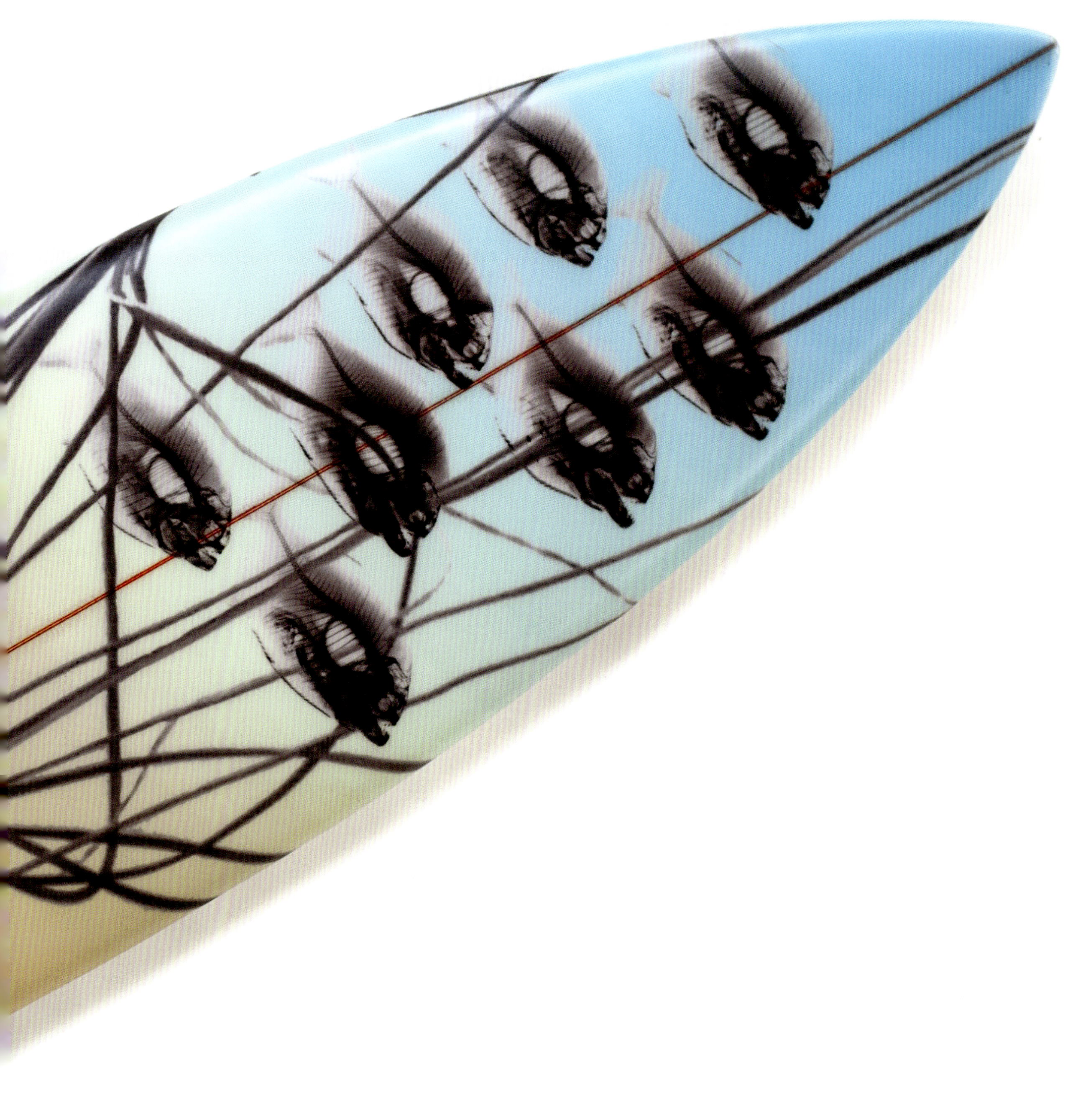

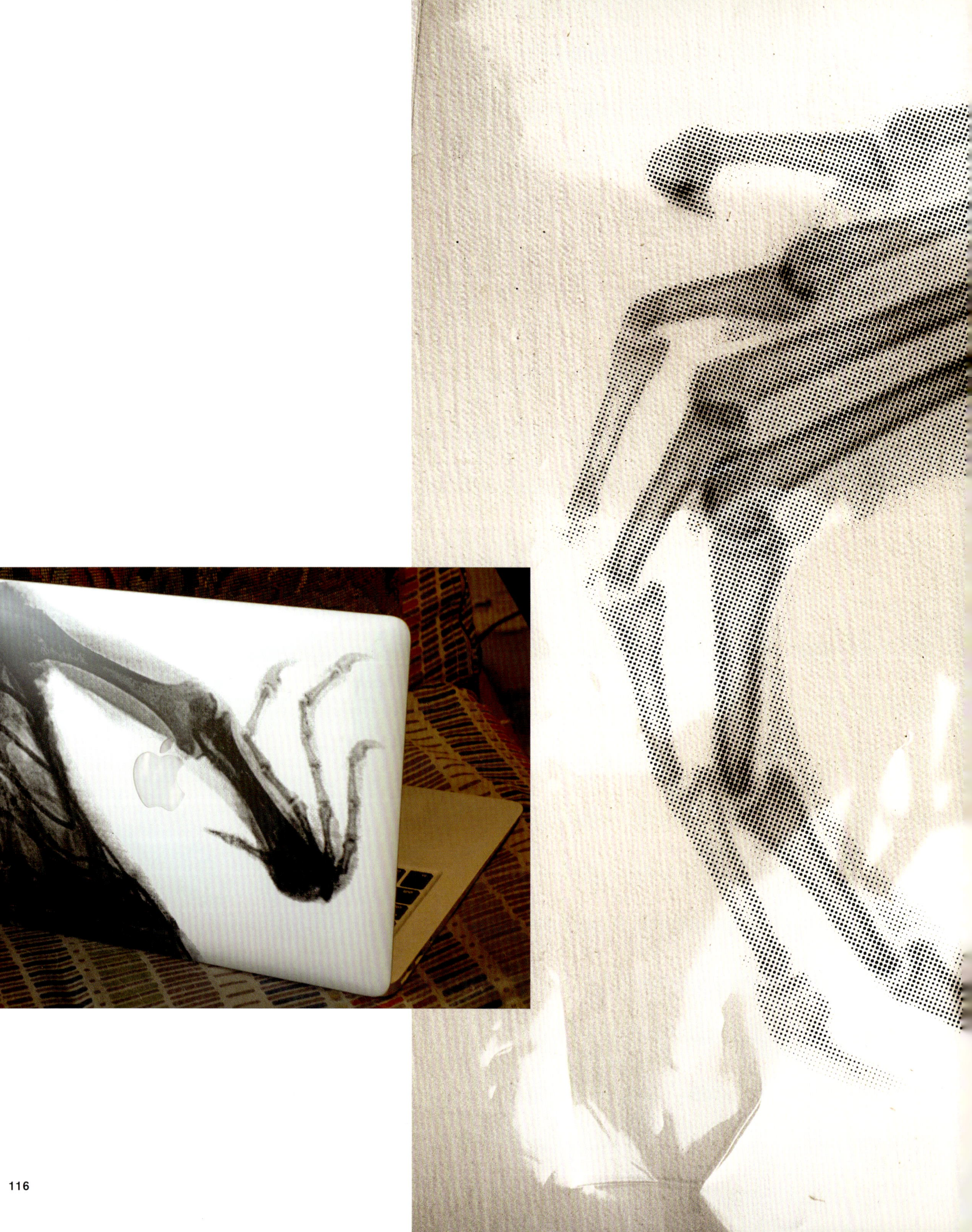

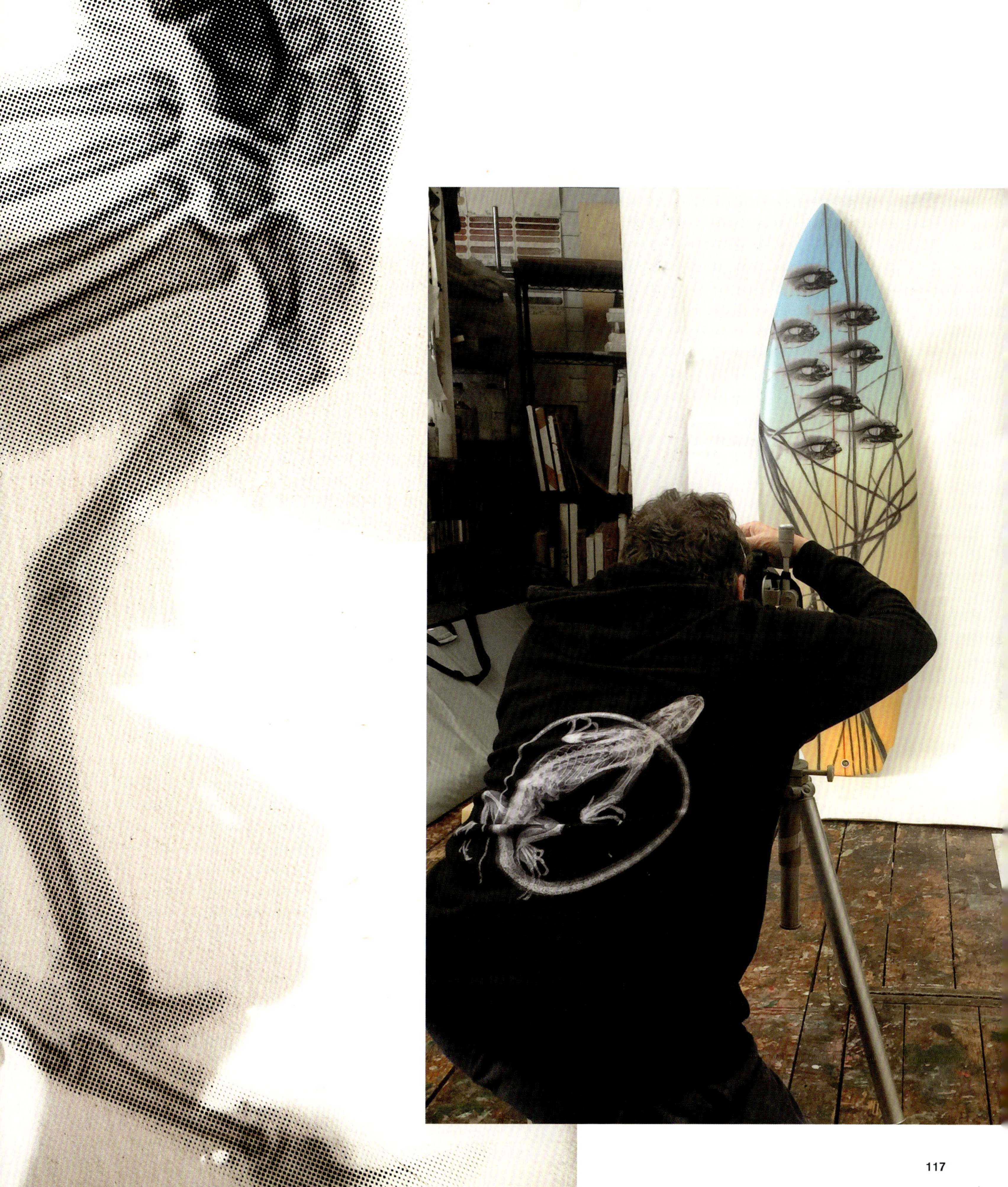

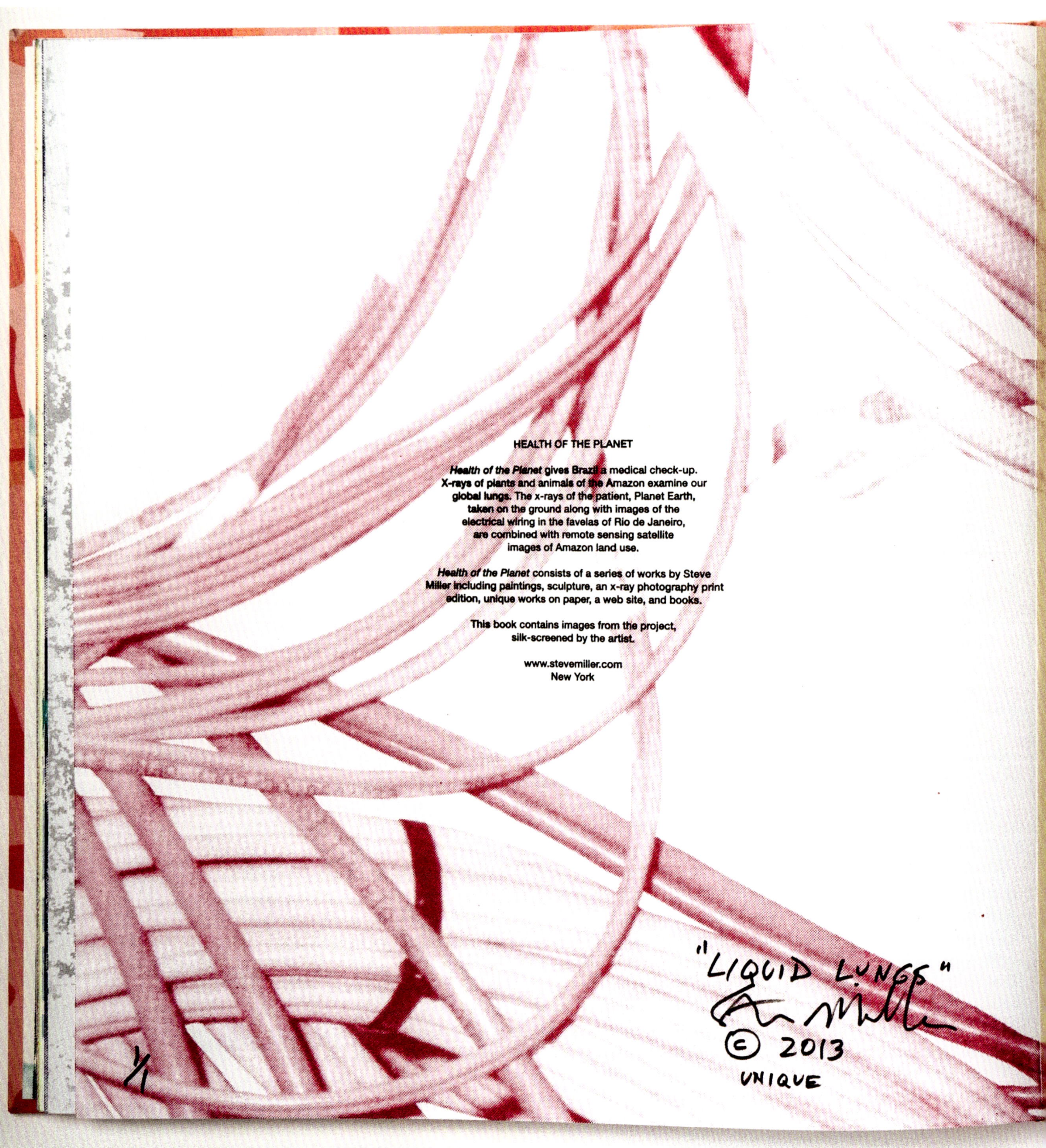
HEALTH OF THE PLANET

Health of the Planet gives Brazil a medical check-up.
X-rays of plants and animals of the Amazon examine our
global lungs. The x-rays of the patient, Planet Earth,
taken on the ground along with images of the
electrical wiring in the favelas of Rio de Janeiro,
are combined with remote sensing satellite
images of Amazon land use.

Health of the Planet consists of a series of works by Steve
Miller including paintings, sculpture, an x-ray photography print
edition, unique works on paper, a web site, and books.

This book contains images from the project,
silk-screened by the artist.

www.stevemiller.com
New York

"LIQUID LUNGS"
© 2013
UNIQUE
1/1

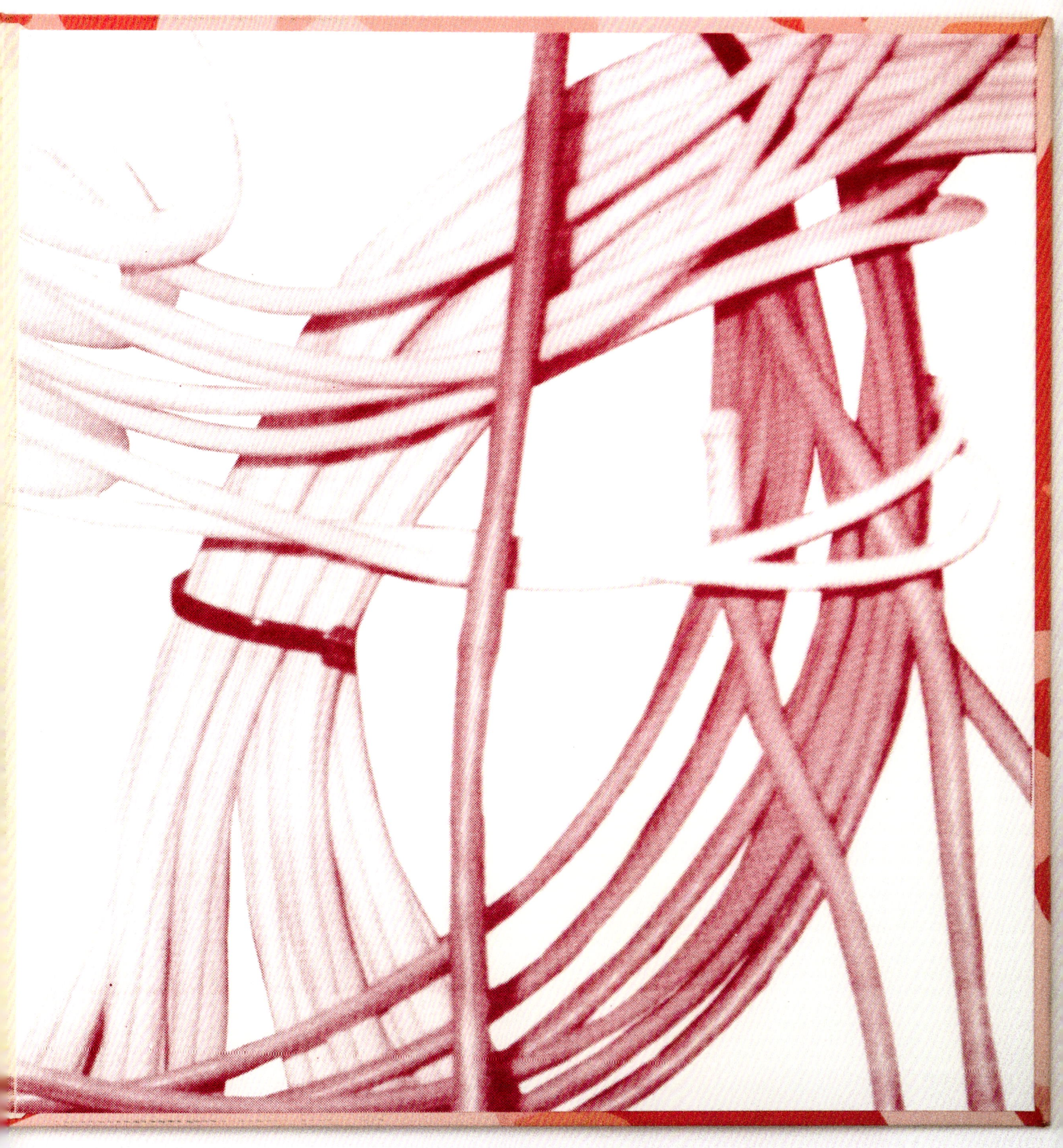

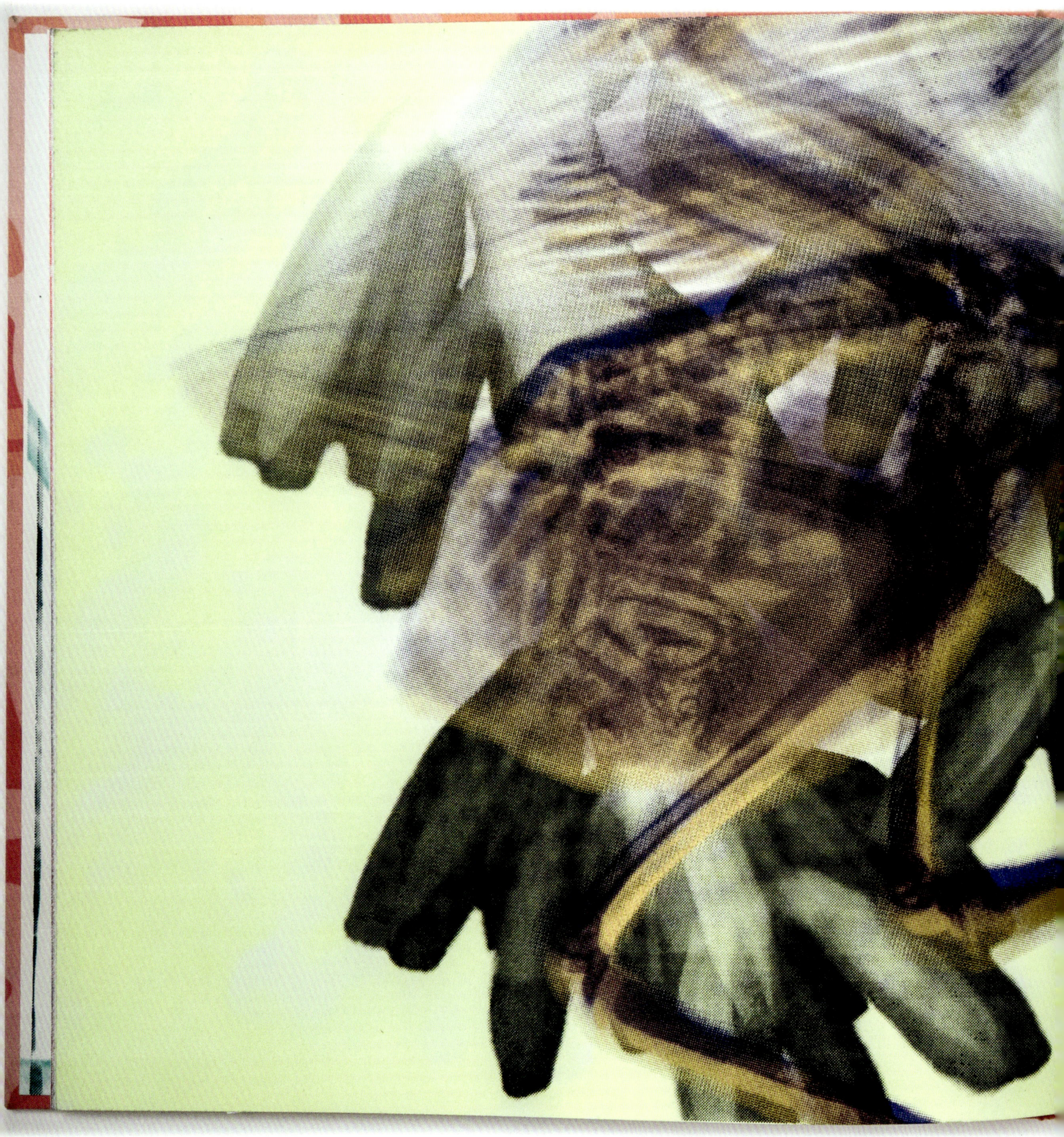

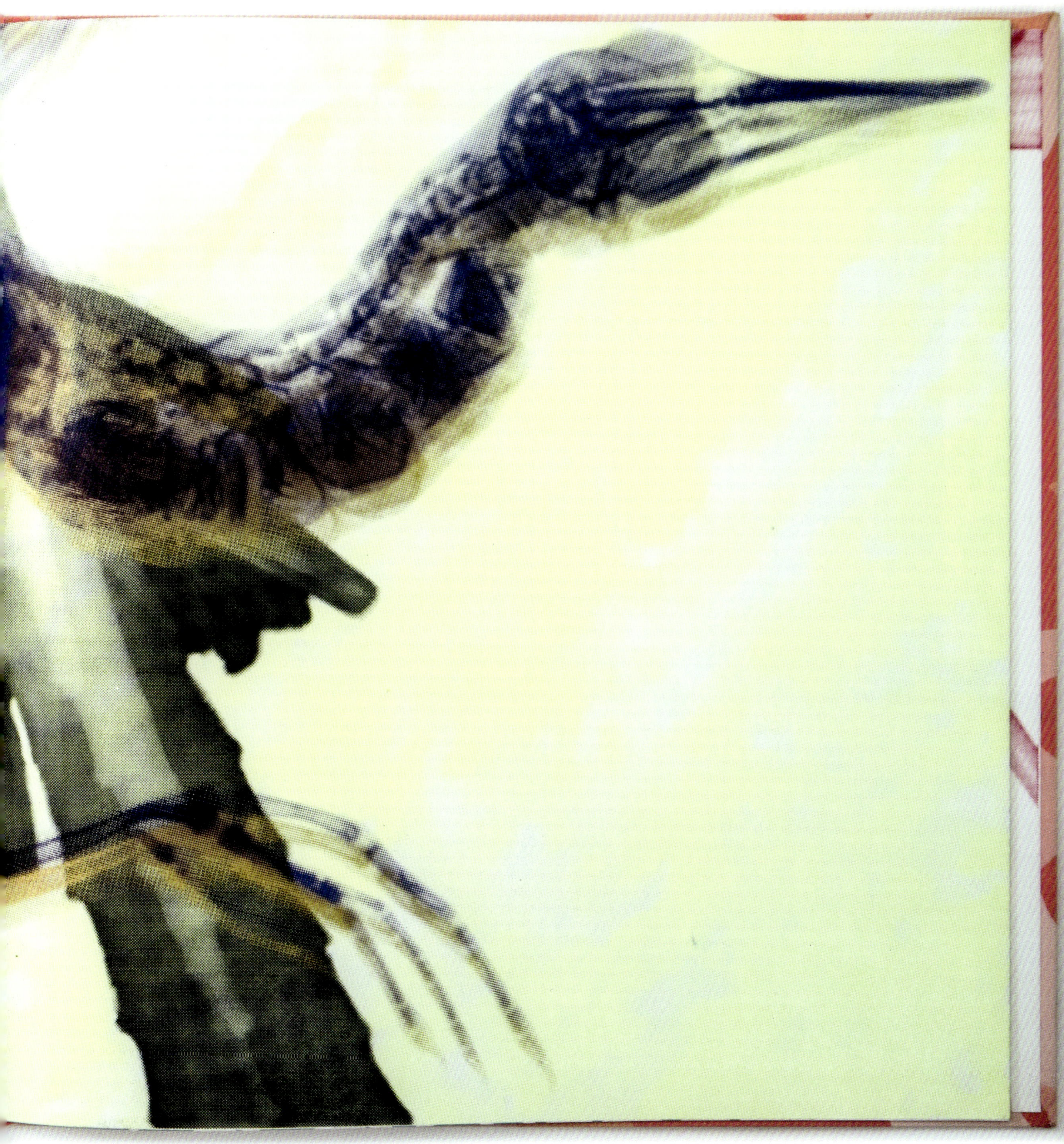

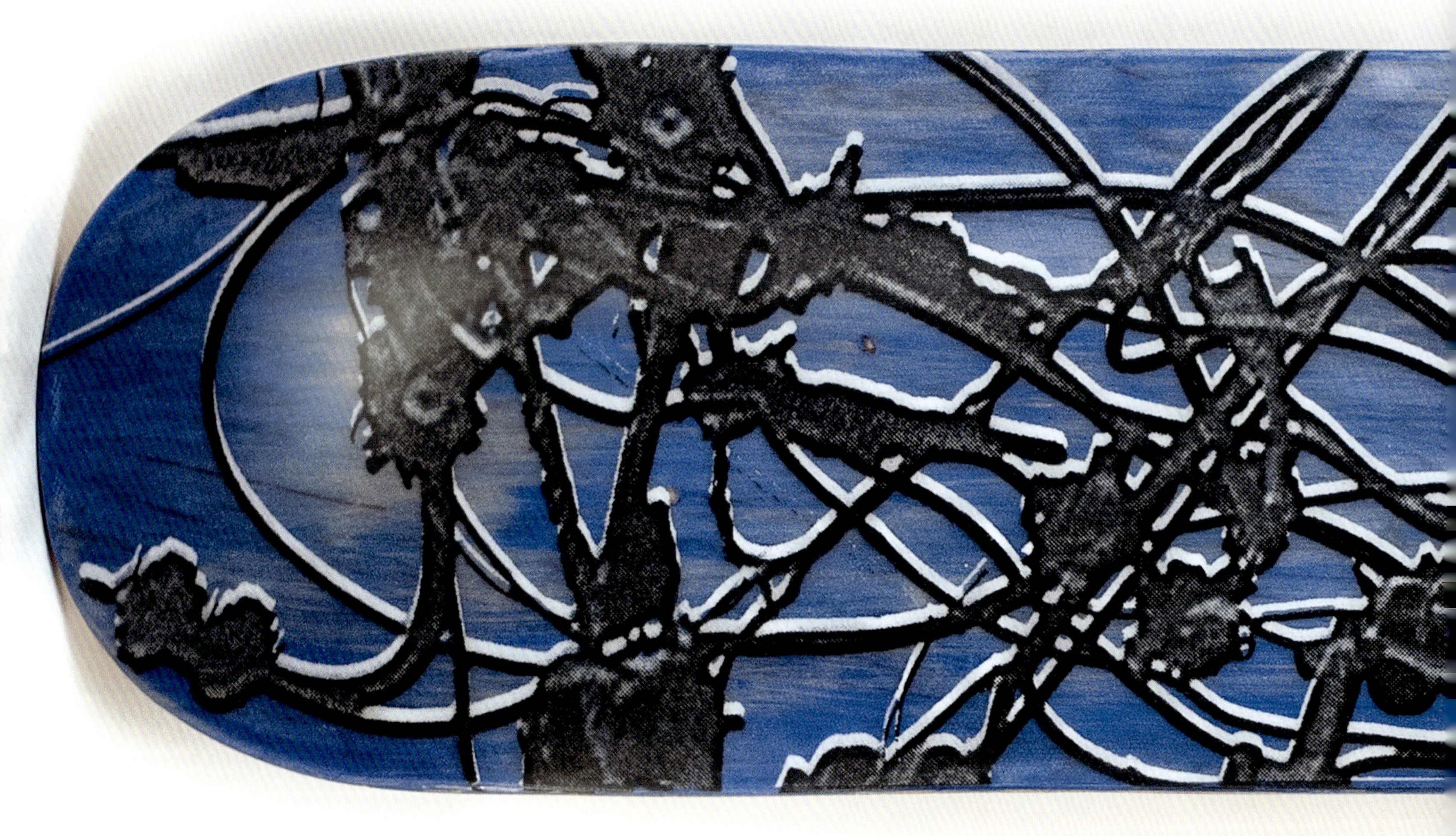

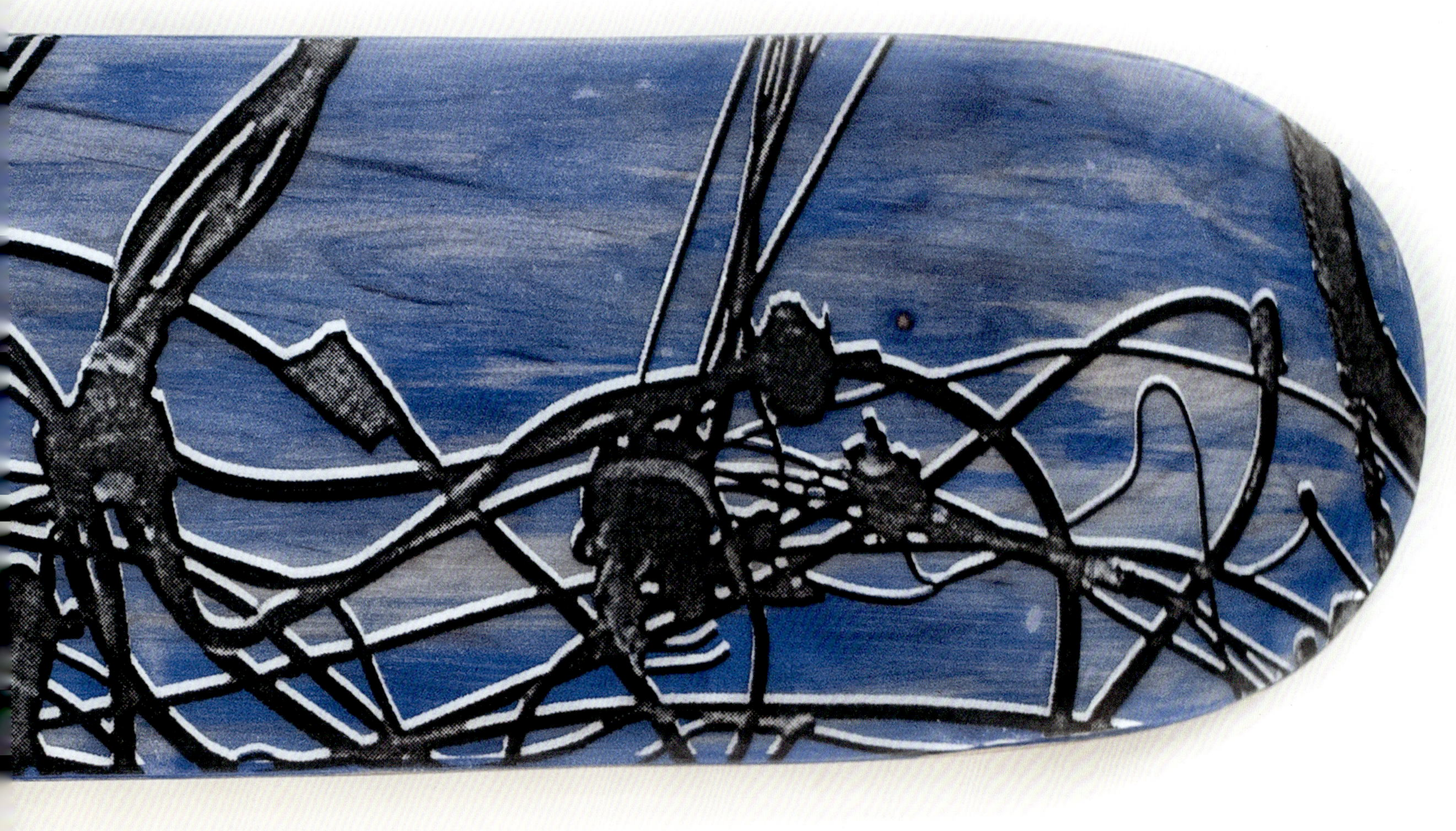

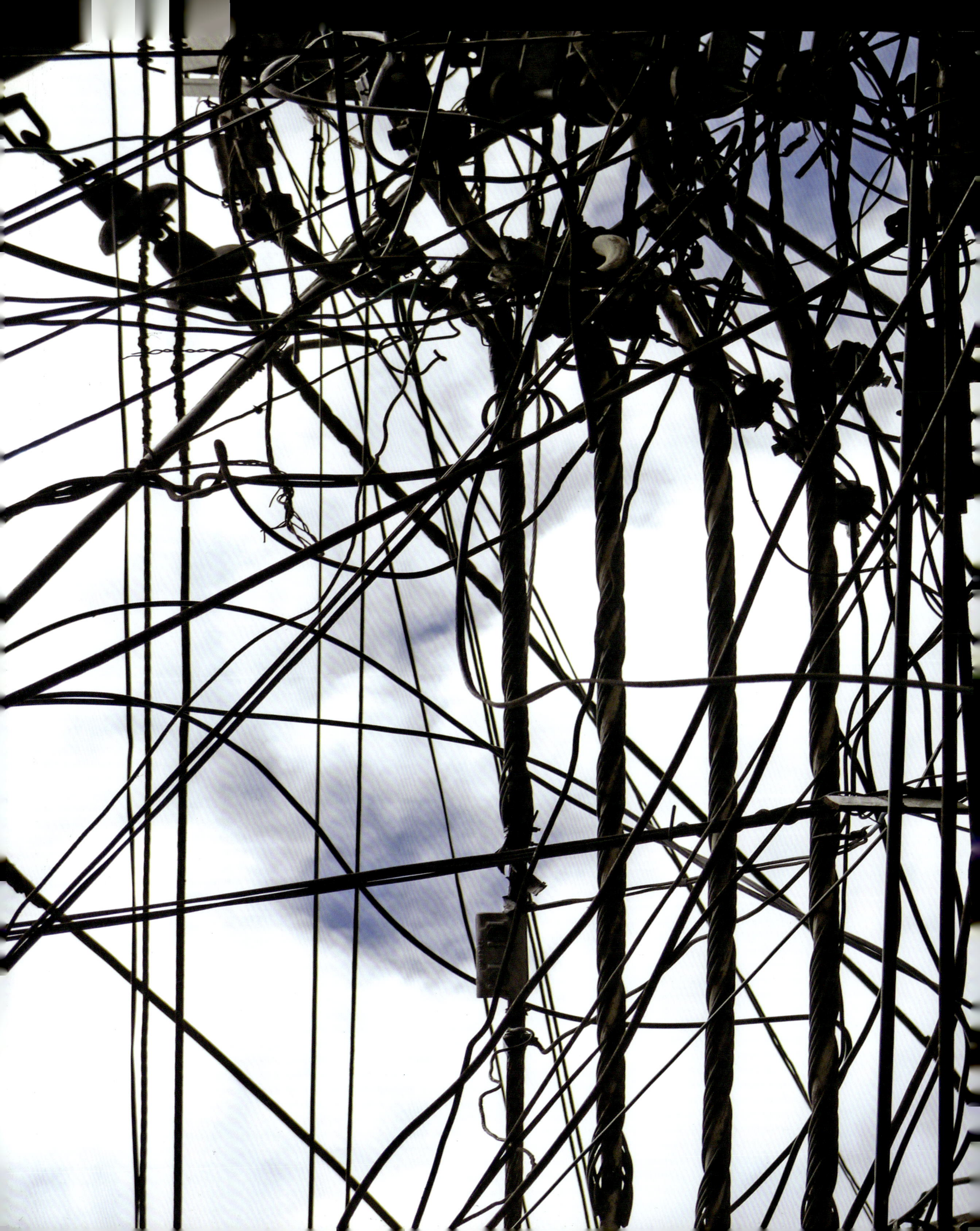

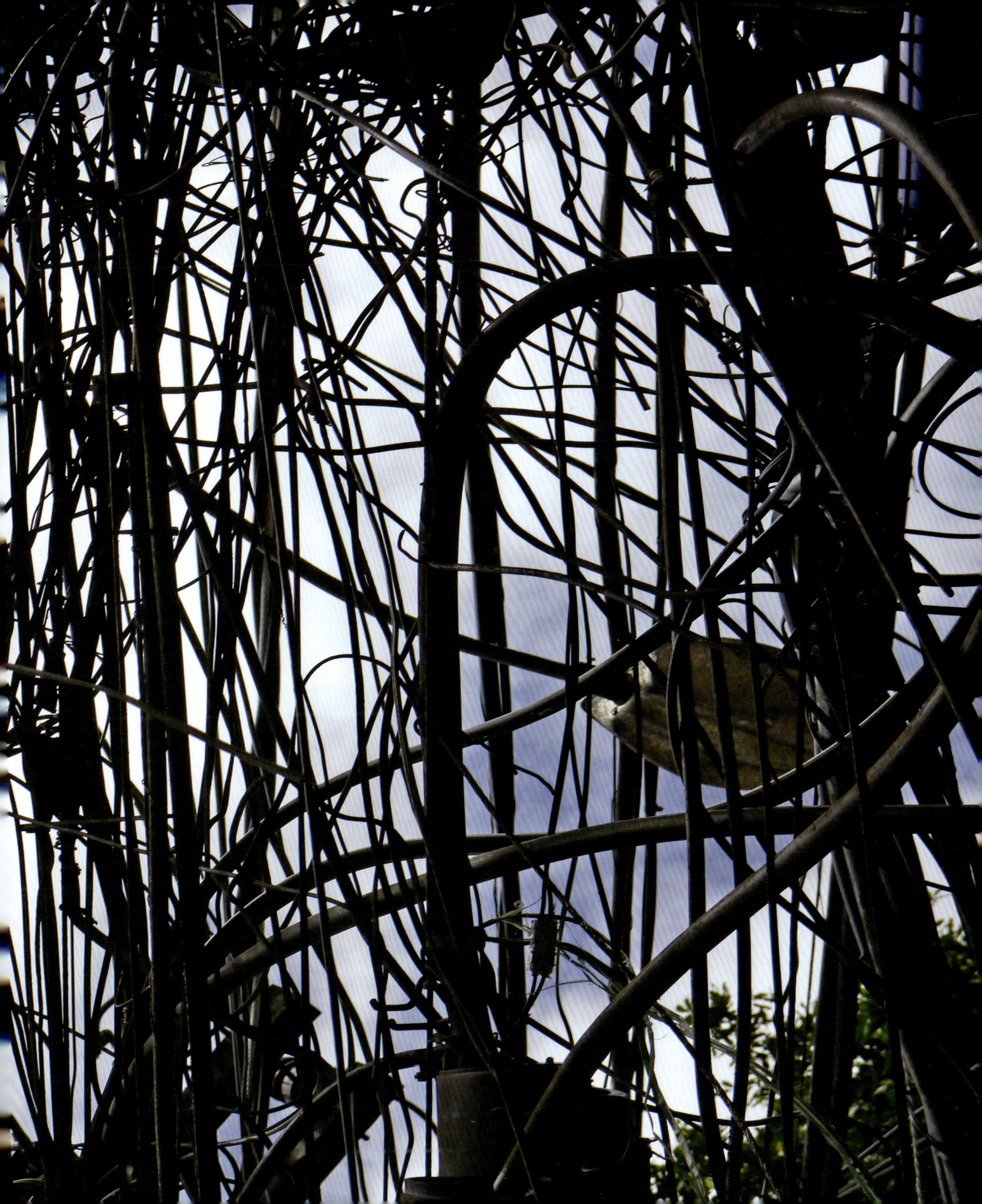

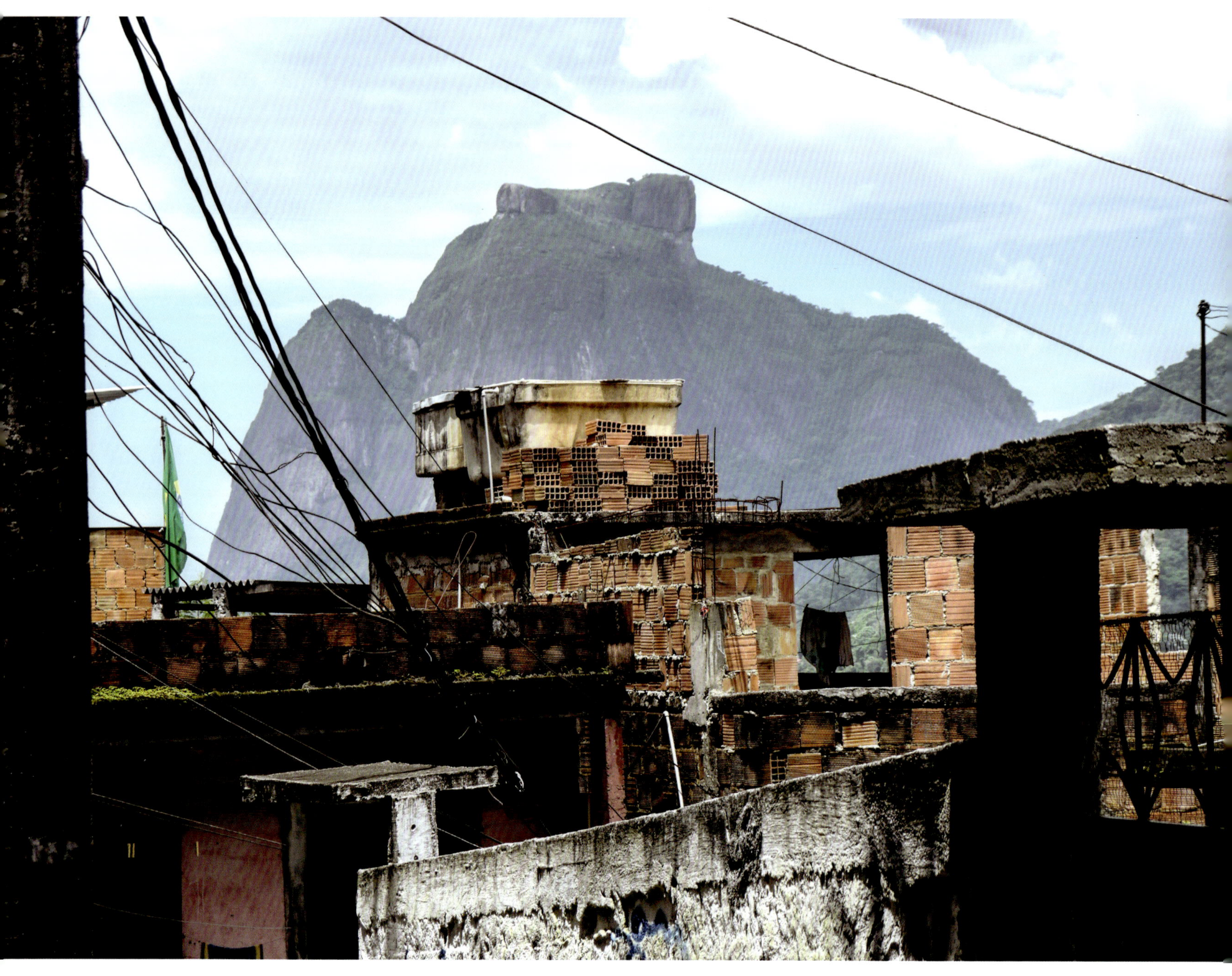

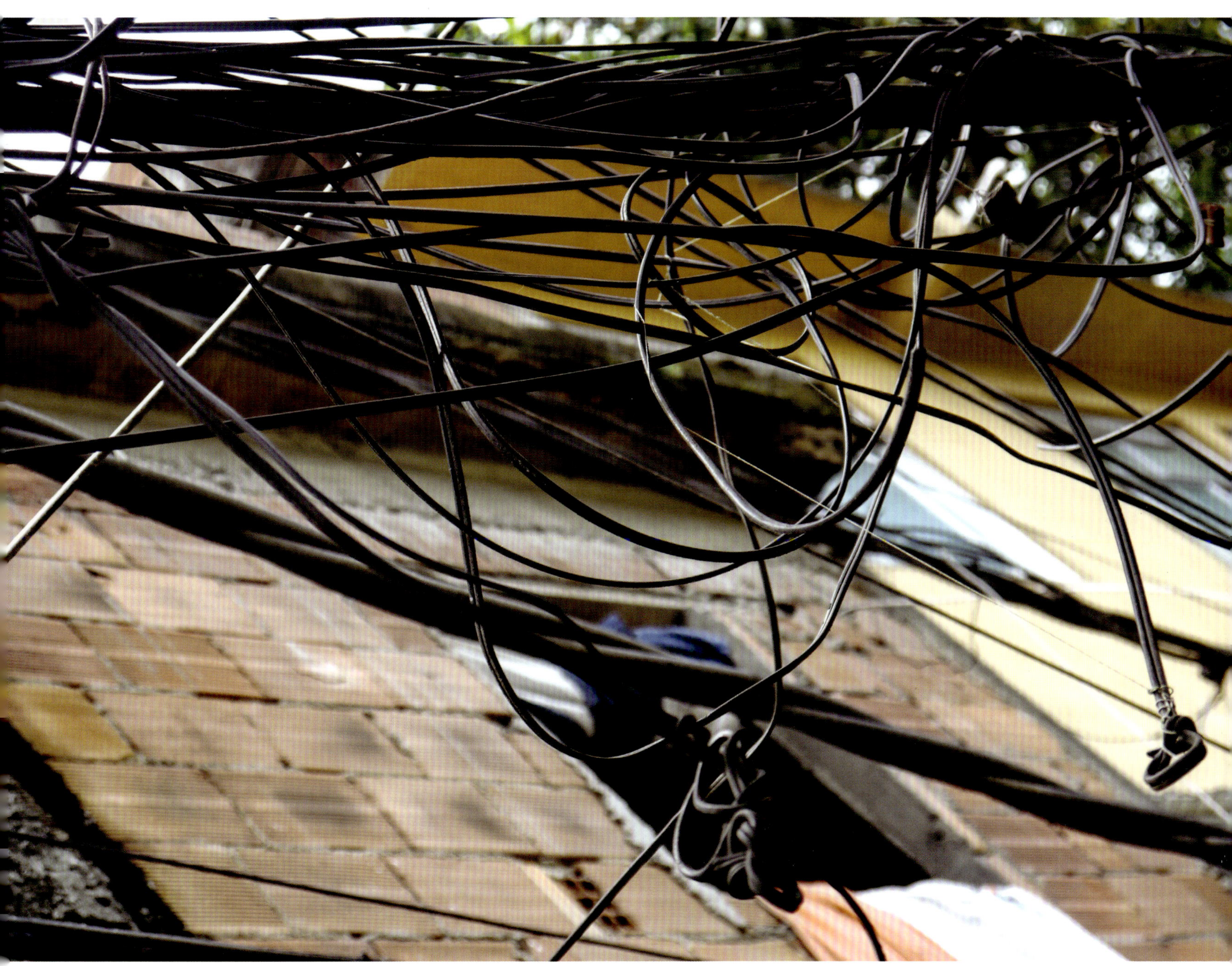

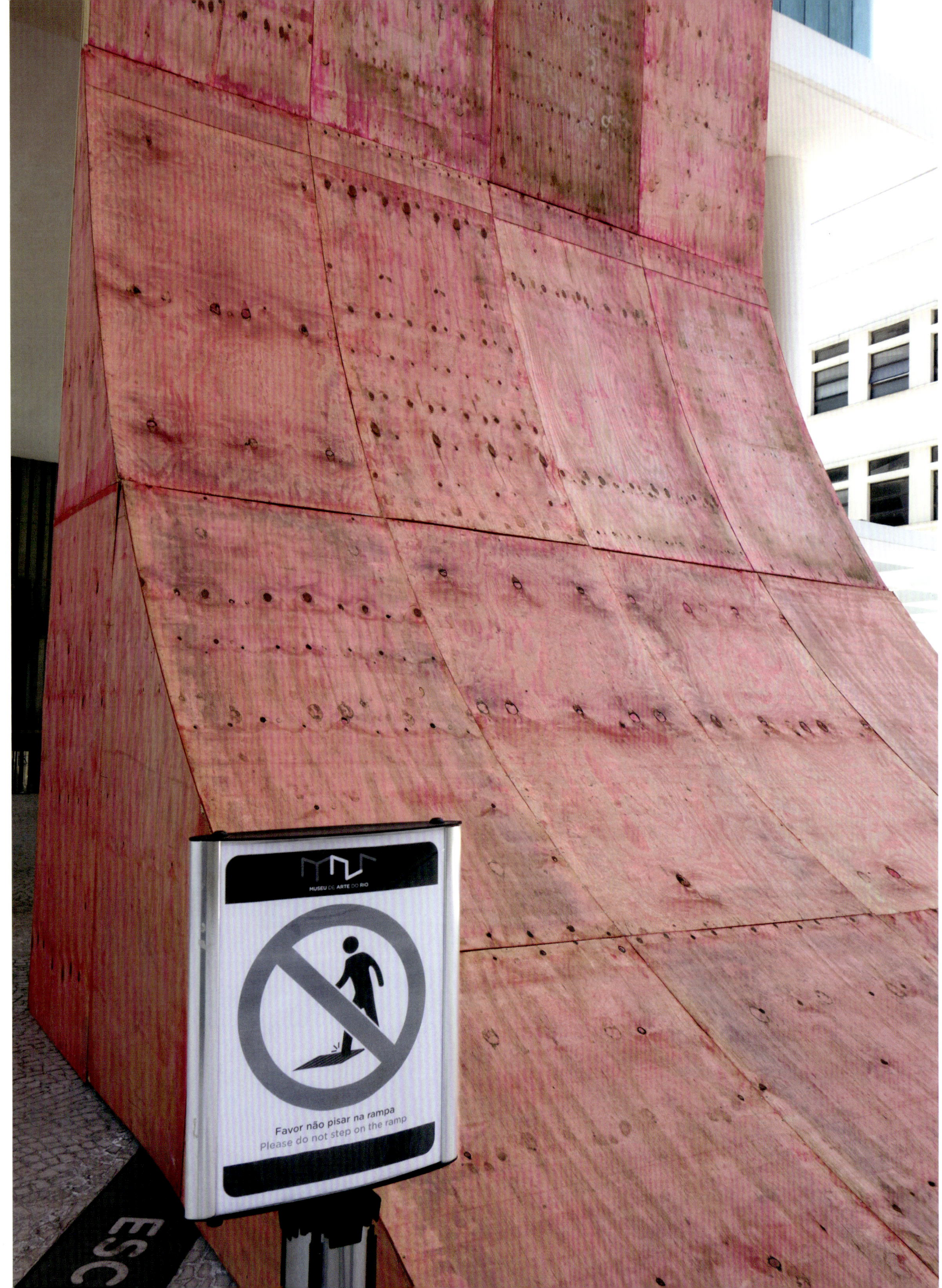

MUSEU DE ARTE DO RIO
Favor não pisar na rampa
Please do not step on the ramp
ESC

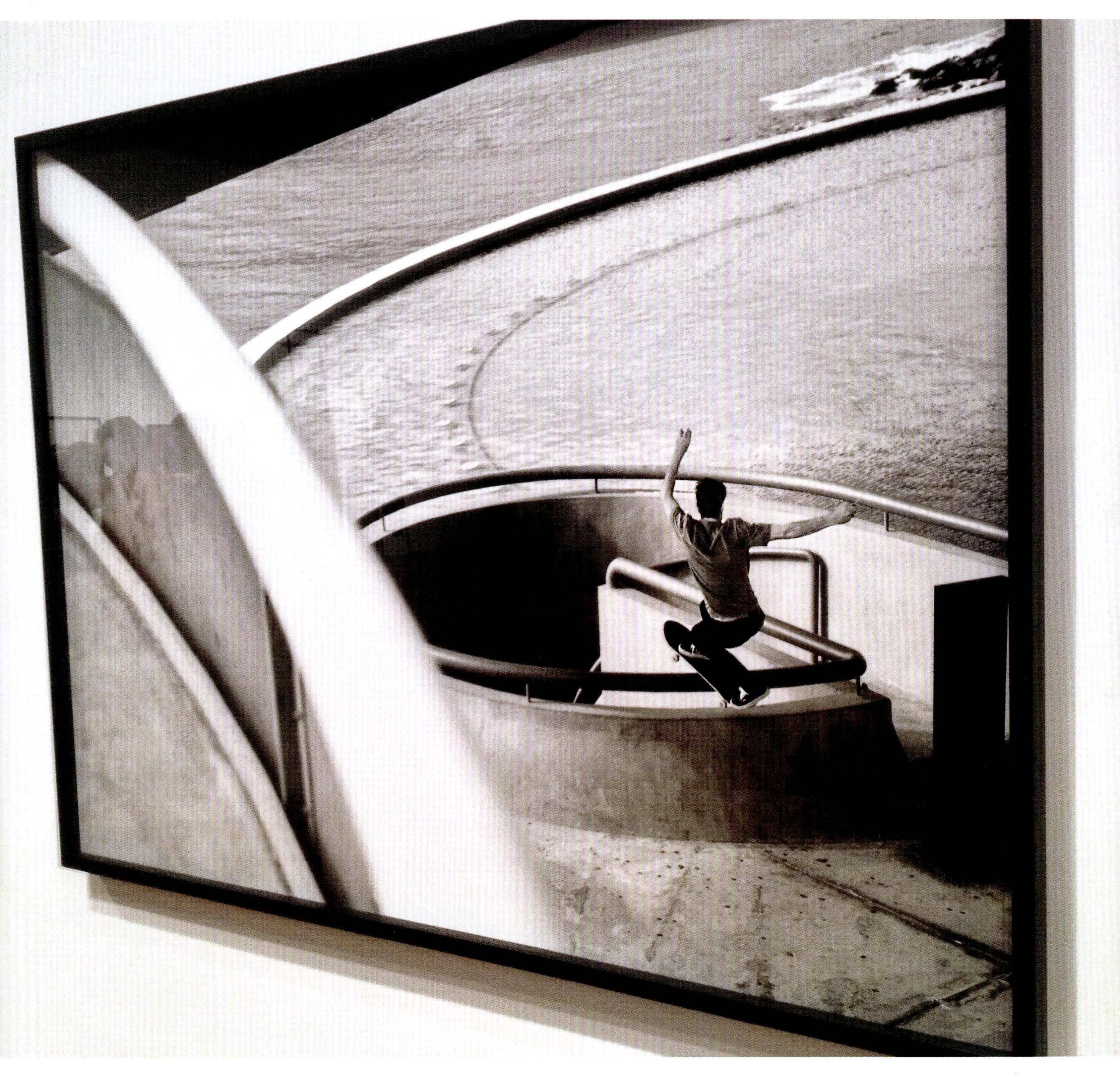

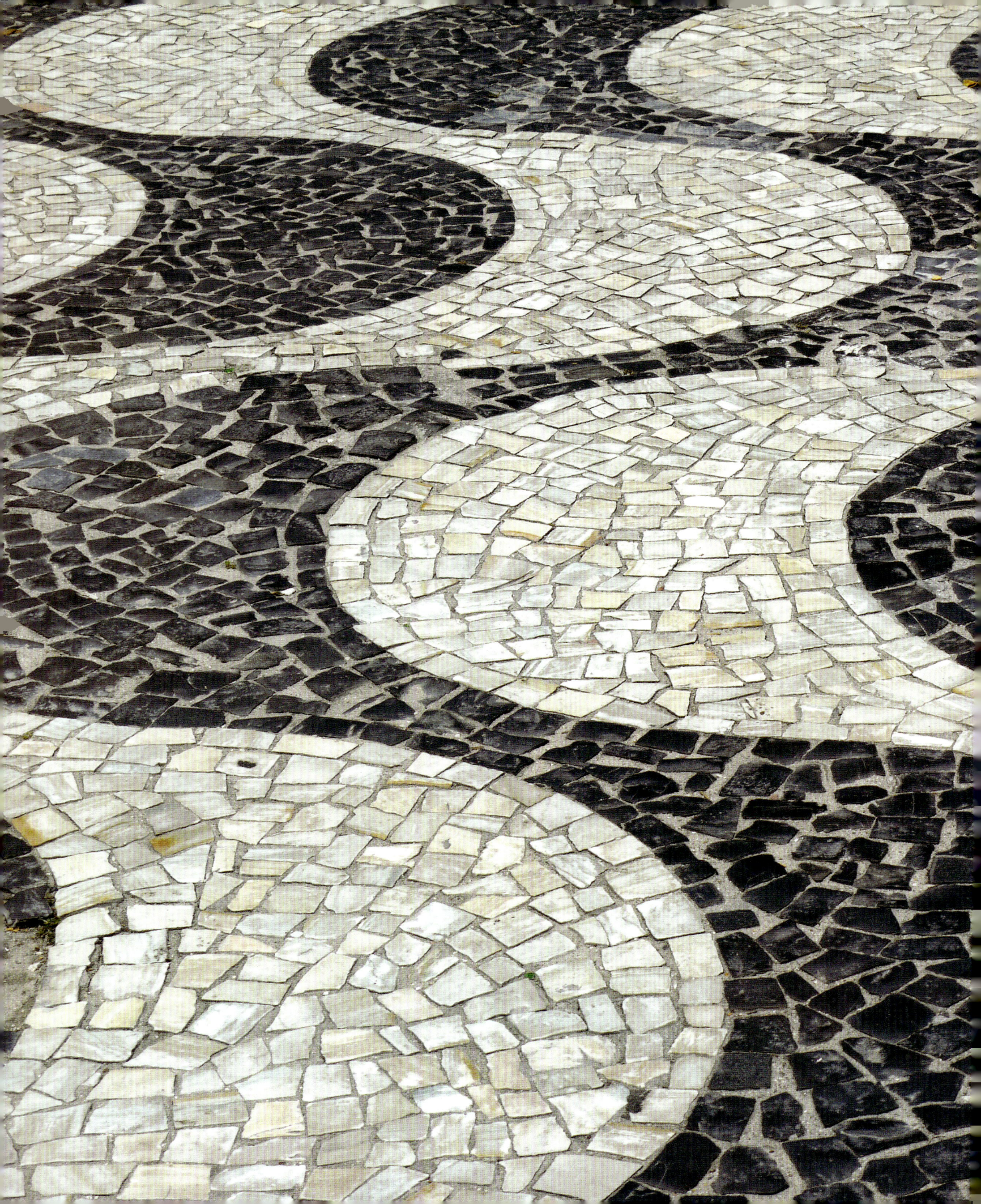

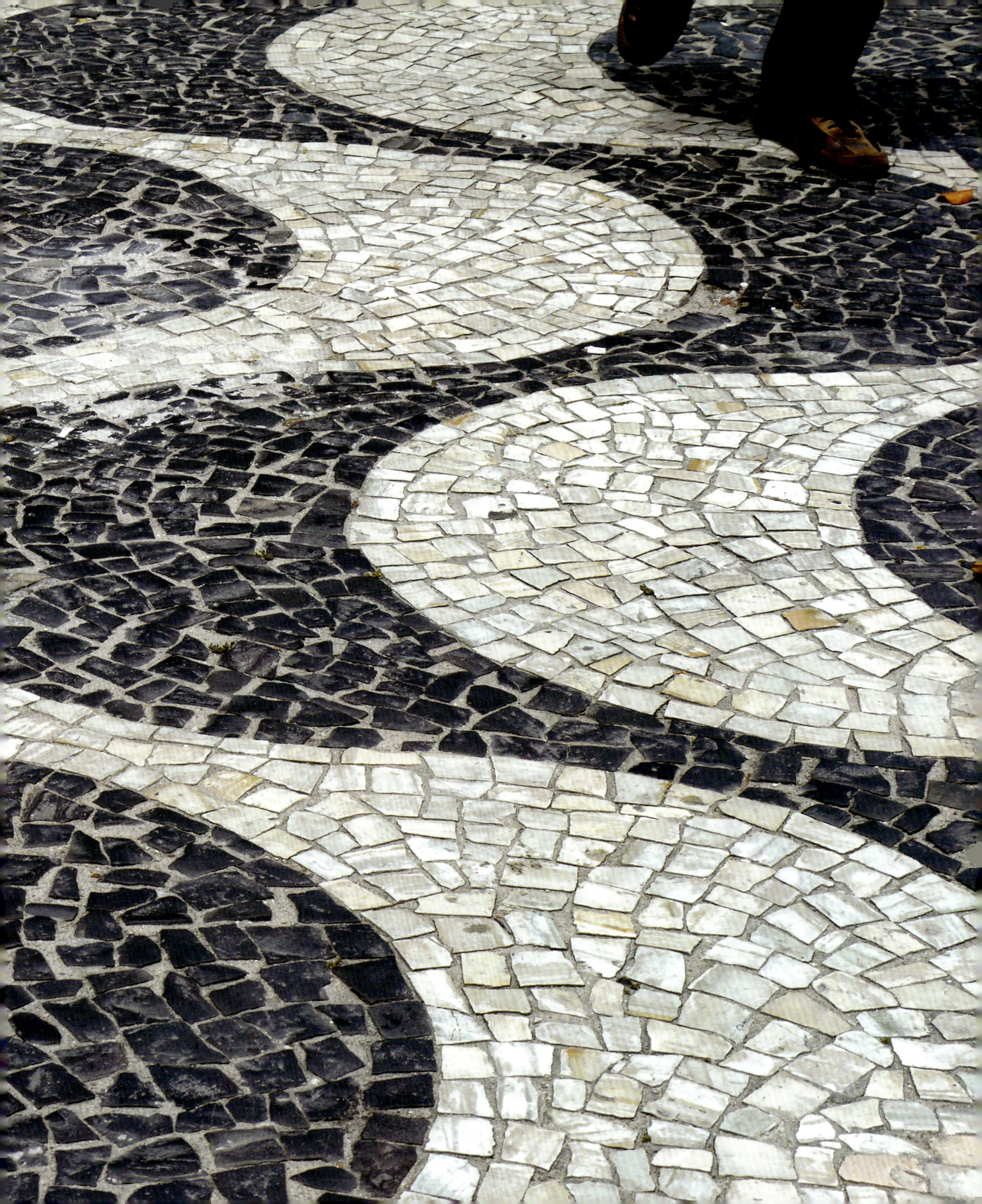

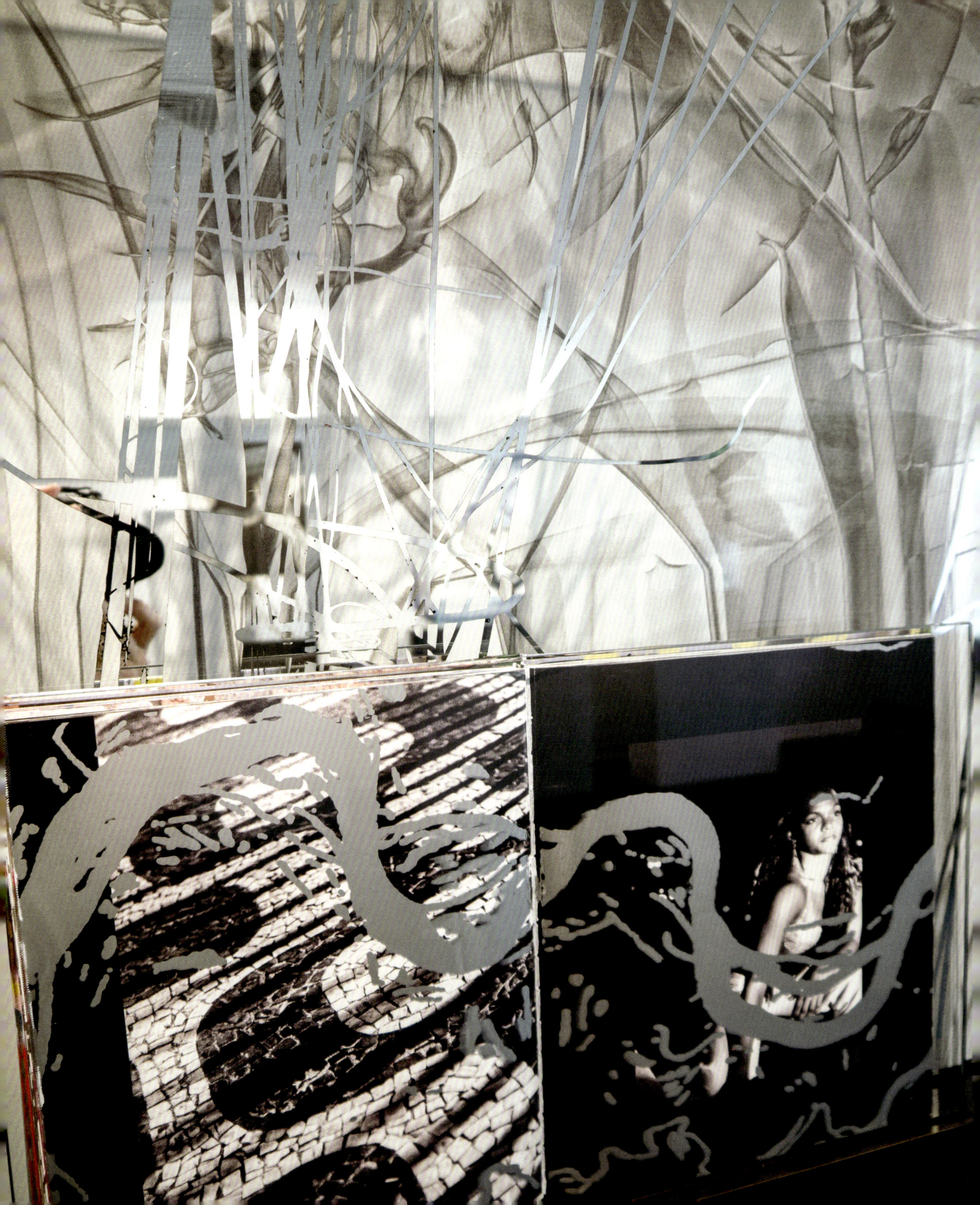

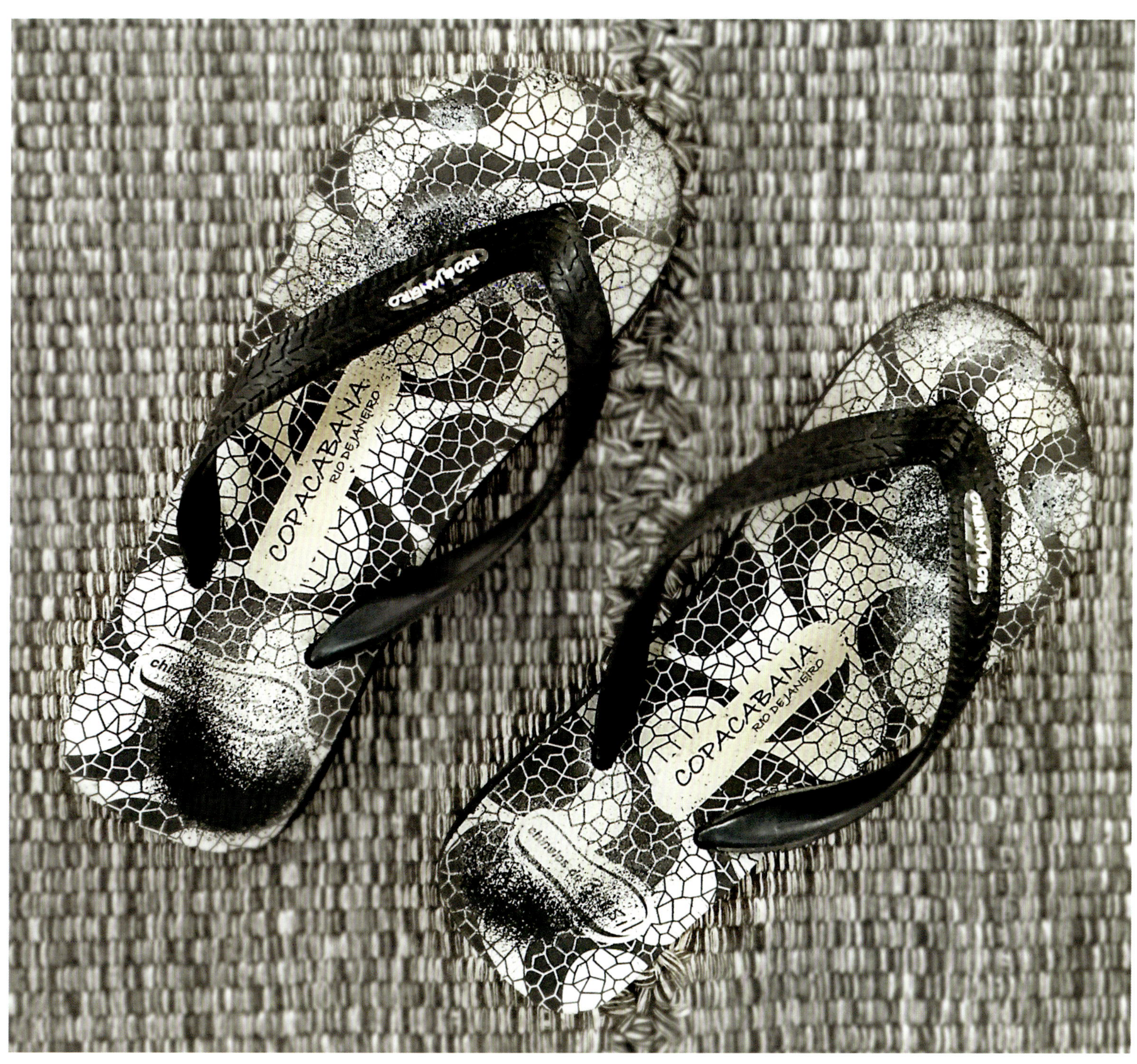

COPACABANA
RIO DE JANEIRO
COPACABANA
RIO DE JANEIRO
RIO DE JANEIRO
RIO DE JANEIRO

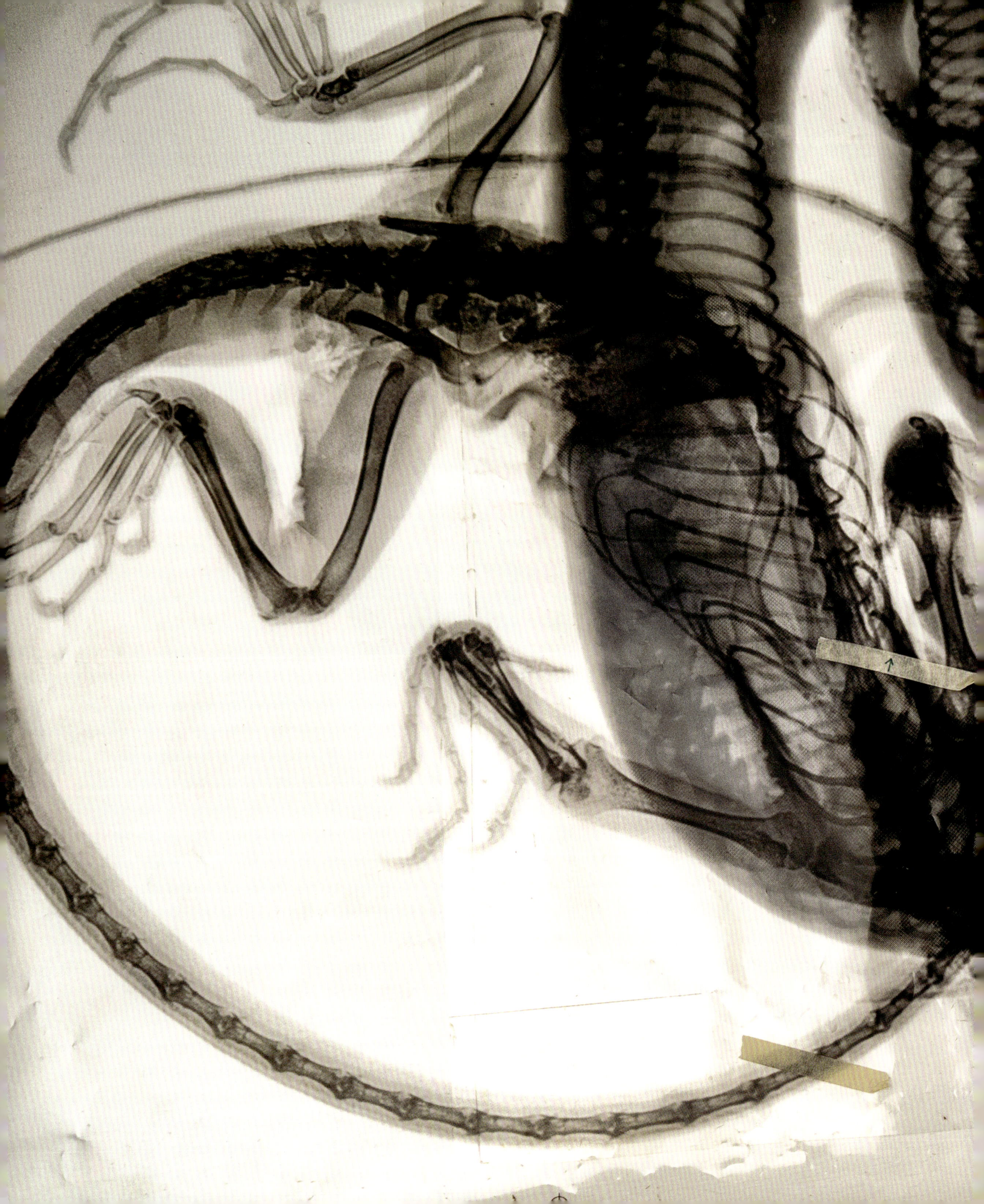

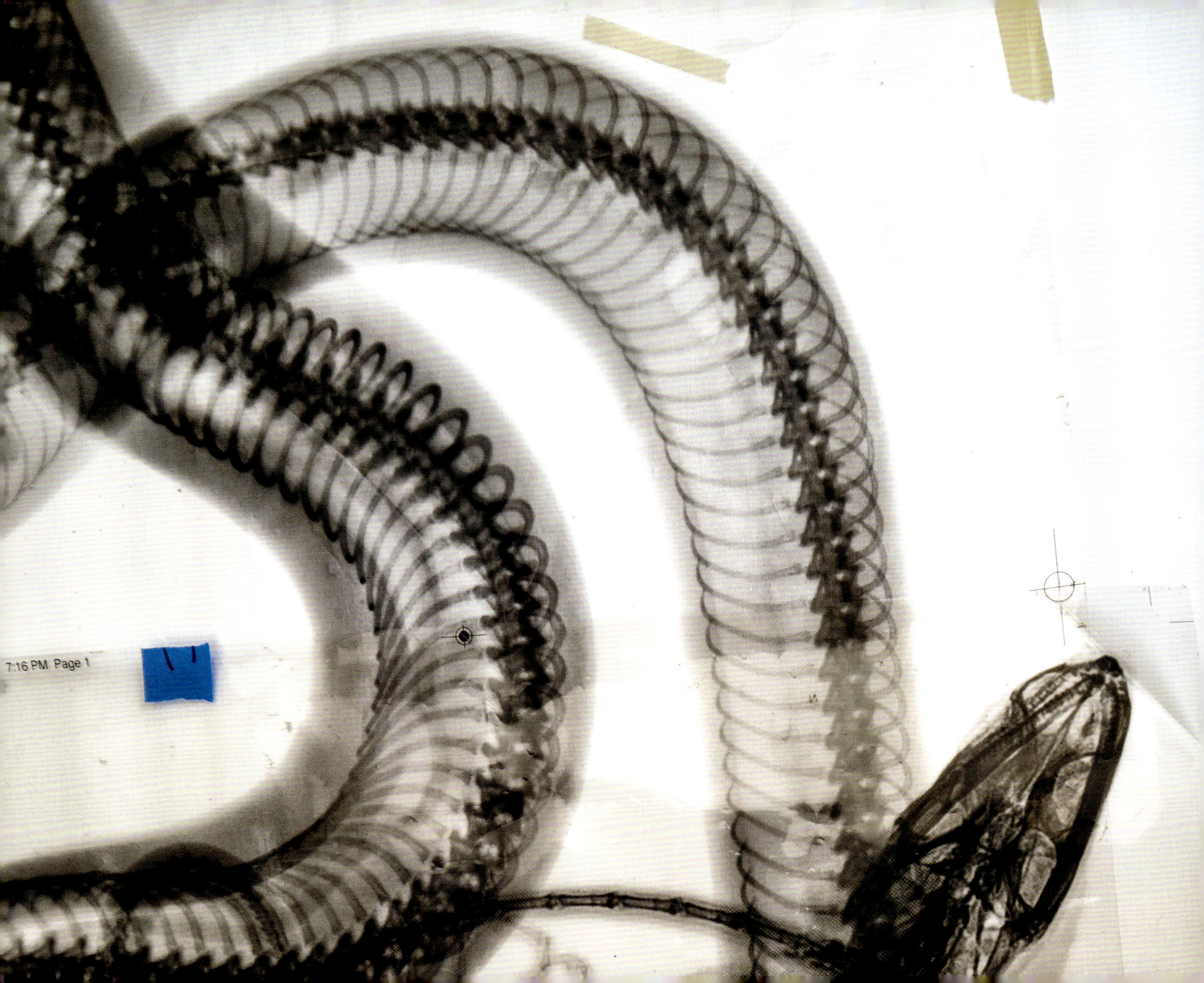
7:16 PM Page 1

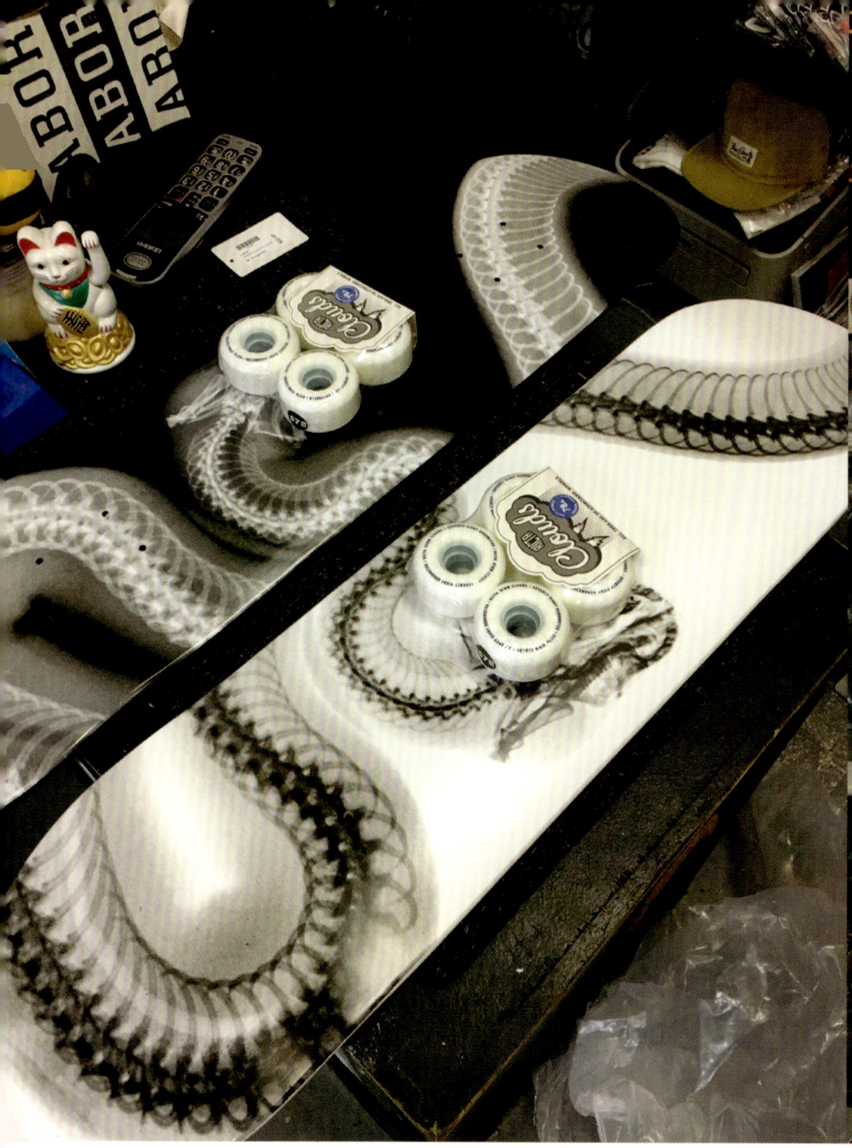
ABOR
ABOR
ABOR
Clouds
Clouds

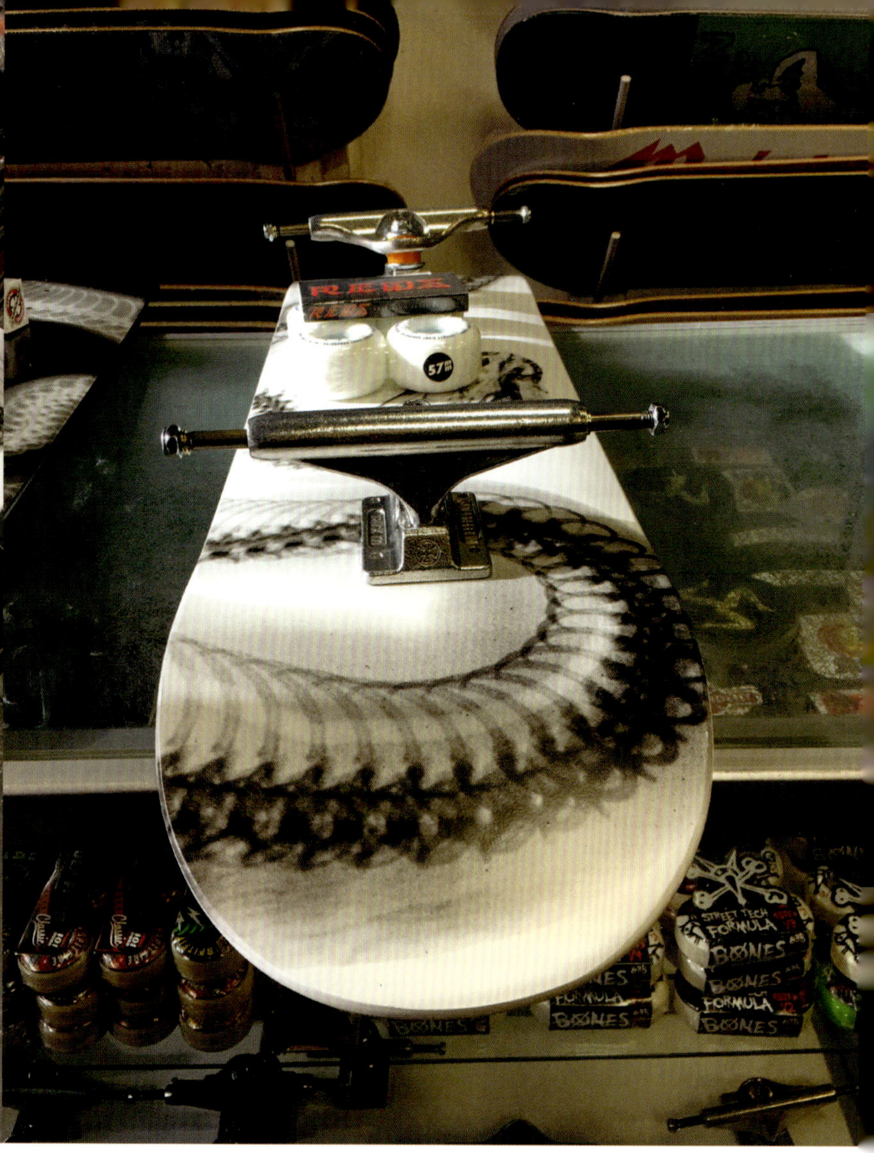
57
STREET TECH FORMULA
BONES
FORMULA
BONES
BONES

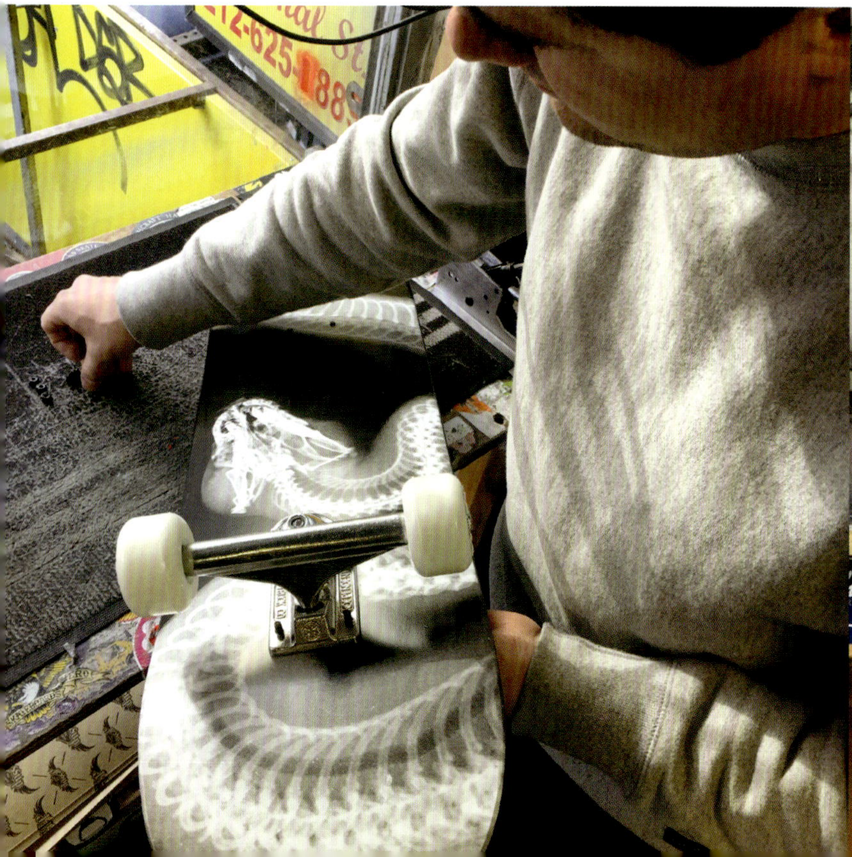

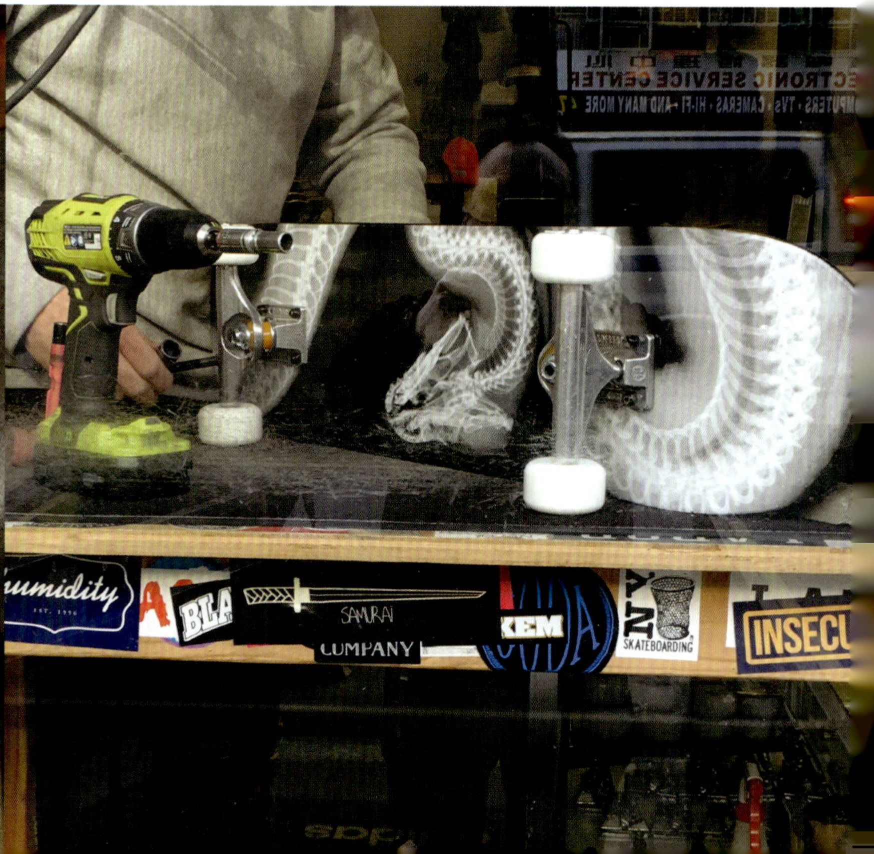
SAMURAI
COMPANY
KEM
N.Y.
SKATEBOARDING

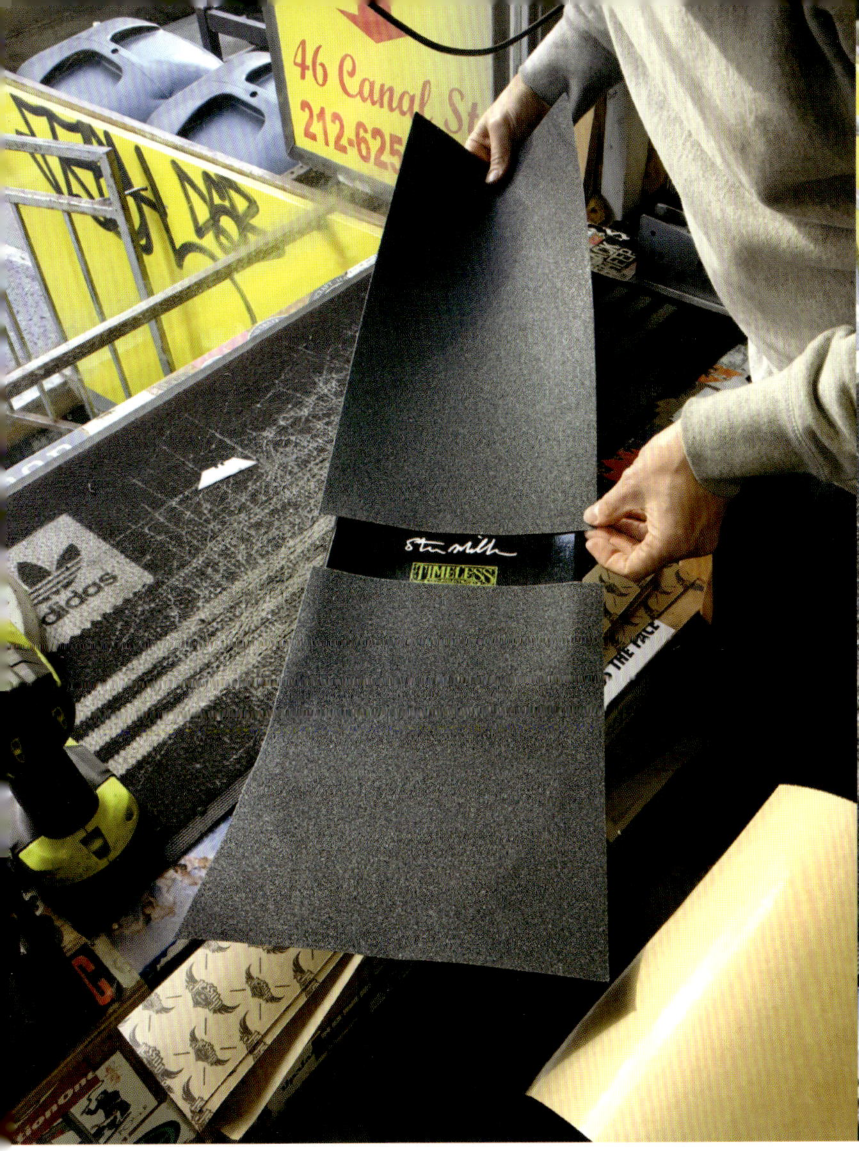

46 Canal St
212-625

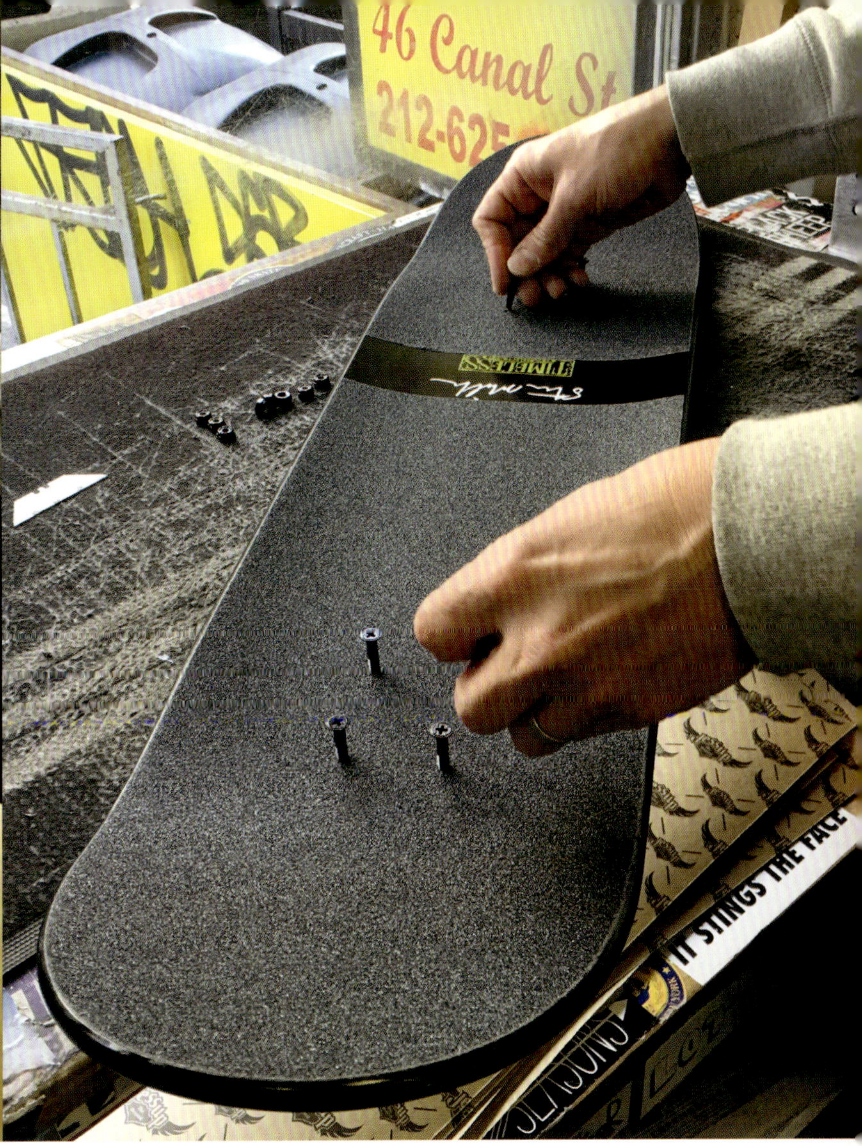

46 Canal St
212-625

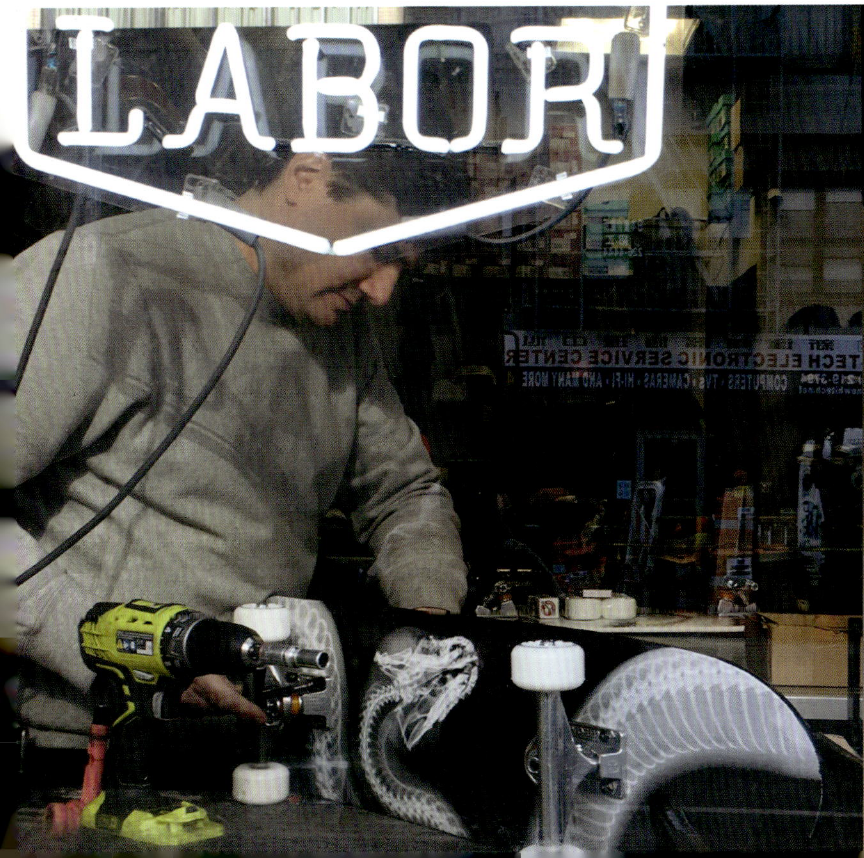

LABOR

TECH ELECTRONIC SERVICE CENTER
COMPUTERS · TVS · CAMERAS · HI-FI · AND MANY MORE

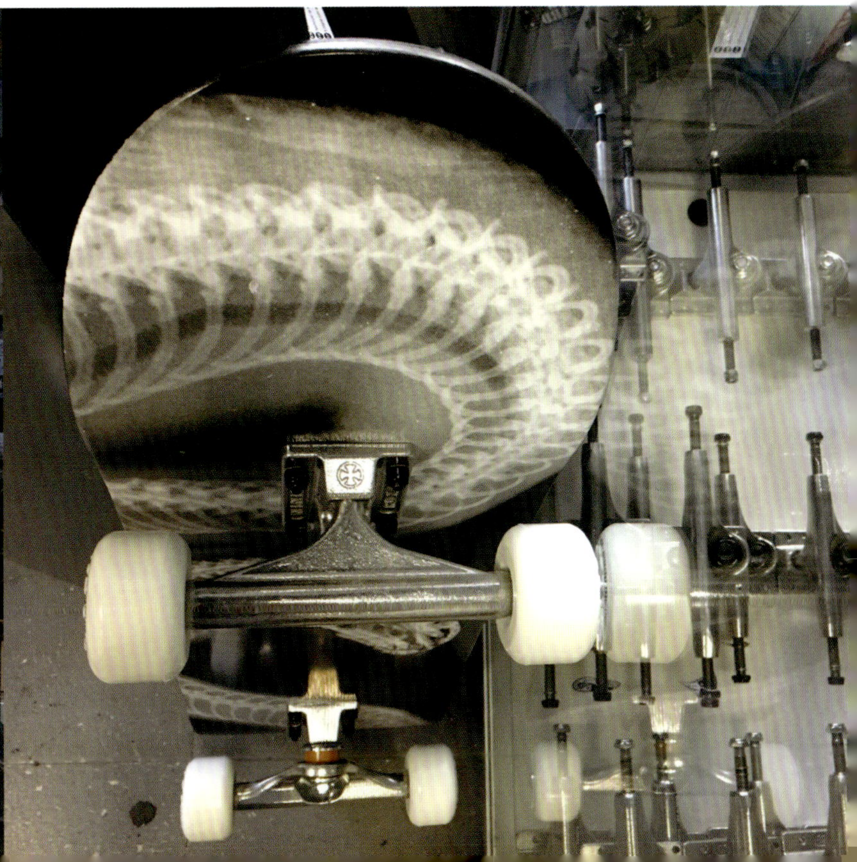

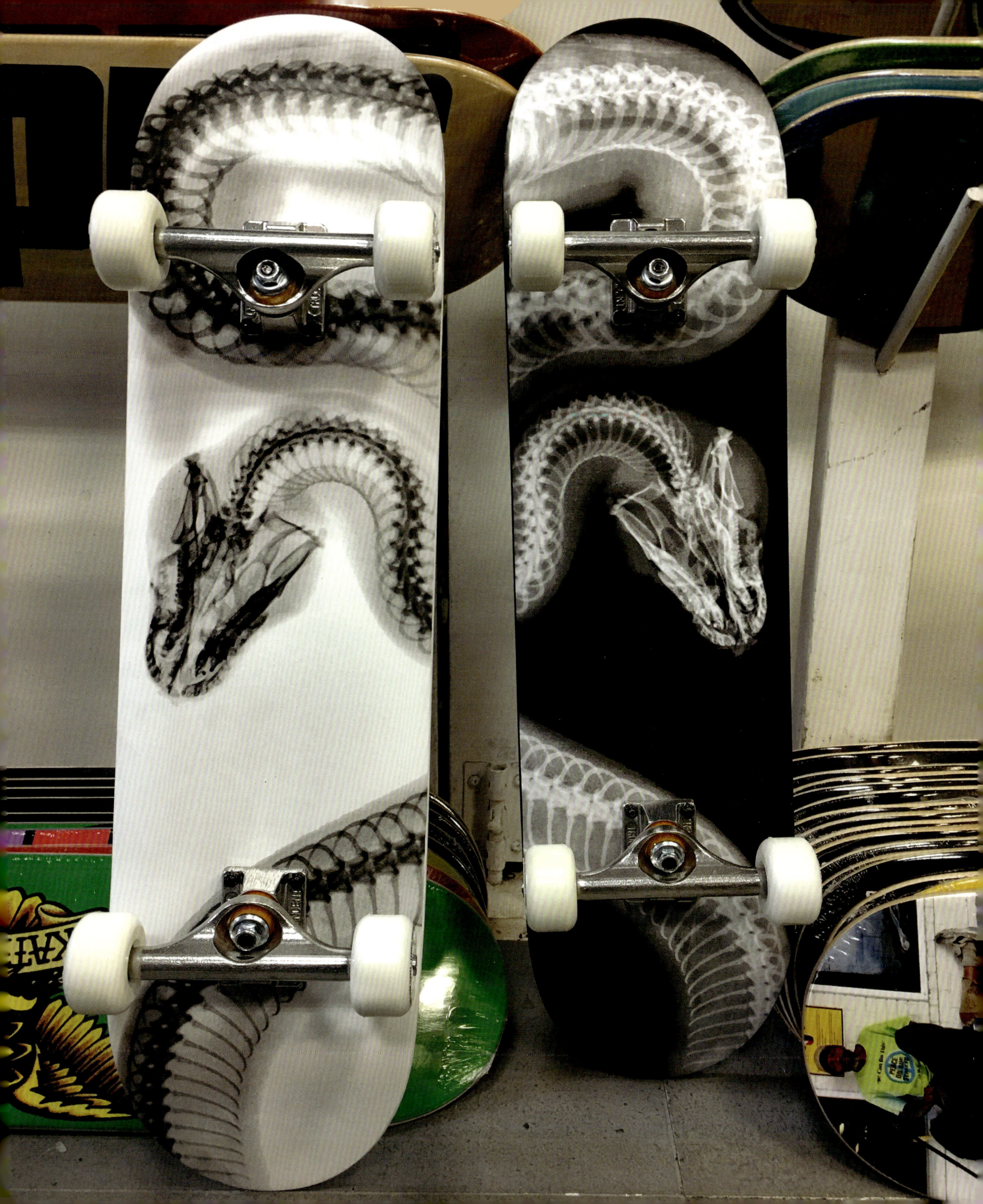

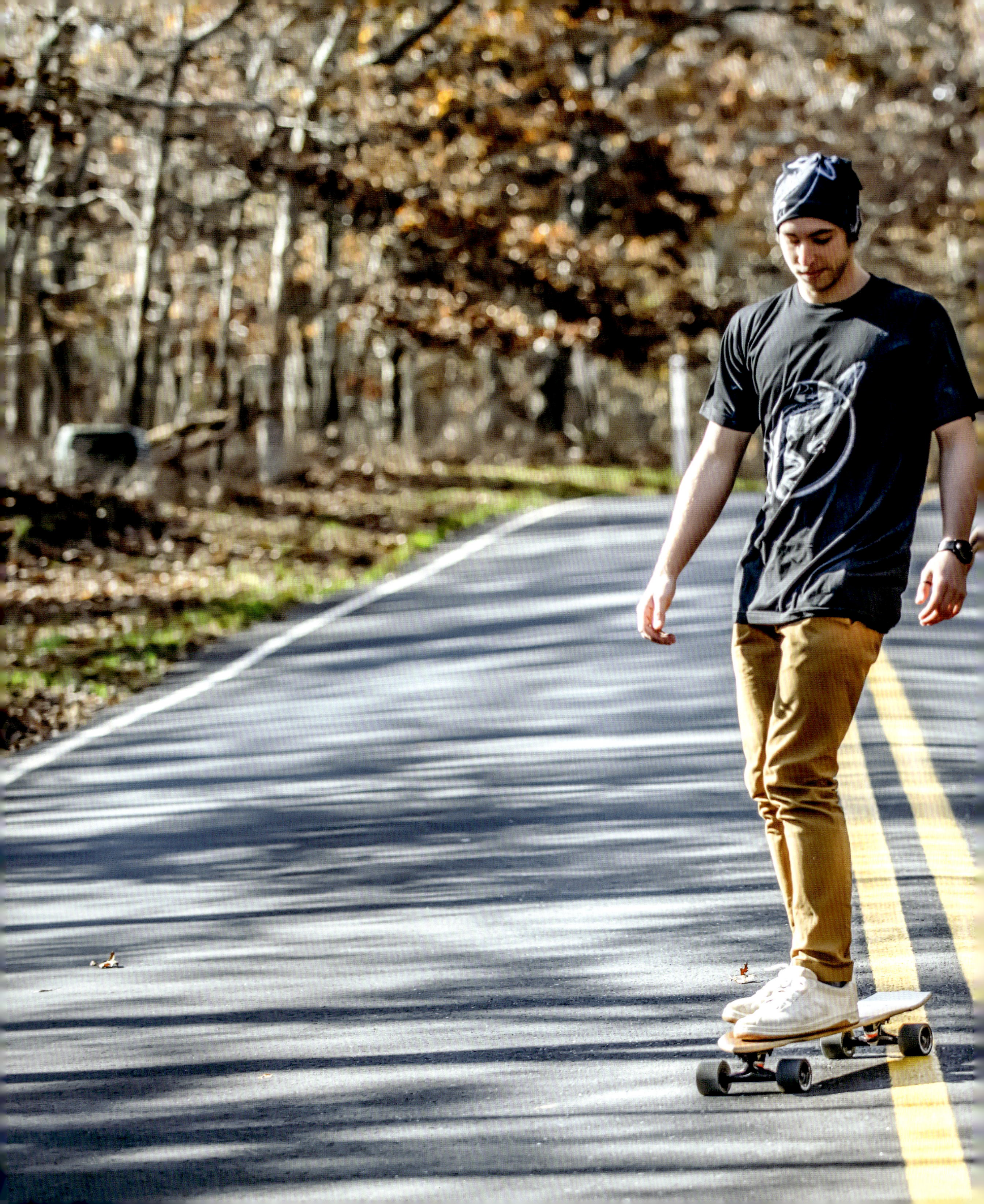

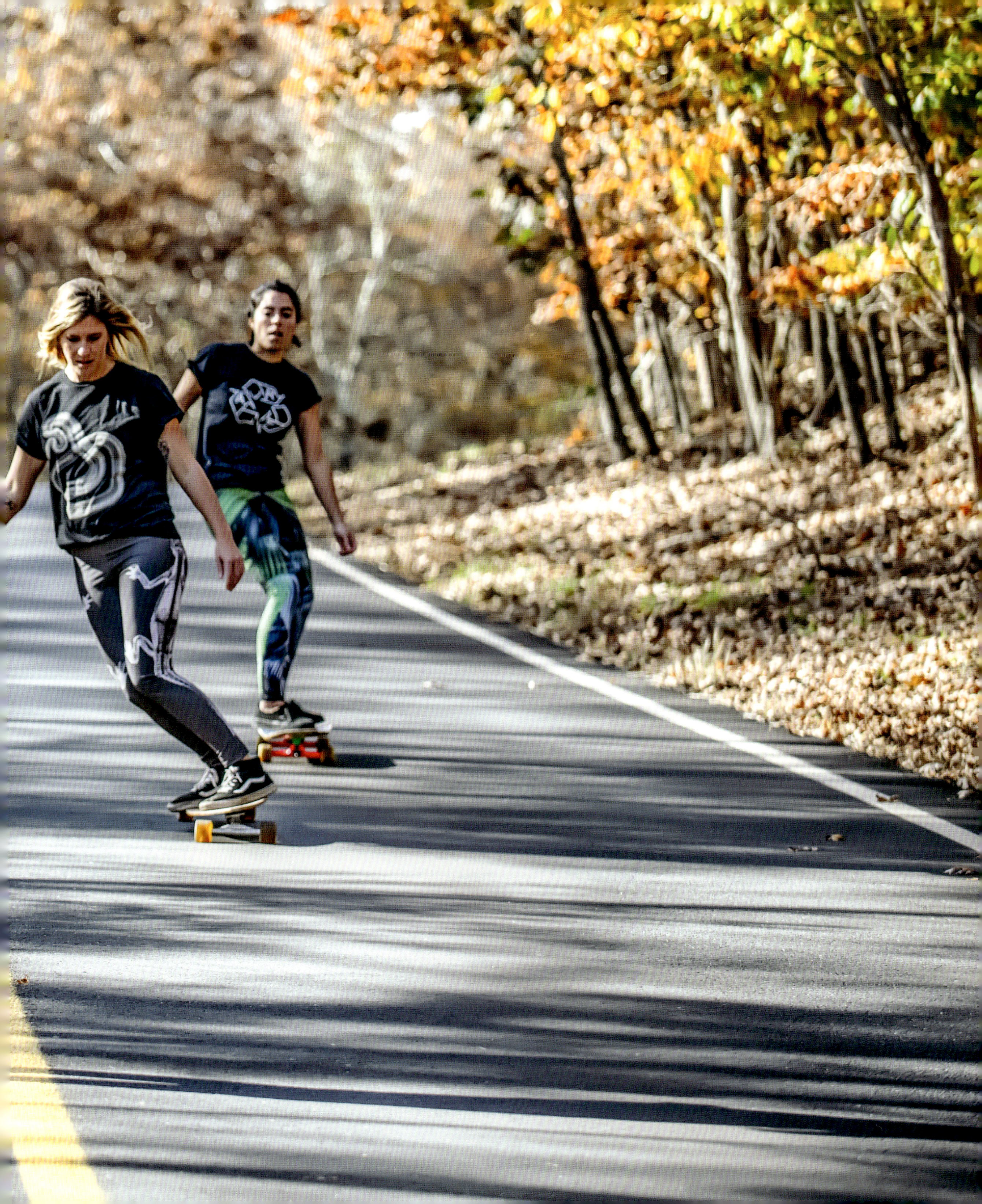

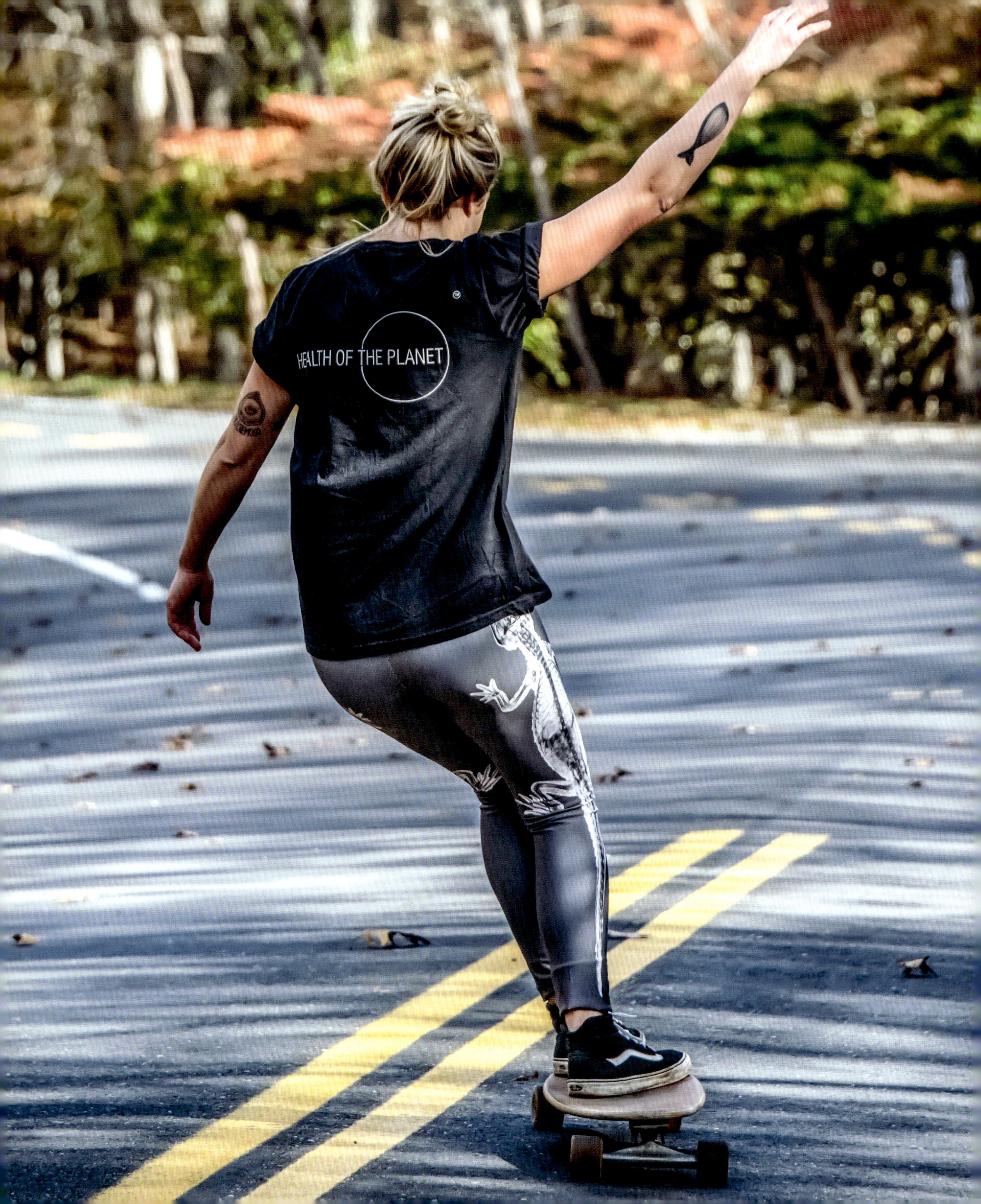

HEALTH OF THE PLANET

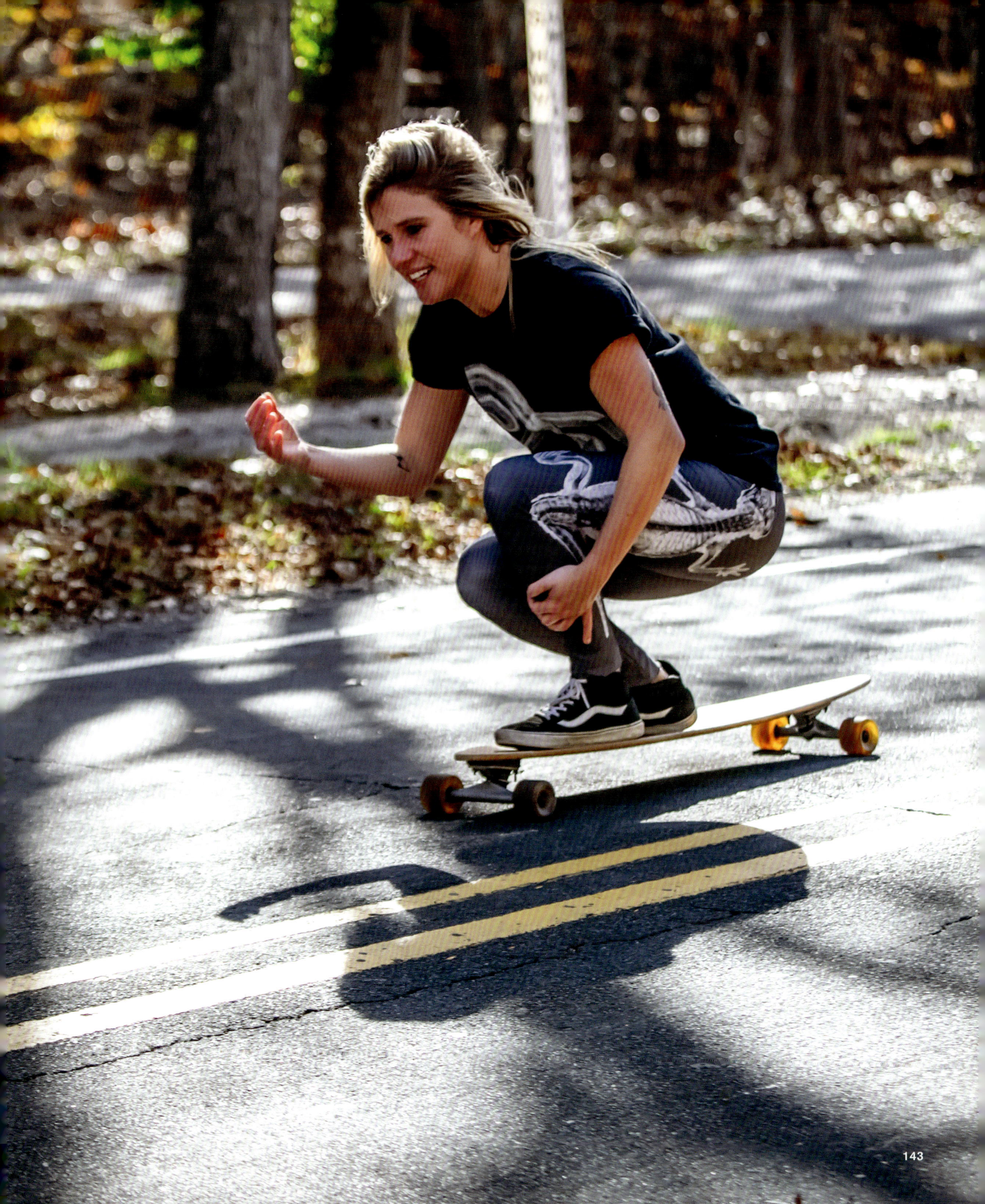

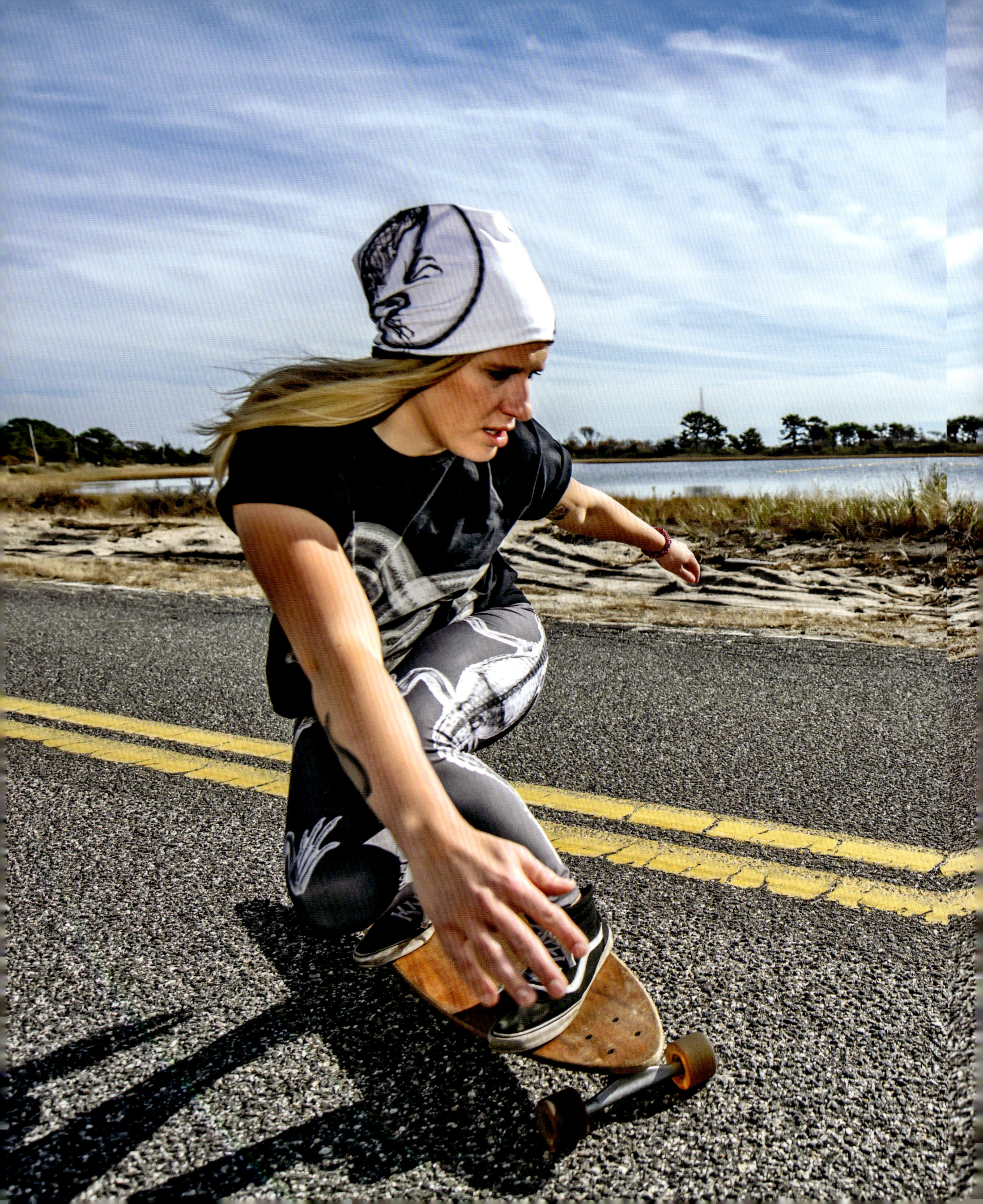

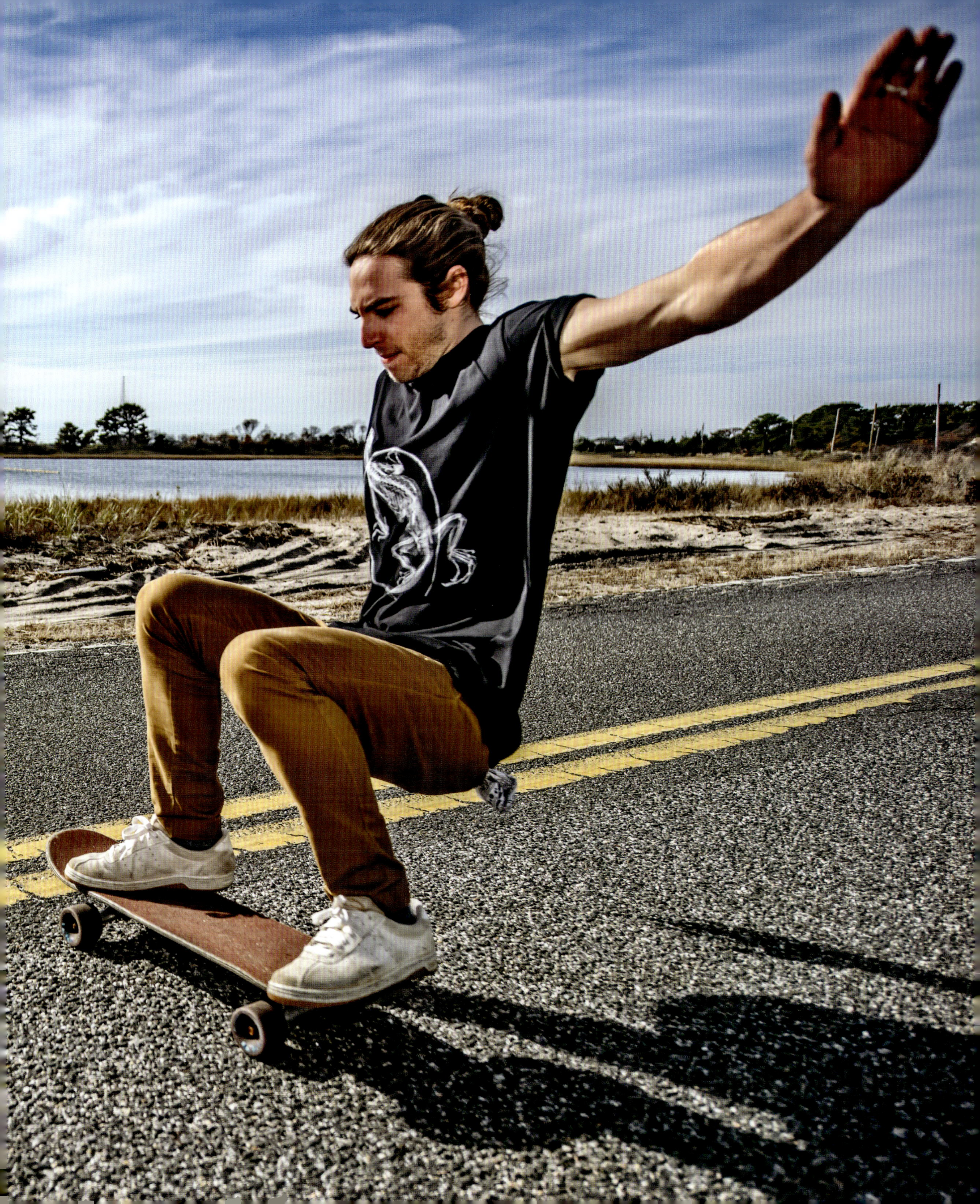

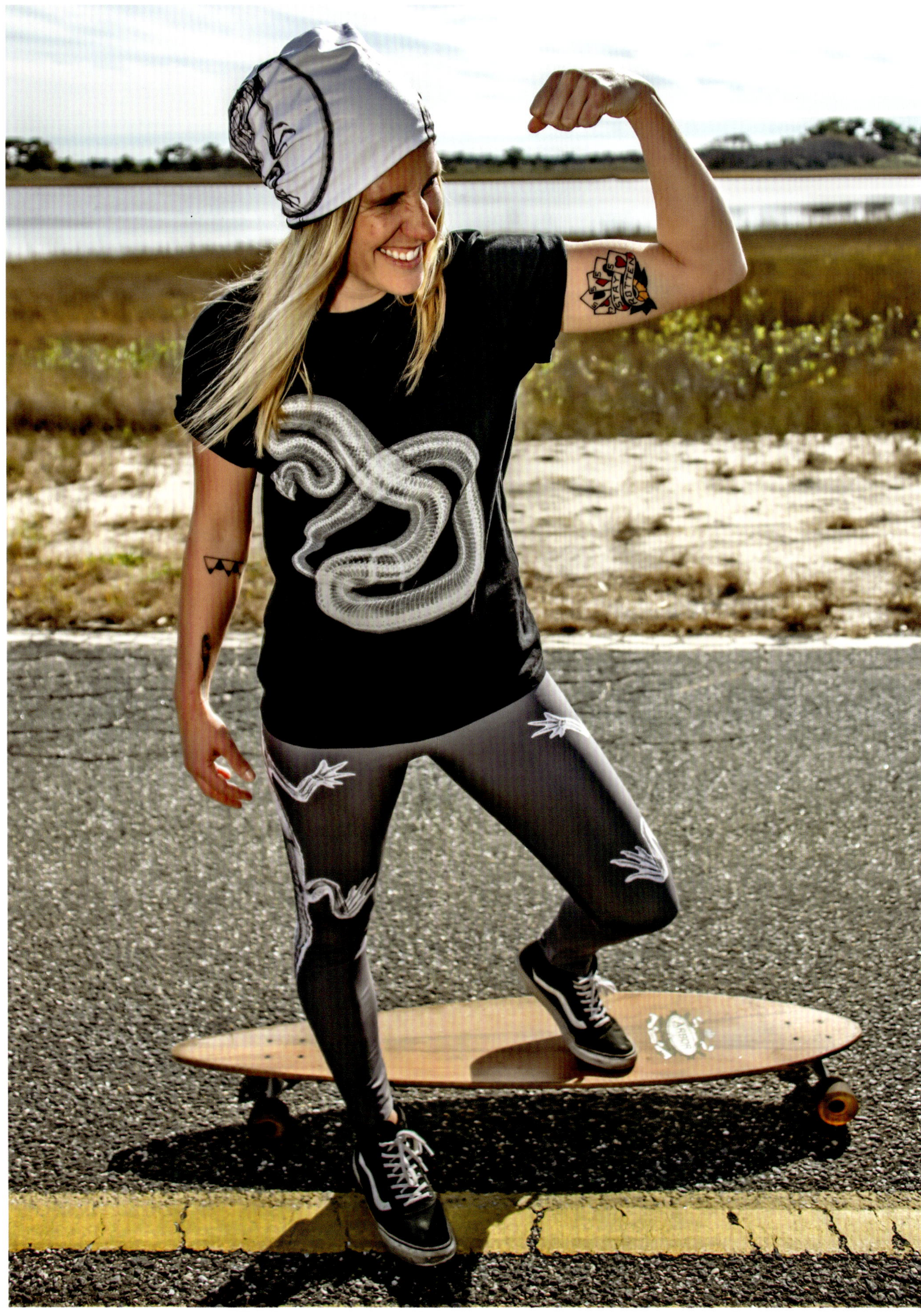

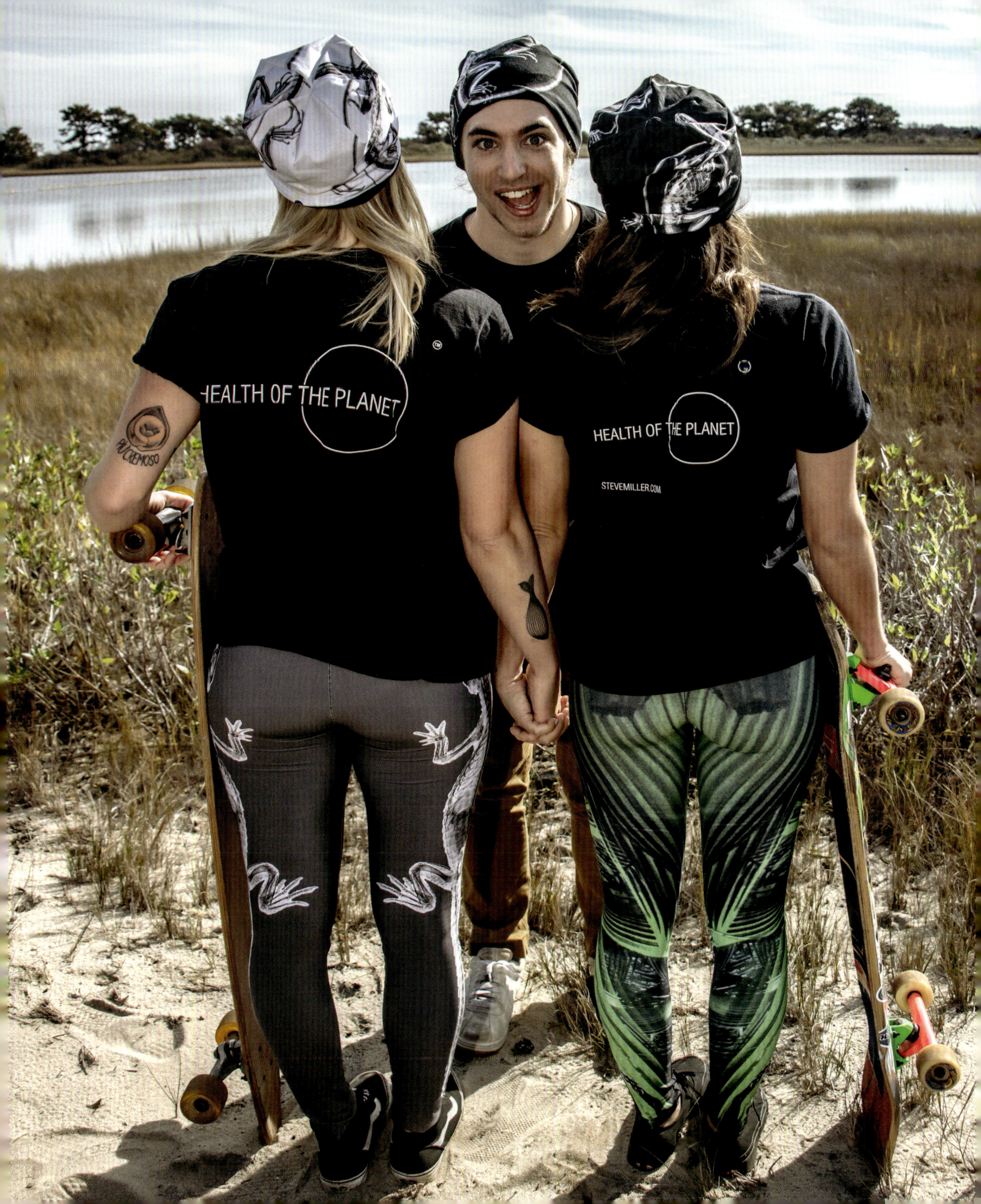

HEALTH OF THE PLANET
HEALTH OF THE PLANET
STEVEMILLER.COM

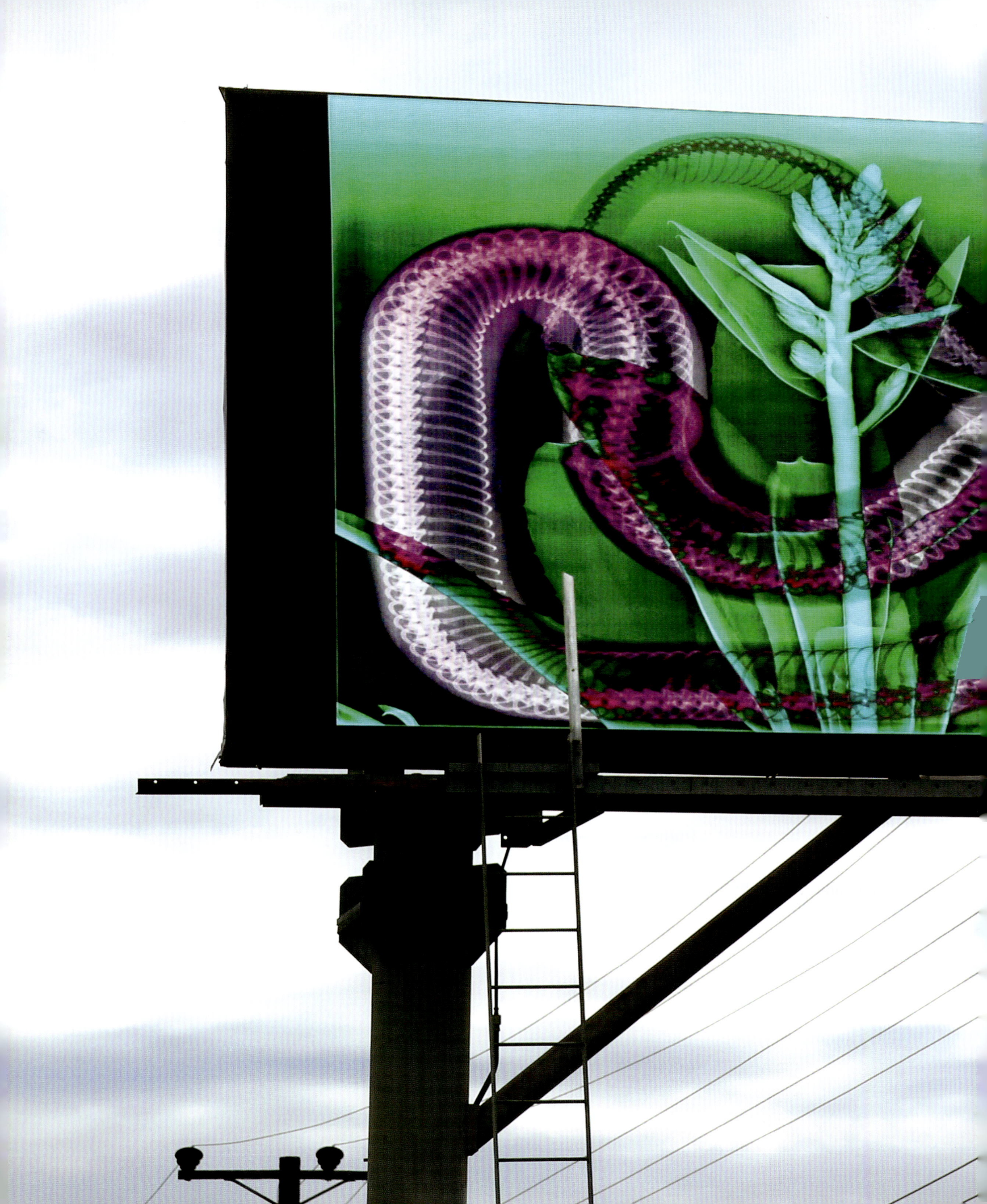

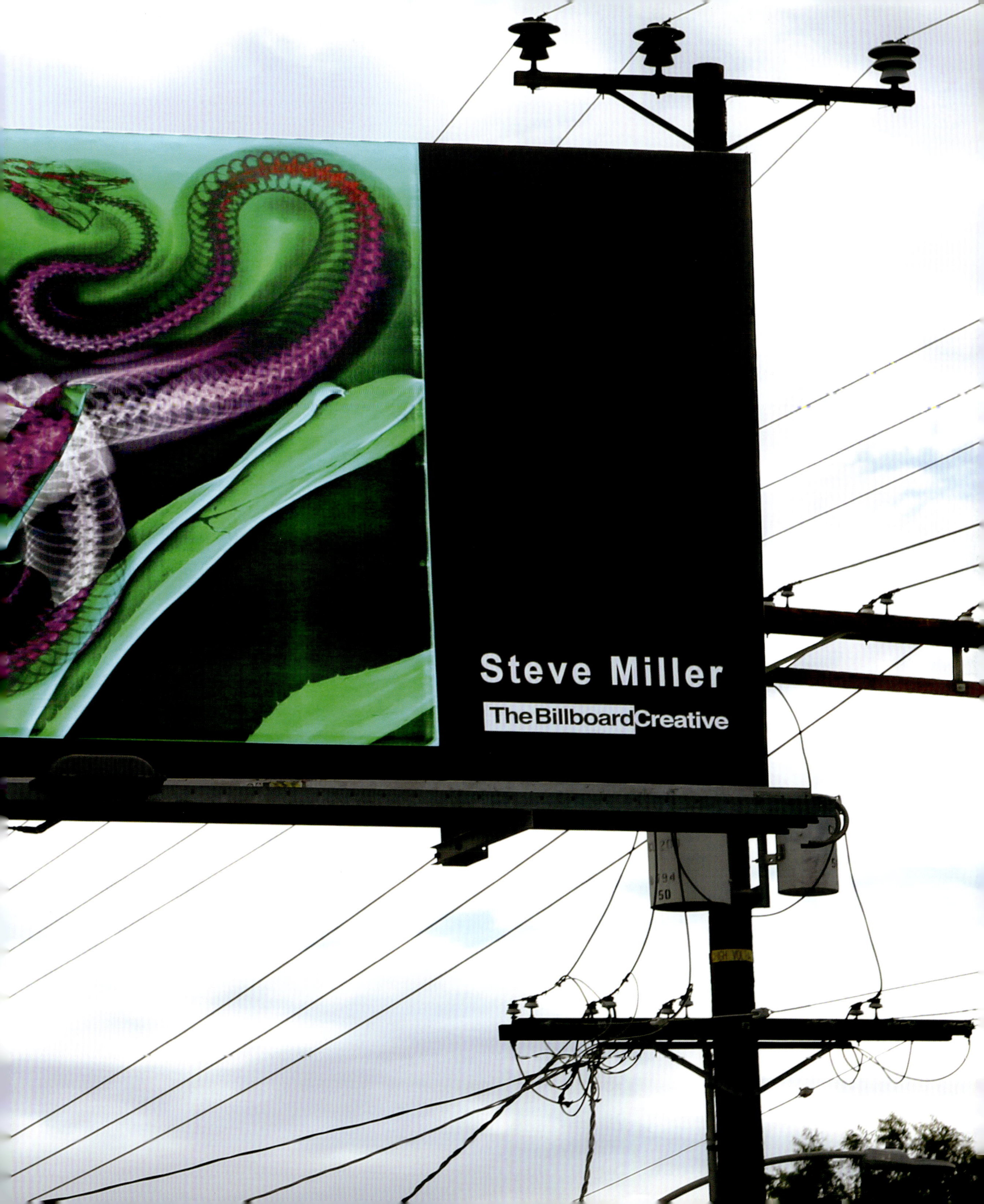

Steve Miller
The Billboard Creative

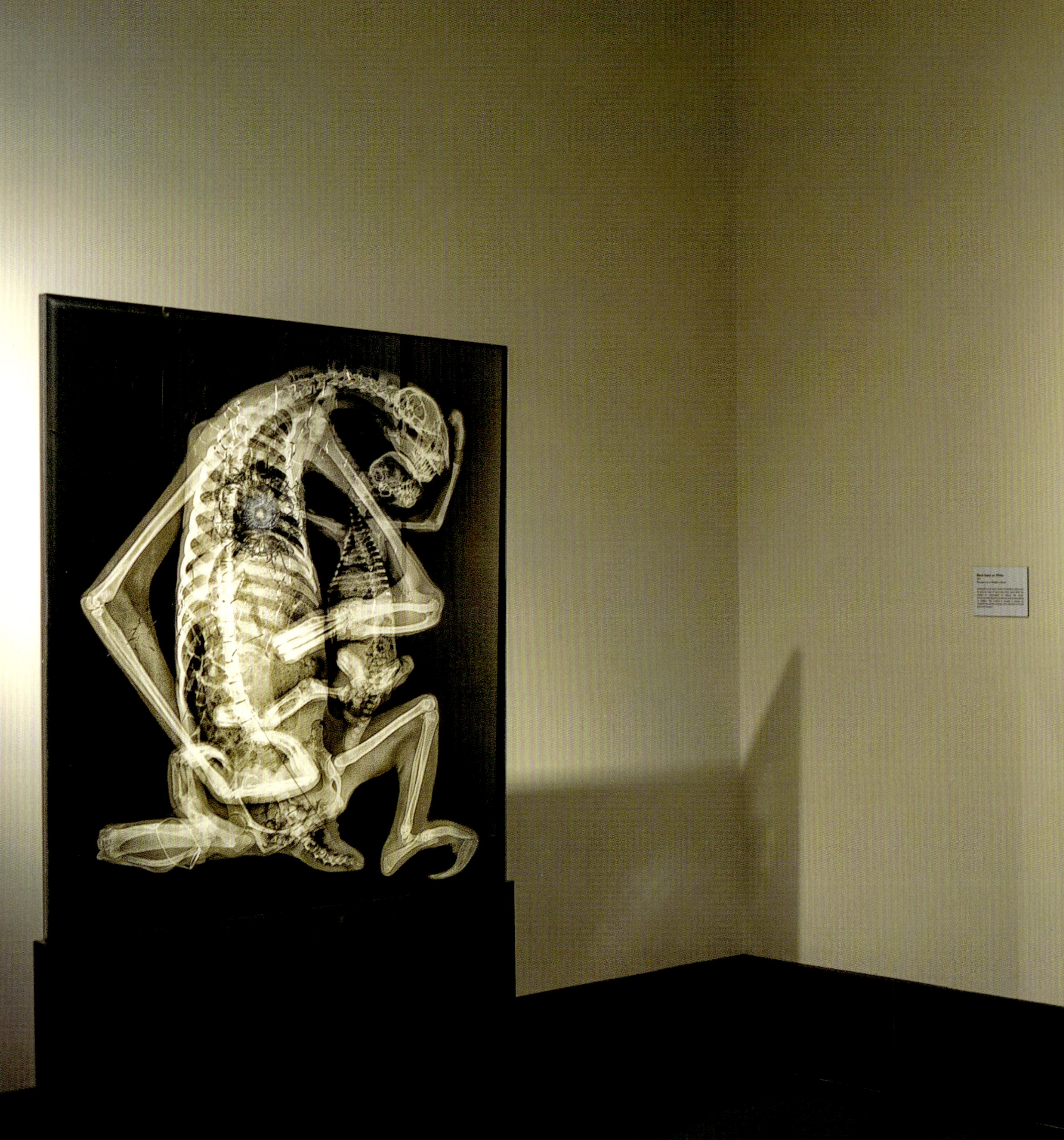

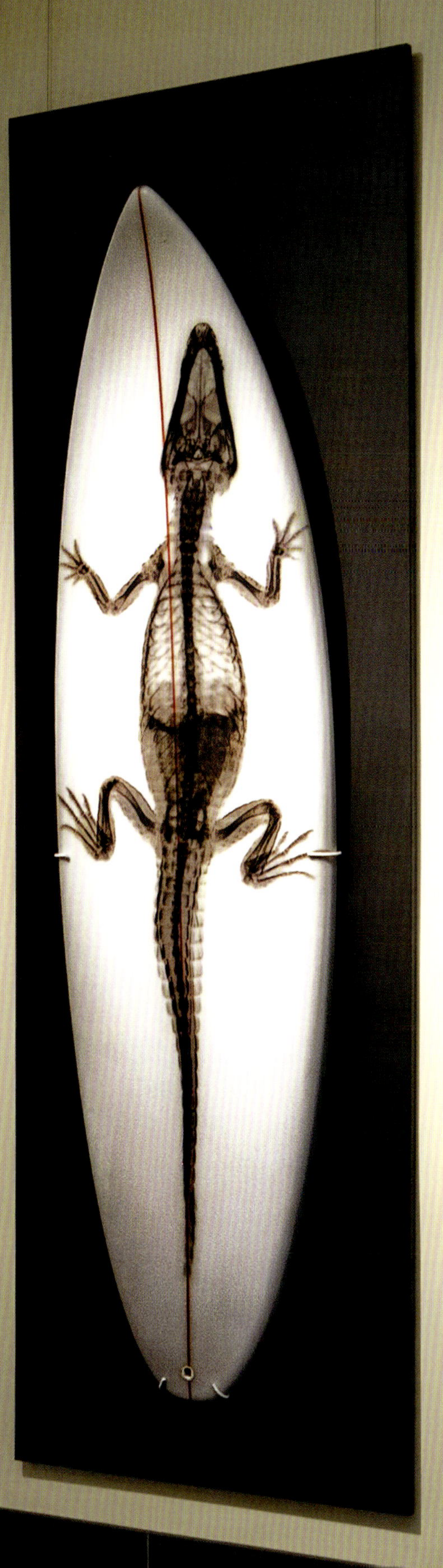

Steve Miller
Health of the Planet

Known as the "lungs of the planet," the Amazon rainforest absorbs an enormous amount of the world's carbon dioxide and produces oxygen. In recent decades, large swaths of the rainforest have been deforested for timber, urbanization, cattle ranching, and plant extracts. Today, roughly one fifth of the Amazon is gone, and scientists cite this deforestation as a major contributing factor to global climate change. Steve Miller explores the impact of deforestation on the Brazilian Amazon rainforest in this exhibition.

On a trip to Brazil in 2005, fascinated by the beauty, biodiversity, and environmental challenges facing the country's tropical environment, Miller began to conceptualize much of the artwork featured here. On subsequent visits, he created x-rays of rainforest flora and fauna, with which he is giving the "lungs of the planet" a metaphorical checkup. He incorporates these x-rays into an unconventional range of media including paintings, prints, glass sculptures, and surfboards. Surfboards are an iconic symbol of Brazilian culture and by printing x-rays of fauna onto them he has created an "eco-trophy" to replace the classic, environmentally-depleting taxidermy trophy. His paintings also include satellite remote sensing imagery of land use and deforestation in the Amazon which he obtained from Woods Hole Research Center on Cape Cod.

Through the juxtaposition of the x-rays and land use imagery, Miller reveals the inner structure and beauty of animals at risk and gives a broader perspective on their dwindling habitats. With his bright colors, energetic painting style, and scientific imagery, Miller wants to enable us to acknowledge our place in the natural world and consequential interactions with it.

Based in New York, Miller is recognized as an early pioneer of the "sciart" (science-based art) movement. He has been exploring scientific concepts and experimenting with new technologies in his artwork since the 1970s.

This exhibition is organized by Cultural Programs of the National Academy of Sciences.

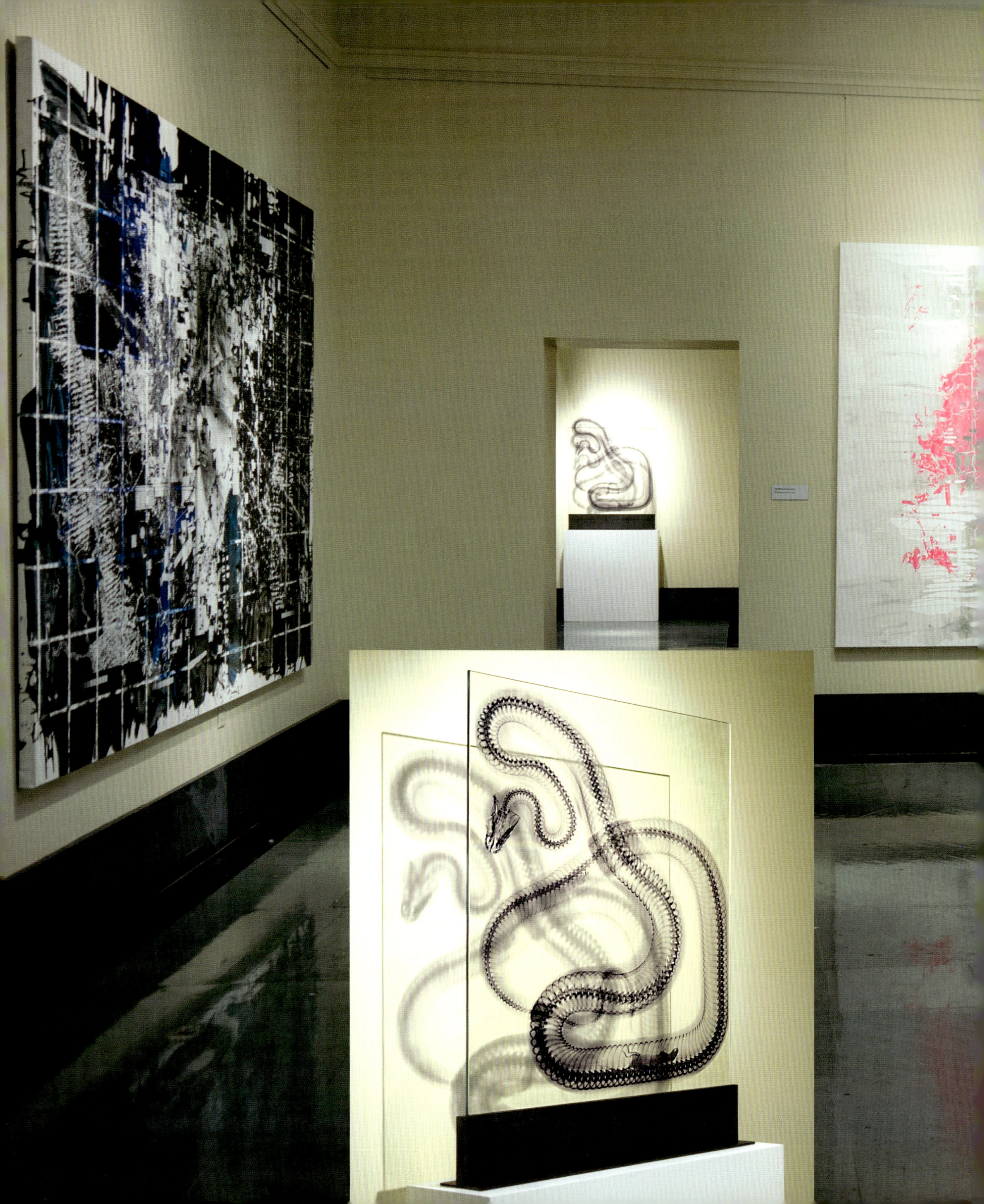

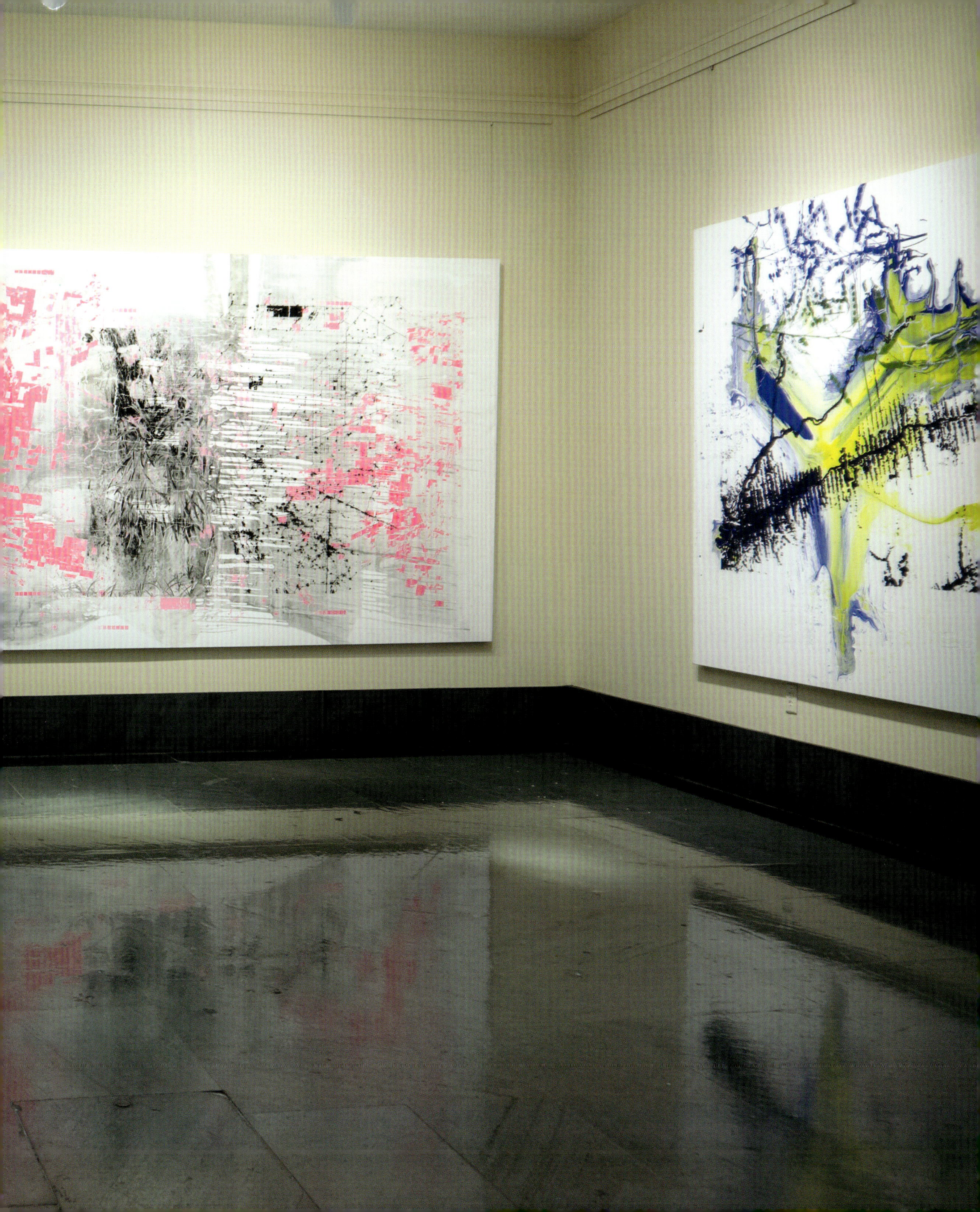

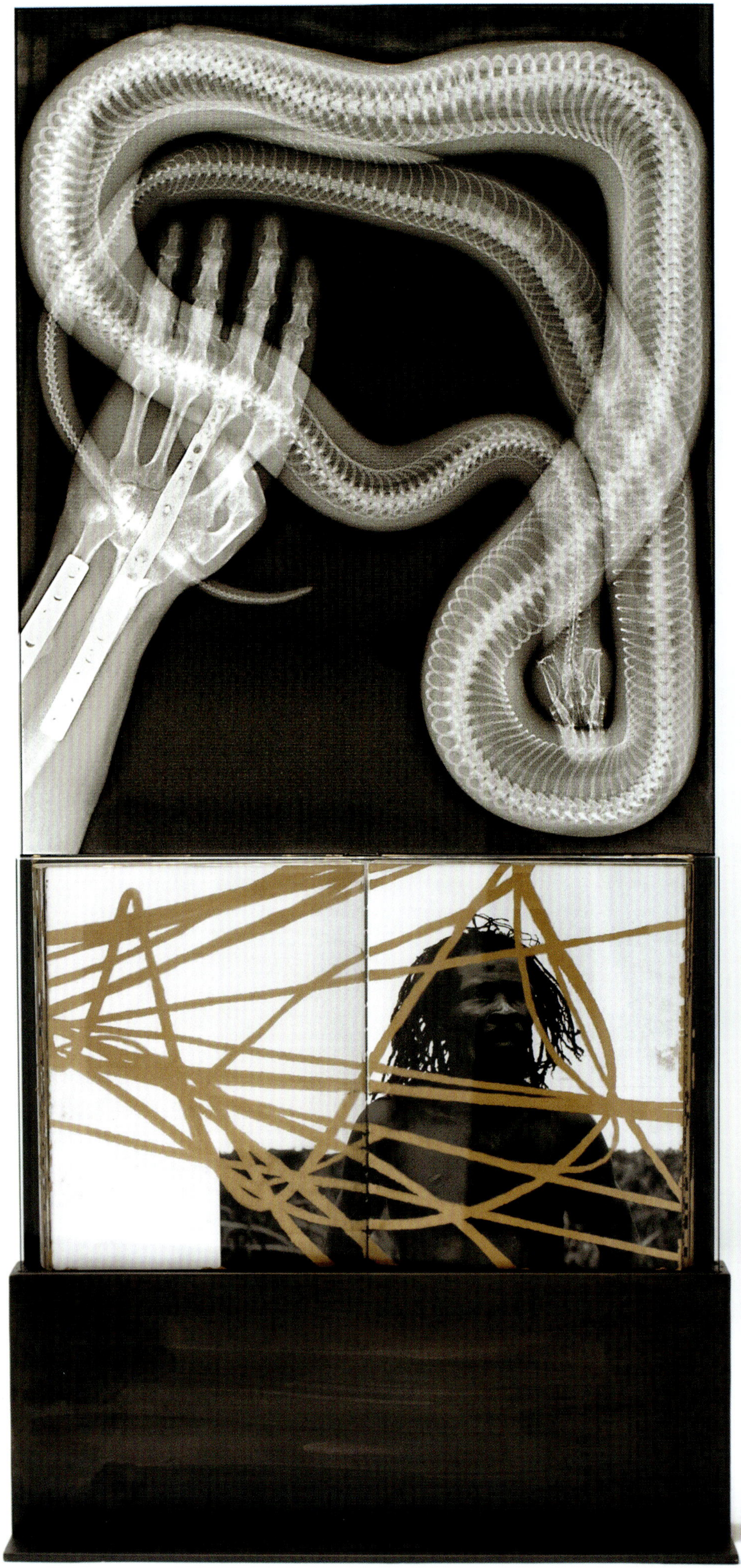

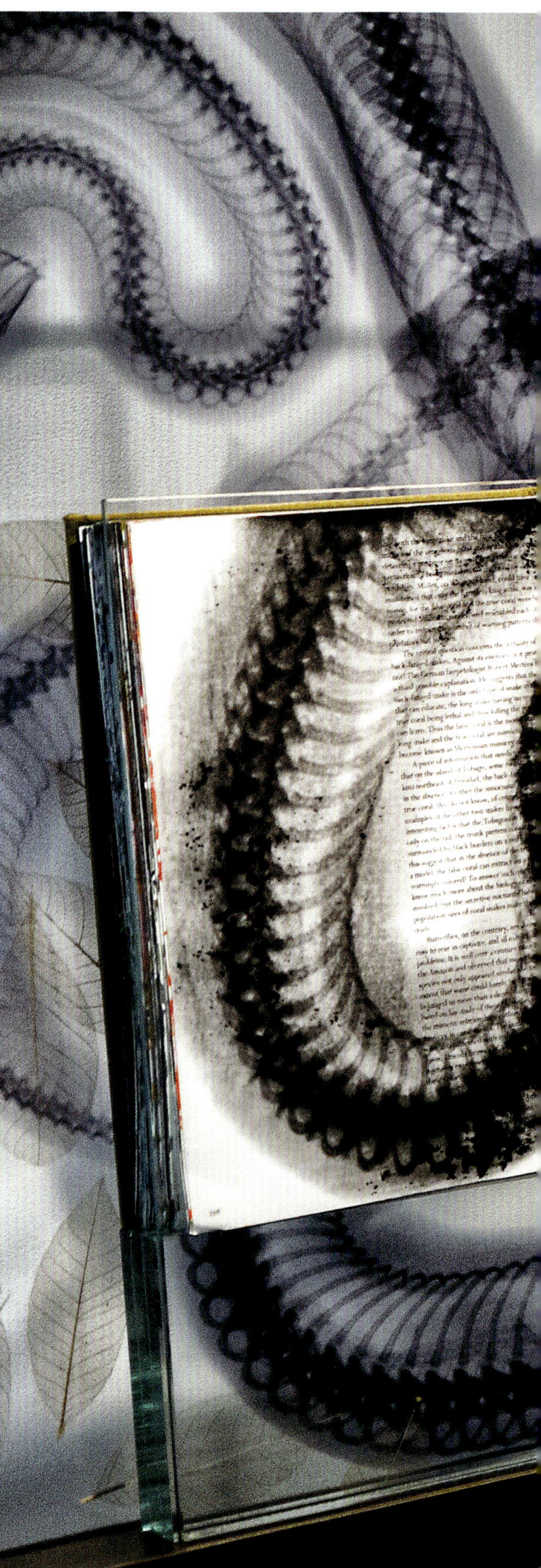

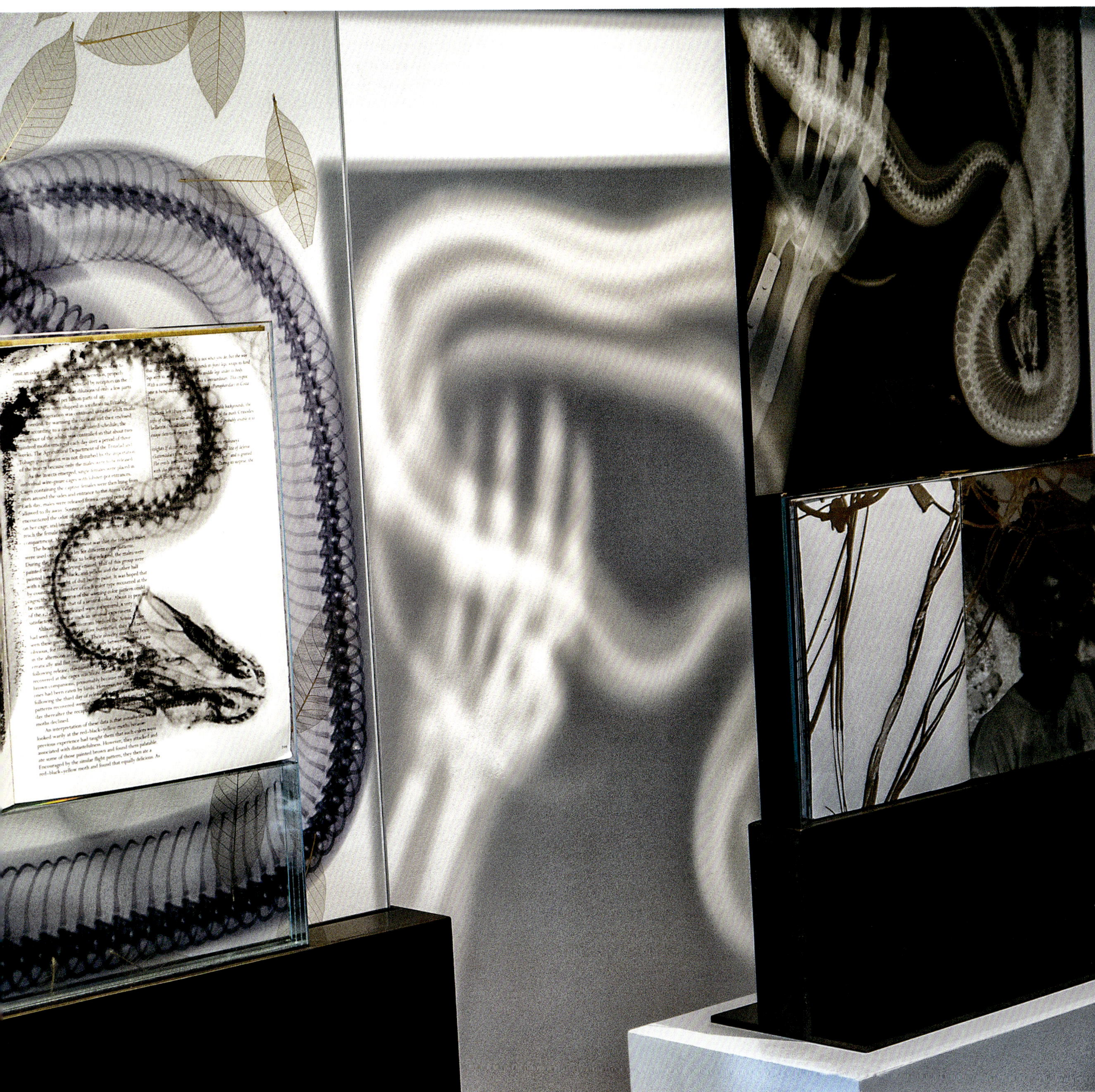

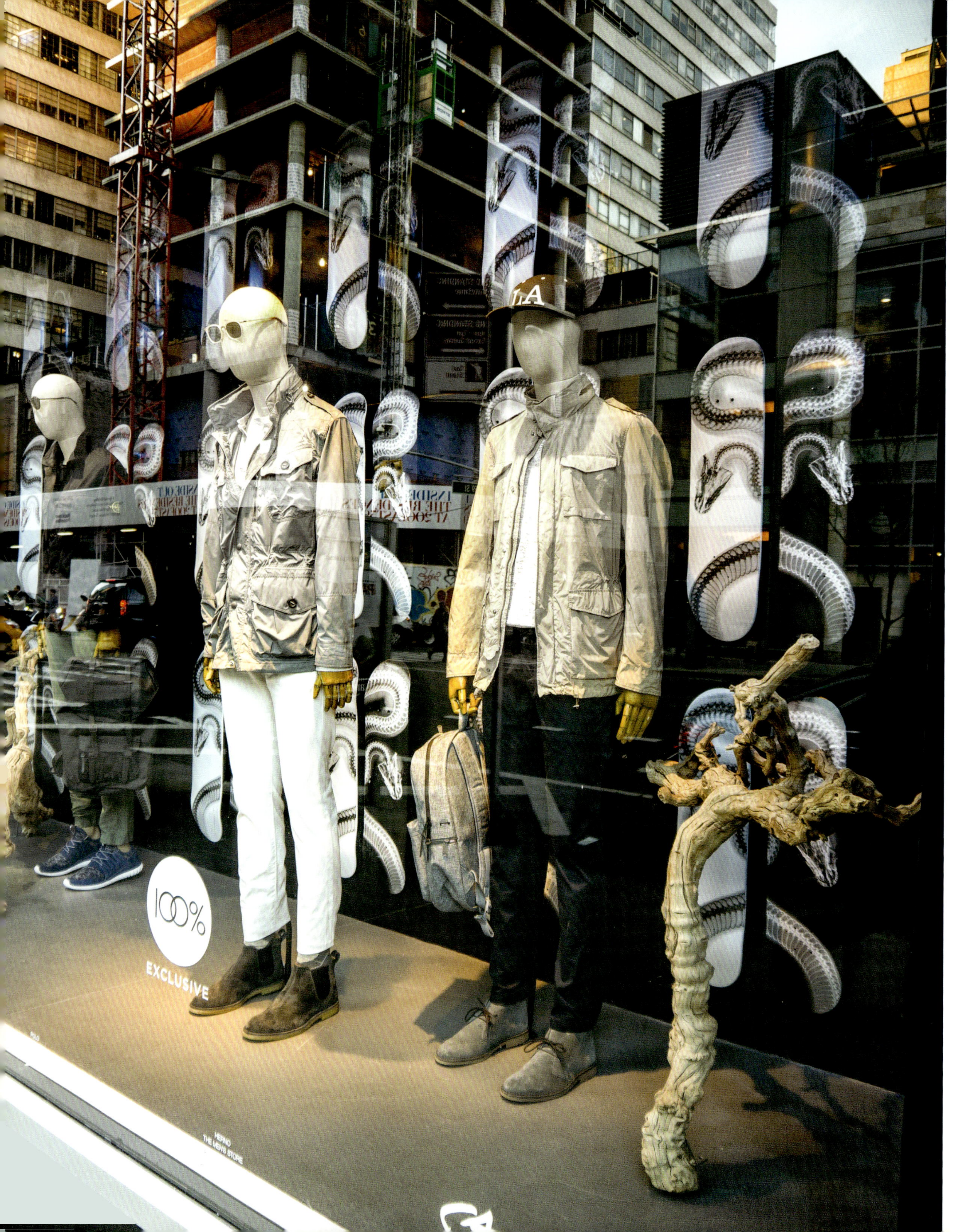

LA
100%
EXCLUSIVE

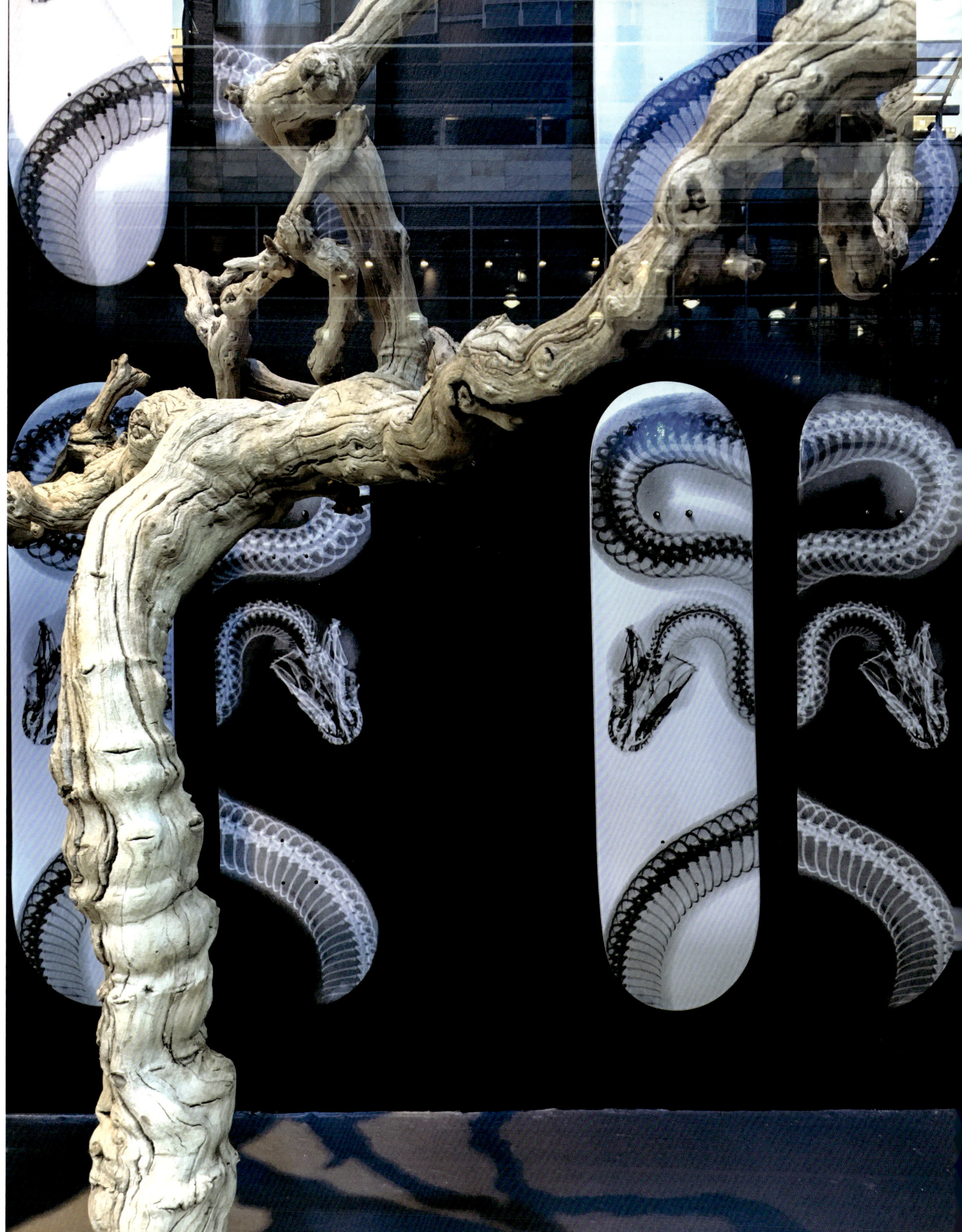

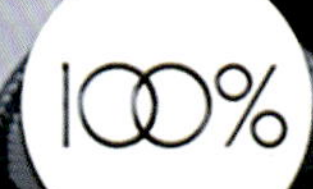

HOW THE WEST WAS WORN
First rule of the desert?
Always come prepared.
100%
EXCLUSIVE
ELEVENTY
LOWER LEVEL
STONE ISLAND
MICHAEL BASTIAN
MICHAEL BASTIAN
THE LAB

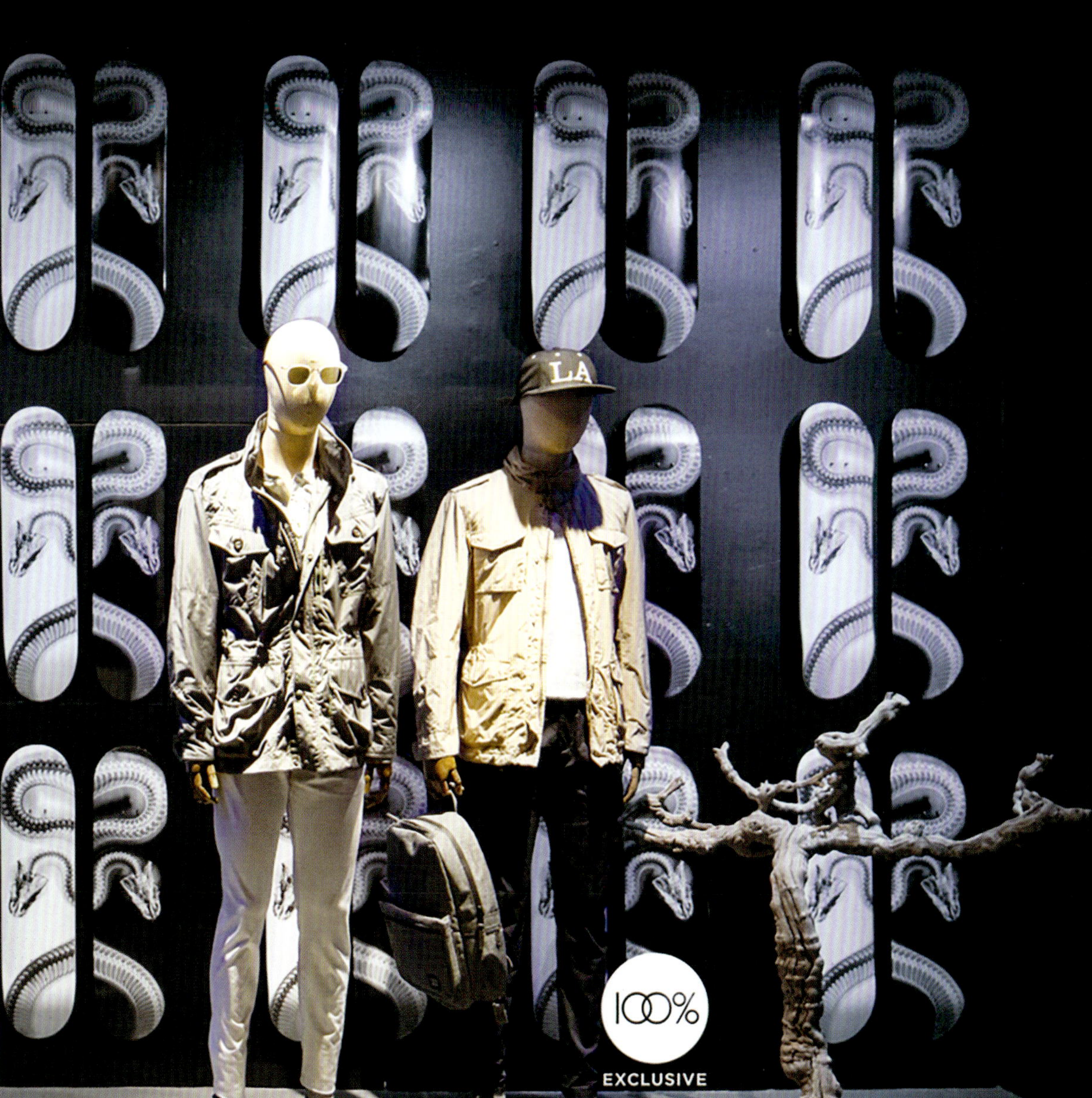
LA
100%
EXCLUSIVE
POLO
RALPH LAUREN
LOWER LEVEL

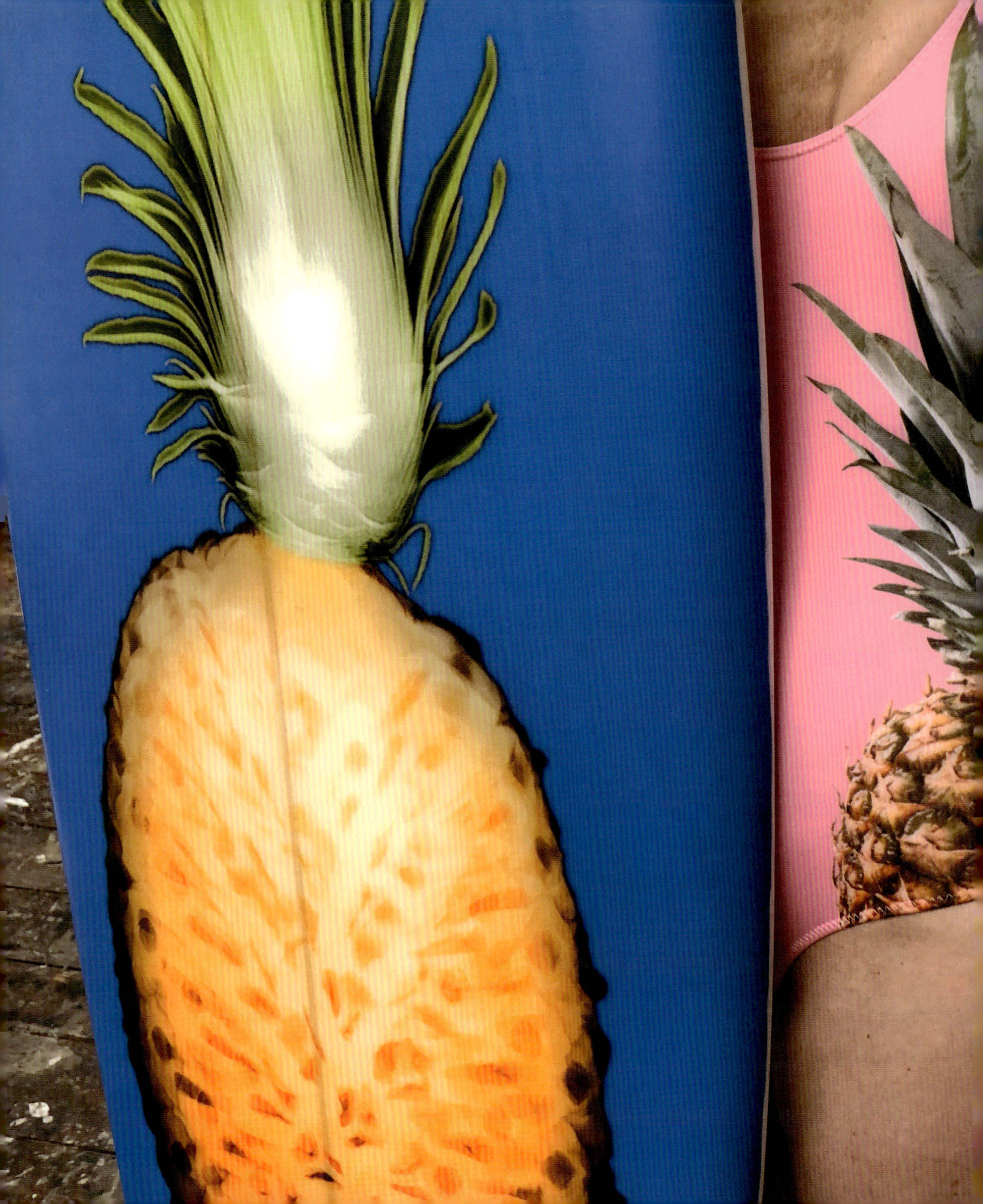

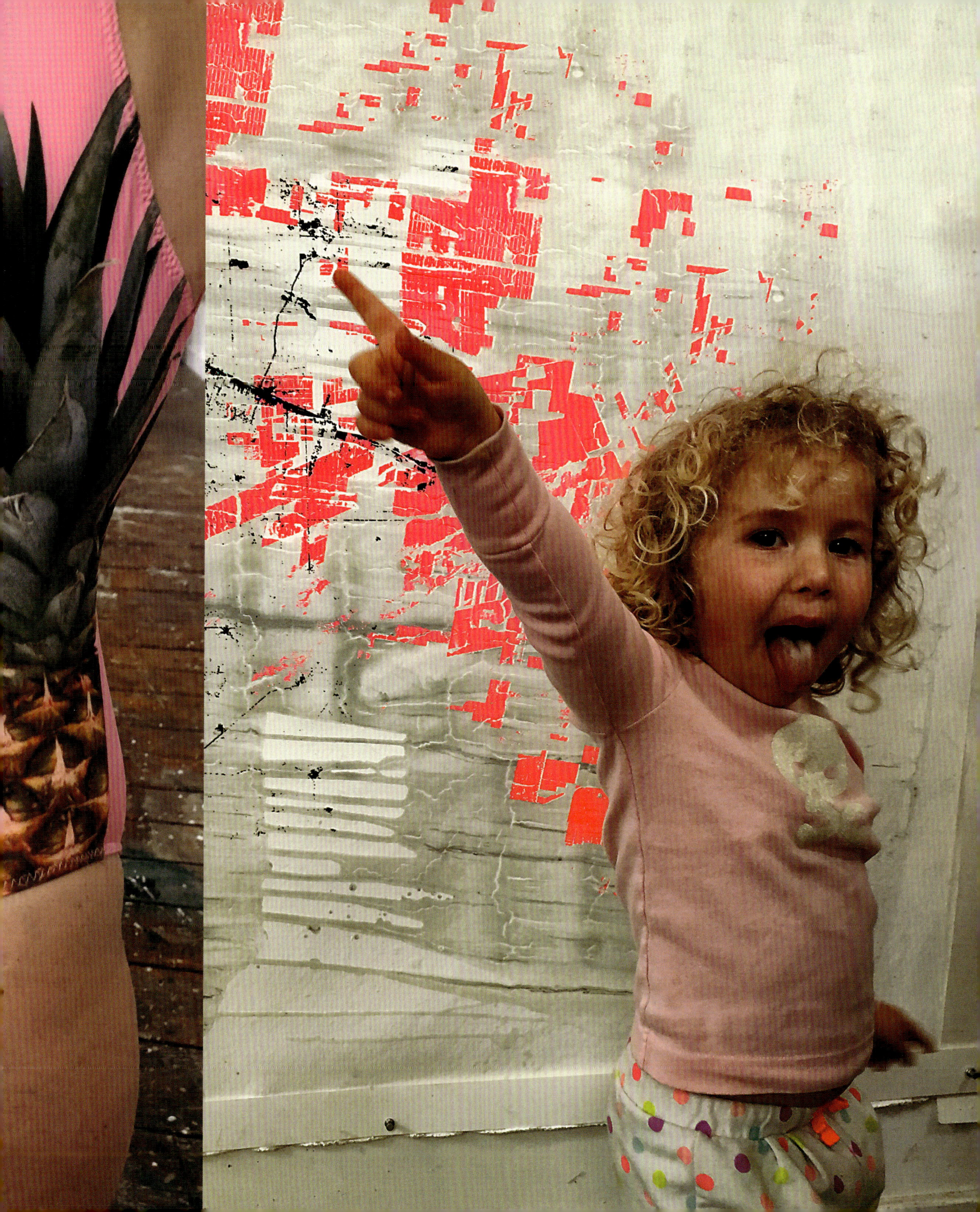

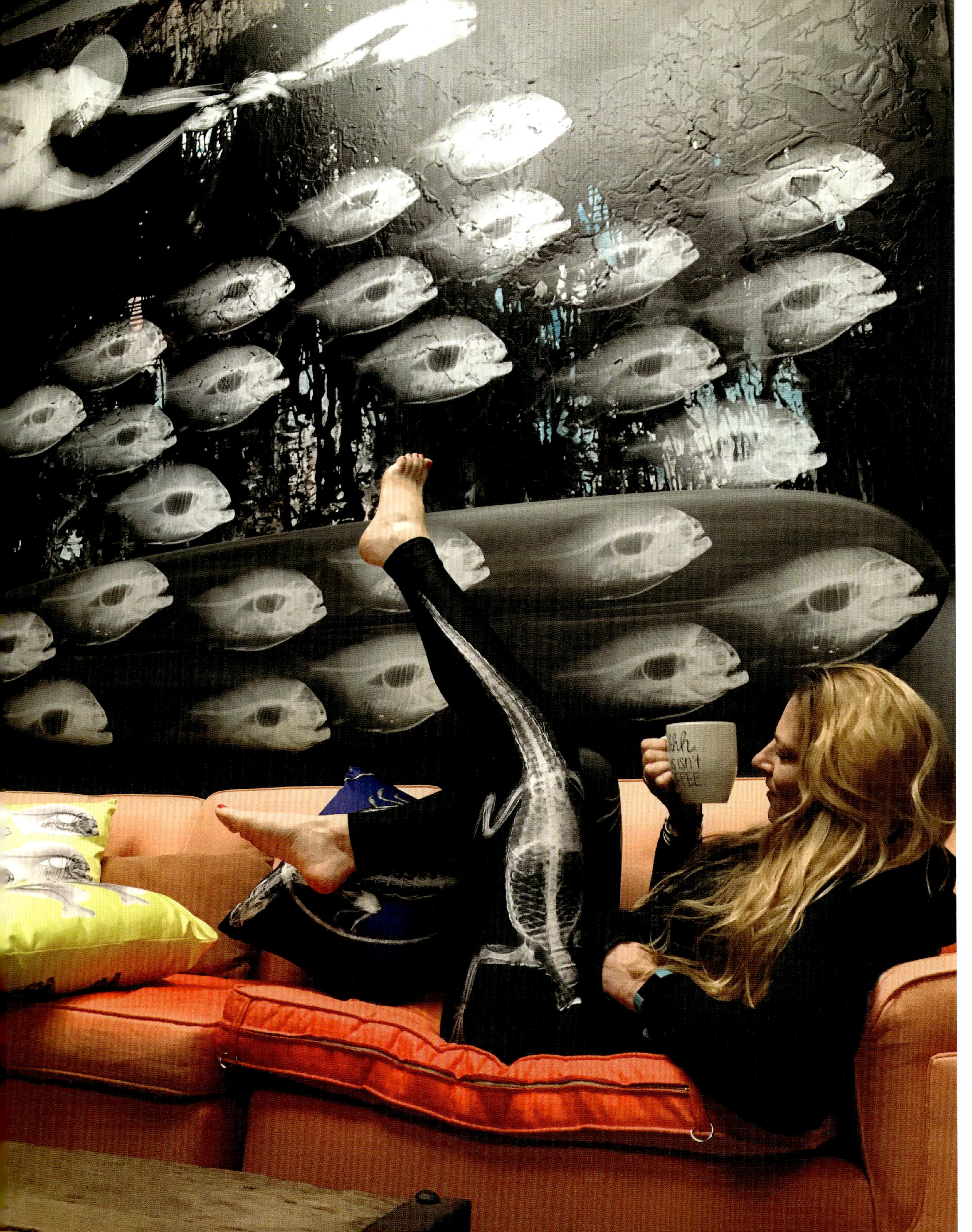
Shhh...
this isn't
COFFEE

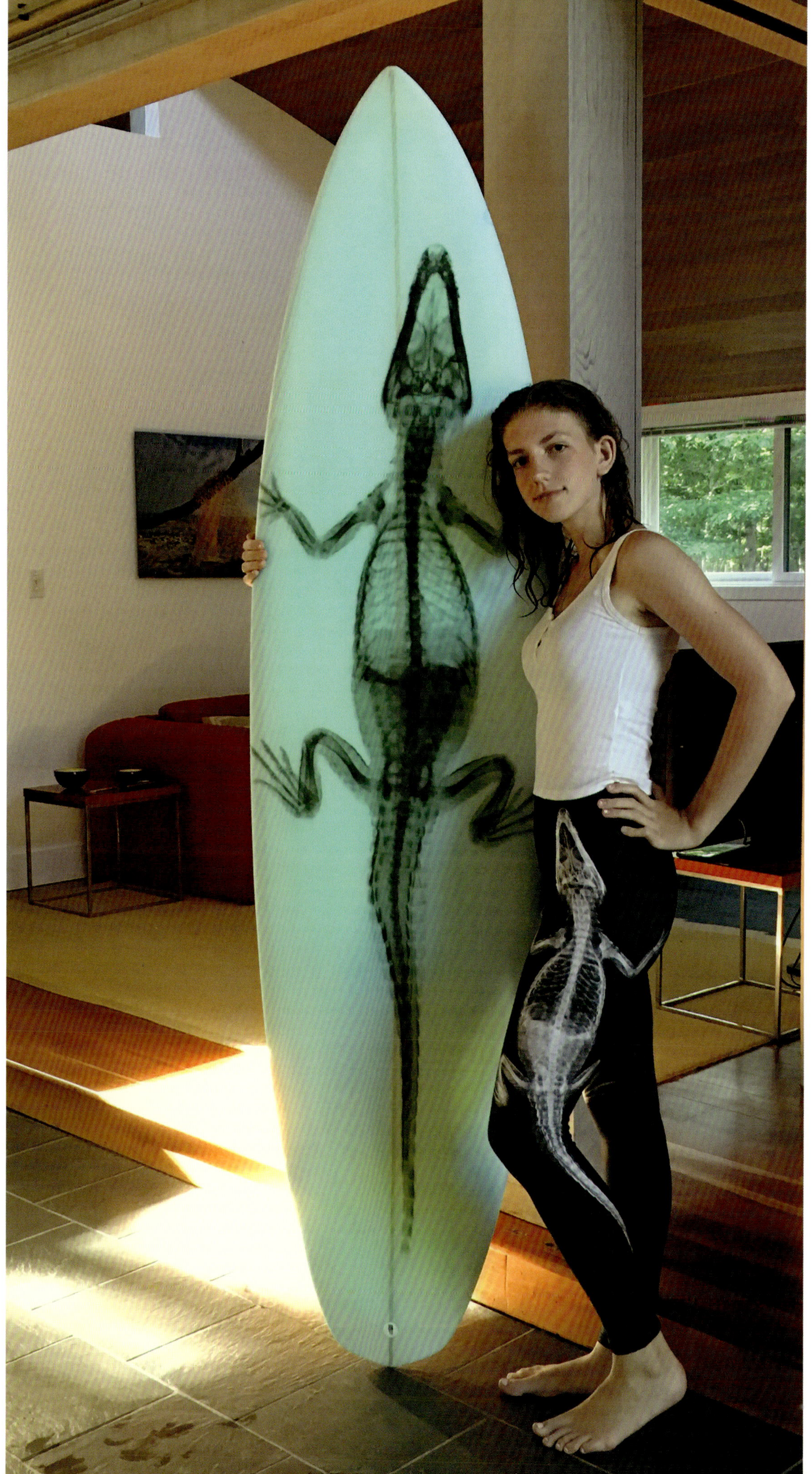

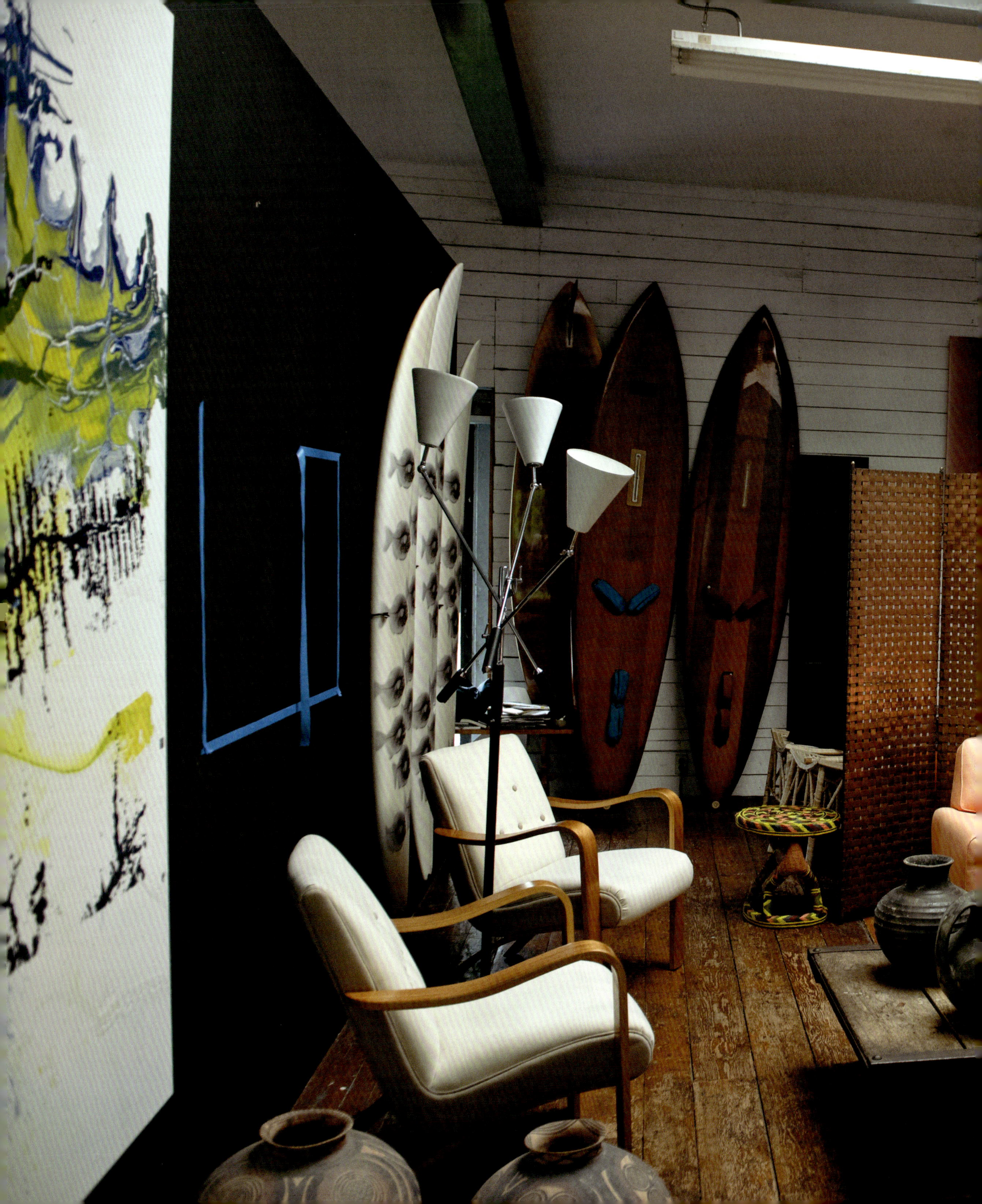

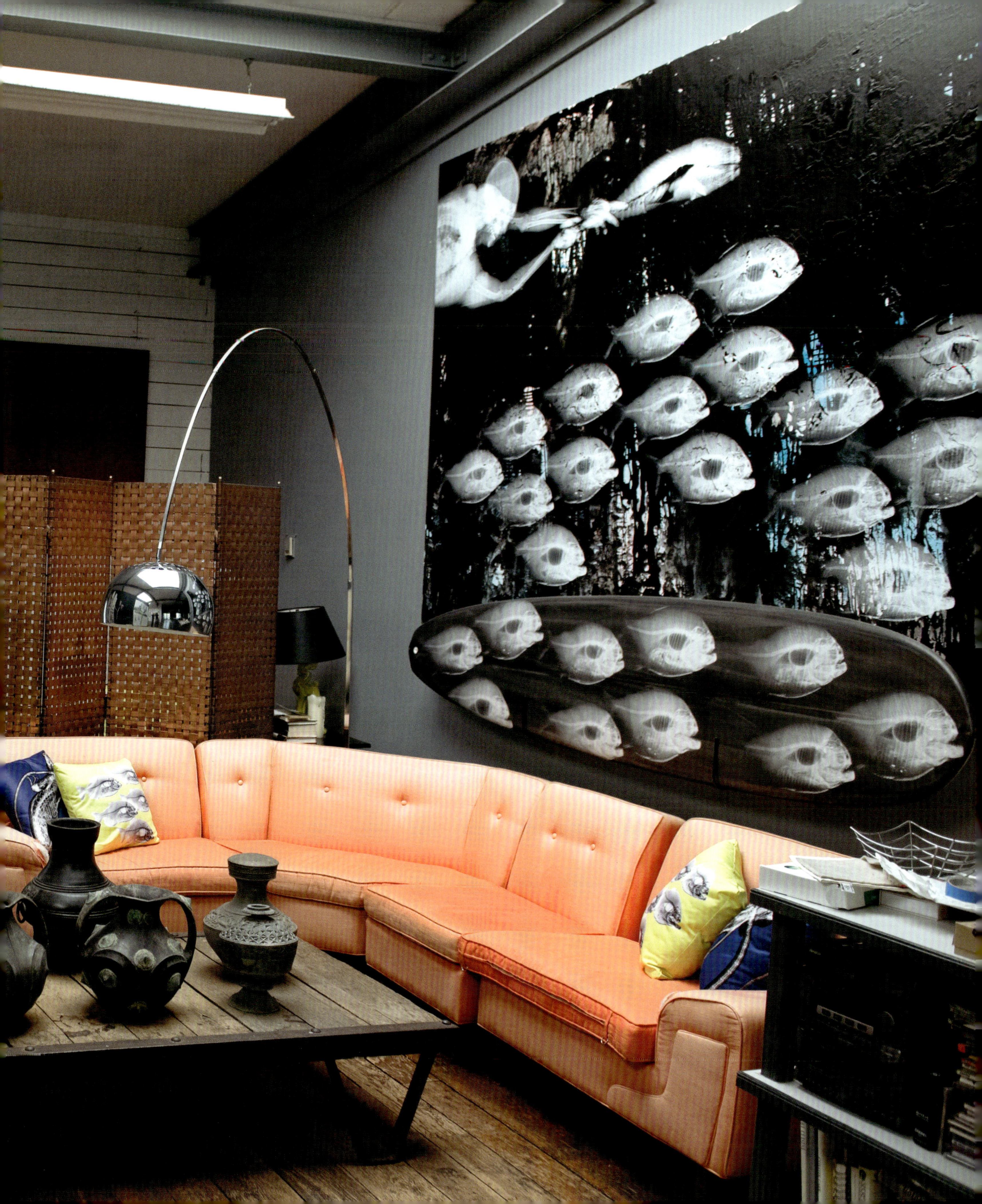

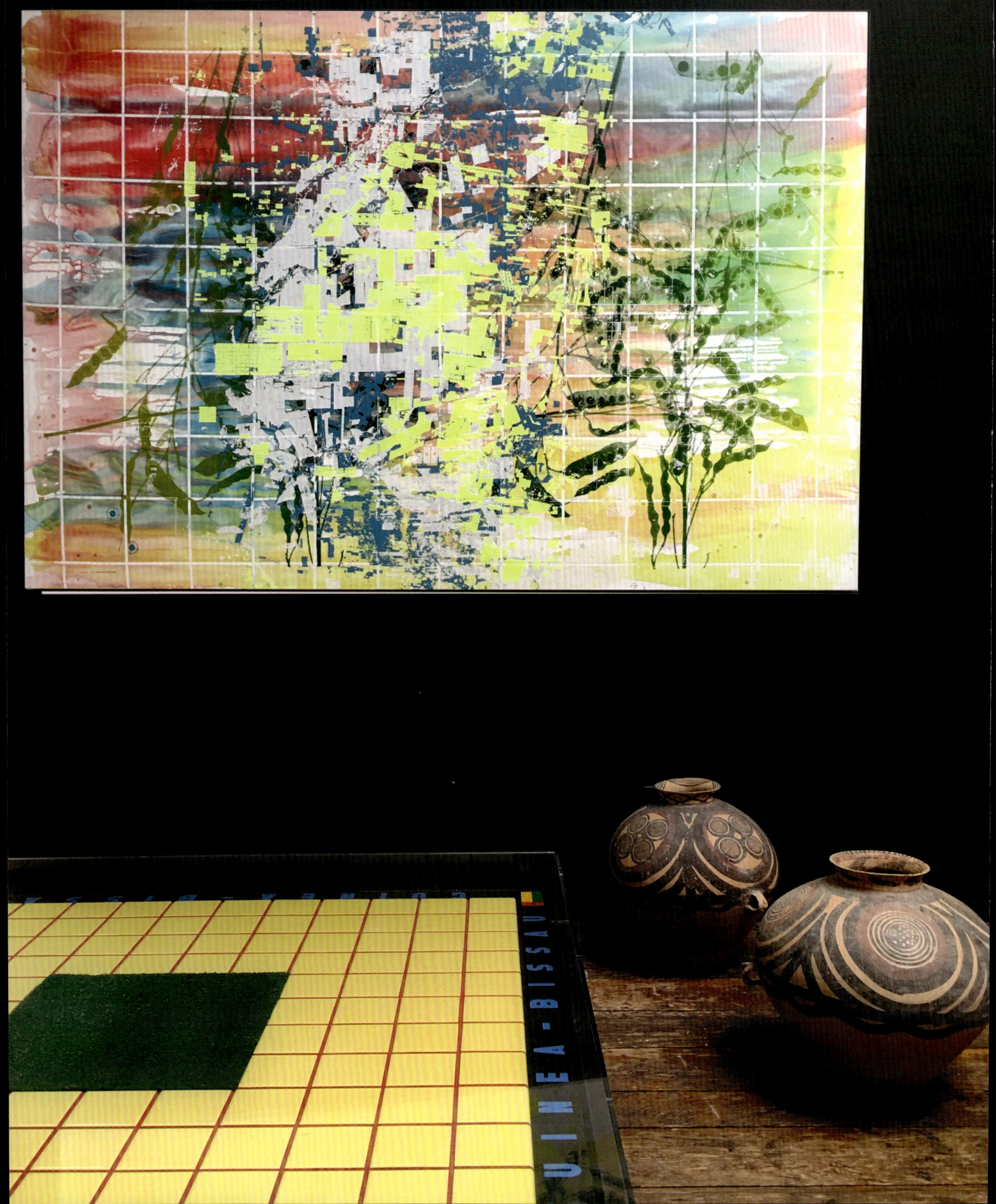

GUINEA-BISSAU

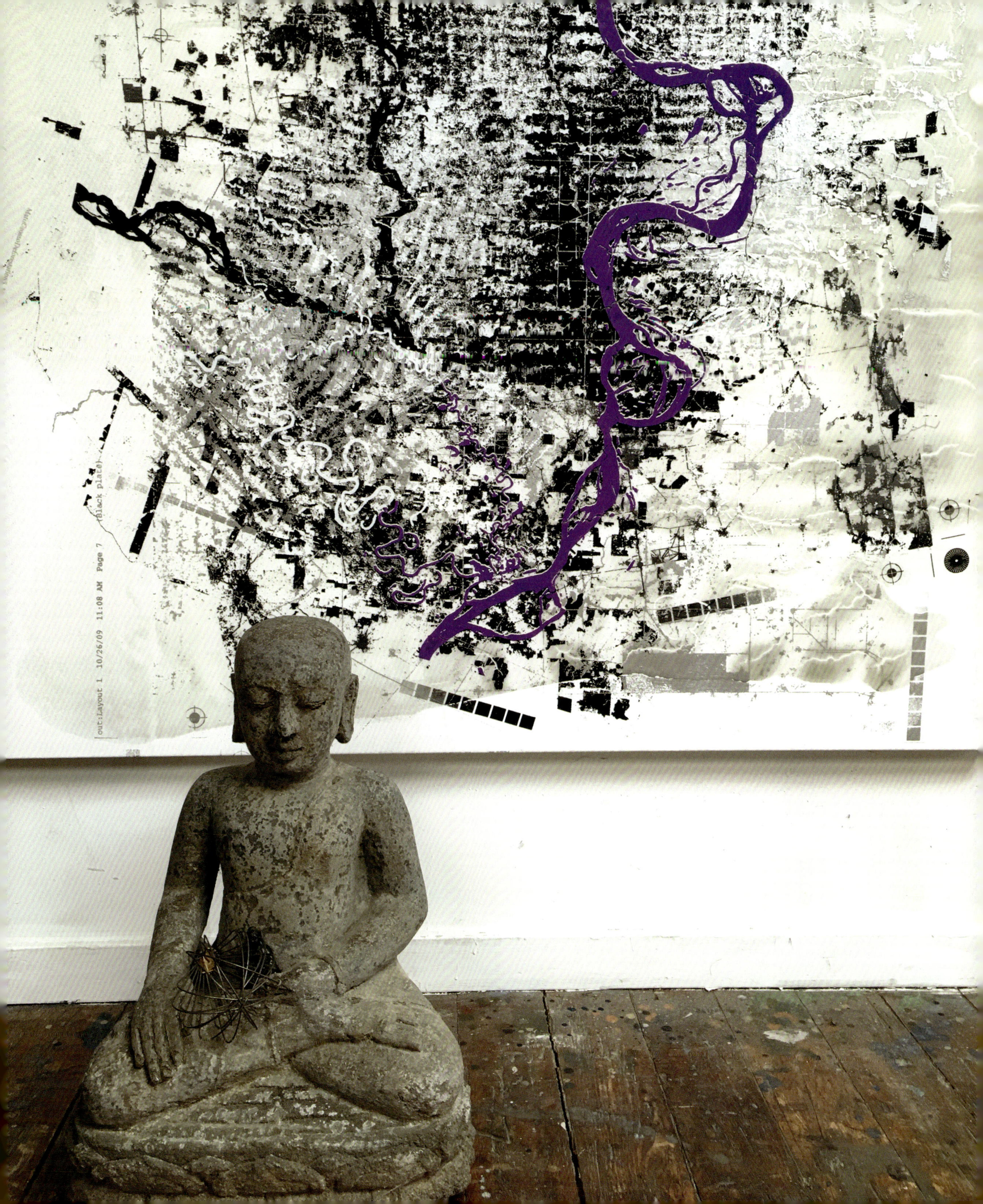
out:Layout 1 10/26/09 11:08 AM Page 7
(Black plate)

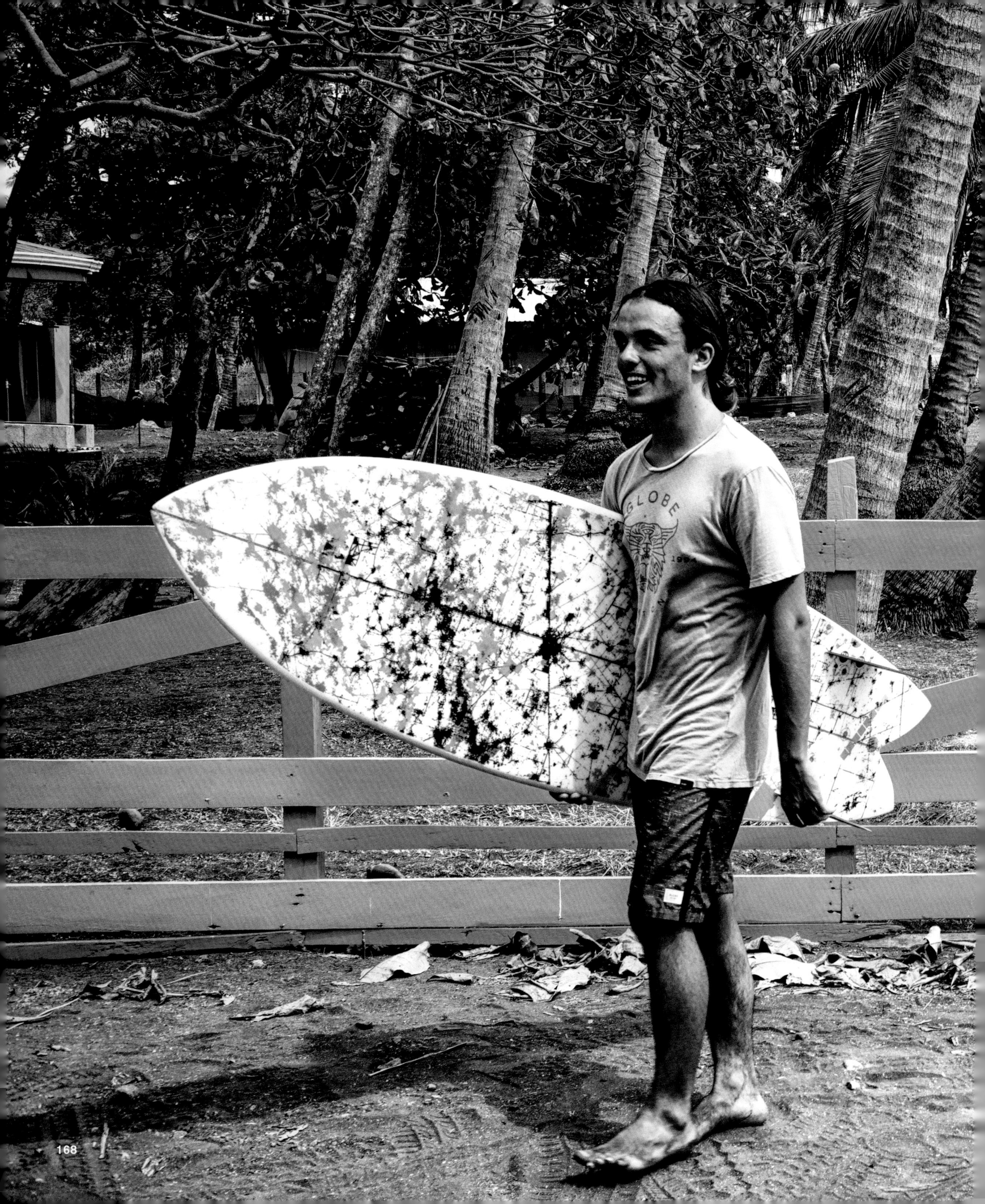

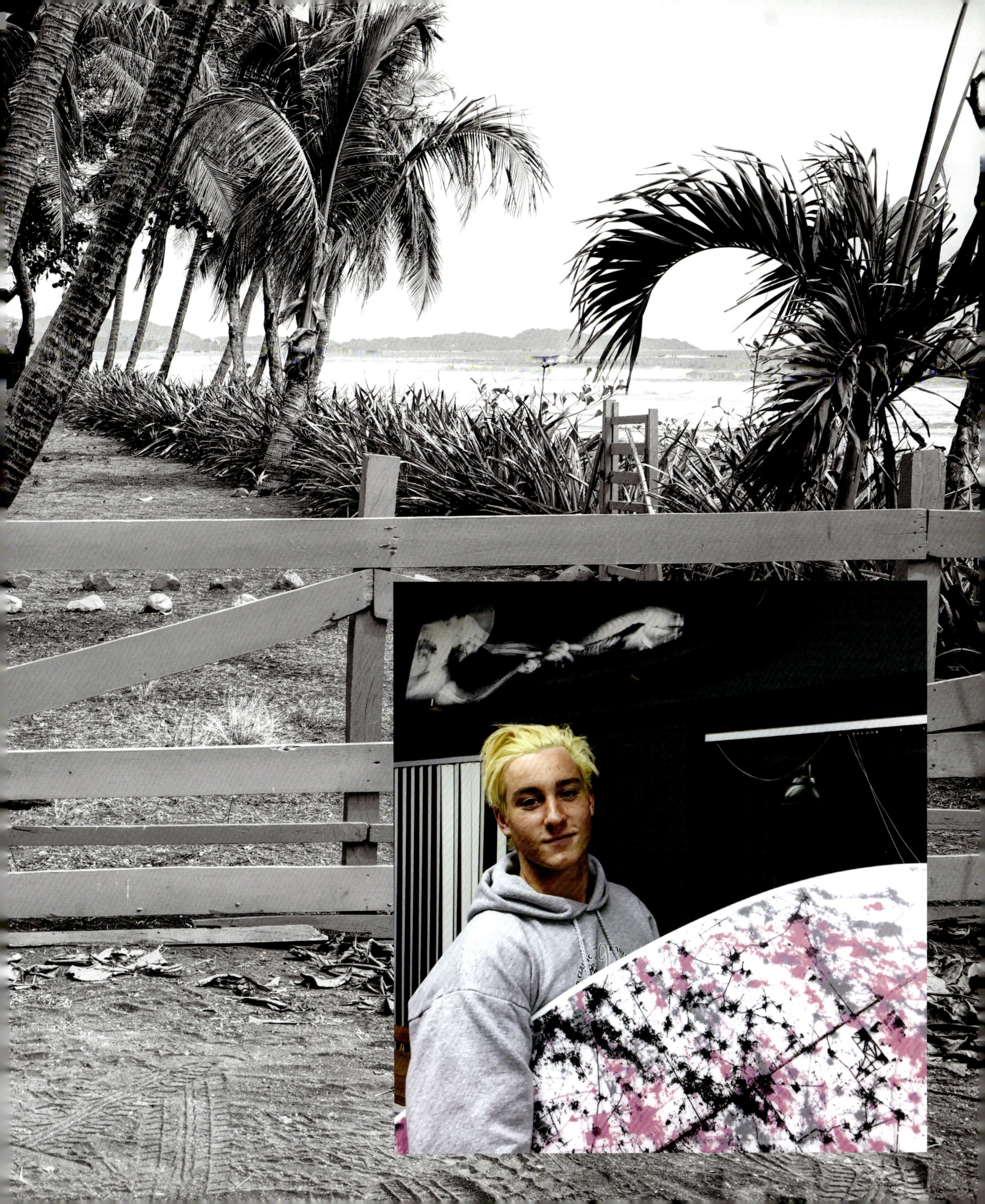

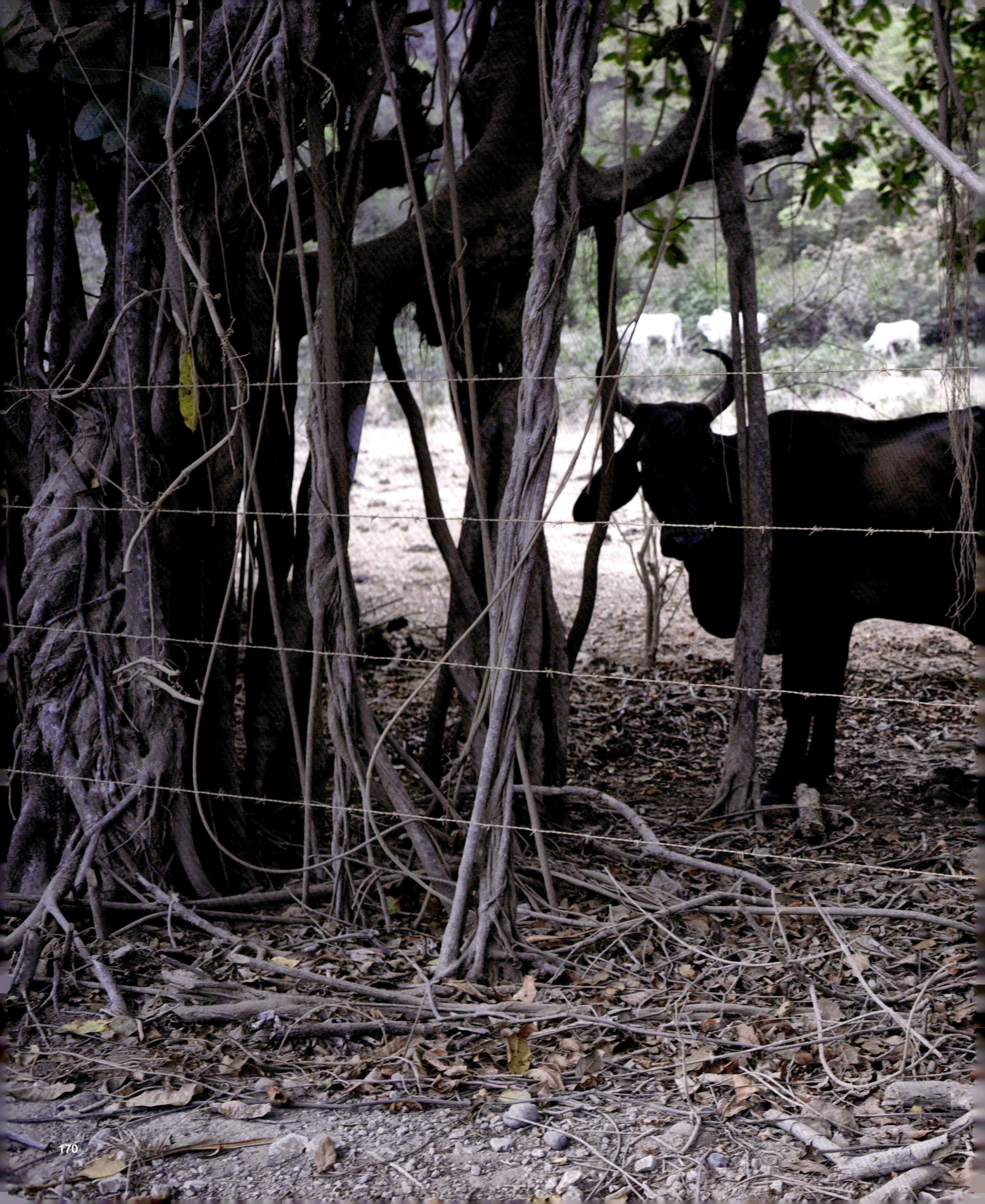

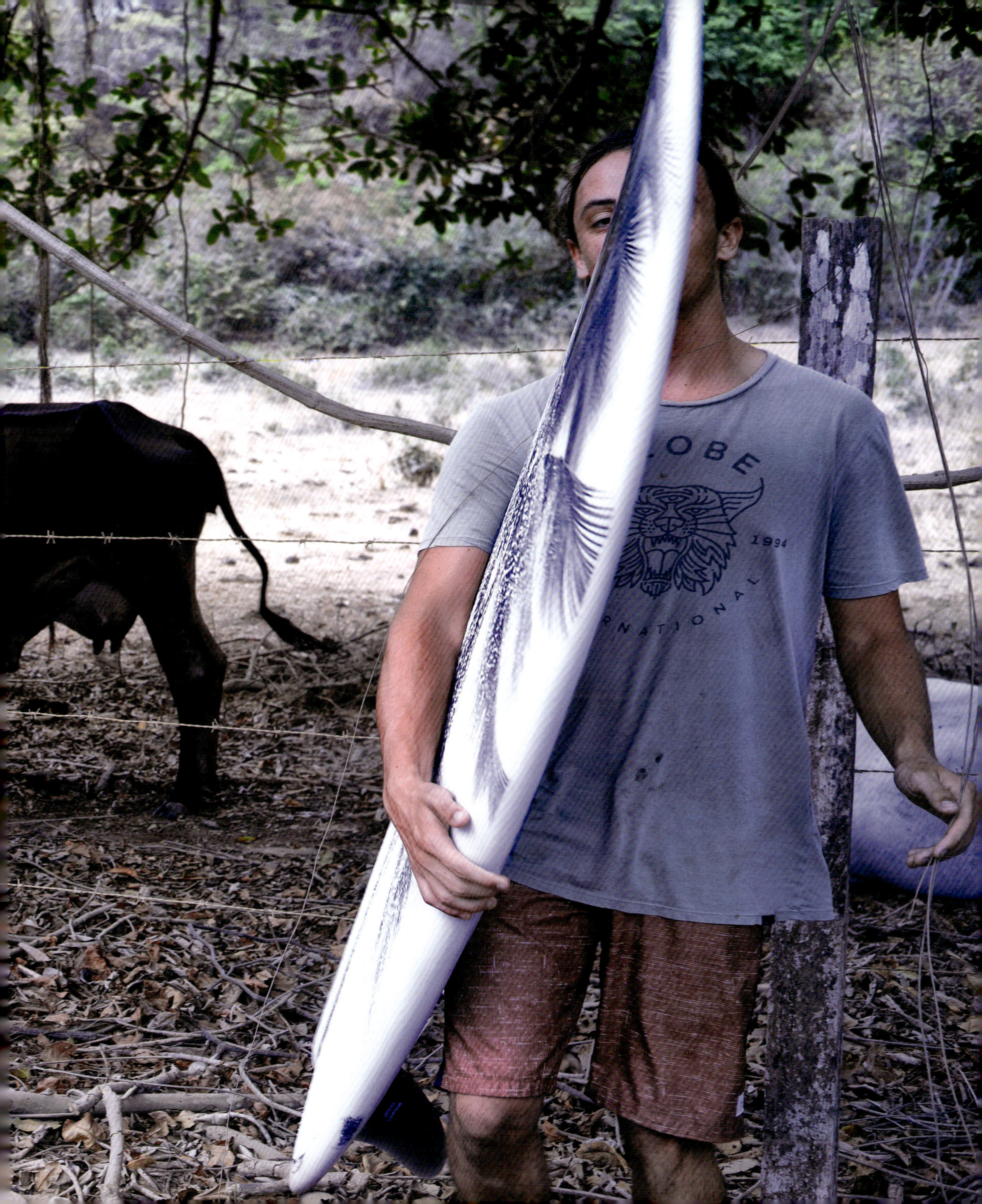

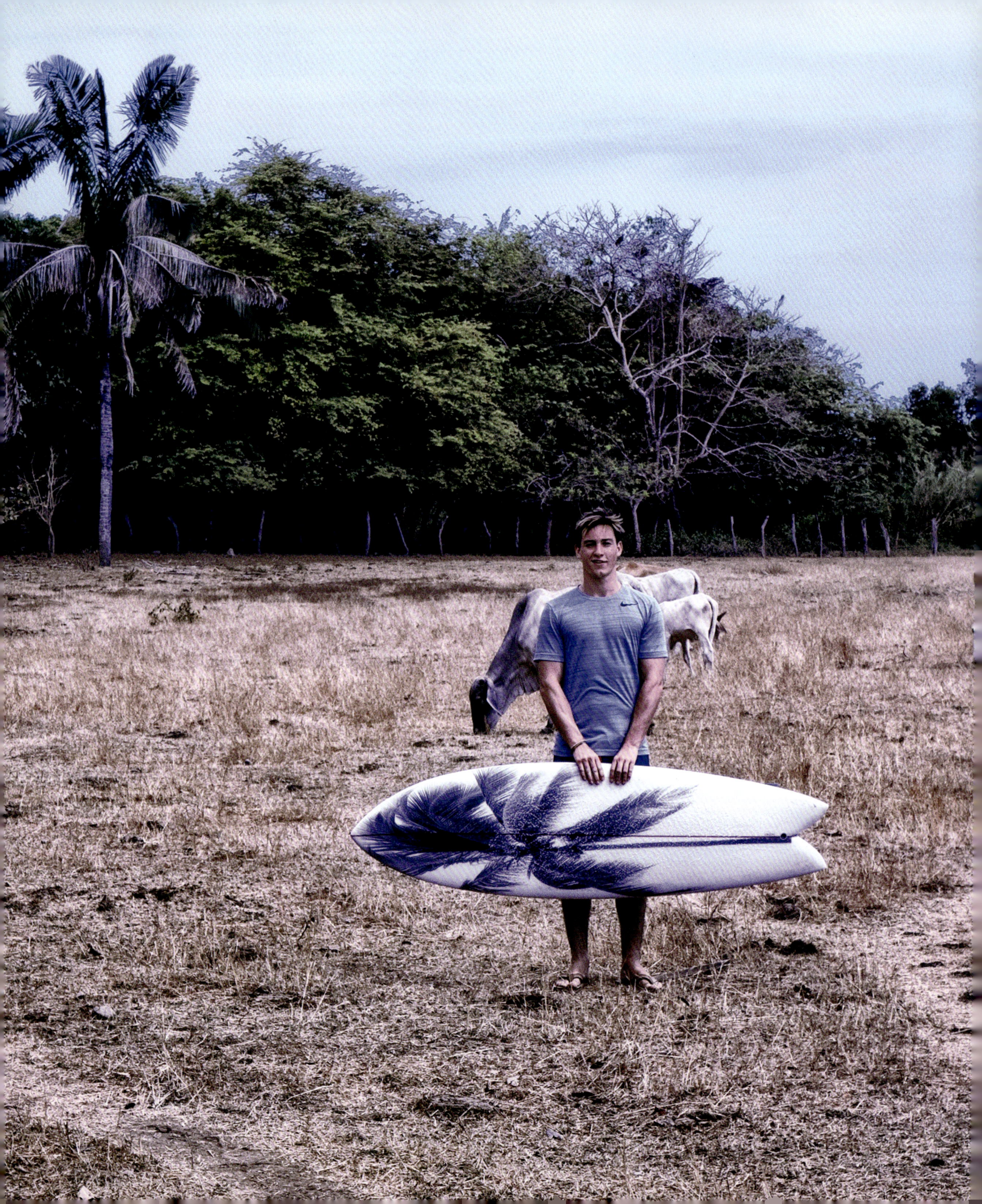

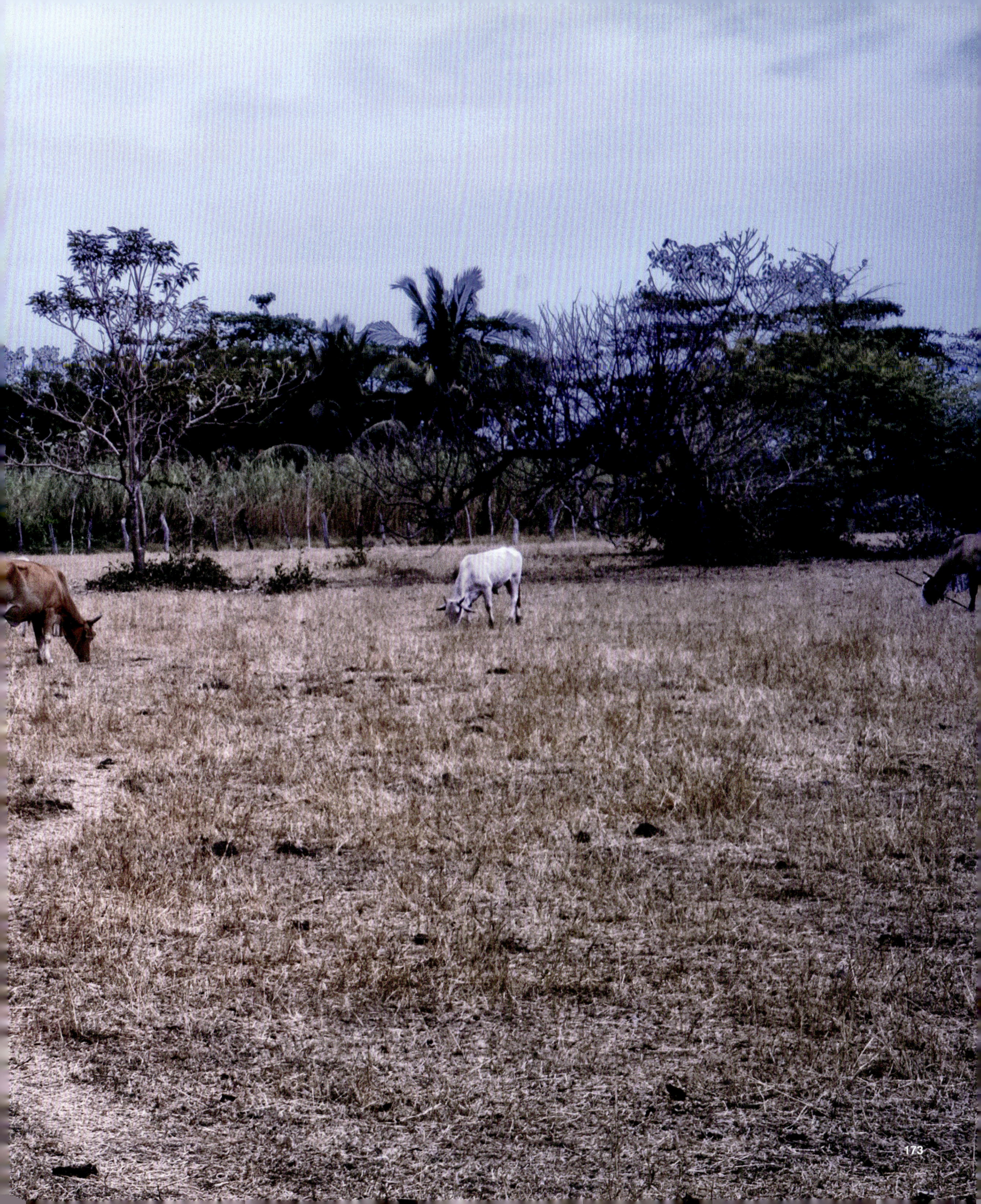

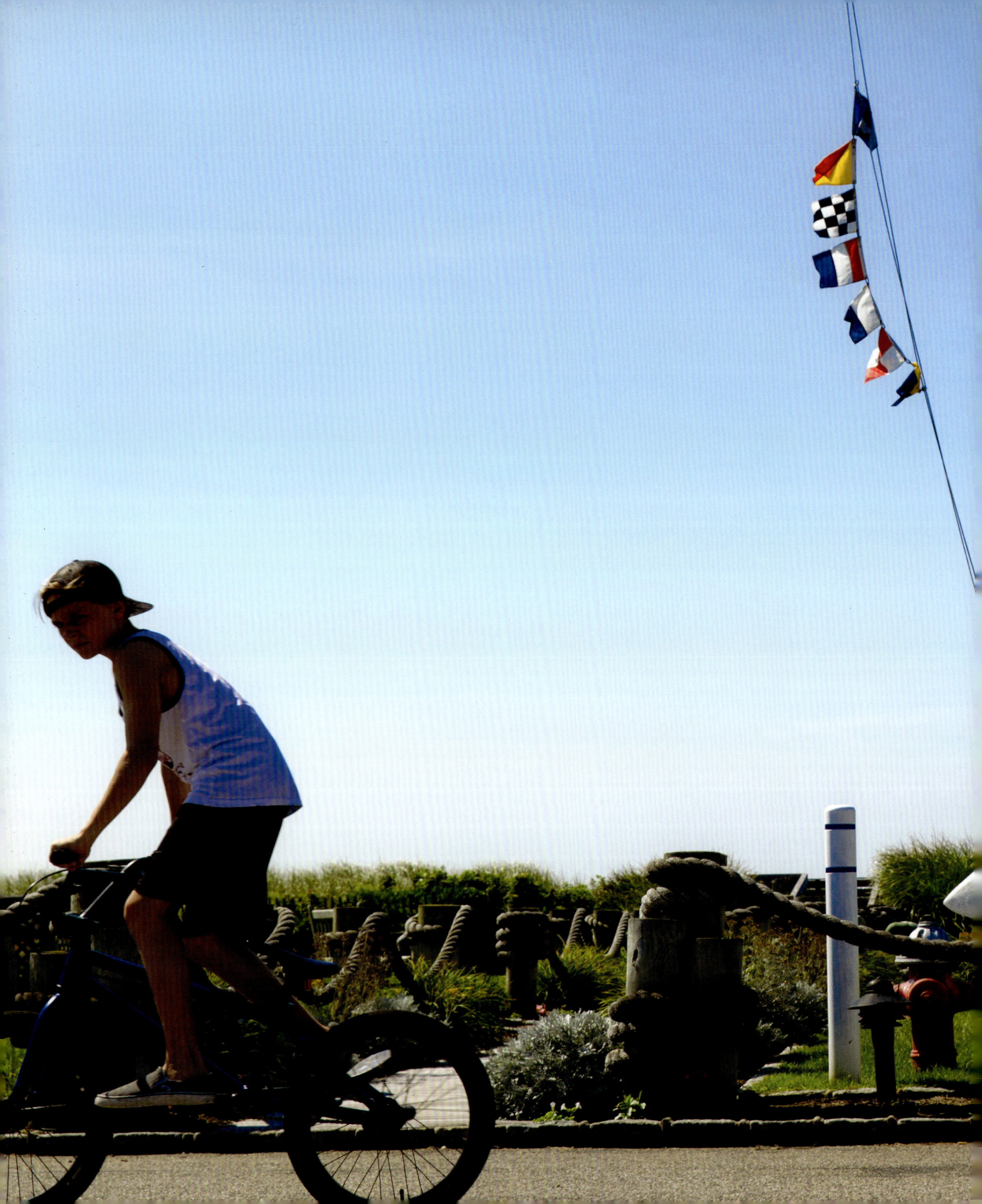

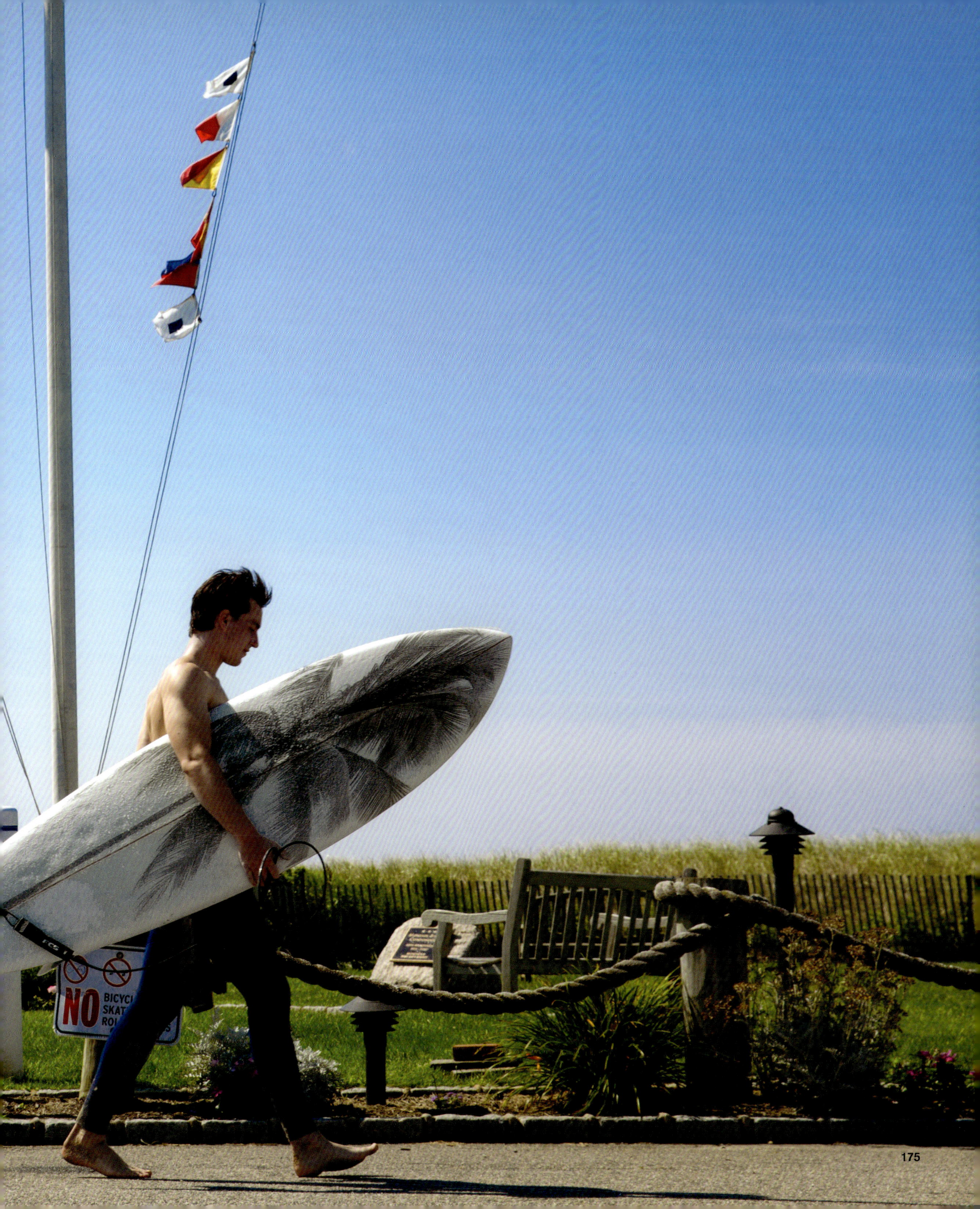

NO BICYCL
SKAT
ROL

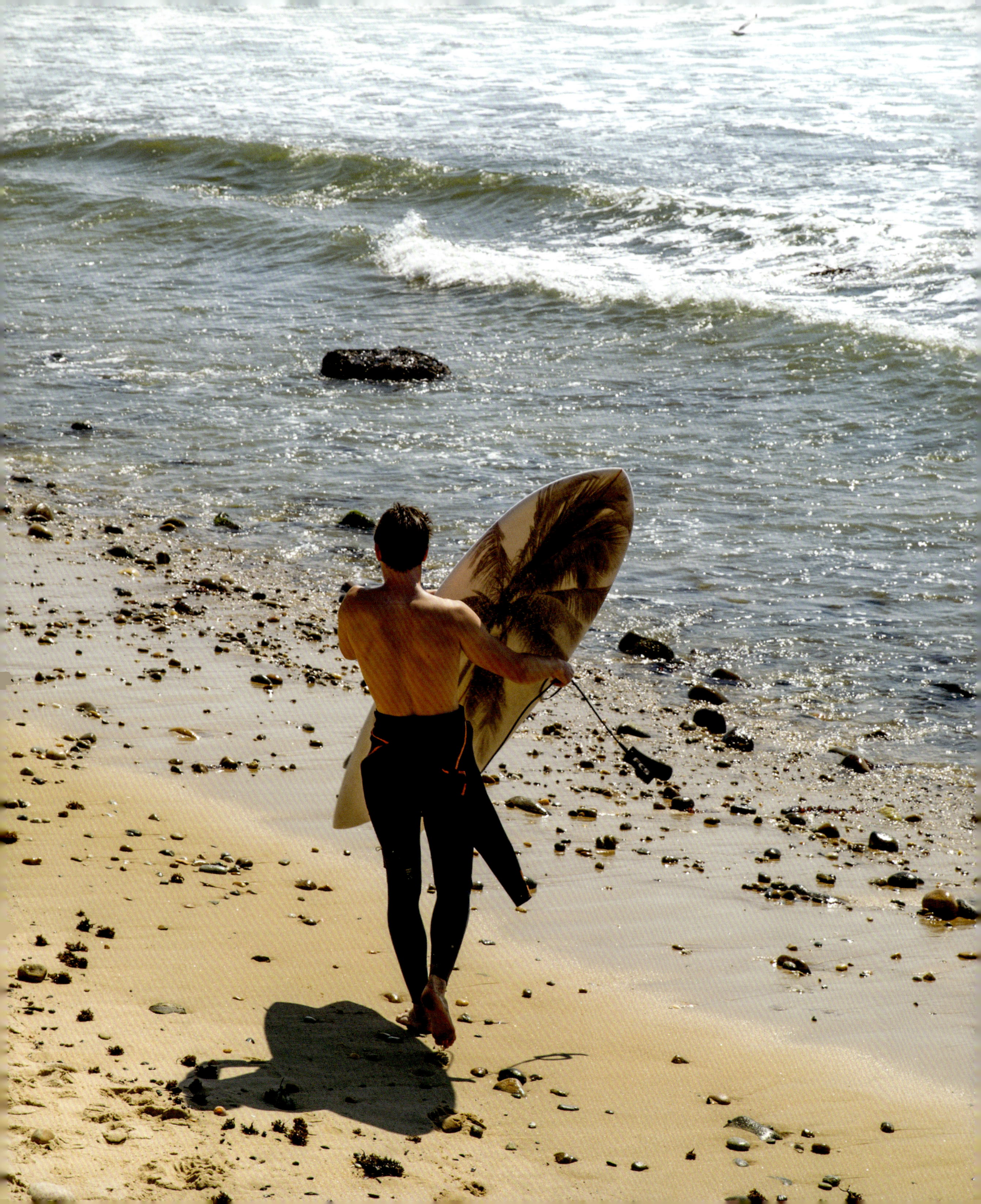

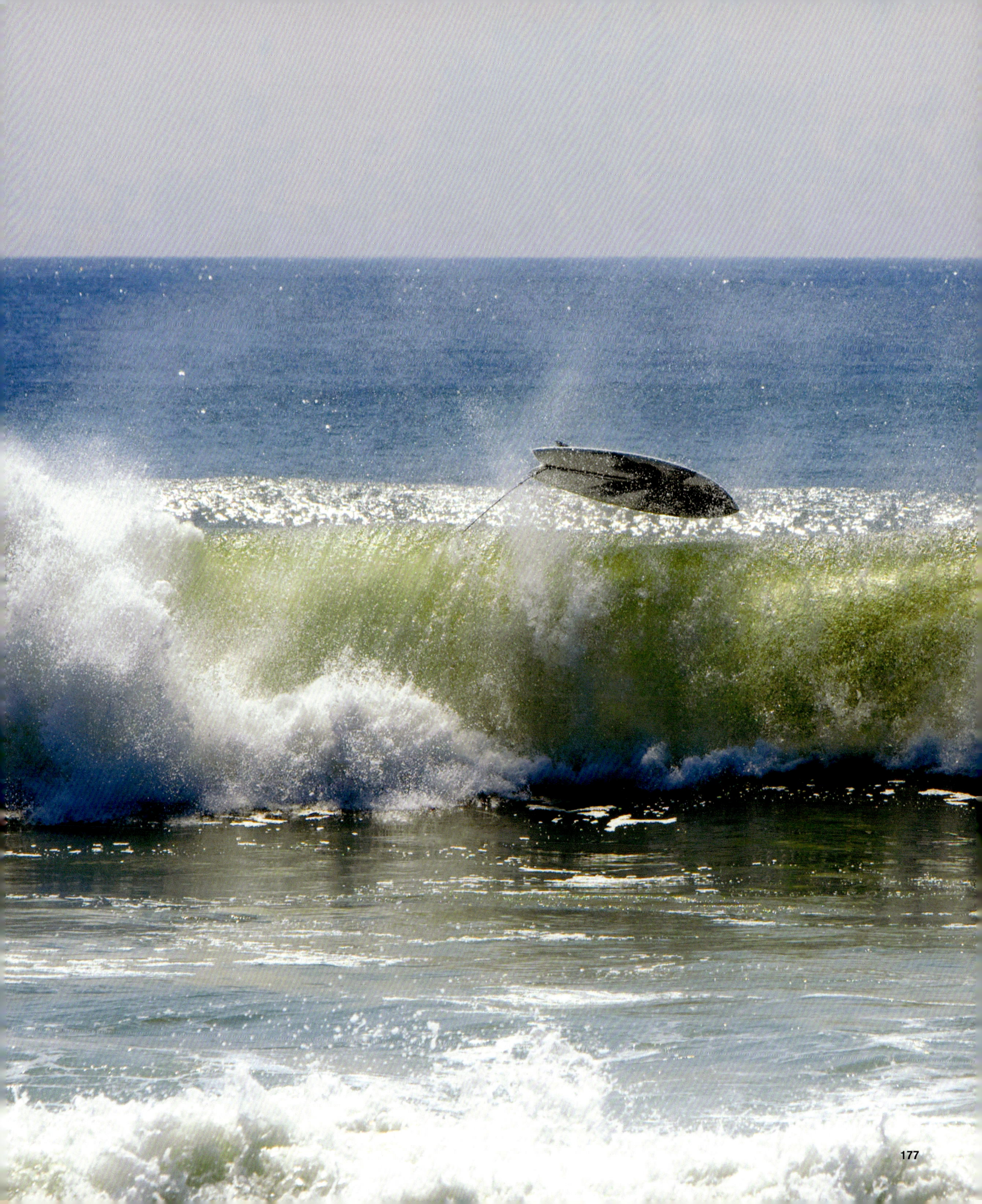

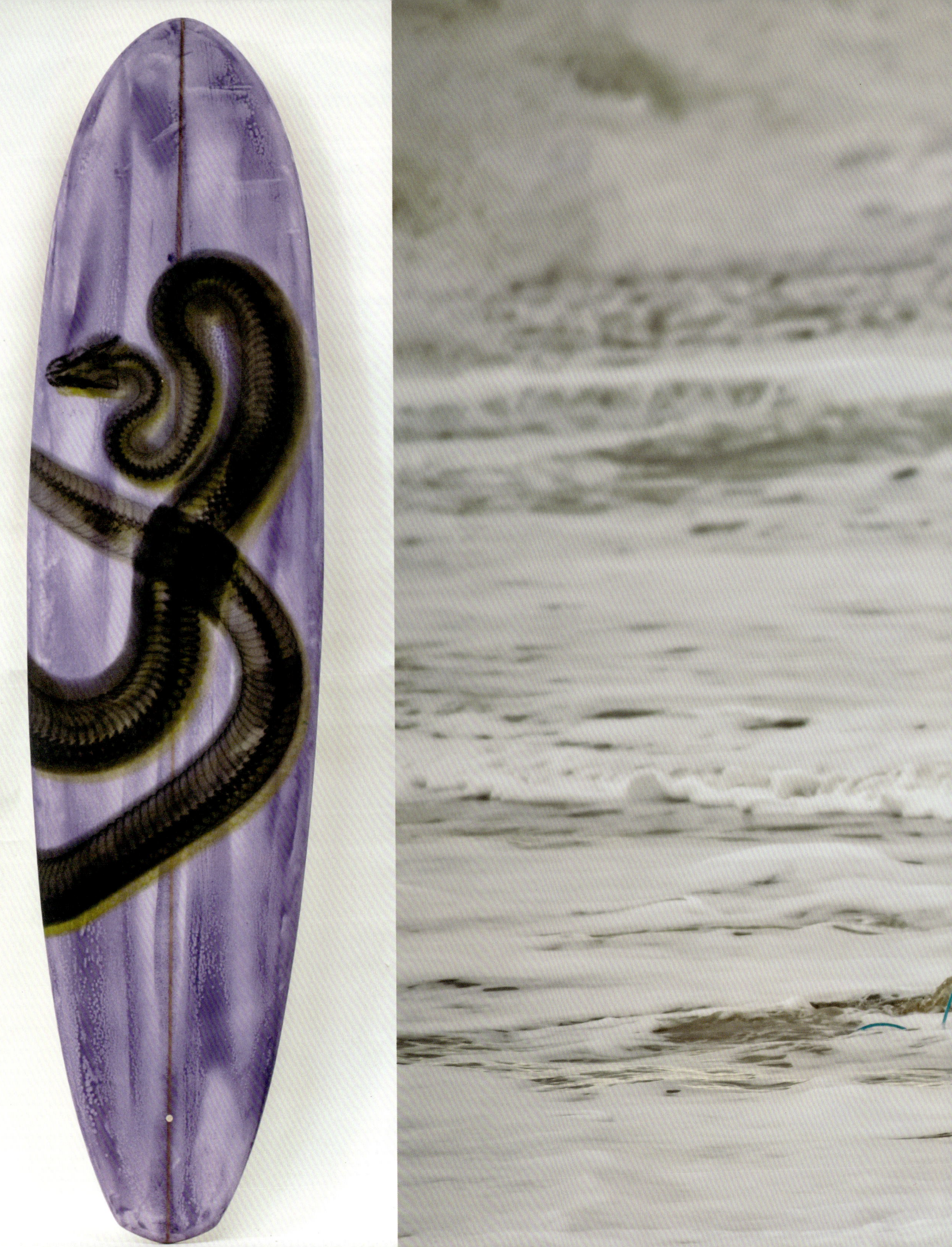

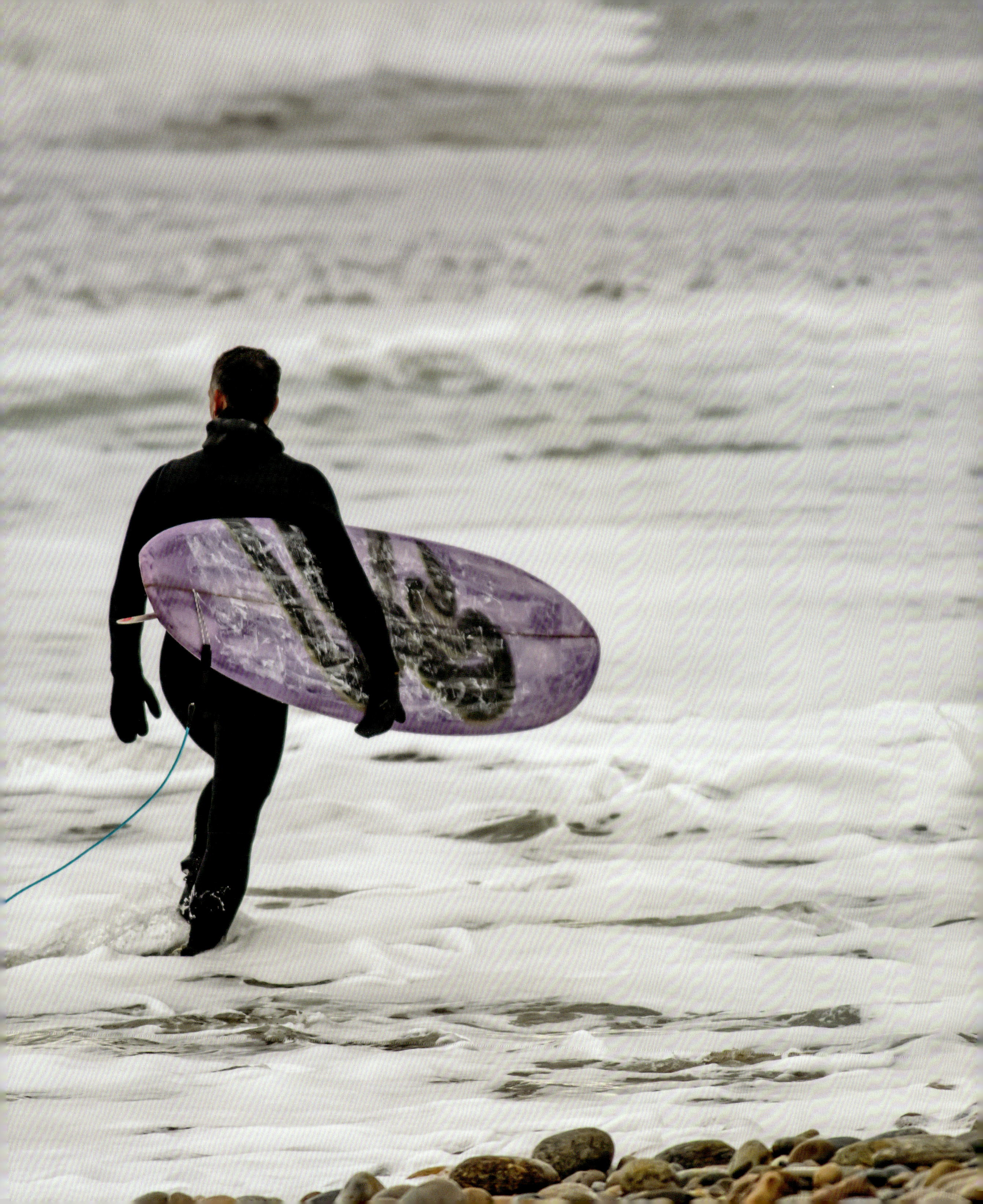

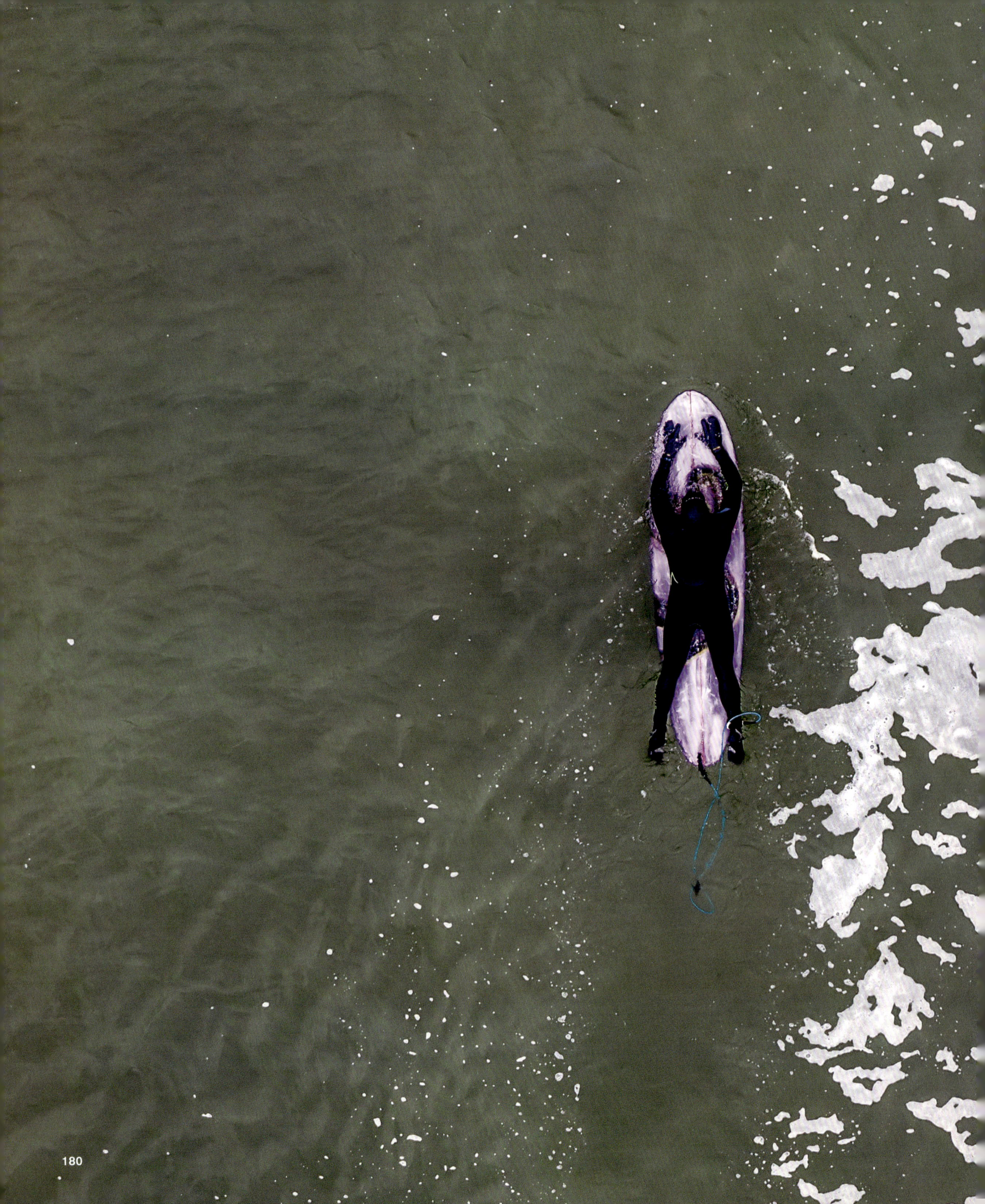

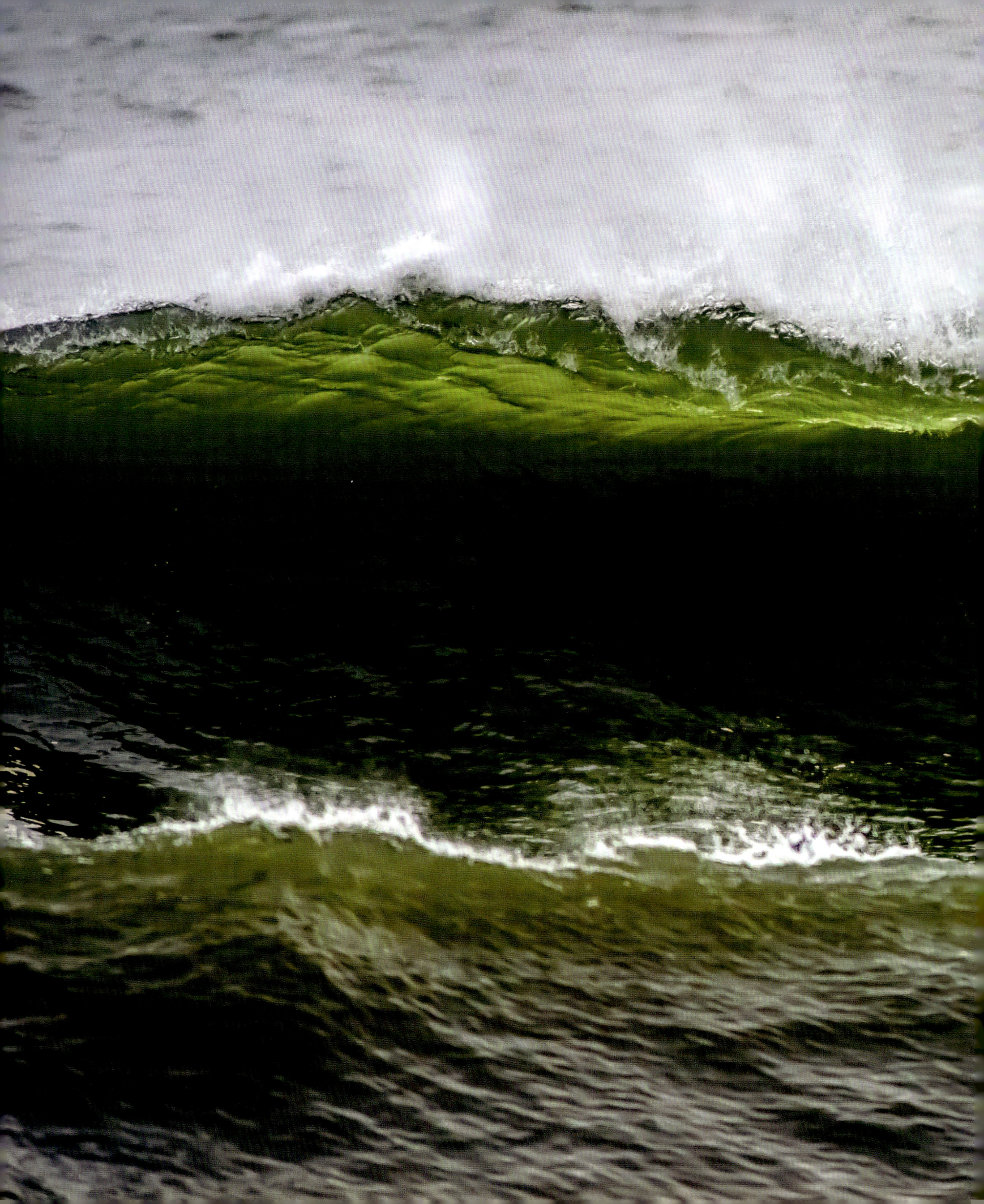

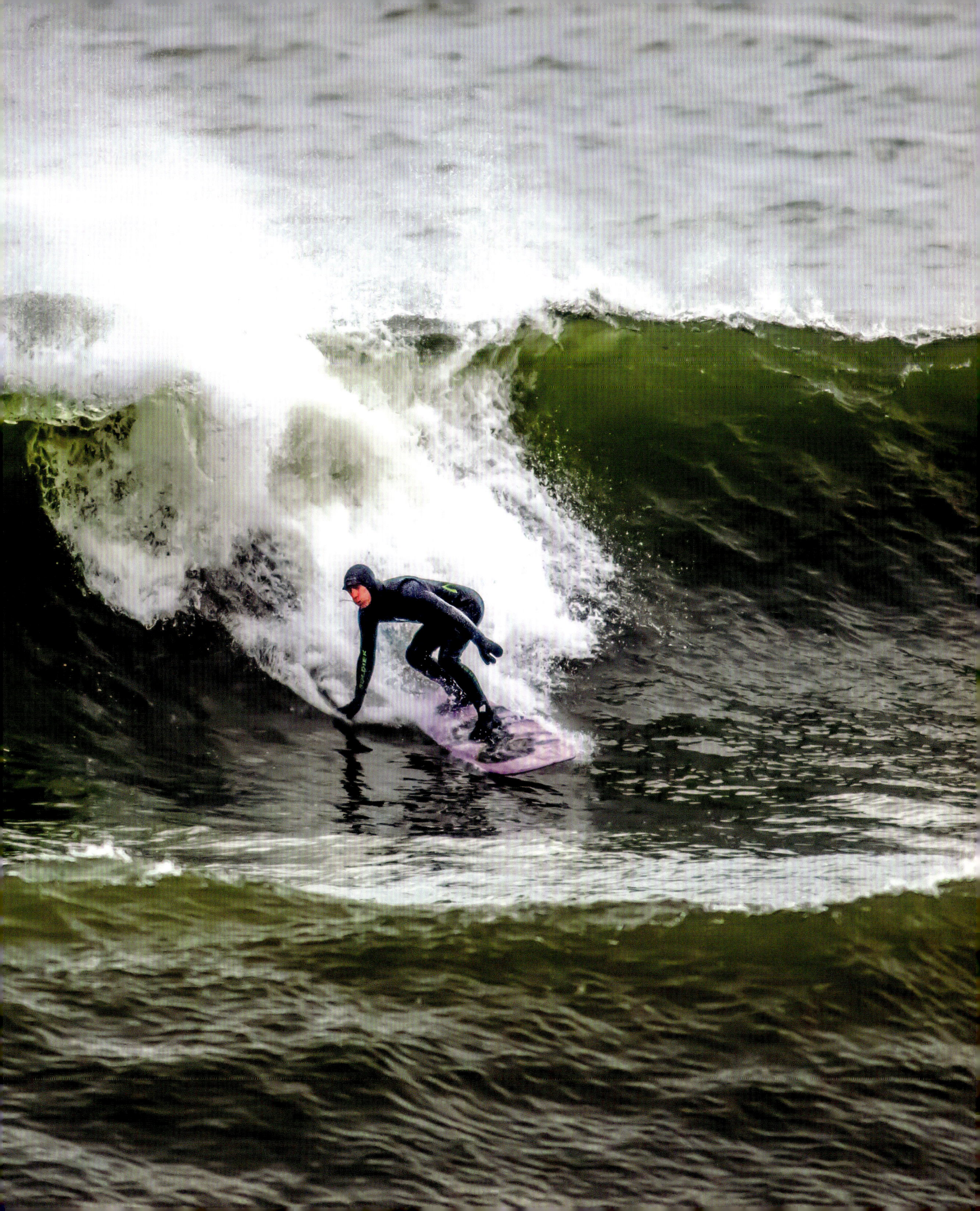

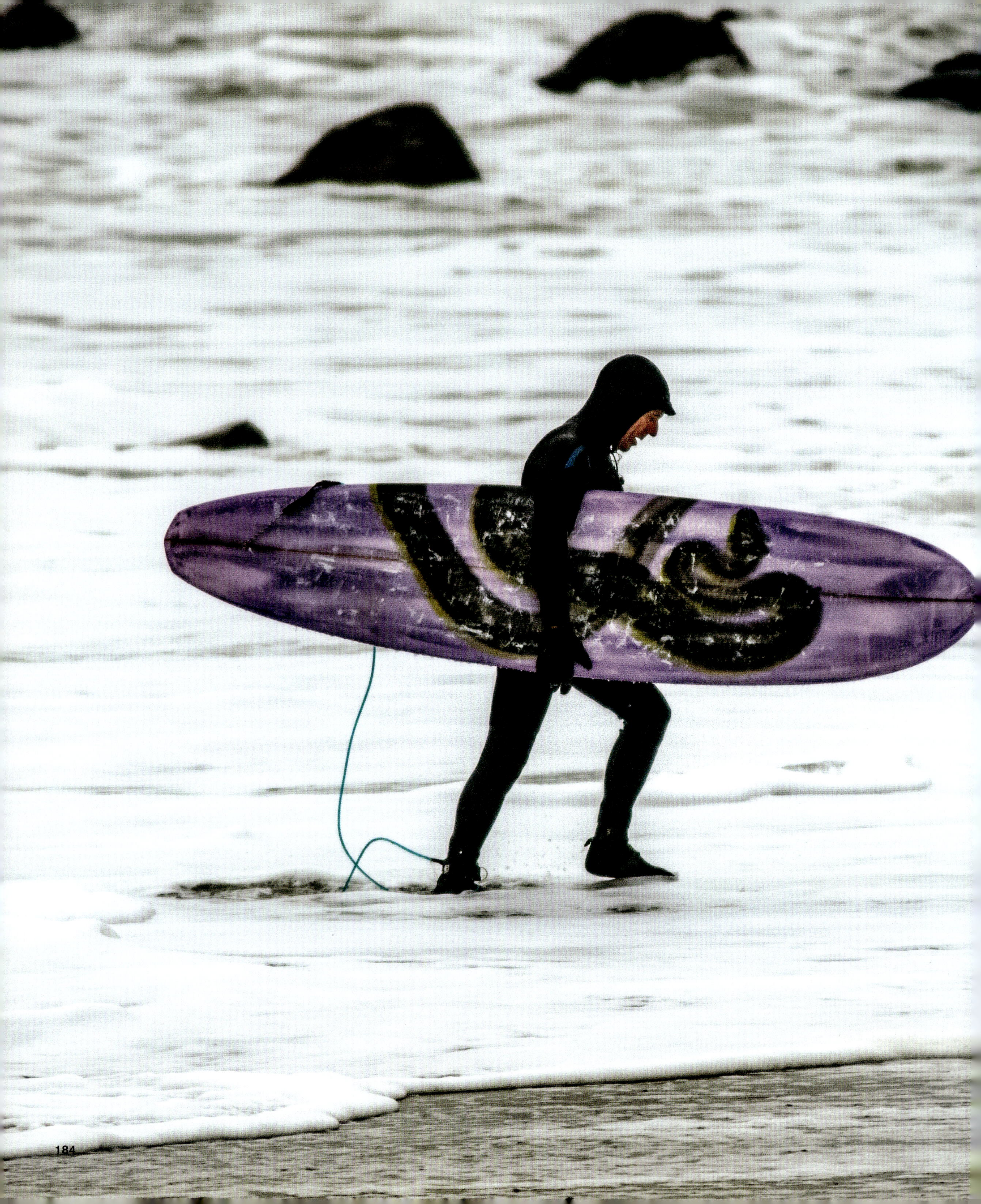

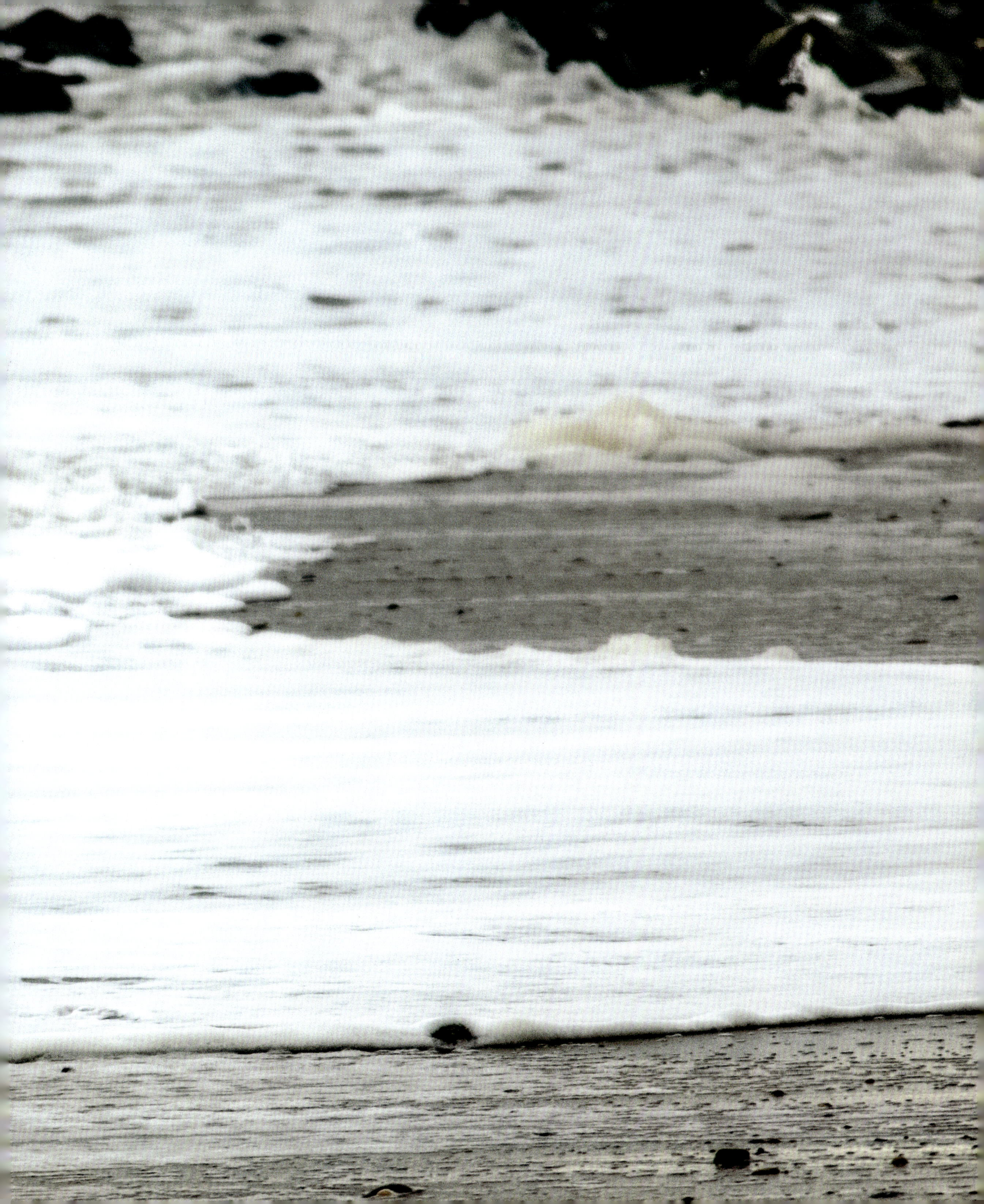

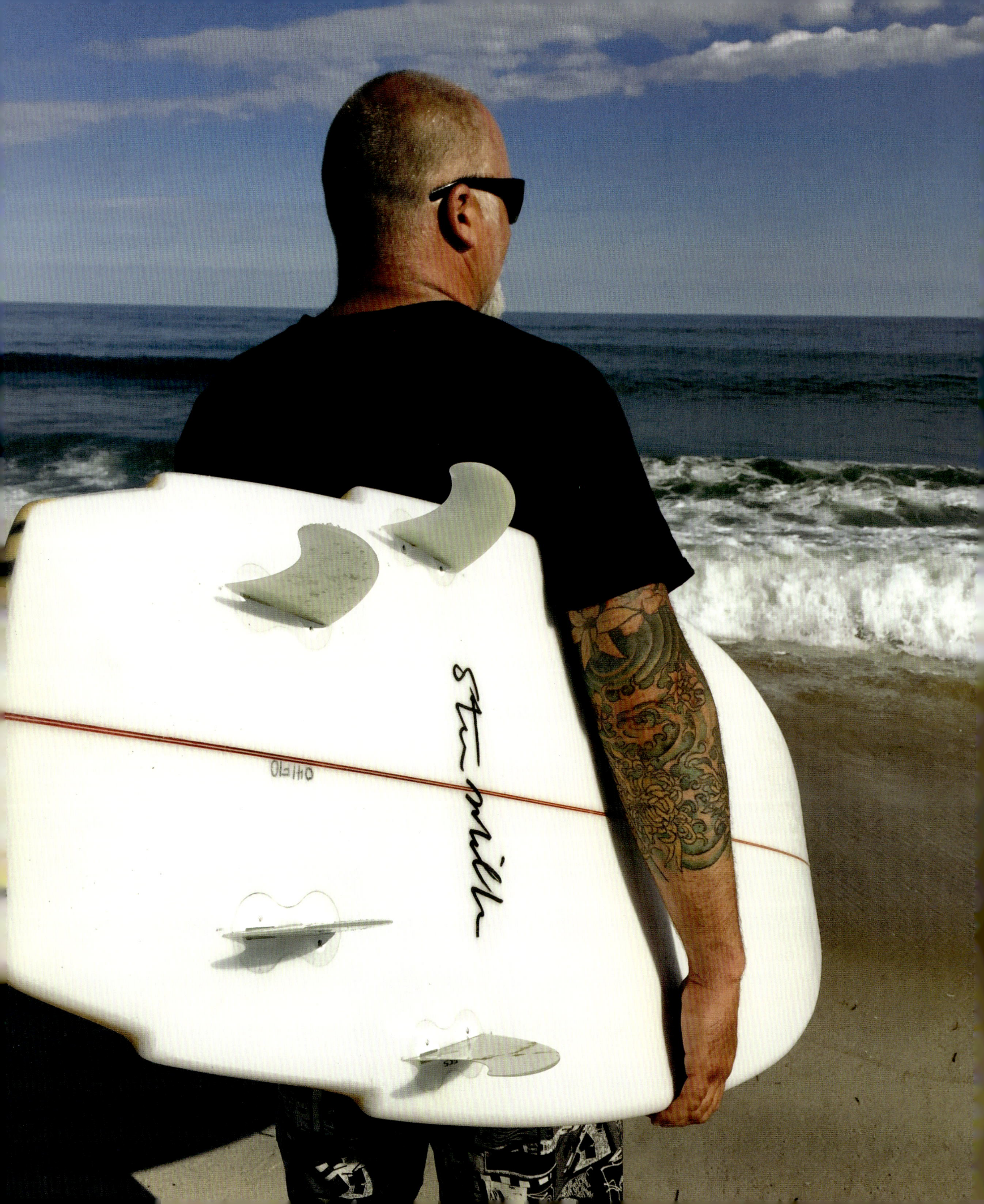

041F10

Personal Data

1951   Born in Buffalo, New York

1973   Middlebury College, Middlebury, VT

1973   Skowhegan School of Painting and Sculpture, New York, NY

Solo Exhibitions

2017   The National Academy of Sciences, Washington, DC
Second Street Gallery, Charlottesville, VA

2016   Robin Rice Gallery, New York, NY
Sara Nightingale Gallery, Watermill, NY
Bloomingdale's, New York, NY

2015   Marsiaj Tempo Galeria, Rio de Janeiro, Brazil

2014   Long House Reserve, East Hampton, NY
Bloomingdale's, New York, NY

2013   National Academy of Sciences, Washington, DC
Arte Rio, Rio de Janeiro, Brazil
Galerie Rigassi, Bern, Switzerland
The Four Seasons Restaurant, New York, NY

2012   Harper's Books, East Hampton, NY

2011   Galeria Tempo, Rio de Janeiro, Brazil

2010   Gallery Maya, London, UK

2009   Robin Rice Gallery, New York, NY

2007   Rose Art Museum, Brandeis University, Waltham, MA

2005   Prudential Center, Bridgehampton, NY

2003   Galerie Lilian Andree, Basel, Switzerland

2002   Galerie Rigassi, Bern, Switzerland

2001   Universal Concepts Unlimited, New York, NY

2000   Universal Concepts Unlimited, New York, NY

1999   Hong Kong Arts Center, Hong Kong
Saks Fifth Avenue Project Art, Southampton, NY

1998   Sagpond Vineyards, Sagaponack, NY
Galerie Karin Sachs, Munich, Germany

1996   Centre International d'Art Visuels CARGO, Marseilles, France
Espace d'Art Yvonamor Palix, Paris, France
CAPC Musée Bordeaux, Galerie Pour la Vie, Bordeaux, France

1994   Espace Art Brenne, Brenne, France

1993   Galerie Karin Sachs, Munich, Germany
Nina Freudenheim Gallery, Buffalo, NY
Galerie AB, Paris, France

1992   Elga Wimmer Gallery, New York, NY

1991   Galerie du Génie, Paris, France

1989   Fiction/Non-Fiction Gallery, New York, NY
Carol Getz Gallery, Miami, FL

1988   Josh Baer Gallery, New York, NY
Galerie du Génie, Paris, France

1987   Josh Baer Gallery, New York, NY

1986   Jack Shainman Gallery, Washington, DC
Josh Baer Gallery, New York, NY

1985   Times Square Electronic Bill Board, New York, NY
Jack Shainman Gallery, Washington, DC
Bette Stoler Gallery, New York, NY

1982   Artist's Space, New York, NY

1981   White Columns, New York, NY

Selected Group Exhibitions

2018   "Not Nature," Madoo Conservancy, Sagaponack, NY
"Midnight Oil," RE Steele Antiques, East Hampton, NY
"EARTH," Lafontaine Contemporary Art, London, UK
"Summertime Salon 2018," Robin Rice Gallery, New York, NY
"Ten Years In," Burchfield Penney Art Center, Buffalo, NY
"Spring Exhibition," Robin Rice Gallery at Beacon Open Studios, Beacon, NY
"*STRATUM*," Cross MacKenzie Gallery, Washington, DC

2017   "Black and White," Nina Freudenheim Gallery, Buffalo, NY
"Summertime Salon 2017," Robin Rice Gallery, New York, NY
"Opening Exhibition," Sara Nightingale Gallery, Sag Harbor, NY

2016   "Water Bodies," Southampton Arts Center, Southampton, NY
"Neo-Psychedelia," Melissa Morgan Fine Art, Palm Desert, CA
"Summertime Salon 2016," Robin Rice Gallery, New York, NY

2015   "Revealing the Parallel: Indian Tantric Painting," Lazypoint Gallery, Amagansett, NY
"Summertime Salon 2015," Robin Rice Gallery, New York, NY
"Entitled," Sara Nightingale Gallery, Sag Harbor, NY

2014   "Summertime Salon 2014," Robin Rice Gallery, New York, NY
"The Irrational Portrait Gallery," Southampton Arts Center, Southampton, NY
"Under the Influence," Sag Harbor Whaling Museum, Sag Harbor, NY
"Armadillo: Soccer, Adversity and the Culture of the Caatinga," Museu de Arte do Rio, Rio de Janeiro, Brazil
"Objectif Arbres," Sotheby's Paris, Paris, France
"Slide," Museu de Arte do Rio, Rio de Janeiro, Brazil

2013   "Machinarium," Oi Futuro, Ipanema, Brazil
"Art Rio 13," Galeria Tempo, Rio de Janeiro, Brazil
"Summertime Salon 2013," Robin Rice Gallery, New York, NY
"Trees in Focus: Anne Fountain Foundation," Sotheby's, New York, NY

2012   "World Cup," MARCO, Monterrey, Mexico
"Bad For You," Shirazu Gallery, London, UK
"Dreams," Galerie Rigassi, Bern, Switzerland
"Group Therapy," Harper's Books, East Hampton, NY
"Open For The Stones," Harper's Books, East Hampton, NY
"Summertime Salon 2012," Robin Rice Gallery, New York, NY

2011   "50th Anniversary Exhibition," Rose Art Museum, Waltham, MA

2010   "Arquivo Geral," Centro de Arte Hélio Oiticica, Rio de Janeiro, Brazil
"Exposição Fotografias," Galeria Mercedes Viegas, Rio de Janeiro, Brazil

"Art/Science Exhibition," Schneider Museum of Art, Ashland, OR

"Summer Time Salon 2010," Robin Rice Gallery, New York, NY

"Group Exhibition," Glenn Horowitz Bookseller, East Hampton, NY

"Moxie and Mayhem: Acquisitions for a New Museum," Burchfield Penney Art Center, Buffalo, NY

"Group Exhibition," Nina Freudenheim Gallery, Buffalo, NY

2009 "Octet," Pera Museum, Istanbul, Turkey

"Deviant Specimens: Amanda Means, Steve Miller and Gary Schnyder," Howard Yezerski Gallery, Boston, MA

"Octet: Codes and Contexts in Recent Art," School of Visual Arts Gallery, New York, NY

"Summertime Salon 2009," Robin Rice Gallery, New York, NY

2008 "10th International Digital Print Exhibition," New York Hall of Science, New York, NY

"I Dream of Genomes," Islip Art Museum, Islip, NY

"Container Exhibition," Long House Reserve, East Hampton, NY

"Summer Time 2008," Robin Rice Gallery, New York, NY

2007 "Coletiva 2007," Mercedes Viegas Arte Contemporanea, Rio de Janeiro, Brazil

"Brasil Des Focus: o olho de fors," Centro Cultural Banco do Brasil, Rio de Janeiro, Brazil

"Summer Time 2007," Robin Rice Gallery, New York, NY

"Small Work," Nina Freudenheim Gallery, Buffalo, NY

2006 "Presentation D'ICONOfly," Christie's, Paris, France

"A Delicate Balance," General Electric Company Headquarters, Fairfield, CT

"Luxury Goods," Kathleen Cullen Fine Arts, New York, NY

"SUMMERTIME," Robin Rice Gallery, New York, NY

"Neuroculture: Visual Art and the Brain," Westport Art Center, Westport, CT

2005 "Finders Keepers," Parrish Art Museum, Southampton, NY

"Abstraction," Burchfield Penney Art Center, Buffalo, NY

"Jameson Ellis and Steve Miller," Peter Marcelle Gallery, Southampton, NY

"Colecoes IV," Galería Luisa Strina, São Paulo, Brazil

"Le Cas du Sac," Musée de la Mode et du Textile, Paris, France

"Collection 2," Foundation Art Contemporain Claudine et Jean-Marc Salomon, Annecy, France

2004 "Colecoes IV," Mercedes Viegas Arte Contemporanea, Rio de Janeiro, Brazil

"Reprotech: Building Better Babies," New York Academy of Sciences, New York, NY

"Touch and Temperature: Art in the Age of Cybernetic Totalism," Deborah Colton Gallery, Houston, TX

"Touch and Temperature: Art in the Age of Cybernetic Totalism," Bitforms Gallery, New York, NY

2003 "Divining Fragments: Reconciling the Body," Center for Photography, Woodstock, NY

"From Code to Commodity: Genetics & Visual Art," New York Academy of Sciences, New York, NY

"Genomic Issue(s): Art and Science," The Graduate Center of the City University of New York, New York, NY

2002 "25th Anniversary Exhibition," The Drawing Center, New York, NY

"Dialogue Between Science & Art", Cultural Center Metropol, Ceské Budejoice, Czech Republic

2001 "Mondial," Le Grimaldi Forum, Monaco

"Digital Printmaking Now," Brooklyn Museum of Art, New York, NY

"The Collector," Universal Concepts Unlimited, New York, NY

"Paradise Now: Picturing the Genetic Revolution," Tang Museum, Saratoga Springs, NY

"Paradise Now: Picturing the Genetic Revolution," University of Michigan Museum of Art, Ann Arbor, MI

"Paradise Now: Picturing the Genetic Revolution," Exit Art, New York, NY

"Foreign Bodies, an intersection between art and medicine," Untitled (Space), New Haven, CT

"Remote Experience Dependency," Universal Concepts Unlimited, New York, NY

"13 Alumni Artists," Middlebury College Museum of Art, Middlebury, VT

"Medicine in Art," College of the Mainland Art Gallery, Texas City, TX

"Rounders," Universal Concepts Unlimited, New York, NY

"CYBERARTS 2000," Prix Ars Electronica, Linz, Austria

1999 "DREAMS 1900-2000," Equitable Art Gallery, New York, NY

"Shoes, Shoes, Shoes," TZ'Art, New York, NY

"100 Years an Arts Community," Fine Arts Work Center, Provincetown, MA

1998 "Out of Portrait," Espace d'Art Yvonamor Palix, Paris, France

"Autour du Mondial," Galerie Enrico Navarra, Paris, France

1997 "Sous le Manteau," Galerie Thaddaeus Ropac, Paris, France

"Autour de Roger Vivier," Agnes b., Tokyo, Japan

1996 "Autour de Roger Vivier," China Club, Hong Kong

"5th Year Celebration," Elga Wimmer Gallery, New York, NY

"Steve Miller and Joseph Nechvatal," Parsons Gallery, Paris, France

1995 "Morceau Choisis, du Fonds National d'Art Contemporain," Centre National d'Art Contemporain de Grenoble, Grenoble, France

"Imaging the Body, an Artistic Diagnosis," New York Academy of Sciences, New York, NY

"Autour de Roger Vivier," Galerie Enrico Navarra, Paris, France

"In Corpus Machina, Keith Cottingham, Steve Miller, Joseph Nechvatal," Espace d'Art Yvonamor Palix, Paris, France

"The Portrait Now," Elga Wimmer Gallery, New York, NY

"Humanism and Technology: The Human Figure in Industrial Society," National Museum of Contemporary Art, Seoul, Korea

"The Outside Inside Gertrude Stein," Dortmunder Kunstverein, Dortmund, Germany

1994 "Gene Culture," Fordham College, New York, NY

"Logo non Logo," Threadwaxing Space, New York, NY

"Les Americains: 50 Annees de Peinture Americaine 1944-1994," Fécamp, France

"Mauvaises Nouvelles De Chine," Galerie Philippe Gravier, Paris, France

"Inaugural Exhibition," Offshore Gallery, East Hampton, NY

"The Outside Inside Gertrude Stein," Elga Wimmer Gallery,
New York, NY

1993 "Compkuenstlerg," Kunstlerwerkstatt Lothringer Strasse,
Munich, Germany

"Gedanken Skizzen Entwurfe," Galerie Karin Sachs, Munich,
Germany

"The Return of The Cadavre Exquis," The Drawing Center,
New York, NY

"Excess in the Techno-Mediacratic Society," Shoshana Wayne
Gallery, Santa Monica, CA

"Excess in the Techno-Mediacratic Society," Galerie Krinzinger,
Vienna, Austria

1991 "Byron, French, Miller, Solomoukha," Elga Wimmer Gallery,
New York, NY

"Art, Science et Materiaux," L'Institut des Materiaux,
Nantes, France

1990 "V.I.P.-Video-Image(s)-Peinture," Galerie du Génie, Paris, France

"Gallery Artists," Carol Getz Gallery, Miami, FL

"Hollywoodland," Fiction/Non-Fiction Gallery, New York, NY

"Not Painting: Goldstein, Miller, Paik, Richter," S. Bitter-Larkin
Gallery, New York, NY

"Komoski, Miller, Minter," Carol Getz Gallery, Miami, FL

1989 "10 Gallery Artists," Nina Freudenheim Gallery, Buffalo, NY

"Chaos," The New Museum of Art, New York, NY

"Invitational With Gallery Artists," Fiction/Non-Fiction Gallery,
New York, NY

"Science/Technology/Abstraction," Wright State University,
Dayton, OH

1988 "Twenty in New York," Nina Freudenheim Gallery, Buffalo, NY

"Digital Explorations: Emerging Visions In Art," Tibor de Nagy
Gallery, New York, NY

"New York," Josh Baer Gallery, New York, NY

1987 "Computer Assisted; The Computer in Contemporary Art,"
Freedman Gallery, Albright College, Reading, PA

"Computers and Art," Contemporary Arts Center, Cincinnati, OH

"Dwyer, Jackson, Miller," Nina Freudenheim Gallery, Buffalo, NY

"Digital Visions: Computers and Art," Everson Museum of Art,
Syracuse, NY

"The 2nd Emerging Expression Biennial: The Artist and the
Computer," Bronx Museum of the Arts, New York, NY

"Group Show," Jack Shainman Gallery, New York, NY

"Art Against AIDS," Baskerville & Watson Gallery, New York, NY

"Dreams of the Alchemist," Carl Solway, Cincinnati, OH

"Group Show," Jack Shainman Gallery, Washington, DC

"New York: New Venue," The Mint Museum, Charlotte, NC

"Monsters: The Phenomena of Dispassion," Barbara Toll,
New York, NY

1986 "Physics," Colin de Land Fine Art, New York, NY

"Layers of Vision," Bette Stoler Gallery, New York, NY

"Dwyer, Lemieux, Majore, Miller, Nagy, Tim Rollins," Rhona
Hoffman Gallery, Chicago, IL

"Spiritual America," CIPA, Buffalo, NY

1985 "Dwyer, Spero, Majore, Miller, Lang," Josh Baer Gallery,
New York, NY

"Belcher, Jaffe, Majore, Miller, Pittu," Bette Stoler Gallery,
New York, NY

"Emerging Expressions: The Artist and the Computer," Bronx
Museum of the Arts, New York, NY

"Past & Future Perfect," Hallwalls Contemporary Art Center,
Buffalo, NY

1984 "Bialobroda, Blair, Miller, Rosenberg," Baskerville & Watson
Gallery, New York, NY

"Between Here & Nowhere," Riverside Studios, London, UK

"Group Show," International With Monument, New York, NY

"The International Show," Baskerville & Watson Gallery,
New York, NY

"Behind Faces & Figures," Philadelphia College of Art,
Philadelphia, PA

"Ars Ex Machina," Bette Stoler Gallery, New York, NY

1983 "A More Store," Jack Tilton Gallery, New York, NY

"Portrait For the 00's," Protech McNeil Gallery, New York, NY

"Language, Drama, Source & Vision," New Museum,
New York, NY

1982 "Nineteen in New York," Nina Freudenheim Gallery, Buffalo, NY

"The Ritz Hotel," Washington Project for the Arts,
Washington, DC

"New Drawing in America," The Drawing Center, New York, NY

"The Crime Show," ABC NO RIO, New York, NY

1981 "Selections Sixteen," The Drawing Center, New York, NY

"The Positive Show," ABC NO RIO, New York, NY

1979 "Six Artists Under Thirty," Burchfield Penny Art Center,
Buffalo, NY

"Dimensions Variable," The New Museum, New York, NY

1978 "Contemporary Reflections," Aldrich Museum, Aldrich, CT

1976 "Member's Gallery," Albright-Knox Art Gallery, Buffalo, NY

1974 "Member's Gallery," Albright-Knox Art Gallery, Buffalo, NY

Public Collections

Albright-Knox Art Gallery, Buffalo, NY

Bloomingdale's, New York, NY

Burchfield Penney Art Center, Buffalo, NY

Chanel, Paris, France

JP Morgan, Chase Bank, New York, NY

Dow Jones & Company, New York, NY

The Dun & Bradstreet Corporation, New York, NY

First Bank System, Minneapolis, MN

Fonds National d'Art Contemporain, French National Collection,
Paris, France

Foundation Hahnloser, Bern, Switzerland

Foundation Salomon, Annecy, France

Eli and Edythe Broad Art Museum, Michigan State University,
East Lansing, MI

High Museum, Atlanta, GA

Museu de Arte do Rio, Rio de Janeiro, Brazil

Musée de la Mode, Paris, France

National Academy of Sciences, Washington, DC

Ralph Lauren, Polo, New York, NY

Rose Art Museum, Brandeis University, Waltham, MA

Santa Barbara Museum, Santa Barbara, CA

PHOTOGRAPHY CREDITS/CAPTIONS

Page 1, ©Steve Miller: Surf shop, Arpoador, Rio de Janeiro, Brazil

Page 5, ©Steve Miller: Jeanine Pepler, NYC loft

Pages 6-7, ©Steve Miller: Amazon caiman x-ray

Page 8, ©Rebecca Rosko: Lindsey Haines, Long Island, NY

Page 11, ©Doug Young: Sagaponack studio, NY

Pages 12, 13, ©Junji Murata: Tohmi Shiroyama, Osaka, Japan

Pages 14-15, ©Steve Miller: Sagaponack studio, NY

Page 16, ©Daniel Gonzalez: Tom Lagrassa Jr., Sag Harbor, NY

Pages 18-21, ©Daniel Gonzalez: Sag Harbor, NY

Pages 22-25, ©Daniel Gonzalez: Montauk, NY

Page 26, ©Rebecca Rosko: Steve Miller with board shaper Joe Flo in studio, Sagaponack, NY

Page 27, ©Steve Miller: NYC studio

Pages 28-29, ©Amie Stoppard: Maggie, Evie, and Esme Stoppard, Sagaponack, NY

Pages 30-31, ©Steve Miller: Amagansett, NY

Pages 32, 33, ©Steve Miller: 2016 Bloomingdale's windows, NYC

Pages 34-35, ©Michael Steele: 2016 Bloomingdale's windows, NYC

Pages 36-39, ©Junji Murata: Tohmi Shiroyama, Osaka, Japan

Page 40, ©Doug Young: Tohmi's skate decks, Ying & Yang

Page 41, ©Steve Miller: Tohmi, Sagaponack, NY

Pages 42-47, ©Steven Brown: Lindsey Haines, Riverhead, NY

Page 48, ©Doug Young: Studio, Sagaponack, NY

Page 49, ©Steve Miller: Goddaughter, Esme Stoppard

Pages 50-51, ©Rebecca Rosko: Selfie, Sagaponack, NY

Pages 52-53, ©Doug Young: Studio, Sagaponack, NY

Pages 54-55, ©Octavio Lobo: MRI portrait, Belem, Brazil

Pages 56-57, ©Steve Miller: School of the Abyss, 2015

Page 58 (top), ©Kristen Chiacchia: Installation at Second Street Gallery 2017, Charlottesville, VA

Page 59 (top), ©Erica Barnes: Installation at Second Street Gallery 2017, Charlottesville, VA

Pages 58-59 (bottom), ©Steve Miller: Charlottesville, VA

Pages 60, 61, ©Steve Miller: Surf clothing for Osklen, Rio de Janeiro, Brazil

Pages 62-65, ©Steve Miller: Cashmere scarves for Ergun Khorchin, Bridgehampton, NY

Pages 66-71, ©Daniel Gonzalez: Tom Lagrassa, Montauk, NY

Page 72, ©Eric Striffler: Missy Hargraves with product placement

Page 73, ©Steve Miller: Amazon x-ray iguana surfboard

Pages 74-75, ©Doug Young: Sagaponack studio, NY

Pages 76, 77, ©Brendan Powell: Sagaponack studio, NY

Pages 78-79, ©Steve Miller, Sagaponack studio, NY

Pages 80, 81, ©Steve Miller: Studio, Sagaponack, NY

Pages 82-83 (inset), ©Steve Miller: Rick Perez with Glock x-ray

Page 83, ©Steve Miller: Rebecca Rosko at work, Sagaponack, NY

Page 84, ©Steve Miller: Shot Sloth Pieta, 2014

Page 85, ©Steve Miller: Shot Sloth Pieta (detail), 2014

Page 86, ©Steve Miller: Piranha x-ray, 2011, Belem, Brazil

Pages 86-87, ©Steve Miller: Piranha silkscreen (detail)

Pages 88, 89, ©Steve Miller: Sagaponack studio, NY

Pages 90, 91, ©Doug Young: Sagaponack studio, NY

Page 92, ©Steve Miller

Page 93, ©Steve Miller: Kickback, 2015

Page 94, ©Steve Miller: 2014 exhibition, "Slide," Museu de Arte do Rio, Brazil

Page 95, ©Rebecca Rosko (3 photos): Silkscreen technique, Studio, Sagaponack, NY

©Steve Miller (bottom right): Shaping studio with silkscreen alligator on paper, Southampton, NY

Pages 96, 97, ©Doug Young: Steve Miller, Sagaponack, NY

Page 99, ©Steve Miller: Joe "Flo" Trizzino in his workshop, Southampton, NY

Page 100, ©Steve Miller

Page 101, ©John Wilton

Pages 102, 103, ©Steve Miller

Page 104, ©Steve Miller: Shaping workshop, Joe "Flo" Trizzino, Southampton, NY

Page 105, ©Steve Miller: Rebecca Rosko, Studio, Sagaponack, NY

Pages 106, 107, ©Steve Miller: Joe Trizzino workshop, Southampton, NY

Pages 108-111, ©Steve Miller: 2014 Bloomingdale's windows, NYC

Pages 112-113, ©Michael Steele: 2016 Bloomingdale's windows, NYC

Pages 112-113 (inset), ©Steve Miller: 2016 Bloomingdale's windows, NYC

Pages 114, 115, ©Steve Miller

Page 116, ©Steve Miller: Apple computer

Pages 116-117, ©Octavio Lobo: Iguana x-ray, Belem, Brazil

Page 117, ©Rebecca Rosko: Sagaponack studio, NY

Pages 118-119, ©Steve Miller: "Liquid Lungs," 2013, Unique artist book

Pages 120-121, ©Steve Miller: "Liquid Lungs," 2013, Amazon bird x-ray, Unique artist book

Pages 122-123, ©Steve Miller

Pages 124-125, ©Steve Miller: Electrical wires in the favela, Rocinha, Rio de Janeiro, Brazil

Page 126, ©Steve Miller: Rocinha with Two Brothers Mountain, Rio de Janeiro, Brazil

Page 127, ©Steve Miller: Rocinha, Rio de Janeiro, Brazil

Pages 128, 129, ©Steve Miller: Museu de Arte do Rio, 2014, Brazil

Pages 130-131, ©Steve Miller: Sidewalk, Copacabana, Rio de Janeiro

Page 132, ©Steve Miller: Brazil, 2012, Book sculpture

Page 133, ©Steve Miller

Pages 134-135, ©Steve Miller: Film positives for making silkscreens

Photography became the means to document the process of creating this body of work, and this book would not have been possible without the generosity of the photographers who contributed to it. Daniel Gonzalez (ably assisted by Raun Norquist) was the catalyst that brought this project to completion with surf and style. And then there were skaters, Tohmi Shiroyama, Lindsey Haines, Anna Wilcoxen, Crystal Carneiro and Tom Lagrassa Jr. Tohmi took a particular relish in destroying my boards which can be seen within these pages. Brendan Powell surfed along with Tom Lagrassa, who got up for any set that came his way.

John Wilton took the first photograph of the x-ray that was sent to Paris, and he has toiled for several years to organize, digitize, Photoshop, and make the InDesign document for this book. My studio assistants, Becky Rosko and Matej Vakula, make projects like this possible. Joe Flo, AKA Joe Trizzino hand shaped every board, and we are moving towards 50 boards as of press time.

The author and film director Michael Tolkin piqued my interest in skating with his movie *Gleaming the Cube*. His reminiscence tapped my own memories of metal wheels on concrete.

On three separate occasions, Anne Keating put the surf and skateboards into the windows of Bloomingdale's. Alanna Quinn and JD Talesek brought the work to the National Academy of Sciences in Washington, DC. Nick Duke opened the door at Second Street Gallery in Charlottesville, VA. Tosha Grantham, the curator at Second Street made the journey from Virginia to Sagaponack, twice, to organize my exhibition.

Finally, for this and other publications of mine, Marvin Heiferman has lent his expertise and insights. His counsel on this book is much appreciated.